The Hollywood Professionals

VOLUME 7

The Hollywood Professionals

VOLUME 7

WILDER & McCAREY

Leland Poague

SAN DIEGO • NEW YORK
A. S. BARNES & COMPANY, INC.
IN LONDON:
THE TANTIVY PRESS

The Hollywood Professionals text copyright ©1980 by
A. S. Barnes and Co., Inc.

The Tantivy Press
Magdalen House
136-148 Tooley Street
London, SE1 2TT, England

First Edition
Manufactured in the United States of America
For information write to A. S. Barnes and Company, Inc.,
P.O. Box 3051, San Diego, CA 92038

Library of Congress Cataloging in Publication Data (Revised)

Canham, Kingsley.
    The Hollywood professionals.

    CONTENTS: v. 1. Michael Curtiz. Raoul Walsh.
Henry Hathaway.—v. 2. Denton, C. Henry King.
Canham, K. Lewis Milestone. Thomas, T. Sam Wood.—
[etc.]—v. 6. Estrin, A. Frank Capra, George Cukor,
Clarence Brown.—v. 7. Poague, Leland. Billy Wilder, Leo McCarey.
    1. Moving-picture producers and directors—United
States—Biography. I. Denton, Clive. II. Thomas,
Tony, 1927-   III. Belton, John. IV. Rosenthal,
Stuart. V. Kass, Judith M. VI. Estrin, Allen.
VII. Title.
PN1998.A2C315   791.43′0233′0922 [B]   72-178
ISBN 0-498-02181-5

1 2 3 4 5 6 7 8 9   84 83 82 81 80

To Betty Ann and Lloyd Allen
And to Susie, Amy, and Melissa
This book is affectionately dedicated.

Contents

PREFACE/
ACKNOWLEDGMENTS

Humility is a virtue little valued in certain critical circles these days. I suppose no humility at all is better than false humility—but, on the occasion of the publication of these essays, I feel humble on two accounts.

First, there are the many debts of kindness and hospitality that cannot possibly be repaid by acknowledgments. To Peter Cowie, I owe the greatest thanks, for his encouragement, his patience, and his diplomacy. Jon and Carol Sanford, Jim Garvey, Mr. and Mrs. James Garvey, Robert and Leone Sanford, Rick and Dorthe Pettigrew, and Lorraine Jenson are all to be thanked for sheltering myself and my family for various periods while I conducted my research. Screenings were arranged with the kind assistance of Patrick Sheehan and Barbara Humphrys of the Library of Congress Motion Picture Section, Charles Silver of the Museum of Modern Art/Film Study Center, and Liz Ancker of the SUNY Geneseo Instructional Resources Center. Thanks to the SUNY Geneseo Faculty Research Committee for financial support and to William Rueckert and Richard Gollin for moral support. Richard Ramsey, Dante Thomas, and Gary Hooper provided expert and much-needed editorial advice. I have also benefited from the suggestions of students both at Geneseo and The University of Rochester: thanks particularly to Glenn Caron and Brett Gold. Illustrations appear through the courteous assistance of George Pratt and the staff at The George Eastman House and Paula Klaw of "Movie Star News." Sections of this book have appeared previously in "Film Criticism" and "Movietone News" and are reprinted with the co-operation of the editors involved, I. Lloyd Michaels and Richard T. Jameson respectively. Thanks also to Sylvia Rucker for her help with translations.

Secondly, I feel a genuine sense of humility before my subject matter, the cinematic art and cinematic artistry of Billy Wilder and Leo McCarey. Both are, indeed, "Hollywood Professionals," in the best sense of both words, and I will account this book successful if it contributes to the ongoing and much needed re-interpretation of the Hollywood cinema.

Hollywood has been much maligned in recent scholarship for purveying "bourgeois ideology," and the present essays ought, I hope, to demonstrate the problematic nature of such assertions. To argue the "vulgar Marxist" contention that the films of Wilder and McCarey (and of nearly everybody else connected with the "classical narrative cinema") are completely and detrimentally determined by the "illusionist" ideology of "bourgeois representation" is to deny any useful or interesting distinctions which might be made between their films or their film-making. And yet, through the course of my research and my writing, two very distinctive and forceful authorial personalities emerged. Of course, the presence of a forceful personal signature is no guarantee of quality (there *are* no guarantees of quality); but the existence of describable authorial "signatures" surely must put to rest arguments of the "studio hack" sort, even if those once buried but newly disinterred moral/political arguments are now couched in the often ill-used critical/technical language of semiotics. Critical language cannot substitute for critical insights. The point of film criticism is clarity, making films *more* intelligible rather than less. It is not to mystify readers with unnecessary jargon.

My goal in these essays, then, has been to generate critical frameworks capable of elucidating the films of both directors. I have not written definitive studies—practical considerations prevented that—but I have been comprehensive, if by "comprehensive" we refer to a certain general applicability. Thus, while I have not said all that might be said about either director's films (that hardly seems possible), I have in each case seen as many films as I could by that artist; have, on the basis of those viewings, constructed an abstract model of the director's general themes, concerns, and stylistic pre-occupations; and have tested that general model repeatedly against specific examples of each man's film-making. To a certain extent the choice of test cases is arbitrary on my part. No doubt a different author would pick a different set of examples. Certain choices, however, reflect the critical context. My decision to discuss *The Awful Truth* at far greater length than *Once Upon a Honeymoon,* for example, reflects my admiration for Robin Wood's "Film Comment" essay on the latter film. Much that I would say he has said. But in no case should readers interpret my choice of examples negatively, as implying a dislike of or disinterest in those films which are not discussed at length. I simply did not discuss them this time around.

The Hollywood Professionals

VOLUME 7

Wilder at work (his frequent collaborator, I. A. L. Diamond, can be seen in the background, at right).

BILLY WILDER

Introduction
(The Lost Wilder)

With a director like Ernst Lubitsch one argues preference for the
German over the American, for the silent over the sound, for the
musicals over the satires, for the sexy over the sentimental. But there
is little doubt that Lubitsch merits the argument. Billy Wilder, on the
other hand, despite his voluminous award-winning output, seems a
different case. At least, for folks like Charles Higham, John Simon,
and Andrew Sarris (Sarris circa 1969), familiarity breeds contempt.
As Higham puts it: "Wilder's films present a uniquely disagreeable
image of a man who sees nothing but evil in life, and is amused at it."[1]
And Simon goes Higham one better: Wilder is, in Simon's estimation,
a "film-maker with false or no morality"; a contention which Simon
then attempts to support by gross misreadings of selected scenes (or
even lines) from three or four Wilder films.[2] Simon at his best is an
excellent critic: his book-length study of *four* Bergman films, "Ingmar
Bergman Directs," is splendidly informative—and supports Simon's
enthusiastic appraisal of Bergman as "the greatest film-maker the
world has seen so far."[3] Simon does not *prove* the contention—such
assertions essentially defy proof—but Simon does a good job of
allowing his enthusiasm to motivate and inform his criticism.
    Therein lies a dilemma, however—a dilemma which tastemakers
cannot escape. If admiration encourages people to write well about
works which they value, encourages them to take the time to argue
that admiration by thorough analysis and explication, then the
reverse will also hold true. That is, people will write poorly about
works which they dislike, and will not take the time to analyse and
explicate. Why bother to write about films which hardly merit
concern? And yet it seems a matter of simple equity that accusations
require more proof than panegyrics. To be fair, Simon and others
like him would have to devote as much time to Wilder as to Bergman,
at least if they expect their attacks to be taken seriously. Better
nothing said than slander said off the cuff.

Which is not to deny that Wilder might well be just as cynical and immoral as Simon and Sarris *et al* make him out to be. It only asserts that Simon and Sarris are unlikely to offer convincing argument to that effect. Nor, for that matter, will I argue the negative case. I have seen every one of Wilder's American, self-directed films, and not one of them has failed to please me. There have been the childish one-liners on occasion; but no less a light than Shakespeare suffered a similar though by no means debilitating malady. As Dr. Johnson put it in his "Preface to Shakespeare": "A quibble is the golden apple for which he will always turn aside from his career or stoop from his elevation."[4] Even Dr. Johnson, however, was forced to admit that Shakespeare's artistic vision—his "just representations of general nature"—more than compensated for the occasional artistic flaw (if genuine flaws they were).

The trouble with Billy Wilder, then, is not so much with Wilder but with the scholarship—or, more accurately, with the lack of it. There have been all too few full and comprehensive critical efforts at elucidating the Wilder vision. And even those few attempts, the Joseph McBride/Michael Wilmington piece in "Film Quarterly" ("The Private Life of Billy Wilder," Vol. 23, No. 4) and Stephen Farber's intelligently reasoned critique of Wilder's career in "Film Comment" ("The Films of Billy Wilder," Vol. 7, No. 4), as helpful as they may be, tend to be sketchy and apologetic.[5] One gets the impression, indeed, that Billy Wilder has been lost behind a smoke-screen of attack and counter-attack. His cynicism has become such a critical issue that other equally important characteristics of the Wilder cinema—characteristics which we will begin to outline in the following remarks—have gone for the most part unnoticed and have accordingly been undervalued.

We can best begin to get at "the lost Wilder" by attending briefly to *The Lost Weekend.* The film is generally praised for its "unusually hard, tense, cruel" realism, for its grimly accurate portrayal of an alcoholic writer's lost weekend, a weekend which was to have been spent taking a country cure ("trees and grass and sweet cider and buttermilk and water from that well"), but which became instead a descent into hell, a descent, specifically, into the delirium tremens which marks advanced cases of the disease.[6] Indeed, Ray Milland was so convincing as Don Birnam that Milland was himself suspected of being an alcoholic.[7] But the film is generally criticised for two separate though related faults. The first complaint, voiced by James Agee, is that we get little sense of the cause behind Birnam's drinking.[8] And the

The Lost Weekend: **Ray Milland, Jane Wyman, Philip Terry.**

second concerns Birnam's "improbable redemption through the love of a good woman (Jane Wyman)."[9]

As far as the first problem is concerned, it is clearly evident that Wilder went to great lengths to develop a sense of Birnam's personality dilemma, to give us the reasons behind Birnam's obsessive drinking. Briefly, as Birnam himself tells us, he is a romantic ("one of the great ones"), a devotee of Shakespeare, who longs to write of life's beauties in appropriately elegant and moving language. He dropped out of college in the flush of first success and moved to the city to become the next Hemingway. Successive manuscripts were less successful, however. He lost confidence, turned to drink to restore confidence, and drank even more to black out the knowledge that drink only dulled his talents. He refuses to accept an everyday job—refuses to lead a routine life of "quiet desperation"—and he sponges off his brother while playing the role of the outcast novelist. Birnam's drinking, therefore, is an attempt to reconcile a romantic vision of himself with a cynical vision of society—a vision which the

film only half supports. It is possible to be a decent human being, as
Nat the barkeep, as Helen, as Wick demonstrate; and it is only Don's
all-or-nothing romanticism which delivers him unto aesthetic bondage. He wishes to rise above social experience, but by so wishing he
inevitably detaches himself from the very source of artistic inspiration. An artist cannot relate to society, cannot survive as an artist
either aesthetically or financially, if he is unwilling to involve himself
in the social arena.

   Which is not to say that personal experience is insufficient subject
for artistic endeavour. Wilder is clearly an intensely personal artist,
however social his concerns may be. But an artist must somehow
relate his personal concerns in a public manner if his experience is to
have aesthetic validity—which is precisely the lesson that Don Birnam
comes to learn in *The Lost Weekend*. His redemption, therefore, comes
about not merely "through love of a good woman," although Helen's
love for Don is not to be undervalued. Rather, Don comes to the end
of his personal rope: he either commits suicide or returns to writing.
He has no other options. And ironically, the very fact of Don's

He would rather drink than write: Ray Milland and Howard da Silva.

desperation provides the subject and the inspiration for his artistic renewal. At last he has a personal experience of real power and purpose to relate, something that really matters.

Indeed, Wilder's direction allows us to understand how much Don's experience matters by requiring that we undergo the experience with him. Don's DT's hallucination is treated realistically and objectively. The mouse in the plaster, the bat's attack, the blood slowly oozing down the wall, all are as "real" to the audience as they are to Don Birnam himself. To be sure, the hallucinations are hallucinations, products of a frustrated imagination and cheap whiskey; but they accurately represent a state of mind, a sort of inward looking paranoia typical of the post-second world war period. And Wilder's point, therefore, is that introspection must be accompanied by public expression. Birnam finds his salvation in the public act of writing, describing his personal experience ("I'm going to put this whole weekend down, minute by minute") with all of the detail and tonality necessary to make it aesthetically "real."

There is much of Wilder in Don Birnam. Like Birnam, Wilder in his heart of hearts is a romantic. His films almost always involve the assertion of will over circumstance, of imagination over actuality, of hope over probability. Norma Desmond plots her comeback in *Sunset Boulevard;* Chuck Tatum attempts to stage manage the story of the century in *Ace in the Hole;* Sabrina seeks to cross class barriers in *Sabrina;* Lindbergh attempts to fly the Atlantic in *The Spirit of St. Louis;* Leonard Vole schemes to subvert justice in *Witness for the Prosecution;* Nestor attempts to clean up the brothels of Paris in *Irma La Douce;* etc., etc. Wilder does not always approve of such assertions, no more than he approves of Don Birnam's alcoholism. But his disapproval falls less on the dreamer than on the dream. That is, dreams *per se* are not only acceptable but necessary. Some dreams, however, are realised only at great cost, to others (there are murders in *Double Indemnity, Sunset Boulevard, Ace in the Hole* and *Witness for the Prosecution*) and ultimately at great cost to the dreamers themselves. Thus in *A Foreign Affair,* for example, the Nazi dream of world domination is seen as utterly self-destroying. Wilder makes the point clear when Colonel Plummer (Millard Mitchell) takes the congressional delegation (there to investigate the morale of occupation troops) on a guided tour of Berlin. We see war memorials, the Reichstag, the Brandenburg gate ("it used to be an arch of triumph until they got out of the habit"), the rubble of the American Embassy, the Reich Chancellery where Hitler commited suicide, and "the balcony where he bet his Reich would last a

Audrey Hepburn in *Sabrina*.

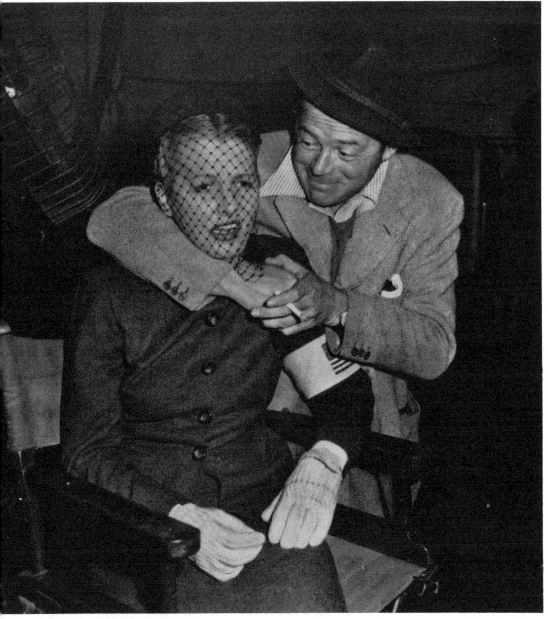

Wilder "brutalizes" Jean Arthur on the set of *A Foreign Affair*.

thousand years." As the Colonel laconically puts it, "that's the one that broke the bookies' hearts."

Romanticism disappointed thus leads naturally to cynicism, to decreased hopes and expectations. To stay with *A Foreign Affair,* we see the people of Berlin living in a cynical world of black markets and rubble, where a mickey-mouse watch sells for $700; and yet amidst the rubble there is time for love. Indeed, while Colonel Plummer comments on the public sights, an indignant Congresswoman, Phoebe Frost (Jean Arthur), takes copious notes in her ever-present black book, cataloguing each embracing couple that they pass by. The cynical fact of her note-taking, however, evidences Miss Frost's own latent romanticism. As it turns out, the Congresswoman "once cried for a man" until her eyes were "half washed out" of her head. And the man, in turn, was a Southern Democrat who represented everything that Iowa Republican Frost "despises." As she puts it: "I loved him insanely, loved the southern syrup of his voice, his mint julep manners." But he was only out to sway her vote. Hence Miss Frost's cynicism, her inordinate fear of sexuality, her up-tight hair do, her veil, her black book; and hence as well her determination to get the officer who is protecting Erika von Schluetow (Marlene Dietrich), a suspected Nazi collaborator who sings at a local off-limits club. All of which has very little to do with Congresswoman Frost's official mission: one corrupt officer does not an immoral army make, but Miss Frost pursues her man-hunt with a certain emotional fervour, indicating (1) a fear that sexual fraternisation with German women will make storm troopers of American G.I.s, a fear clearly based on her own romantic misadventures; and (2) her growing interest in Capt. Pringle (John Lund), the officer who accompanies Miss Frost on her midnight stake-outs. At one level, then, Phoebe Frost is a cynic, suspicious and self-righteous. But at a deeper, more legitimate level, she is a romantic, afraid of love, but longing for the emotional freedom ("the midnight ride of Paul Revere") that love allows.

In *A Foreign Affair,* as elsewhere in Wilder, there is a delicate balance at work, between hope and fear, between surviving and thriving. Thus the implicit comparison between Phoebe Frost and Erika von Schluetow: both are (or pretend to be) in love with the same man, Capt. Pringle; both are cynical, each in her own way; and both are doing their best to stay physically and emotionally alive under the circumstances. Indeed, both had allowed themselves to be wooed by ideologically abhorrent suitors, the Democrat in Phoebe's case, Hitler in Erika's. The difference, obviously, is that Phoebe "filibustered" (shades of *Mr. Smith Goes to Washington*) while Erika smilingly offered her hand to Hitler's kiss (we see this in newsreel footage uncovered in Frost's investigation). And Wilder clearly holds out, then, not for surface propriety, but for genuine ethics. Indeed, meeting Phoebe provides John Pringle with the chance to revive his Iowa farm-boy soul, to recognise the value of hay rides, of sitting and holding hands,

Jean Arthur does her farm-girl best in *A Foreign Affair*.

of whistling "Shine on Harvest Moon." And Erika's derisive laughter, her contempt for Phoebe and Iowa, confirms John's feeling that Erika's "love" is only a racket, to get extra rations, to get to America. Wilder does not condemn her for that; Richard Corliss is correct to assert that Wilder "celebrates the German survival instinct in the midst of hunger and humiliation . . . as the European equivalent of America's pioneer individualism"; but Capt. Pringle and Billy Wilder correctly assert a moral position which prefers a humanised, Ninotchka-like Phoebe Frost to the elegant insincerity of Erika von Schluetow.[10] Erika may be more interesting on the surface, all jewels and decadence; but Wilder is romantic enough, and moral enough, to value Phoebe's naïveté.

Finding such an appropriate balance between naïveté and cynicism, between innocence and experience, is a problem that Wilder continually struggles with. The tendency, as Don Birnam demonstrates in *The Lost Weekend,* is to let the balance get out of hand; and Wilder's occasional *faux pas* are of this very out-of-hand sort. But, for the most part, Wilder, like Don Birnam, deals with this difficult issue by means of art, by publicly and repeatedly confronting it, lest the issue be forgotten and a realistic sense of perspective be lost. Thus there is a continual dialectic of confession and confrontation in Wilder; and the very process of maintaining that dialectic comes to have paramount importance. As Wilder put it: "I do not have in my cellar prints of my old movies. I don't read my old screenplays. I don't live in past glories. That was last week—what have we done this week?"[11] Thus the activity of film-making is more important to Wilder than the finished films themselves, which explains, perhaps, his eye for the box office: he has to make commercially successful films or he will stop making films altogether.

Wilder thus places a certain ethical value on action, a value which allows him to admire prostitutes, con-artists, crazies of every description, who have at least the guts to act in a world where fear can reduce people to drunken stupors. Nobody's perfect, as Joe E. Brown tells Jack Lemmon at the end of *Some Like It Hot,* and imperfection is forgivable in Wilder if not carried to extremes of the Nazi variety. Indeed, it is this very sort of imperfection-in-action which Wilder celebrates, and John Simon castigates, in *One, Two, Three.* Specifically, Simon objects to James Cagney's snappy one-line put-down of Comrade Piffl ("Look at it this way, kid: any world that can produce the Taj Mahal, William Shakespeare, and striped toothpaste can't be all bad") as being completely senseless and pointless. As Simon puts it:

If it is meant as a defense of Western culture, what is the Taj Mahal
doing there? If it is meant as a defense of democratic culture, again,
why the Taj Mahal? If it is intended as a defense of American
culture and its striped toothpaste, what are the Taj and Shakespeare doing there? If it is ridicule rather than a vindication of
America, what is the whole thing doing in that context?

Simon clearly asks the right question here—the appropriateness of
the line does depend on our understanding of its context—but he
completely misrepresents (or misreads) that context in his rush to
condemn Wilder's "immorality."

To begin with, Wilder can hardly be said to be defending a specific
ideology in *One, Two, Three:* everyone in the film, from Communist
border guards and American M.P.s on up, is on the make. Clearly
Wilder prefers by a slight margin the more open sort of capitalist
greed for being the less hypocritical variety; but he is careful, within
the film's farcical context, to have everyone be equally self-centered.
It is this sort of democratic leveling which comrade Piffl objects to
when he sees that the Russian trade commissar has defected: "Is
everybody in this world corrupt? Maybe we should liquidate the
whole human race and start all over again?" But it is Piffl's nihilistic
desperation that Cagney rejects in his "can't be all bad" remark. It is
the human race, in all of its glorious imperfection, that Cagney and
Wilder defend. There was a Will Shakespeare, there is a Taj Mahal,
and yes, there is striped toothpaste. Perhaps we would not need the
toothpaste if we drank less Coca Cola (Cagney runs the Berlin bottling
plant); but soft drinks are clearly preferable to atom bombs.

Nor is it the case that Wilder unquestioningly approves of Cagney's
maniacal energy. All is not wrong with the world, but all is not right
with the MacNamara marriage. MacNamara (Cagney) and his wife,
Phyllis (Arlene Francis), have reached the end of the marital line. She
is "fed up" with her husband's get-ahead schemes; she constantly and
ironically refers to him as "mein führer"; she sides with the boss's
daughter and the daughter's East German boyfriend in their attempts to circumvent Mac's authority; and she finally declares her
own independence ("Aloha"). Thus overmuch action of the wrong
sort, for the wrong reasons, and in the wrong direction, threatens to
destroy an otherwise vital familial/sexual relationship.

The problem, however, is not simply Mac's overcharged lifestyle.
Phyllis had acquiesced to it (she "didn't want to be one of those
nagging American wives") so that Mac's energy expands to fill the
power vacuum created by Phyllis's sexual/political reticence. Mac's

Conquering the world for Coca-Cola: James Cagney and Lilo Pulver in
One, Two, Three.

attempt to break up the Scarlett/Piffl romance, however, sensitises
her to the precariousness of her own situation. Mac can be "a first class
heel with oak leaf clusters" when circumstance demands it, the "rat"
in the "rat race," and Phyllis unilaterally decides to withdraw from
Berlin, from the marriage, and to return with the children to Atlanta.
Mac's sudden burst of energy, first to annul the marriage of Scarlett
and Otto, and then to "remodel" Otto into an acceptable capitalist
son-in-law when it is discovered that Scarlett is pregnant, requires an
equal burst of self-assertion on Phyllis's part, and she decides to leave.

It is ironic but appropriate, then, that Mac's own family should be
breaking up at the very moment when Mac labours so mightily to
insure harmony among the Hazeltines, their daughter, and their new
son-in-law. Like Dave the Dude in Capra's *Pocketful of Miracles,* Mac
seems to be working at cross purposes.[12] But Wilder's moralism is, in
personal terms, benevolent; and Wilder expresses his sympathy with
Mac by allowing circumstances to set Mac straight. That is, Mac is

Remodeling Otto (Horst Buchholz) in *One, Two, Three:* **Cagney and Arlene Francis (right).**

himself remade in the process of remodelling Otto. He indulges his frenetic energy to the nth degree in his Herculean attempt to make Otto a member of the Hazeltine family, and the effort both exhausts and rejuvenates him. On the one hand, Mac passes the torch of fanaticism on to Otto, who gets the management job that Mac had so aspired to. Put another way, Mac burns himself out by doing his job too well. But, on the other hand, Mac comes to value the sort of family security that his efforts have secured for Otto. Mac may not get the London job—but he is not at all sure that he wants it any longer. Furthermore, Phyllis has shown just the sort of energetic spunk that will make family life not only secure but interesting. So Mac willingly accepts promotion to a do-nothing post in Atlanta, forswears his dreams of world conquest (recall the world map in his Berlin office), and he does so in the service of domestic (rather than political) tranquillity. Like *Ninotchka, One, Two, Three* does not attempt a genuine political solution—Wilder is not that sort of romantic—but

Greta Garbo and Melvyn Douglas in *Ninotchka.*

both films assert the comic value of energetic sexual relationships as being the cornerstone of a vital and open society.

All of which may be conservative to a point—satiric comedy tends generally in that direction—but it is neither nihilistic nor immoral, as critics like Simon and Higham assert. Billy Wilder is, when properly understood, a film-maker of strict morality and often delicate feeling, a romantic at heart, a man who values courage and conviction, but who values action—courage at work in the social arena—as well. Wilder is thus realistic without being overly or debilitatingly cynical. He lives in the material world—there is no other—but he never loses sight of life's legitimate value, of its drives, its rhythms, of its tenuous and therefore precious continuity. Wilder argues life's case with a certain brash eloquence; and we need not feel shame for admiring the cinema of Billy Wilder.

The Search for Certainty (Great Expectations):
Double Indemnity, Sunset Boulevard, Stalag 17

Double Indemnity is, next to *Sunset Boulevard* and *Some Like It Hot,* Wilder's most written-about film. Charles Higham and Joel Greenberg, for example, are not alone in considering *Double Indemnity* "one of the highest summits of *film noir*" (p. 28); and, stylistically speaking, such descriptions are accurate: the world of *Double Indemnity* is a world of dark city streets and swerving headlights; a world of fearful shadows, of harsh dusty afternoons. Indeed, Wilder employs the iconography of *film noir*—the clanging telephones, the neon desk lamps, the dictaphones, the black sedans, the empty hallways—with a certain ruthless precision in his portrayal of progress gone berserk. But the film's reputation as a *genre* classic, however well deserved, tends to discourage a genuine understanding of the film's complexities. It is not enough to describe *Double Indemnity* as a "cynical and corrosive" meditation upon greed in which "a blonde, Phyllis Dietrichson (Barbara Stanwyck) sets out to seduce an insurance man, Walter Neff (Fred MacMurray) so she can dispose of her unwanted husband for the death money" (pp. 28-29). Such a description gives us no sense of the film's finely tuned ambivalence. The world of *Double Indemnity* may seem a world of blacks and whites, of morality and immorality, of innocence and experience; but the characters we most attend to—Neff, Phyllis Dietrichson, Barton Keyes (Edward G. Robinson), the claims investigator who is Neff's closest friend, and Lola Dietrichson (Jean Heather), step-daughter to Phyllis—embody a complex set of motives and methods, giving rise, through the course of the film, to an equally complex though hardly pitiless understanding of the human condition. *Double Indemnity* is high tragedy, concerned ultimately with the value and meaning of life, and its point, though hard-headed in the best *film noir* tradition, transcends the limits of cynicism.

We can best understand the complexity of *Double Indemnity* by attending to the interplay of risk and distance. Every character in the film seeks security in one form or another. Lola Dietrichson, at one extreme, seeks to escape the hateful atmosphere of the Dietrichson household for the tenuous emotional security of marriage to Nino Zachetti (Byron Barr), an angry ex-medical student with a king-size chip on his punk's shoulder. Barton Keyes, at the other extreme, seems to have rejected the emotional security of marital relationships for the safe but vicariously exciting position of claims investigator for Pacific All Risk Insurance. Robinson's Keyes even manages to inject a genuine measure of romanticism into the job. As he tells Neff: "To me a claims man is a surgeon, that desk is an operating table, and those pencils are scalpels and bone chisels, and those papers are not just forms and statistics and claims for compensation, they're alive, they're packed with drama, with twisted hopes and crooked dreams—a claims man, Walter, is a . . . is a doctor and a bloodhound and a cop and a judge and a jury and a father confessor, all in one." Robinson's staccato delivery of the lines testifies to Keyes' sincerity, both in his commitment to the job and in his desire that Neff become his assistant ("you're too good to be a salesman"). Indeed, the Keyes/Neff relationship, symbolised by a masculine ritual of the match and the cigar (Keyes never has a light—Neff always strikes the match), seems the only positive relationship Keyes has in life. Keyes had once been on the verge of matrimony—but the "little man" in his gut got to him, he investigated his fiancée, and she proved to be "a tramp from a long line of tramps." Wilder does not condemn Keyes for his caution—even if Keyes does earn an ulcer for his trouble. If anything, Wilder admires his energetic integrity. Furthermore, as the film demonstrates, even vicarious experience can be meaningful and significant, to a point. Keyes overhears Neff's confession, as we "overhear" it (Keyes stands in the office doorway as Neff records his

On the verge of death: Fred MacMurray and Edward G. Robinson in *Double Indemnity*.

confession on Keyes' dictaphone), and the film succeeds to the degree that we (Keyes included) comprehend and then apply the lesson learned. As Keyes laconically puts it at the film's conclusion, "You can't figure them all, Walter."

"Figuring" is, therefore, a central theme in *Double Indemnity;* and the ability to figure, to comprehend, is seen as a function of distance. Keyes could not figure out the Dietrichson case because he was too involved with Neff. In a way, they loved each other. In the film's closing moment, a dying Neff, now slumped across the Pacific All Risk doorway, draws his own moral: "You know why you couldn't figure this one, Keyes? The guy you were looking for was too close, right across the desk from you." Keyes replies, "Closer than that, Walter." And Neff concludes the litany by saying "I love you too." It is said offhand, almost sarcastically, but it expresses Neff's genuine respect and affection for Keyes.

A similar sort of "professional" relationship exists between Neff and Phyllis Dietrichson. Initially, of course, at least as Neff perceives it, his relationship to Phyllis is almost completely physical. When Neff first stops at the Dietrichson home, to see about renewing Diet-richson's auto insurance, he sees Phyllis, standing at the head of the stairs, clad only in a bathrobe. Neff (in close-up) flashes a boyish smile and when Phyllis explains that she has been sunbathing cracks an adolescent joke ("no pigeons around, I hope"—he winces). He is clearly attracted to her—and the physical nature of that attraction is emphasised when Neff slowly paces the Dietrichson living room while waiting for Phyllis to get dressed. Wilder's camera follows Neff's movements while Neff in voice over describes the room's physical atmosphere: the smell of cigar smoke, the dusty sunshine, the Venetian blinds, the piano and the family photograph (of Dietrichson and his daughter by his first wife), the goldfish bowl on the table. But Neff "wasn't a whole lot interested in goldfish right then."

This Chandleresque attention to detail continues when Phyllis makes her entrance. We first see her high heels coming quickly down the stairs (Neff in voice over: "I wanted to see her again, close"). Wilder then tracks back to pick her up in medium shot as she buttons the bodice of her dress and steps before the mirror to put her "face on straight." Even at this point in the film Phyllis is aware of and plays upon Neff's sexual expectations in order to further her own pur-poses. She wants to talk about insurance while Neff wants to talk about her ("That's a honey of an anklet you're wearing, Mrs. Dietrichson"). Phyllis gives him a good eyeful (recall the way she

Getting down to business: MacMurray and Barbara Stanwyck discuss insurance in *Double Indemnity*.

crosses her legs to "hide" the anklet) while pretending to talk business. Neff quickly catches on and shifts his metaphor. Phyllis reluctantly reveals her first name. Neff comments that he "thinks" he likes it; Phyllis retorts, "But you're not sure"; and Neff offers "to drive it around the block a couple of times."

This rhetorical shift can be seen to carry ominous implications. Neff had come to the Dietrichson house to sell car insurance. His metaphor equates Phyllis with an automobile (she then accuses him of exceeding the "speed limit"). Cars figure prominently in the murder plot. Neff leaves his car with his garage attendant in order to establish an alibi. Neff hides in the back of Dietrichson's car when Phyllis drives her crippled husband to the railway depot, and he murders Dietrichson en route. Neff, impersonating Dietrichson, then boards the Southern Pacific while Phyllis drives the car bearing Dietrichson's body to the rendezvous. Neff then jumps from the train, drags Dietrichson's corpse to the tracks (we never see the body, only Neff's face as he strains to pull the dead weight), and then Neff and Phyllis make their suspenseful getaway in the self-same auto.

Dietrichson, therefore, is literally "driven" to his death—and the issue of "transportation," both physical and psychological, thus becomes important. Indeed, according to Keyes, the murder plot can itself be understood as a demonic and ill-fated vehicle. "They've committed a murder," Keyes explains, "and it's not like taking a trolley ride together where they can get off at different stops. They're stuck with each other and they've got to ride all the way to the end of the line." Keyes is right, of course. The murder, once committed, sets in motion a train of events that can only stop at death—but, as Keyes indicated by his own rushed syntax, the train-ride deathward can be exhilarating and meaningful in its own way. To be sure, Neff and Phyllis do not set out to commit some sort of elaborate double suicide. They do not believe they will be caught or that the plot will go off the track. But the attempt to beat the odds, the attempt to accept (and therefore deny) all risk (and Neff works for Pacific All Risk) is, in its grandeur and temerity, a marvellous undertaking, however self-defeating.

What binds Neff and Phyllis together is not, therefore, the desire for money. As Neff records it on the office dictaphone, he could not stop thinking about the possibility of murdering Dietrichson because it was all tied up with something he had been "thinking about" for years, long before he ever ran into Phyllis Dietrichson:

> You're like the guy behind the roulette wheel, watching the customers to make sure they don't crook the house. And then one night you get to thinking how you could crook the house yourself, and do it smart because you've got that wheel right under your hands, you know every notch in it by heart, and you figure all you need is a plant out front, a shill to put down the bet. Then suddenly the doorbell rings and the whole set up is right there in the room with you.

We see here the sense of fatalism which pervades the film. Neff implies that he would not have committed the murder were the perfect opportunity not presented. It is as if Neff had been invited to beat the odds. Indeed, Neff seems incapable of refusing the invitation. At best he can only hope that fortune will find a way of cancelling the party. Perhaps Dietrichson's broken leg is fate's way of letting Neff off the hook. But the roulette wheel metaphor, though accurate to a point, is clearly self-serving as well. Even Phyllis employs a similar

The scheme breaks down: Phyllis and Neff confront each other at the supermarket.

tactic when things start to fall apart. She tells Neff, as they face each other across a sterile, too-perfect supermarket shelf: "You planned the whole thing—I only wanted him dead." To be sure, once the bet is down, once Dietrichson is dead, fate does seem to close in on them. But prior to the murder they both seem very strong willed and self-possessed, capable certainly of enacting alternative scenarios.

That they choose to go through with the murder, therefore, indicates a genuine, almost childlike belief in their ability to bring it off. Neff is the best salesman at Pacific All Risk, and he clearly sells himself on the proposition that Phyllis loves him and that her love justifies homicide. He is convinced, furthermore, that he can avoid all negative consequences. As he tells Phyllis in his apartment, on the night when they decide to go through with the murder, "This is going to be perfect, you understand, straight down the line." This last phrase ("straight down the line") becomes, indeed, a sort of oft-repeated litany, ominous when considered in the context of the death-train metaphor but expressive, at least for Neff and Phyllis, of their mutual determination to commit the perfect crime.

Neff's motives in this are therefore clear: he wants to outwit the universe and his love for Phyllis provides the excuse. Phyllis's motives, however, are less self-evident, at least from Neff's point of view. And the problem involves Phyllis Dietrichson's capacity for dissimulation. For example, after her husband's body is found, Mr. Norton, the President of Pacific All Risk, calls Phyllis into his office to contest the coroner's verdict of accidental death. Norton expresses his pro forma regrets, and then plunges "straight into business." And business, for Norton, involves a financially motivated sort of emotional terrorism. He argues very stridently and at length that Dietrichson's death was a suicide—in which instance the company is "not liable." But his heavy-handed, moralistic rhetoric quickly gives way to the language of corporate expediency ("What I want to suggest is a compromise on both sides—a settlement"). It is a disgusting performance, crass, cold, and unfeeling. And Phyllis's angry response rings with a genuine sort of outrage: "You want to bargain with me, at a time like this. I don't like your insinuations about my husband and I don't like your methods. In fact, I don't like you, Mr. Norton." Her outrage is legitimate and her disfavour well deserved: Norton does not have a moral leg to stand on (as Keyes puts it). That Phyllis is equally culpable does not change the situation. She may feign ignorance of the accident policy, innocence in the matter of her husband's death—but we can hardly describe her response to Norton as "acting." Her tactic, here as elsewhere, is to orchestrate the contexts of her life so that her legitimate feelings—her disgust with Norton, her hatred for her husband—serve to further her illegitimate purposes.

But what about her feelings for Walter Neff? I have argued that the Neff/Phyllis relationship is not motivated by mere greed. At the very least, their relationship is one of mutual expediency: Phyllis provides Neff with the chance to crook the system while Neff gives Phyllis the opportunity to gain her independence of Dietrichson. But I believe that there is more to it than that, despite Phyllis's last minute assertion that she never loved Walter or anyone else. To be brief about it, I believe that Phyllis comes to love Neff unknowingly and despite herself. Her life before meeting Neff has been a search for financial security (hence all the talk about new hats and new dresses). She had been a private nurse, in which role she had hastened the death of the first Mrs. Dietrichson; and once married to her former employer she begins scheming to rid herself of his hated presence while holding on to his fortune. That fortune, however, evaporates soon thereafter, upon Dietrichson's entry into the petroleum racket. At which point Phyllis starts thinking seriously about the possibility of the accident insurance gambit: she can be rid of her husband and gain financial security in one well-calculated move.

Such is the situation when Neff first calls at the Dietrichson house. Initially, then, Phyllis encourages Neff's attentions for the purpose of acquiring the necessary accident insurance. During Neff's first visit, indeed, she is careful not to push the issue too hard; and Neff leaves with sex rather than murder on his mind ("I felt like a million"). Phyllis then arranges Neff's next visit so they can be alone—and she raises the question: can she get accident insurance on her husband without her husband being aware of the transaction? Neff catches on immediately—Phyllis backs off and she eventually follows Neff to his apartment with the intention of covering her tracks: "I must have said something that gave you a terribly wrong impression—you must never think anything like that about me, Walter." And her manner is as important as her words, here: she does seem sorry that she ordered Neff out of the house that afternoon. Most of the conversation, however, focuses on the relationship between Phyllis and her husband. As Phyllis tells Neff: "He keeps me on a leash so tight I can't breathe." And again her sincerity comes through—she really does hate Dietrichson—and she effectively enlists Neff's sympathy by aligning her "role" with her emotions.

Doubtless, Phyllis sees her "seduction" of Neff as a master-stroke of calculation. Not only does she get the insurance but she gets an insurance expert to participate in planning and executing the murder. As the plan evolves, however, we see something more than murder taking place. Phyllis may begin by feigning love for Neff ("I'm crazy about you, Walter")—but that love becomes real (as her inability to pull the trigger eventually indicates), and real for very good reason. Phyllis has literally met her match in Neff. Both are salesmen of a sort; both are schemers on a grand scale; both are dedicated to the assertion of ego over circumstance. For once in her life self-interest and love come into alignment: Phyllis sees herself in Neff. And it is this sense of shared identity which allows us to account for those moments in the film when Phyllis seems genuinely ecstatic with herself, with Walter, and with their scheme.

For example, after Neff surreptitiously gets Dietrichson's signature on the policy, Phyllis walks Neff to the door. She bids Neff a polite "good night" as she watches her husband climb the stairs to the bedroom. She then ducks out the door and confers with Neff in the shadows. Neff confirms the signature, the date of Dietrichson's trip to Palo Alto, and he tells Phyllis that Dietrichson must not drive: she must make sure he takes the train. Phyllis asks why, and Neff explains "double indemnity" in a rushed whisper: "they pay double for certain accidents, the kind that almost never happen—like, for instance, if a guy is killed on the train." Neff thus goes Phyllis one better (Neff: "we're hitting it for the limit") and the look on her face after Neff leaves indicates the high degree of her admiration for him. There is no one there to catch her act—she smiles spontaneously and to herself—and it is clear that Neff has inspired her respect. There are other such moments, as well—when Phyllis calls Neff after the incident in Norton's office, for example—and there are moments later in the film when her attitude verges on disgust for Neff's weakness. The point, however, is that her relationship with Neff is sufficiently ambiguous—she is not sure herself how she feels—that her hesitation to kill Neff is not unmotivated. As the role is written, Phyllis may be completely heartless; but, as Wilder directs it and Stanwyck enacts it, Phyllis is clearly torn between the extreme instincts of self-preservation (she tries to kill Neff) and love (she begs him to hold her close).

At the film's conclusion, then, all of its metaphors and concerns come together. Phyllis and Neff have reached the end of the line. Their "perfect" scheme has come unravelled, as Keyes had predicted it would. In attempting to outwit the universe they only outwit themselves. In attempting to deny the probabilities against success they only increase the certainty of failure. As Keyes puts it to Neff: "They may think it's twice as safe because they're two of 'em; but it isn't twice as safe—it's ten times twice as dangerous." Great expectations therefore collapse of their own corrupt accord—and the collapse is punishment enough. Indeed, Wilder does not bear down on the immorality of their action because he does not have to: murder is its own punishment and Phyllis and Neff become their own executioners.

Wilder is basically optimistic in this. People may be corrupt; society of the get-rich-quick Southern California sort may encourage their corruption; but the universe, as is generally the case in tragedy, remains basically just. Wilder's detractors take him to task, however, because Wilder refuses to be judgmental in a simple-minded fashion. Wilder allows us to get close to characters like Neff and Phyllis because even their failures are quintessentially human. Even in their corruption they are interesting because their corruption represents only a slightly displaced, though clearly self-destructive, version of more common desires. All of us long for security of one sort or another, though some strategies hold out more hope for success. Neff and Phyllis simply seek more security than the universe has to offer: hence the insurance metaphor—nothing is sure but death. And, if we feel betrayed, it is because intimacy always requires risk.

Indeed, that is the point of *Double Indemnity*. Life can never be perfect. We cannot figure them all. We have to take chances. Ultimately, love is twice as risky as hate, but we must accept uncertainty as the price we pay for getting close to people. It is ironic that it takes murder to bring Neff and Phyllis together. But once together, no matter how perverse their initial motives, they encounter a depth of feeling and consciousness which is almost worth the price they pay. Phyllis finally becomes aware that love is possible, though it requires embracing her executioner. And Neff sets Zachetti straight about Lola even though it requires confession: Neff must admit his own guilt to Keyes if Zachetti is to be kept out of the gas chamber. In both cases it is a matter of self-sacrifice. We hardly expect it of Phyllis, though when it comes it seems perfectly logical, but her decision not to fire the second shot and Neff's decision to confess rather than escape express between them a genuinely positive sense of value.

As is generally the case in tragedy, however, the value of life only becomes evident when the fact of life is at hazard. Indeed, the film's narrative structure—flashbacks enclosed by a framework of relatively brief duration—is simultaneously a process of dying and understanding. Neff begins his dictation near midnight and concludes near 4:30 a.m. By recounting the story of his relationship with Phyllis, Neff gains the distance necessary for understanding. Thus, at the beginning of his narrative, he argues greed and love as probable motives: but as he continues he realises that neither love nor greed were motive enough for his actions. There was more to it than that. Neff was really out to crook the universe. Simultaneously, however, while Neff laboriously dictates his four hour confession, he slowly bleeds to death. Toward the end he complains, "It's cold," wonders forlornly if Phyllis is "still lying alone up there in that house," and he then concludes his confession as Keyes walks into the room. As originally written, Neff does not die in the Pacific All Risk doorway—he recovers, stands trial, and is executed—but as finally released, *Double Indemnity* leaves us with the impression that Neff pays for awareness with his life. It is a chilling vision of existence (so is "King Lear" for that matter), but such visions serve their purpose if we accept vulnerability as a necessary condition of living in the material world.

* * *

Sunset Boulevard bears an interesting relationship to *Double Indemnity*. Both films employ a flashback structure to raise issues of self and self-consciousness. In both cases, self-consciousness comes simultaneously with dying: Walter Neff narrates *Double Indemnity* while bleeding to death and Joe Gillis (William Holden) narrates *Sunset Boulevard* while floating face down in that Sunset Boulevard swimming pool. In both cases, the sequence of events culminating in death is initiated almost by chance: both Neff and Gillis are out driving through the Los Angeles hills and both decide on the spur of the moment to turn into a driveway (Neff for business reasons, Gillis for the sake of escaping from the finance company boys). Neff thus comes face to face with Phyllis Dietrichson and therefore face to face with himself. Similarly Joe Gillis comes face to face with a pathetically ageing, illusion-bound, but still self-assertive silent movie queen, Norma Desmond (Gloria Swanson), a meeting which eventually results in Gillis's confession-like narrative. Furthermore, the "story" in each case involves a questionable sexual relationship. However we ultimately read the Neff/Phyllis relationship in *Double Indemnity,* it clearly begins as an expression of lust (on Neff's part) and calculation (on Phyllis's). Likewise, in *Sunset Boulevard,* the relationship between Gillis, a down-and-out screenwriter with a "couple of B pictures to his credit," and silent-star Norma Desmond begins as an expression of fear (Norma fears, without saying it, that her original screenplay for *Salome* will not pass muster at Paramount without the help of a card-carrying screenwriter) and as an expression of financial cynicism (Gillis figures he can "concoct a little plot" of his own by doing a "patch up job" on Norma's "silly hodgepodge of melodramatic clichés"—at the rate of a quick and dirty $500 a week). In each case, the central male/female pair is set against (and threatens) a more normal, more innocent, though hardly perfect sexual relationship: Lola and Zachetti in *Double Indemnity,* Betty Schaefer (Nancy Olson) and Artie Green (Jack Webb) in *Sunset Boulevard.* And, in each case, the central character asserts his better self through self-sacrifice. That is, Neff confesses to Keyes in order to save Zachetti; while Gillis confesses to Betty in the hope that she will go back to Artie.

The primary difference between the two films, therefore, is a matter not of structure but metaphor. *Double Indemnity* employs the flashback form as a means of coming to terms with a certain type of romantic obsession. Neff and Phyllis both set out to crook the universe by committing the perfect crime. The attempt is doomed, of course, but it allows the characters to express their humanity in a more genuine fashion than either had thought possible. *Sunset Boulevard* makes use of a similar structure, again for the purpose of coming to terms with a form of romantic obsession—but the obsession in *Sunset Boulevard* has less to do with crime than with immortality and art. That is, Norma Desmond attempts to confound time, to return from the dead in effect, and the vehicle for her return, as it was for her coming, is cinema. She wants to resurrect the good old days, to return to Paramount ("without me, there would be no Paramount"), to Mr. DeMille, and to the legions of adoring fans who have "never forgiven" her "for deserting the screen." Her profession certainly encourages this belief that time can be arrested. Her over-opulent mansion abounds with photographs of a younger Norma Desmond ("Norma Desmonds, more Norma Desmonds and still more Norma Desmonds," as Joe puts it), and Norma frequently spends her evenings indulging in a bizarre form of self-worship, sitting tensely on the sofa beside Joe as they watch her silent self upon her private screen. Cinema is therefore a completely appropriate and powerful metaphor for the desire to deny mortality; and the cinematic metaphor allows Wilder to explore basic ontological issues.

Wilder undertakes this exploration by examining various "styles of being," particularly as those styles do (or do not) exhibit an appropriate awareness of the relationship between mutability and art. Age is, therefore, as Richard Corliss points out (pp. 147-150), a central concern. At one extreme we have the Old Hollywood of Norma Desmond, Max von Meyerling (Erich von Stroheim), and the rest of Norma's Hollywood waxworks (including H. B. Warner and Buster Keaton). And at the other extreme we have the New Hollywood of Joe Gillis, Betty Schaefer and Artie Green. Each generation has a different style, a different mode of existence and creation. The Old Hollywood thrived on silent melodrama, on the heroic gesture, on star worship (Norma still consults astrologers). The New Hollywood values a socially conscious sort of literary realism, martyrdom as creativity is stifled by studio bigwigs and insensitive agents, and a hard boiled, behind-the-camera, true-to-life stance. To some degree, it is a matter of the image (the silent cinema) vs. the word (the talkies)—and yet the film does not argue word and image as antithetical. It is

New Hollywood (William Holden) *vs.* Old Hollywood (Eric von Stroheim) in *Sunset Boulevard.*

possible, as DeMille (playing himself) demonstrates, to change with the times, to move from the silents to the talkies, without betraying or denying the value that images may have. And, similarly, it is possible, as Betty Schaefer demonstrates, to move from before the camera to behind it. She began as an actress but switched to production, working her way up the studio ladder from mail room to reader's department, when it became clear that acting was not her strong suit.

And yet, despite the superficial differences of style and manner, the two Hollywoods share a common impulse—the drive for success and security, as success is defined at any given point in time. Even Betty Schaefer, who serves as the (relatively) innocent third party in the Norma/Betty/Joe triangle, longs for success as a screenwriter. She is third generation Hollywood ("Grandma did stunt work for Pearl White") and she seizes the opportunity presented by one of Joe's backlogged scripts to urge a collaboration. She has a producer "hopped up" over the story, realises that she cannot finish the script unaided, even though Joe grants her the prerogative ("it's all yours"), and she gets genuinely angry at Joe's lack of enthusiasm. As she tells him at Schwab's drugstore: "I kind of hoped to get in on this deal—I don't want to be a reader all my life." To be sure, Wilder does not condemn Betty's ambition *per se:* we rather expect 22-year-olds to look to the future. But Wilder does raise the issue of her sexual loyalties, at least to the extent that Betty's sexual interest seems to shift, rather conveniently, with the change in her professional situation: through the course of their clandestine collaboration Betty proceeds to fall in love with Joe. It does not seem coy or calculated, Betty is herself troubled by the change, but the issue of mixed motives remains unresolved. Ultimately, of course, we come to understand how readily shared goals (mutual self-interest) can lead to emotional involvement—and yet Betty's action still seems tainted.

Our sense of discomfort, however, is not a function of Betty's action by itself. Rather, her action seems tainted for recalling, in no small detail, Joe's behavior *vis-à-vis* Norma. In each case the younger person undertakes to rewrite or rework the older person's original script; and in both instances collaboration—which involves shared activities and shared goals—leads to love of a sort. On balance, Betty's love for Joe seems the purer for breaking fewer taboos. We do not cringe when they embrace on the balcony outside Betty's office, as we do cringe when Norma's boney hands and bandaged arms clutch Joe and pull him down to "celebrate" the New Year. Yet the issue of expediency remains: in neither case can we neatly separate affection from self-interest. And, furthermore, the equation works in both directions. If the relationship between Betty and Joe seems tainted by its similarity to the relationship between Joe and Norma, then the relationship between Joe and Norma gains legitimacy when placed against the Joe/Betty relationship. They differ only in that Norma needs Joe more than Joe needs Betty (Norma's love, indeed, borders on hysteria), and in that Joe is more aware than Norma that love entails not only self-interest but responsibility. In each case the older partner (Norma/Joe) views the younger partner (Joe/Betty) as a link with the past: loving Joe makes Norma feel young again, loving Betty allows Joe to shed some of his cynicism and regain a youthful enthusiasm for writing. And in each case the older partner rejects the younger in accord with a particular style of "being in time." That is, Joe rejects Betty and by so doing asserts the value of "realism" as well as a genuine sense of personal responsibility. Likewise, Norma rejects

Joe (by shooting him) as an equally genuine assertion of "illusion": she is a star, nobody walks out on a star, and therefore Joe becomes nobody, becomes a corpse grotesquely afloat in Norma's floodlit swimming pool. It all follows a concise though perhaps brutal logic. And both assertions are simultaneously melodramatic and self-destructive—Joe dies, Norma goes mad.

Wilder's point, however, is that both styles of being are equally valid when seen within the larger context of time. Joe, of course, would like to think otherwise. Joe-as-narrator begins the film by positing a ready distinction between reality (which he views as grotesque) and illusion (reality distorted and made glamorous by the news media), and he offers to recount "the facts, the whole truth" before it is "all distorted and blown out of proportion." His tone of voice here, and throughout the first section of the film (up to the point of Norma's suicide attempt), rings with a smug, self-serving detachment, as if Gillis were somehow superior to the drama he relates. And it is not simply a matter of the voice-over narration. A voice from the dead ought, perhaps, to be granted a certain privilege. But Joe employs this pseudo-cynical stance from the very beginning of his association with Norma. He feels himself superior to her and to Hollywood in general (the studios, he explains sarcastically, turned his dust bowl epic into a torpedo boat tale), sees Norma as an easy mark, a crazy old lady that he can readily manipulate, and even after moving into Norma's mansion he sports a whore's ethics—physically involved while trying (or pretending) to be mentally and emotionally above it all.

The film clearly argues against such a stance—at least to the degree that Joe interprets his New Hollywood brand of cynicism as more genuine, more legitimate, more realistic, than Norma's time-bound egomania. To begin with, of course, Joe clearly underestimates Norma—underestimates her cunning in the service of self-preservation (she manipulates Joe far more than Joe manipulates her), and underestimates the degree to which Norma is correct in her evaluation of the Hollywood present: in a way, she is right: "It's the pictures that got small." And secondly, Joe quite mistakenly overestimates the degree of his own immunity to the Hollywood ethos. Like each of the three novice writers in the film, Joe longs for the limelight—even if that light is only a few seconds of flickering screen credits: "Screenplay by, original story by. . . ." As Joe tells us in the opening sequence, he "always wanted a pool."

But there is more to cinematic success than crazy mansions and Isotta-Fraschini automobiles. Norma's passionate desire to return to the screen is not a function of poverty: she is a millionaire (as she tells Joe on New Year's Eve). Rather, her passion is indicative of an almost frantic desire to "be"—to be loved, to be recognised, to be actively at work. Her dilemma, of course, and hence her fear of time, results not from a particularly pathological fear of ageing—although ageing is hardly to be seen as a painless process—but from the fear that time has passed her by, has made it impossible for her "to be in the world" because the world no longer has room for her style of being. It is not just a matter of words replacing gestures in the vocabulary of cinema, however, even if Norma would like to think that such is the case. It is rather that the cinema has remained true to the cult of youthful faces that Norma had herself helped to initiate. If Norma had a youthful Betty Hutton face she would be working regardless of changes in film technology.

Joe can sympathise with Norma, therefore, for being in an analogous position. Both the "has been" and the "never was" (Corliss, p. 149) exist on the periphery of the Hollywood system, and each longs to gain (or regain) celebrity, acclaim, and a sense of purpose. This sense of shared circumstance allows us to account for the gradual change in Joe's attitude and position vis-à-vis Norma. At first Joe sees her as a cuckoo old lady—someone he can exploit and desert at will. But as he settles step by step into the routine of life on Sunset Boulevard, he slowly discovers, almost despite himself, that Norma's eccentricities are not a matter of self-indulgent grotesquerie. On the contrary, they serve to mask a deep and genuine sense of despair, very akin in its genesis to Joe's own brand of snappy sarcasm. Joe finds Norma fascinating, therefore, as an only slightly distorted reflection of his own hopes and fears: and his imprisonment, at least until the night of Norma's wrist-slashing episode, is clearly self-imposed. He may get genuinely upset when the finance company boys haul his car away (it is, he argues, a matter of "life and death"); but when Norma professes her love for Joe in her drunken New Year's Eve fit he does not let the lack of wheels prevent his leaving: he just walks out to Sunset Boulevard and thumbs a ride.

Very early on, then, it is clear that the Norma/Joe relationship reflects more than mere exploitation—Joe stays because he finds Norma interesting, because she is, in her way, very much like Joe himself. Furthermore, there is the matter of gratitude. When Joe returns to Norma, after learning of her suicide attempt, he tells her: "You're the only person in this stinking town that has been good to me." This is not totally accurate—Artie Green does his best by

Joe—but it clearly expresses the feeling on Joe's part that Norma has not genuinely ill-treated him. Her worst sin, after all, is that she allows herself to fall in love with a younger man. Again, our initial reaction is at one with Joe's—horror. But we come to understand, as Joe comes to understand, much to his own astonishment upon learning of Norma's desperate attempt to end it all, that Norma really means something to him: note how he rushes through the crowd at Artie's party and rushes through the door at Norma's mansion. However illusion bound Norma may be, Joe now begins to comprehend the necessity for the illusion—and his own responsibility to help maintain it. He may not "love" her in any normal sense of the word, but he suddenly finds himself in a position of power: he can kill Norma simply by walking out on her, and he chooses not to do so, at least not until Norma forces his hand for reasons of jealousy.

All of which indicates that *Sunset Boulevard* is not a film devoid of ethics, love, or pity—although in each case such virtues are expressed instinctively and in accord with a particular "style" of behaviour. Norma's life style, for example—her mansion, her bizarre wardrobe, her hand-made automobile, her paramour—represents after all a form of integrity, an assertion of self in defiance of time. Even her suicide attempts have a certain heroic legitimacy to them—"a great star has her great pride"—and Norma would rather cease living than live in accord with a meaningless and hopeless present. Or consider Max, Norma's butler/chauffeur, her first husband, and the director who discovered Norma as a 16-year-old girl. At first, we tend to concur with Joe in our evaluation of Max: he and Norma are a matched set of crazies (as, for instance, when the two of them bury the dead chimp in the garden). And yet, as the narrative progresses, we come to understand that Max is less a servant than a guardian. He writes the fan letters that keep Norma busy; he makes sure that Norma's eyeshadow is balanced; and he serves as a rock solid buffer (Wilder often films von Stroheim in profile closeups which emphasise this solidity), standing between Norma and the present (as, for example, when he demands to be admitted at the Paramount studio gate or, later on, when he "directs" her "farewell appearance"). His motive in every instance is clearly kindness of a sort, and when he stoops to retrieve Norma's bejewelled veil, which she had thrown off lest it come between Joe and herself, we sense the agony and the empathy of his position: he straightens, steps back, and gazes eye-straight ahead, lest he lose emotional control. Seeing her in love with Joe is almost more than he can bear; but even worse would be the destruction of Norma's fantastic universe and the concommitant destruction of her equally fantastic yet majestic sense of self. As Max expresses it to Joe in the darkness of the garage, he found "everything unendurable" after Norma had left him—and Max therefore accepts the butler role quite willingly in order to be close to Norma, in order to be sure that Norma never learns the truth.

The film's illusion/reality conflict finally comes to a head when Norma, her nerves "torn to shreds" by the pressure of her rejuvenation regimen, and desperate at the thought that Joe is seeing another woman, anonymously calls Betty to tell her the story of Joe's sordid relationship with an older, wealthier woman. Norma thus reveals an unexpected degree of self-awareness: when her illusion threatens to fall apart she is not beneath employing something like the truth to gain her ends. And by so doing she also eliminates any possibility that Joe can escape the necessity for "facing facts." Indeed, Joe enters the room in the background and overhears Norma's morbid narrative. His hand is now forced. Joe grabs the phone and invites Betty to come

The has-been and the never-was: Gloria Swanson as Norma Desmond and William Holden as Joe Gillis.

by the mansion—then she can see for herself how Joe lives and with whom.

The entire situation has a very tragic cast to it. Norma is the unwitting victim of her past and of her own past success. She understands very clearly the allure of young beautiful faces, understands that Joe has fallen in love with just such a young and beautiful woman, and understands further that her attempt at rejuvenation is bound to fail. Thus she begs Joe's forgiveness and pleads that she needs him more than ever before: "Look at me, look at my hands, look at my face, look under my eyes—how can I go back to work if I'm wasting away under this torment." Again her rhetoric is self-serving. She looks old, she argues, not because she is old but because Joe's infidelity has driven her to the verge of a mental and physical breakdown. Norma therefore endeavours to accommodate her anxiety within the context of her personal "style of being." As a result, however, she only forces Joe to revert, at least in part, to his earlier "realistic" stance.

Throughout the central section of the film Joe's attitude towards Norma has been compassionate. His wise cracks are no longer directed at Norma (he rather complains about audiences who believe that actors make up their lines without the aid of writers), and he collaborates with Max in maintaining the fiction that DeMille really wants to use Norma (rather than her automobile). In other words, Joe adapts himself to Norma's style of being—he learns how to play bridge, dance the tango, how to lead the life of a well-dressed companion to a well-heeled older woman. But by so doing Joe does not express cynicism. It is ironic that being kind to Norma is the most significant and purposeful course of action open to Joe, but his instinctive decision to be kind is very much to his credit.

In any case, Norma's phone call to Betty forces Joe to shift styles. He can no longer maintain the fiction that he "loves" Norma, or at least he cannot maintain it in the melodramatic terms that Norma requires. And he can no longer hide from Betty the fact of his questionable involvement with Norma. Yet it quickly becomes clear that Joe's realistic "face the facts" style depends as much on illusion as Norma's romantic style. Thus, when Betty arrives at the mansion, Joe takes her on a guided tour of sorts, showing her the grand living room with its hide-away movie screen and its pipe-organ and its countless framed photographs. Furthermore, he describes in very unflattering terms his relationship with Norma ("an older woman who's well to do—a younger man who's not doing too well"), and he invites Betty to fill in the gruesome details. But Joe clearly speaks in half truths here, leaving out altogether the fact of his compassion, a fact which radically changes the picture. And Joe knows he is lying. Throughout his speech Joe walks around the room, away from Betty, not looking at her. When he completes the circuit and stands once again face to face, Betty pleads with him to pack up and leave ("if you love me, Joe"). At that Joe turns his back once again on Betty and walks to a closeup in the lower left hand quadrant of the screen. He tells her "to be practical" and argues that he has "a good deal here—a long term contract with no options." It all sounds glibly realistic, as Joe no doubt intends it to sound, but the pained expression on his face (an expression hidden from Betty) measures his agony: like Virgil Smith

Bing Crosby in *The Emperor Waltz.*

(Bing Crosby) in *The Emperor Waltz,* Joe expresses his integrity by pretending to be his worst self. Only by so doing can Joe convince Betty to leave and to return to Artie.

Clearly, then, Joe's "realistic" stance, at least by this point in the film, has become a "style" in every sense of the word, a pattern of action motivated from within, as an expression of personal ethics and priorities. Joe's rejection of Betty is therefore an ethical decision, realistic from Joe's point of view for acknowledging his own sense of self-disgust. And his decision to leave Norma is similarly motivated. He is nobody special, certainly not an immortal of the cinema, just a hick newsman from Dayton, Ohio, and thus it is perfectly in keeping with Joe's hardbitten style that he retreat to the journalistic trenches. To do so, as Joe sees it, is simply to acknowledge reality: there is no room in Hollywood for Joe Gillis. For that matter, however, there is no room in Hollywood for Norma Desmond, and as Norma becomes more frantic at the prospect of Joe's departure (he literally packs his bags and returns Norma's presents), Joe is forced, somewhat against his will, to disillusion Norma as well. He remains compassionate, but he becomes convinced that her interests are better served by acknowledging the facts of the situation. There are no fan letters, there isn't going to be any picture, and there is no audience to mourn Norma's passing should she make good her promised suicide attempt.

Again, Joe miscalculates, carried away as he is by his own martyr-like New Hollywood style of doing things. Once more he assumes the superiority of a particular mode of being—and to some degree, perhaps, he is justified in this. Joe is clearly more comfortable playing the down-and-out writer role, and by assuming that role he re-asserts his own independence, his own identity. But by so doing he also loses his identity by inviting the now deranged Norma to shoot him in the back, by inviting her to carry the *Salome* role to its proper aesthetic conclusion. Joe assumes that the truth will set him free, that reality will overcome or defuse illusion. And he fails to account for the possibility that illusion has a reality of its own, a reality powerful enough to pitch him headlong into oblivion. Indeed, he fails to understand the degree to which he is enacting his own fondest fantasy. He literally becomes the martyred poet, stabbed in the back by the Hollywood system.

At the film's conclusion, then, Joe-the-narrator finally comes to acknowledge the power of fantasy. His tone of voice remains bitter as he condemns "the heartless so-and-sos" who gather at the murder scene as if it were opening day at a supermarket. But he comes to

Enfolded by the dream: the cameras roll once more for Norma Desmond.

understand Norma's madness as a legitimate if desperate method of dealing with a world that insists on describing her as a "star of yesteryear." Norma's ritualistic, wide-eyed insistence to the contrary—"stars are ageless"—represents a genuine attempt to deny time, to deny mortality, to conquer the imperfection of the flesh. In fact, it cannot be done. But imagination has its own resources: thus Norma Desmond finally regains the limelight and finds herself once more before those magic cameras. As Joe puts it: "Life, which can be strangely merciful, had taken pity on Norma Desmond. The dream she had clung to so desperately had enfolded her." Norma's obsession thus becomes a timeless form of reality. By going mad she freezes time and prevents any further deterioration of her emotional position. As in *Double Indemnity,* we do not have in *Sunset Boulevard* a pleasant vision of normality. But the process of the film, for us as well as for Joe Gillis, requires that we acknowledge the humanity and integrity of those who dare to follow the high road of risk and imagination.

*   *   *

In formal terms, Wilder's films fall into two large groups—those narrated largely in flashback, which includes not only *Double Indemnity* and *Sunset Boulevard* but *Stalag 17, The Lost Weekend,* and *The Private Life of Sherlock Holmes,* and those whose narration is chronologically straightforward. Generally speaking, the flashback films tend to bear down on a sense of loss, a sense of the past—and they tend in generic terms to be tragedies of romantic obsession, fables of failure which counsel accommodation to the facts of life. Such is clearly the case in *Double Indemnity* and *Sunset Boulevard,* although the metaphor is different in each instance. There are exceptions to the rule of course. *The Lost Weekend,* for example, is a flashback film that feels like a tragedy but which becomes instead an ironic comedy, at least to the extent that Don accepts a realistic though not pessimistic picture of himself and thereby re-asserts his relationship with Helen. And romantic obsession as a theme occurs repeatedly in the more straightforward films. Indeed, Wilder's most powerful metaphor for obsession—Nazism—is used more frequently in straightforward narratives like *Five Graves to Cairo, A Foreign Affair,* and *One, Two, Three* than in the flashback films. This probably results from the fact that first person narrative almost always requires (or generates) some sympathy for the narrator—and it seems unlikely that an Austrian émigré like Wilder could be that sympathetic toward National Socialism. The only Nazis who attract a real measure of Wilder's admiration are Erika von Schluetow in *A Foreign Affair*—as played by Dietrich, she is a woman of wit and style whose participation in the Nazi experiment was primarily passive (letting Hitler kiss her hand)—and Erwin Rommel (Erich von Stroheim) in *Five Graves to Cairo,* whose Nazism seems subsidiary to his sense of military professionalism and personal loyalty.

Stalag 17 is interesting, then, in that it combines the fascist metaphor and the flashback structure. To be sure, the two seem literally at odds: the character who narrates (who *is*) the flashback is an American POW, and the tale he tells involves the conflict between the POWs and their German captors. But, as the narrative progresses and as it becomes clear that there must be a collaborator or a spy among the prisoners, we come to see that the narrator's behaviour (the narrator as character within his own story), and indeed the behaviour of all of the American POWs, takes on a decidedly fascist aspect, and becomes all the more fascist as the Nazis escalate their efforts to undermine prisoner morale.

Above, Erich von Stroheim (centre) as Erwin Rommel in *Five Graves to Cairo.*

Right, Marlene Dietrich as Erika von Schluetow in *A Foreign Affair.*

Immediately, then, a simple good-guy/bad-guy reading of *Stalag 17* is undercut. Indeed, the narrator, Cookie (Gil Stratton Jr.), himself rejects romanticism (or attempts to reject it) in the film's voice-over prologue: "It always makes me sore when I see those war pictures, all about flying leathernecks and submarine patrols and frogmen and guerillas in the Philippines. What gets me is that there never was a movie about POWs, about prisoners of war." As is generally the case in Wilder's flashback films, the prologue and its import take on additional and sometimes shifting meanings through the course of the film, and we will have occasion to return to Cookie's opening remarks. But the general thrust of Cookie's first person account, his condemnation of Hollywood heroics, encourages a "realistic" reading of *Stalag 17*.

In visual terms, such a reading is clearly justified. The film is by turns drab, foreboding, and harsh, taking full if depressing advantage of the black/white spectrum and of our tendency to read black-and-white as denoting a documentary sort of "reality." There are few long shots, and those serve primarily to emphasise the film's sense of enclosure. The camp is hunkered down in a barren forest, beneath a leaden, slate-grey sky, surrounded by mountains that seem inert without ever seeming majestic: they exist, but only as one more barrier between the prisoners and freedom. For the most part, however, the film is shot within the camp (we see the muddy, snow-patched yard) and within Barracks Four (we see rough-hewn bunks stacked one atop the other). The camera set-ups, accordingly, are determined by the same physical constraints that delimit prisoner activity—and there seems little room for heroics.

A similarly forceful sense of realism, bordering at times on cynicism, seems to motivate the film's central character, Sefton (William Holden), entrepreneur in residence at Stalag 17, who recalls—in his arrogance, his apparent capacity for selfishness, and his anger—the Joe Gillis character (also played by Holden) in *Sunset Boulevard*. Both men, we should remark, are washouts, Joe from Hollywood, Sefton from flight school. Both men, furthermore, are set against more authoritative has-beens, ex-film-star Norma Desmond in *Sunset Boulevard,* and ex-cavalry officer, now turned bitterly sarcastic camp commandant, Col. von Scherbach (Otto Preminger) in *Stalag 17*. And there is a tendency, with both films, to perceive the conflict of has-been with would-have-been as expressing Wilder's sense of nihilism.

Such a reading seems far more plausible for *Stalag 17* than for

Otto Preminger (right) as Colonel von Scherbach in *Stalag 17:* **Harvey Lembeck (left) and Don Taylor (center).**

Sunset Boulevard. In the earlier film, as I have argued, Joe's decision to return to Norma after her suicide attempt makes it clear, midway through the narrative, that their relationship embodies, however paradoxically, a sense of shared goals and genuine feelings: Joe is not drawn to Norma for her money. In *Stalag 17,* on the other hand, the apparent collaboration between von Scherbach and Sefton seems to reflect each man's dedication to self-service.

Von Scherbach, for one, is clearly concerned with camp security, not for the contribution that a secure Stalag 17 might make to the German war effort but for the fact that a perfect record will further his own career. Indeed, von Scherbach takes a certain malevolent pleasure in asserting his own power and identity, which he accomplishes by tormenting his captives. Thus, for example, he launches into an extended, self-satisfied, hands-on-hips monologue, complete with sarcastically friendly references to the weather ("I so much hoped we could give you a white Christmas, just like the ones you used to know") to announce the capture/execution of Manfredi and Johnson, the two POWs who had attempted to escape in the film's opening sequence. As von Scherbach almost gleefully puts it, just before ordering a guard to lift the tarp from the bodies so that the assembled prisoners might witness his lethal handiwork: "They had the good sense to rejoin us again so my record would remain unblemished."

Sefton's selfishness, on the other hand, expresses itself not through murder (though he will be accused of collaborating in the "murder" of Manfredi and Johnson) but through dedication to "private property" and private enterprise. Sefton's status as the camp's most well-heeled prisoner is established in the opening sequence. While Manfredi and Johnson make their way through the tunnel, Sefton bets against their success—not, we should note, for motives of greed alone (it is clear, when Cookie obediently opens Sefton's footlocker to get sufficient cigarettes to cover the bets, that Sefton lacks for nothing)—but as a means of countering the facile optimism expressed by the other prisoners. And yet it is possible to interpret Sefton's irritation here as expressing an opportunistic sort of cynicism. That is, he may not need cigarettes, but winning them may serve to reinforce Sefton's sense of superiority. Indeed, such an interpretation gains strength the next morning, after roll call, when Sefton cooks himself a hard-to-come-by egg for breakfast. His envious barracks mates razz Sefton as he prepares to eat his meal, and Sefton brings the issue out in the open: "What's the beef, boys? So I'm trading. Everybody is trading. So maybe I trade a little sharper." At which point, Duke (Neville Brand), Sefton's prime nemesis and accuser, breaks in, argues menacingly that Sefton is a "lot sharper," and Sefton replies: "Listen, stupe, the first week I was in this joint somebody stole my red cross package, my blanket, and my left shoe. Well, since then I've wised up. This ain't no Salvation Army. This is everybody for himself, dog eat dog."

All of which would seem to support a taker/taken reading of *Stalag 17:* there are those characters who win, who get what they want regardless of the consequences to others, and there are those who get taken, who lose, because they were not sharp enough or self-centered enough to get their share. But such a reading does not hold up and is not supported by the evidence of the film. To begin with, the POWs cannot be described as a gang of heartless thugs, despite the fact that they beat Sefton to a bloody pulp after convincing themselves that he is the collaborator. As the camp's most proficient trader, he is the most logical candidate: he could trade information as easily as silk stockings or cameras. As a group, however, the prisoners generally demonstrate a remarkable *esprit de corps,* recalling that of the French prisoners in Renoir's *La Grande Illusion* and *Le Caporal Epinglé.* Everyone may be trading, as Sefton points out, but such trading is only incidental. The primary activity and concern of the Stalag 17 prisoners is the maintenance of their sanity and equilibrium, the maintenance, in other words, of their humanity, despite their dehumanising circumstances: witness their spontaneous humour, their concern for crazy Joey, witness the teamwork involved in their escape attempts, and particularly the teamwork required to snatch Lt. Dunbar (Don Taylor) from the S.S. before the S.S. can get Dunbar out of camp.

It is important to keep in mind, furthermore, just who started the war, for it is the difference between initiating and improvising which serves to define the moral issue in *Stalag 17.* Like Hitler, von Scherbach asserts his own personality over and above the common good. Carried to the Nazi extreme, this sort of self-assertion at the expense of human life is clearly to be rejected. The prisoners, by contrast, Sefton included, harbour no such ambitions—as individuals they are occupied not by dreams of conquest but by thoughts of home: hence the importance of mail call, of the Christmas tree, of their pin-ups (Betty Grable), of their home-made radio. And as a group they struggle to continue their improvised but purposeful opposition to the oppressive and inhuman Nazi regime. Thus Cookie's complaint in the prologue that movies only celebrate the heroism of "flying leathernecks" is not a condemnation of heroics *per se.* On the contrary, Cookie and his mates long for the opportunity to take significant action, even if it means throwing rocks at low-flying German aircraft. Indeed, it is only when their efforts to counter von Scherbach's lust for perfection are frustrated (i.e., when von Scherbach arrests Lt. Dunbar for sabotage) that they settle on Sefton as their scapegoat.

Put another way, *Stalag 17* pits a jackbooted ringmaster and his sideshow henchmen against a crew of children (Joey and Blondy) and comedians (Hoffy describes Harry and Animal as "the barracks clowns"). Indeed, much is made of this clown metaphor, which serves to embody the democratic and existential spirit of improvisation, both slapstick (Harry and Animal "paint" their way into the women's compound) and serious (Lt. Dunbar blows up a German munitions train with a jerry-rigged cigarette-and-matchbook time bomb). Thus, for example, when Animal, angry over the deaths of Manfredi and Johnson and angrier still at von Scherbach's patronising offer to supply Christmas trees for each barracks ("You will like that"), heaves Joey's ocarina into a mud puddle at von Scherbach's jack-booted feet, von Scherbach offers to "give the funny man exactly five seconds to step forward." Everyone (Sefton included) steps forward—as von Scherbach puts it: "I see, six hundred funny men." And later, when Schulz confiscates the radio, he ducks the embittered wisecracks by declaring that "everybody's a clown." Schulz then turns good-naturedly to Lt. Dunbar and wonders aloud how the Allies expect to win the war with "an army of clowns." And Dunbar's reply ("We sort of hope you'll laugh yourself to death") is indicative of the prisoners' determination to have the last laugh even if the Nazis had the first.

It is important to remark, then, that the camp's biggest clown, the man who makes the most significant single contribution to the maintenance of prisoner morale, even before he uncovers the collaborator in their midst, is Sefton. Every one of his schemes for self-enrichment serves to ease the burden of imprisonment. His rat races, his "killer diller" still, his peep show (a telescope view of a steaming bathhouse window in the women's compound)—all function to make prison life more bearable for Sefton's mates. In other words, Sefton does not profit at the expense of anyone else, and this in contrast to von Scherbach, whose advancement is predicated on maintaining an oppressive and dehumanising prison camp status quo. Sefton thus serves a valuable social function in Stalag 17, and this would be true even were Sefton genuinely to believe in "every man for himself."

And yet it is clear from the film's opening moments that Sefton is deeply and genuinely concerned for his fellow prisoners. His ridicule of the first escape attempt, for example, is founded on fear for its failure, not merely upon a desire to be contentious. As he puts it to Manfredi and Johnson: "Just one question—did you calculate the risk?" And he implies, thereby, that such attempts—under the circumstances—senselessly endanger human life. He is proved accurate in his evaluation of the situation. Manfredi and Johnson die. But Sefton takes little satisfaction in being so vindicated. On the contrary, when the machine gun bursts cut through the silence, Sefton responds by tossing his cigar down in disgust: he would rather have lost the bet. And likewise, the next day, when the coffins bearing the bodies of Manfredi and Johnson are carted out of camp, Sefton makes a similar gesture, angrily smashing his cigar out against the wash house wall.

But in both of these instances, as in many others, Sefton's fellow prisoners are too caught up in their own outrage to recognise Sefton's real motives. Thus, when Sefton throws his cigar to the barracks floor no one sees the gesture—they are all looking out the window. And when Sefton smashes his cigar out on the wash house wall, the tendency is to ignore his anger and to focus on the fact that he does not remove his flight cap in respect to the dead until after the cigar is extinguished. Or when, after Duke challenges Sefton's integrity, a challenge precipitated by Sefton's fried egg, Sefton complains of indigestion and gives the egg to crazy Joey, there is a tendency to interpret his move as a matter of cynical calculation, designed quite consciously to gain a theatrical advantage.

Yet the pattern of Sefton's behaviour is completely consistent for those who have eyes to see it. When push comes to shove, whenever it really matters, Sefton sides with the children and the clowns: hence his kindness to Joey, his many rackets, his refusal to inform against those who beat him up, his concern that the real collaborator, Price (Peter Graves), a German plant who is, ironically, the barracks security officer, be appropriately dealt with (merely blowing his cover would only get Price transferred to another camp where he could endanger additional allied lives), and hence, ultimately, Sefton's decision to escape with Lt. Dunbar. Like many a Wilder cynic, Sefton is a romantic at heart (he had wanted to be a flyer) whose cynical facade must be understood as a defence against a world that does not match up to romantic expectations. Note, however, that Sefton's cynicism is only skin deep, despite the fact that his fellow prisoners give him reason enough to become a collaborator. Furthermore, Sefton's romanticism and his realism are not contradictory or mutually exclusive. Unlike von Scherbach and Price—indeed, unlike the other prisoners—Sefton never lets his romanticism overcome his caution. Sefton's insistence on calculating the risk is perfectly consistent with a willingness to act—he simply refuses to act foolishly, refuses to act like a conventional war hero. It is Price who plays that role. And thus Sefton's decision to take Dunbar out of camp does not represent a change of heart. It is the situation that has changed, and changed significantly. For one thing, it is far more risky for Dunbar to stay in camp than to escape, risky for all of the prisoners who collaborated in the abduction, not just for Dunbar himself. Furthermore, for the first time in the film, the escape can go forward without

**Animal (Robert Strauss) and Sefton (William Holden) in Barracks 4 of
Stalag 17.**

fear of an informer. Price has been exposed. And finally, there is the
fact that Sefton has a diversion to cover his escape—Price will be
thrown out into the compound with cans tied to his legs. The
Germans will have someone other than Sefton and Dunbar to shoot
at.

And it is the issue of Price's death that lends the film's conclusion a
sense of moral force. Wilder's *mise-en-scène,* which alternates long
shots of Price, caught in the web of searchlights, with tight medium
shots emphasizing the agony of his death, does not allow the
emotional satisfaction of easy vengeance. Death is a horrible circumstance, whether it be the death of Manfredi and Johnson in the
film's beginning, or Price's death in the film's closing moments—and
it attests to Wilder's sense of moral balance that he does not indulge in
a simpleminded sort of dramatic justice. In other words, Price does
not die simply to satisfy the need for a scapegoat (and the fact that

most of the prisoners treat him as a scapegoat demonstrates how pervasive the instinct for irresponsibility can be). To the contrary, Price earns his death and contributes to his own downfall. It occurs neither to von Scherbach nor to Price that there are limits to the exercise of power. They therefore make the fatal mistake of assuming that Price can operate with impunity among the prisoners, no matter how suspicious they might become. Thus von Scherbach has Schulz confiscate the radio for the sake of demonstrating his omniscience, not because the radio posed a genuine threat to camp security. Indeed, by so doing, von Scherbach only makes it easier for the prisoners to locate the informer: it has to be someone in Barracks Four. Of course, the POWs, with Price's sustained encouragement, mistakenly brand Sefton the collaborator, but by allowing Sefton to be so branded, and by forcing Sefton out of the group, Price only serves to precipitate his own downfall. It is only because Sefton is forced to keep his distance, is forced to keep himself apart from the other prisoners, is forced to become a spectator to prisoner activities rather than a participant in them, that Sefton has motive and opportunity to observe the routines of barracks life, one of which, the tying and untying of the lamp cord overhanging the barracks chess set, serves as the signal between Price and Schulz that the mail (messages hidden in the black queen) is to be picked up. Thus, at the very moment when Price and von Scherbach are most confident of their power, their confidence effectively betrays them (as it betrays so many other Wilder characters). Von Scherbach stages one too many mock air-raids in his attempt to get the details of Dunbar's sabotage activities, and Sefton, who hides in the shadows of the barracks while all the other prisoners evacuate to the trenches, gets a front row seat as Price explains to Schulz the secret of Dunbar's home-made incendiary.

Thus, like earlier murderers in Wilder (like Walter Neff in *Double Indemnity,* for example), Price effectively murders himself through over-confidence. It is not that Price is evil *per se* but that Price and von Scherbach are too caught up in themselves to see the likely consequences of their actions. Sefton, on the other hand, while seeming self-centered, is very careful to account for probability. Thus Sefton *does not* expose Price immediately upon discovering his true identity. As a cool-headed Sefton puts it to Cookie, exposing Price will only get Price transferred to another camp where he can repeat his act, and killing Price will only invite reprisals. Rather, Sefton is content to wait, and to obstruct Price's attempts to communicate with Schulz and von Scherbach, until opportunity presents itself to deal with Price and the threat he represents. And that opportunity presents itself when the time comes for Dunbar to escape. Price has been unable to tip off von Scherbach about the plan to break Dunbar out. In desperation Price grabs the dogtag that Harry has extracted from Hoffy's flight cap and volunteers to take Dunbar out himself. Sefton's moment has arrived. Price must now be exposed and dealt with. And Sefton's plan for dealing with Price, tossing him out into the compound, will serve a double purpose: it will provide a diversion to cover the escape, thus improving the odds for success, and it will eliminate Price without inviting Nazi reprisals (von Scherbach will have all the trouble he needs explaining the fact that his own guards killed his prize informer).

None of which is intended to deny the fact that Sefton enjoys the hell out of turning the tables on Price and on the rest of the POWs. It argues, however, that Sefton is completely consistent (Sarris notwithstanding).[13] Sefton retains his cynical facade: indeed, he has to appear cold and calculating in order to call Price's bluff. But by calling it, and by volunteering to take Dunbar out of camp, Sefton demonstrates a genuine sense of solidarity with the other prisoners. He has been on their side all along—and hence his salute as he ducks into the trap door.

Unlike *Double Indemnity* and *Sunset Boulevard*, then, *Stalag 17* does not focus on a central narrative presence. The earlier films are *about* consciousness and conscience, and it is the main character's sense of morality and reality which is called into question. In *Stalag 17* on the other hand, as I have demonstrated, the central character, Sefton, is basically right-minded from the start. Sefton respects probability and takes an appropriately sceptical stance, refusing to indulge in foolish or self-destructive behavior of the sort that kills Neff and Phyllis in *Double Indemnity* or Leonard Vole in *Witness for the Prosecution* (to take just two examples). The *Stalag 17* narrator, on the other hand, though peripheral in terms of the film's action, functions as the middle term in a three term metaphor. On the one hand, as Sefton's sidekick, Cookie is a spectator, always on the sidelines (and Sefton's affection for the camp stutterer evidences once again his basic right-mindedness). On the other hand, even Cookie comes to doubt Sefton's integrity, despite the fact that he knows Sefton better than most. Therefore, Cookie's willingness to brand Sefton a scapegoat on the evidence of appearance rather than fact aligns him and the other prisoners, and ourselves as well, with Price and von Scherbach. In other words, *Stalag 17* serves to challenge the sort of perceptual/

Witness for the Prosecution: **John Williams, Tyrone Power (as Leonard Vole), and Charles Laughton.**

ideological habits which encourage or allow the rush to easy, self-serving, and ultimately self-destructive judgments. As observers we can be fooled if we let our emotions get the better of our insights and attentiveness. Metaphorically speaking, at least, there is a bit of von Scherbach in all of us, and *Stalag 17* is Wilder's warning that romanticism even of the normal sort can get out of hand under stressful circumstances. Again, it is not a matter of cynicism: it would be foolish to warn those who won't listen, and the American POWs are generally portrayed as men of conscience (they don't string Sefton up, after all). The point, however, is that even good men can let circumstances get the better of them. And we must therefore be constantly sceptical, not of the world, or of life's possibilities, but of ourselves and our estimations. Thus, critics who rush to condemn Wilder's cynicism in *Stalag 17* only serve to prove the importance of Wilder's point—and they argue Wilder's case with unintended eloquence.

Questions of Identity:
The Major and the Minor, Some Like It Hot, Kiss Me, Stupid

Axel Madsen describes Wilder's first self-directed American film, *The Major and the Minor,* as a comedy "in the escapist vein of the early war years with a frothy coating of patriotism and 'doing our duty' " (p. 62). I will argue that the film is neither escapist nor frothy—but Madsen's description accurately summarises the tone of the film, its general sense of good-heartedness and romance. Comedies generally take place in a benevolent universe, and it attests to the optimistic streak in Wilder, even in films like *The Apartment* and *Kiss Me, Stupid,* that he generally abides by this comic rubric. Indeed, the optimism in *The Major and the Minor* is largely a function of a benevolent providence: we are led to feel that the universe is run by laws which allow people the opportunity to lead meaningful lives no matter how meaningless or stunted life may at first seem. More importantly, perhaps, at least in *The Major and the Minor,* it is providence which allows people to understand their proper role in life, and it is by means of "role playing" that people come to accept their place in the scheme of things.

Susan Applegate (Ginger Rogers), for example, plays several roles through the course of the movie. At the film's beginning she is a hair care specialist on a house call ("Revigora system, hair treatment and scalp massage"). She is also a very self-possessed and beautiful woman. The doorman watches her as she walks into the apartment building; the elevator boy lets out a wolf-whistle and wonders about getting his own scalp massaged; and Mr. Osborne, her evening's client, keeps up a rather lame line of sexually loaded patter—all of which testify to the strength of Susan's appeal. Indeed, it is Osborne's sexual interest in Miss Applegate that eventually sends her back to Iowa. Mrs. Osborne is attending an air-raid drill ("She keeps telling me we're going to get into this war") and Mr. Osborne hopes to use the opportunity to indulge in a little "drinky poo, bitey poo, rhumba poo"—or such is his design. Susan, however, is fed up with life in the city; she has been "stared at, glanced over, passed by, slapped around, brushed off [and] cuddled up against"; and Mr. Osborne's threat ("I don't know how much influence I have with your employers . . .") is the last straw. After "one year and twenty-five jobs in New York" Susan Applegate decides to sign off, to return to Stevenson, Iowa, where people "walk on two feet," where cars have "four wheels," and where the grass is "plain green." Stevenson may be "dull," as Susan puts it in a burst of indignant rhetoric, but the unrelieved sexual cynicism of New York City is just as "boring" and a good deal more predatory.

From Susan's point of view, then, her choices are limited: rural boredom or urban boredom. But the real issue, as Susan's confrontation with Osborne defines it, has to do with the conflict of purposeful and purposeless activity. Susan is a woman of energy and drive, willing to smash eggs in people's faces when necessary, and marriage to "plain, honest, slow-witted" Will Duffy, the man who runs the Stevenson Feed and Grain, is unlikely to provide the sort of meaningfully energetic relationship that Susan deserves. Thus Susan's decision to leave the city is clearly a move in the right direction—but she risks boredom no matter which move she makes.

Susan's willingness to take risks, however, is very much in her favour. She had the courage to leave Stevenson for New York in the first place; and when the time comes she willingly packs her bags and heads for Grand Central Station to catch a train homeward. Unfortunately, or so it seems, fares have increased since her arrival in the city, and the $27.50 she had salted away will not pay for her return trip ticket. Fate is on her side, however, and she is given opportunity to make good her escape when she overhears a mother purchase half-fare tickets for her children. There is risk involved—she might not get away with it—but Susan rolls up her skirt, washes off her makeup, rips the veil from her hat, puts on a pair of flats, and adopts a new *persona*. She is no longer the gorgeous hair care specialist but an overgrown twelve-year-old of "Swedish stock."

Susan's "baby snookums" act is equally humorous and dangerous: dangerous in that she might get caught (though one suspects her punishment would hardly be debilitating—a confession and a phone call home to mother), and humorous in that Susan is constantly torn between her adult reactions (she starts to shout at the passenger who pops her balloon) and the demands of her school girl role (she checks the shout and starts to blubber). At a deeper level, however, it is vitally important that the conductors *do* catch on: otherwise Susan would return safely home to Stevenson and would marry Will Duffy. But fortune once again comes to Susan's aid. The conductors catch her smoking on the observation platform, and Susan is forced to run pell mell through the train—finally seeking shelter in the compartment of Major Philip Kirby (Ray Milland).

It is important to emphasise, as Wilder emphasises by use of long shots down the hallway of the sleeping car, that Susan could have ducked into any of a number of compartments. That she ducks into Kirby's is therefore fortunate in two respects. On the one hand, it is a matter of pure chance. And on the other, it is clear that Susan and Kirby must come together, for both their sakes. Kirby is a man of action and principle; he is returning to Wallace Military Academy

Ginger Rogers as a twelve-year-old "Sue-Sue Applegate" in *The Major and the Minor*.

from Washington where he had petitioned for return to active duty; and the concern he shows for Sue-Sue's welfare is in marked contrast to the "wet clothes/dry martini" ethos of Mr. Osborne. She is clearly attracted to Kirby; she even finds his naïveté rather charming (recall the way she scratches her head after Kirby "puts her to sleep" by counting dwarves); and she wants very much to reveal her true identity to him. He is, from her vantage point, a man neither dull nor jaded, a legitimate and attractive alternative to both Will Duffy and Osborne.

But it is equally important that Susan remain incognito. Had she told Kirby the truth, their relationship would very likely have been terminated with a handshake and an apology. Kirby would doubtless have returned to Wallace Military Academy and to his fiancée, Pamela Hill (Rita Johnson), the commandant's daughter, who would have seen to it that Kirby's transfer never came through. As Pamela's inquisitive younger sister, Lucy (Diana Lynn), puts it to Susan: "Pamela's picked out the husband she wants, and she wants him right here at Wallace Military." Fortunately, Susan is denied the opportunity to confess. The tracks ahead are flooded, the train has been forced to stop, and Pamela insists on driving "twenty-seven miles over suicidal roads" to pick Kirby up ("We certainly can't leave him on the train all by himself"). She arrives to find Susan in Kirby's berth, and, before things can be set straight, Susan (as Sue-Sue) must agree to accompany Kirby to the military school. Unless Kirby can prove that the "woman" in his room was really a twelve-year-old girl, he is very likely to be drummed out of the service—and will probably lose Pamela as well.

Far more dangerous, however, is the possibility that he will *not* lose Pamela. Again, it is a matter of role playing. Kirby wants to play an active role in the fight against Hitler. Pamela pretends to play a supportive role in Kirby's effort to be assigned to active duty ("If you get this transfer, I go with you wherever you go"), but she works behind the scenes to insure that Kirby will remain at Wallace Military Academy. Kirby is not really needed there, however. The cadets seem unusually self-sufficient—even a bit too worldly wise for their young years (although it is appropriate for children to mimic adult behavior). If anything, Kirby is immature in his own way on occasion—note the difficulty with which he attempts to caution Sue-Sue about moths and light bulbs and natural instincts—and his desire to be transferred indicates an awareness on his part that he needs to find a more purposeful role to play, one which will encourage more responsible, more adult behaviour. Pamela, however, as evidenced by her twenty-seven mile dash to the train and her determined efforts to prevent Kirby's transfer, clearly intends to prevent his assuming responsibility. Thus she does her motherly, finishing-school best to establish a secure domestic empire—Kirby will succeed her father as commandant, and Pamela will continue to run the Wallace Military show. But, as the cadets continually point out to Sue-Sue, the fall of the Maginot Line to the German armies demonstrates the futility of stationary defences, and it is therefore appropriate that Susan—a woman who. is adept at changing with changing circumstances—should be the one to win the sexual war.

This sex/war metaphor is far more profound than Madsen's

"frothy coating" remark would seem to indicate. The war as a fact of history is kept constantly before us. Mr. Osborne mentions it at the film's beginning (his wife is at an air-raid drill); Pamela mentions it in her letter to Washington (a letter which Lucy steams open); even the cadets refer to "the present war" in their Maginot line seduction routine. The conflict between Pamela and Kirby is essentially a conflict between her desire for security (a desire we see frequently in Wilder) and Kirby's sense of foresight and responsibility. That is, Kirby sees the war as inevitable (he is not eager to see it, but see it he does) while Pamela wants to shut the war (and the world) out of her life. Wilder's point, however, is that one must take risks in life if life is to have meaning. As Susan demonstrates, one must risk identity to find it—before the film is over she plays not only the career girl role but the little girl role, the young-boy role (she lowers her voice while working the academy switchboard), the Pamela Hill role (she mimics Pamela's voice and her "beguiling" vocabulary in order to help Kirby get his transfer) and finally she impersonates her own mother at the film's end when Kirby shows up in Stevenson to deliver Lucy's tadpole-turned-frog to Sue-Sue. Indeed, Susan actually "gives up" her adult identity, at least as far as Kirby is concerned. She had intended, as soon as Kirby's transfer came through, to reveal her true identity to him. But Pamela finally catches on to Susan's masquerade and threatens to ruin Kirby if Susan goes through with her transformation from school girl to adult. Susan rightly continues her masquerade, then, as a genuine expression of her love for Kirby, and she leaves Wallace Military without saying goodbye or revealing her identity.

By so doing, however, Susan asserts a genuine sense of moral identity; and her integrity is rewarded when Kirby shows up in Stevenson. He is headed overseas, despite Pamela's efforts to the contrary. Like Susan, Kirby understands the necessity of risking identity—in war as in love—for the sake of preserving identity. Indeed, Kirby's acceptance of his military responsibility is simultaneously a rejection of Pamela and her domestic isolationism. And Kirby can assert his better self because Susan came into his life. This is true on two levels and for good reason. Dramatically, Susan is the one who makes the crucial phone call to Washington. Thematically, however, Susan is the one who reinvigorates Kirby's sense of self, who gives him the courage to defy Pamela.

Of course, Susan does much to invigorate life in general at Wallace Military. Even the jaded cadets prefer her unassuming self-confidence to the Veronica Lake pretensions of Mrs. Shackelford's girls. At the Saturday night dance (which recalls, in a charmingly scaled down fashion, the embassy ball in Lubitsch's *The Merry Widow*) Susan is by far the most sought-after partner (we see this in long shot as the cadets crowd around her). As Kirby puts it to Susan later, thinking she is Mrs. Applegate: "Those three days she spent with us, it seemed as if, well, as if spring had enrolled at Wallace Military; everything came alive from the youngest cadet to the oldest cannon." More importantly, however, Susan forces Kirby to recall his own youthful proclivity for romance and for self-assertion. When they first meet, in his railway berth, Kirby tries to rest her little girl fears by assuring her that "it's just like travelling with your grandfather or your uncle." And until the film's closing moments—when Sue-Sue miraculously becomes Susan Catherine Applegate—Kirby maintains this "Uncle Philip" relationship with her. To be sure, Philip is quite obviously a young man—but his assignment to Wallace Military Academy makes him feel as if he has been put out to pasture. All of his colleagues are old men, and even Pamela treats him like a childish old dotard who does not know what to do with himself or his life. Indeed, Pamela's taste for old men is eventually satisfied when she marries the father of Cadet Wigton.

Susan's presence is important, therefore, as a catalyst: just seeing her with the cadets raises issues of youth and sex for Kirby. He even wonders aloud why youth should be wasted on the young. And at the ball it becomes clear that Kirby's concern for Sue-Sue is something more than fatherly. As Kirby tells Pamela, "It's amazing the appeal that kid has." Given the fact that Kirby remains blind to Susan's true identity and age, it is to his credit that he adopts a chaperon's stance, wondering why Sue-Sue would want to waste the third waltz on him. The problem, however, is more profound than whether or not Kirby ought to dance with a twelve-year-old. As Kirby puts it to Sue-Sue, "I warn you, I can't reverse"—a comment which applies beyond the context of dance steps. That is, Kirby's continued fatherly demeanour settles him more firmly into the old dotard role that Pamela intends for him. And yet the fact of Kirby's ill-timed "crush" on Sue-Sue recalls an earlier ill-timed love affair—between a twelve-year-old Kirby and his forty-year-old dancing instructor. And when the course was over, rather than shake hands and bow from the waist and say "thank you," Kirby "kissed her smack on the lips." Kirby tells the tale after his break with Pamela, and he tells it to demonstrate that he is "always off schedule twenty or thirty years," either with his dance

The minor (Ginger Rogers) and the Major (Ray Milland) at the Saturday Night Dance.

instructor or with Sue-Sue. The point of the fable, however, is that Kirby had once been courageous enough to defy convention and assert his sense of commitment. Such assertions are not without risk—the twelve-year-old Kirby faints dead away from the sexual shock—but it is a similar willingness to take risks that allowed Kirby to tell Pamela that his "decision is made." Either she accepts the fact of his transfer or the marriage is off. Kirby had seen it coming, has sensed that his interests and Pamela's were at cross purposes—but the break is far less painful than he had imagined it would be. As he describes it to Sue-Sue upon returning to the dance floor: "I've just been through an experience I thought would break my back and weigh me down like lead, but look at me—I'm filled with helium." Indeed, as Kirby and Sue-Sue dance he reverses his feet as readily as he reversed his position *vis à vis* Pamela—and Wilder accentuates this ease of movement by panning very gently back and forth in time to

Sue Sue "grows up": the depot scene in *The Major and the Minor*.

follow the major and the minor as they celebrate Kirby's declaration of independence.

Like Capt. Pringle in *A Foreign Affair,* Major Kirby in *The Major and the Minor* is faced with a choice that is simultaneously moral and sexual. But Kirby wrongly perceives it as an either/or situation: either Pamela and the role of the fatherly military has been, or active service and celibacy. As he tells Susan ("Mrs. Applegate") in the Stevenson scene: "As I see it now, Pamela was absolutely right. No man in my position has any business to marry, going away goodness knows how far into what I believe will be war." Susan, however, challenges Kirby's estimation of the situation: "I think you underestimate us, Major Kirby—perhaps all a woman wants is to be a photograph a soldier tacks above his bunk, or a stupid lock of hair in the back of his watch." Out of context, perhaps, Susan's assertion might seem to smack of home-made jam and weeping willows—but the issue in *The Major and the Minor* concerns a willingness to take risks and make sacrifices, a completely necessary willingness given the historical situation. As Susan Catherine Applegate tells Kirby at the railway depot, she is headed west to marry a soldier: "He's going to war so that this country will be spared what happened to France." And the legitimacy of her position seems hardly questionable. All human beings are faced with the necessity of risk taking—even in their personal lives, as Susan demonstrates at the film's beginning. Kirby's willingness to go to war should be understood therefore as a logical extension of a completely proper and surprisingly self-aware stance. Human beings are equal in their capacity for self serving behavior, as Mr. Osborne and Pamela demonstrate. But they are capable of self-sacrifice as well: thus Susan and Kirby both put self-hood on the line in the service of others.

The film's Cinderella/Prince Charming conclusion, Susan and Philip embracing on the Stevenson railway platform, therefore, provides an appropriately comic image of fruitful human relationships. Such relationships are precious, particularly in a world at war, and Wilder does not deny that fact. If anything, Wilder's *mise-en-scène* tends to emphasise the miraculousness of the Susan/Philip fairy tale. In the moonlit evening Susan and her white dress stand brilliantly out from the darkness (she wore black at the film's beginning). We see her from Kirby's point of view, in long shot, and though we are, unlike

Kirby, fully aware of Susan's identity (we have known all along), we nevertheless share the exhilaration of recognition. Philip is no longer bound by either childishness or premature senility; Susan is no longer the cynical career girl; both find identity in commitment to each other; and together they embody a genuine sense of social responsibility. Wilder therefore escapes nothing. He rather celebrates the miraculous power of love to renew those who willingly open themselves up to the risks and rewards of living. Strawberries will grow yearly (Susan's mother sells preserves); tadpoles will be transformed into frogs; and life can continue if people are willing to commit themselves to purposeful action in the world.

*   *   *

Some Like It Hot can best be understood as a marvellously elaborate set of structural and thematic variations on the security/risk/identity issues first set forth in *The Major and the Minor*. Both films begin in the city (New York/Chicago) where the central character or characters are engaged in a fruitless search for some sort of financial and emotional security. In the case of Susan Applegate, however, it is unrelieved sexual cynicism that drives her to catch the next train homeward; it is financial insecurity (the lack of sufficient train fare) that leads to her masquerade; and it is her masquerade, as luck (and Wilder) would have it, that leads Susan to Philip Kirby, the man she will eventually marry. In *Some Like It Hot*, on the other hand, the central characters, Joe (Tony Curtis) and Jerry (Jack Lemmon), are content to have jobs as musicians, Joe on sax, Jerry on string bass, in a speakeasy dance band. They have been out of work for months, they owe money to every girl in the chorus, are behind on their rent, and Jerry looks forward to getting a tooth filled. Even without the difficulties which soon befall them, however, their security would be tenuous: ever the operator, Joe wants to bet their first week's wages on a dog named Greased Lightning, and no doubt Jerry would have gone along with the scheme (as he eventually does, under other circumstances). But the presence of Pat O'Brien—the archetypal Irish cop—in the audience is preface to a police raid on the joint and Joe and Jerry are lucky enough to escape the police dragnet by climbing down the fire escape. Joe then convinces Jerry to push their luck: they hock their overcoats, bet the money on the dog. The dog loses, so once again Joe and Jerry are forced to make the rounds of musical agents in search of a gig.

Here too luck is at work—although "luck" now becomes associated with the sort of sexual cynicism that drove Susan Applegate out of New York City. Joe and Jerry knock at the right door, find the right secretary filing her nails, and that secretary, angry at being stood up by Joe, sends the boys in to see the boss, telling them that Poliakoff (Billy Gray) has need of a sax and a bass for a Florida-bound dance band. The joke, or so it seems, is on Joe and Jerry. They play the right instruments but are "the wrong shape." It's an all girl band that needs the sax and bass. And while Jerry, anxious to trade Florida sunshine for Chicago snow storms, argues that they can and should take the job ("We could borrow some clothes from the girls in the chorus . . . a couple of second hand wigs . . ."), Joe nixes the idea.

At this point Poliakoff gets a phone call. He has a one night stand lined up in Urbana and the job is Joe and Jerry's if they can get the

Poliakoff (Billy Gray) has a job for Jerry (Jack Lemmon) and Joe (Tony Curtis)—in an all girl dance band.

transportation. Which raises, once again, the sexual issue: Joe puts the make on Nellie, the secretary, asks her what she is doing that evening, and asks her for her car when she says she's "not doing anything." And thus sexual exploitation (e.g., Joe's treatment of Nellie) finally becomes associated with death. When they go to pick up Nellie's car at the local garage, Joe and Jerry become unwitting witnesses to the St. Valentine's Day Massacre. Indeed, they almost join the victims. But luck of a sort is once again on their side. Spats Columbo (George Raft) and his "Harvard men" are a little too confident. They fail to finish off Toothpick Charlie with the first blast (Charlie was the man who tipped off the cops who raided Columbo's speakeasy). And when Charlie lurches for the telephone Joe and Jerry have the chance to run for their lives. Of course, their lives are not worth much if they can't get out of Chicago, so Joe changes his mind about the Florida gig. Joe and Jerry have no choice. Like Susan Applegate, they haven't got the money to get out of town on their own. Their only avenue of escape is disguise. It's either high heels and false chests or certain death.

Unlike Susan Applegate, however, Joe and Jerry are very much responsible for their own predicament. As I have already noted, it's Joe's love-'em-and-leave-'em sexual philosophy which is directly responsible for the fact that Joe and Jerry are on the run. And therefore it is ironically appropriate that Joe should find salvation in skirts. Jerry is not quite so responsible for the situation as Joe. But Jerry almost always acquiesces to Joe's schemes, admires Joe's sexual *savoir faire* ("Isn't he a bit of terrific?"), and so he too earns an appropriate comeuppance by being forced to play the female role. The point, however, is not simply that Joe and Jerry are somehow being punished. It is rather the case, as it was in *The Major and the Minor,* that Wilder admires those like Susan and Joe and Jerry who have the will, the energy, the intelligence, and the vitality to survive in a world full of death-dealing mobsters. And by forcing them to play roles he provides opportunity for those characters not only to escape unhealthy circumstances but to find greater and more legitimate security than they had ever thought possible.

Joe and Jerry are not the only characters in the film, however, and they can best be understood as occupying complementary places on a scale of characters which extends from Spats Columbo at one end, through Joe, Osgood Fielding III (Joe E. Brown), and Jerry to Sugar Kane (Marilyn Monroe) at the other. Thus Spats Columbo represents a principle of unbridled self-assertion. Like other Wilder fascists—

the jack-booted von Scherbach in *Stalag 17,* for example—Spats
revels in the exercise of power, and particularly in exercising the
power over life and death. Indeed, Spats dreams of "retiring" Little
Bonaparte and taking over as top mob boss. But again, like von
Scherbach in *Stalag 17,* or, to a lesser degree, like Pamela in *the Major
and the Minor,* Spats overestimates his ability to control events.
Specifically, he assumes he can rub out Toothpick Charlie with
impunity, as if it were of no consequence that Toothpick Charlie and
Little Bonaparte had been choir boys together. But it is not simply a
lapse of foresight on Columbo's part. There was no real necessity for
rubbing out Charlie, no more necessity than was involved in von
Scherbach's attempts to get the goods on Lt. Dunbar in *Stalag 17.*
Rather, in both cases, it is a matter of self-assertion beyond the
demands of circumstance. Indeed, it is almost as if Spats had rubbed
out Charlie for the purpose of calling Bonaparte's authority into
question. Charlie is, like Price in *Stalag 17,* only a pawn in someone
else's power game. And hence the necessity that Columbo catch up

Rubbing out Toothpick Charlie: George Raft as Spats Columbo in *Some Like It Hot.*

with Joe and Jerry. As witnesses, of course, Joe and Jerry represent a genuine threat to Columbo's freedom. More importantly, however, their escape underlines the fact that Spats is not all powerful. As long as they are at large, Columbo's credibility is at hazard. Indeed, at the film's conclusion it is clear that Bonaparte still maintains the loyalty of the mob and that Columbo's challenge to his authority is more bluff than substance. That Spats blithely sits down to a last supper without suspecting any possibility of danger is testimony to the self-destructive nature of overmuch self-confidence and self-interest.

At the other end of the character scale is Sugar Kane, née Kowalcik (Marilyn Monroe), a down-and-out torch singer whose emotional malaise results from a past history of passionate and compulsive liaisons with unscrupulous tenor sax players. As she puts it to Joe in the privacy of the Florida Limited lady's washroom: "All they have to do is play eight bars of 'Come to Me, My Melancholy Baby' and my spine turns to custard, I get goosepimply all over, and I come to him." But it is not the liaisons so much as their seemingly inevitable consequence that has driven Sugar to seek refuge in liquor, in the celibate safety of an all girl band, and in the prospect of marrying a "helpless," near-sighted, yacht-owning millionaire when she finally gets to Florida. Everytime she falls for a sax player she winds up with "the fuzzy end of the lollipop." All that's left behind, as she so eloquently puts it, "is a pair of old socks and a tube of toothpaste—all squeezed out." And she is tired of letting her emotions get the better of her. Indeed, she reveals her past sexual history as evidence to support the contention that she's "not very bright." But being "bright" in this context involves the denial of emotion in the service of a reverse sort of sexual exploitation. That is, Sugar is tired of being the victim of saxophone sexuality, always the hard loving loser, and if sex is going to be a matter of commercial exploitation ("The next thing you know, they are borrowing money from you—they're spending it on other dames and betting on horses"), then Sugar has decided to get the sweet end of the lollipop for once in her life.

In her own way, then, Sugar adopts (or tries to adopt) an emotional stance very similar to Spats Columbo's—the self comes first, the lives and feelings of others do not matter. Such, indeed, is the vision of life embodied in Sugar's first song, "Running Wild." According to the song, Sugar has a "carefree mind, all the time." She is, therefore, "never blue." She will "love nobody," because "it's not worthwhile." And by avoiding love, by running wild, she attempts to deny life's agonies. In other words, she "don't care." Not caring, however, is seldom rewarded in Wilder. It gets Spats Columbo killed, if we understand "care" to imply a certain responsiveness to others and to external circumstance. And thus it is appropriate and logical that the only millionaire (or would-be millionaire) under seventy-five that Sugar encounters should be (or should pretend to be) impotent. Indeed, by playing the role of an impotent, Cary Grant-style playboy, Joe demonstrates an intuitive though somewhat self-serving awareness of the nature of Sugar's dilemma. As Joe tells the tale, his impotence is the result of nearsightedness. He had been in love once, had spent a beautiful summer with Nellie at the Grand Canyon, and in a fit of sunset-inspired passion both had removed their glasses in order to kiss—at which point Nellie stepped off the canyon rim. And the fable carries a double moral in context. On the one hand, it pays to attend to the emotional terrain. Too little attentiveness, too little caution, can get you killed (this happens to Spats). And on the other hand, too much caution can have much the same effect. In the terms of Joe's fable, overmuch caution can be like a "heart shot full of novocain." Joe-the-millionaire cannot get close to women for fear that getting close will result in emotional disaster. Likewise, in Sugar's very real case, she forswears love for fear that love will once again lead to exploitation and desertion. Rather no love at all than run the risk of disappointment.

Much to her credit, however, Sugar never ceases to be emotionally honest, however much she might try to squelch emotion in the quest for financial security. Thus, for example, her performance of "Running Wild" concludes with the untimely appearance of her flask on the floor—and the flask, the contents of which Sugar depends on to help deaden the blues, directly contradicts the devil-may-care attitude of her song. Or consider her open-faced enthusiasm for "Shell Oil Jr."—his money matters far less than his apparent kindheartedness. As Sugar describes him to "Josephine": "He's a real gentleman—you know, not one of these grabbers." Indeed, her second song, "I Want to Be Loved by You," makes it clear, not only by means of the lyrics but by means of her full spirited performance, that she hasn't given up on love at all. Rather, she seeks to avoid the sort of lover who exploits her naïveté. Or consider her unfeigned concern for Joe's ersatz sexual dilemma ("talk about sad!"). That he "can't fall in love" strikes Sugar as a tragedy of the highest order ("How can you think about food at a time like this") and she does her Marilyn Monroe best to remedy the situation. By so doing, however, she once again falls head over toothpaste tube in love and once more runs the risk of disappointment—a greater risk now than ever before, given the nature of her expectations. Indeed, as her "I'm Through with Love" number (which she sings after Shell Oil Jr. jilts her for the daughter of a company president) indicates, Sugar's expectations may have risen so high that her fall could prove emotionally fatal.

To be sure, Sugar's impotent millionaire is neither wealthy nor impotent, but that in no way denies the legitimacy of Sugar's selflessness. If anything, Wilder admires Sugar's will to love as much as he admires Joe's will to survive. Thus Sugar provides the opposite term to Spats in the character scheme: Spats loves no one but himself while Sugar loves everyone but herself. Both stances are dangerous—Spats is killed and Sugar risks emotional handicap. But Wilder clearly prefers Sugar's sort of risk taking for being more generous, more honest, and more humane. Therefore Wilder eventually rewards her integrity by providing her with a sax man who comes genuinely to value and appreciate Sugar for her virtues.

In terms of this selfish/selfless character scale, then, Joe—the saxophone player that Sugar eventually winds up with—can be seen at first as a sexual gangster analogous in his selfishness to Spats Columbo. Indeed, as his relationship with Sugar indicates, he can be dangerous in the extreme, allowing his own impulses (his passion for Sugar) to genuinely endanger others. His seduction of Sugar could result only in her disappointment were he to continue his love-'em-and-leave-'em habits. But to Joe's credit he feels genuinely rotten for stringing her along. It is not clear how he would have broken off with Sugar were the romance to have run its natural course, although he would clearly have broken her heart whatever the circumstances. As Joe puts it to Jerry, arguing the inevitability of heartbreak: "You can't make an omelette without breaking an egg." But when Columbo and Company show up at the hotel to attend the "Friends of Italian Opera" convention, Joe is forced to bid Sugar a hasty and not too tactful adieu. And yet, as Joe talks to Sugar on the phone, he comes to realise the gravity of the situation: Sugar once again will get the fuzzy end of the lollipop. It is more than Joe can take. And, at the very least, he feels compelled to present Sugar with the diamond bracelet that Osgood had given to Jerry. That diamond bracelet represents Joe and Jerry's ticket out of town—their security—and that Joe gives it to Sugar, sacrificing his financial security for the sake of Sugar's emotional security, testifies to his new-found sense of sexual reality. Thus, by playing the female role, Joe comes to understand the dynamics of sexual politics: when the sax man walks out, the torch

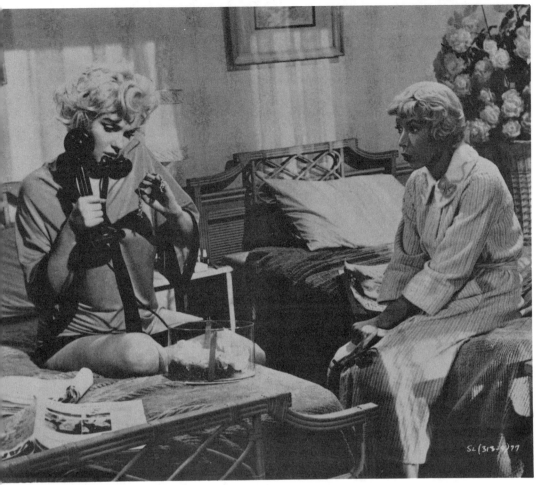

The fuzzy end of the lollipop: Sugar (Marilyn Monroe) gets the bracelet from Joe in *Some Like It Hot*.

singer suffers. And even Joe can see that, in Sugar's case, "No man is worth it." He is wrong, of course. The very fact that he says it to Sugar—quite literally at some risk to his own life (Columbo's thugs are after him)—proves that one man, at least, is worth it. And Sugar, not quite so dumb after all, has the courage and the insight necessary to reach the same conclusion: hence she follows Joe down to Osgood's boat, knowing full well the risk involved, but willing to run it nevertheless for the sake of love.

Jerry, in his turn, can therefore be understood as a complement to Joe. In fact, Jerry serves almost to parody Joe's egocentricity—although Jerry's egocentricity is for the most part a matter of fantasy. In practical terms, though, and under ordinary circumstances, Jerry is generally content to be Joe's sidekick, despite the fact that he is constantly berating himself for acquiescing to Joe's schemes. Indeed, he goes along with those schemes, as Wilder goes along, because he admires Joe's intelligence and ability. But, as soon as Jerry enters into his make-believe role as "Daphne," he gives free though somewhat dangerous reign to his own romantic inclinations. Thus, as soon as they get on the train, Jerry compares his present situation—as a male in the midst of an all-girl band—to a childhood dream, being locked up overnight in a pastry shop: "And there were goodies all around . . . sponge cake and Boston cream pie and cherry tarts. . . ." At which point Joe interrupts to remind Jerry that they are both "on a diet." Joe's point is well taken though not sufficiently attended to. If Jerry blows their masquerade by indulging his taste for sweets (or, specifically, for Sugar), it might well mean death. As Joe puts it to Jerry a few moments later in the washroom: "One false move and they'll toss us off the train. Then there'll be the police, the papers, and the mob in Chicago." In his own naïve way, then, Jerry aspires to be a sexual gangster like Joe—and by being so blatant about it he serves to underline the potential dangers implicit in sexual conquest. Indeed, by being so blatant he forces Joe—heretofore the sexual aggressor—to advise abstinence.

Furthermore, once they get to Florida, Jerry again demonstrates the danger of sexual exploitation. At Joe's insistence, Jerry romances Osgood Fielding III so that Jerry can use Osgood's yacht to put the make on Sugar. And Jerry almost loses his sexual identity in the process ("I'm a boy, I'm a boy—I wish I were dead"). He gets so carried away, in fact, that he concocts a hare-brained scheme of his own: he will accept Osgood's proposal, will go through with the marriage, will tell Osgood the truth thereafter, and will collect, or so he thinks, a monthly alimony cheque once the marriage is annulled. It makes little sense, of course—men don't collect alimony from men—but it is not that much more senseless than Joe's scheme *vis-à-vis* Sugar: both relationships are grounded in falsehood. And thus Jerry's relationship to Joe on the character scale is analogous to Sugar's relationship to Spats. Jerry and Sugar are generally selfless, while Joe and Spats are generally egocentric—but in each case the selfless character reveals a capacity for selfish behaviour.

And right in the middle of all this, both literally in terms of the film's action and figuratively in terms of the character scheme I have been proposing, is Osgood Fielding III. Fielding is like Spats to the degree that he has the money and the power to indulge his fantasies. He is also like Spats in that he is subject to higher authority: where Spats pledges (or pretends to pledge) allegiance to Little Bonaparte, Fielding pledges (or pretends to pledge) allegiance to "Mama."

Fielding is like Sugar, however, in that his fantasies are not concerned with the exercise of power. Rather, Fielding has a thing about showgirls just as Sugar has a thing about sax players. Indeed, Fielding has married so many showgirls that he's lost count ("Mama's keeping score").

Unlike Sugar, however, Fielding never lets failure get him down. If anything, Fielding rather enjoys the rituals of courtship (recall his tango scene with Jerry) and has the wherewithal to be exploited without suffering financial hardship (his escapades have cost his "family quite a bit of money"). None of which pleases "Mama"— who has packed Osgood off to Florida for the season in hopes that Osgood will catch deep sea fish rather than chorines. But by so doing, however, she only guarantees that Osgood will become bait for Florida bound golddiggers like Sugar and Daphne. And the point, once more, has to do with the interplay of risk and security. Mrs. Fielding wants Osgood to avoid the wrong sort of girl. So Osgood gets a guy. Furthermore, Osgood's blithe acceptance of Joe's gender ("Nobody's perfect") evidences the fact that sexual and financial security are not unrelated. It seems clear that Sugar's sexual malaise is made all the worse by the precariousness of her financial situation. She is not only defrauded of affection but of her money as well. No wonder, then, that she comes to associate love with sexual/financial exploitation: as a girl singer in a male band she is powerless to fight it. Osgood, on the other hand, has the money to indulge his relatively harmless taste for bizarre sex—a contortionist here, a drag queen there, it's all one to him. And it's all one because Osgood has the financial security that Sugar lacks. In which case, *Some Like It Hot* can be seen as a fairly pointed critique of capitalism and sex—not simply as a cynical series of fag jokes. Osgood hurts no one. Indeed, he saves two if not three lives. Spats Columbo, on the other hand, perpetrates a massacre. And it is that sort of lifetaking egocentricism that is the ultimate perversity in Wilder.

Like *The Major and the Minor*, however, *Some Like It Hot* is not merely a critique of any particular economic ideology. As Wilder demonstrates in *One, Two, Three* (which clearly resembles *Some Like It Hot* in pace and purpose), both capitalism and socialism can be perverted to egocentric ends. Rather, *The Major and the Minor* and *Some Like It Hot* are both concerned very deeply with more basic issues of "personal style." To a large degree, everyone plays roles—not simply those in costume. Put another way, every character in *Some Like It Hot* is searching for the right costume, the right style, a way of being in the world that will provide an adequate measure of emotional security. Some characters wear the wrong costume: we recognise Columbo's body by his spats as he slides under the table, for example. Some people are forced to wear costumes that seem at first an ill fit (Jerry tells Joe that he feels "naked" before they board the Florida Limited) but which eventually allow them to become their better selves. Thus Joe gets Sugar honestly and openly—no more subterfuge, no more heartbreak. Thus Jerry gets . . . well, we're not sure what Jerry gets. But like Joe, Jerry is forced to be honestly himself, no matter what the consequence *vis-à-vis* Osgood. If anything, it is clear that Jerry will now have to chart his own course, take his own risks, will now have to become truly responsible because he won't have Joe to emulate or depend on in the future: Joe now has a new room-mate. And then there are characters like Osgood and Sugar who are essentially themselves right from the start. Sugar may try to play the golddigger role but we never doubt the integrity of her feelings nor the humanity of her instincts.

Some Like It Hot must ultimately be understood, therefore, as a celebration of emotional and sexual integrity. It is ironic but true that even critics who care about Wilder tend in discussing *Some Like It Hot* to focus on parts rather than on the whole—on performances, or on Wilder's various references (or debts) to Howard Hawks rather than on the Wilder vision. Ultimately, of course, there is no real issue here. Any director worth his salt will take into account the iconographic values of a given actor or actress and will encourage the most appropriate performance for his purposes. This is particularly true of "classical" directors like Hawks, Ford, and Wilder. And *Some Like It Hot* is surely graced by some of the most significant and appropriate performances in screen history—particularly Marilyn Monroe's transcendent performance as Sugar Kane. But Wilder has orchestrated those performances to suit his own expressive ends and it seems no injustice to anyone that Wilder be given his due in this respect. Indeed, the "intensity" of performance found generally in Wilder seems a clear reflection of Wilder's own intense personality— as if he would have acted all the roles himself had that been possible.

Likewise, Wilder's copious references to Hawks ought not to be seen as an abdication of authority or as a failure of imagination. Such references can serve a variety of purposes (see my discussion of *The Front Page*), but in *Some Like It Hot* Wilder uses the Hawks motifs as a costume of sorts. After the straight adventure of *The Spirit of St. Louis,* after the Lubitsch-like grace of *Love in the Afternoon,* after the Agatha

An "effeminate" Cary Grant in *I Was a Male War Bride* by Howard Hawks.

Christie intrigue of *Witness for the Prosecution,* Wilder may have felt the
need for a change of pace and what better method of changing pace
than to emulate the energetic hijinks of Howard Hawks. Of course,
Wilder and Hawks can hardly be described as having antithetical
visions: the Wilder/Brackett/Hawks collaboration on *Ball of Fire*
proves that. But in *Some Like It Hot,* I would argue, Wilder borrows
certain Hawksian motifs—transvestism; the golddigging blonde; the
shy, ineffectual Cary Grantish character—just as Joe and Jerry
borrow clothes from the girls at the speakeasy, in order eventually to
re-assert his better self. Indeed, in each case Wilder shifts the context
(and hence the import) of those motifs to suit his own purposes. Sugar
is never sincere in her golddigging, for example, while the Marilyn
Monroe character in *Gentlemen Prefer Blondes* is serious in the extreme.

Barbara Stanwyck and Gary Cooper in *Ball of Fire* (directed by Hawks from
the screenplay by Brackett and Wilder).

And the result is that *Some Like It Hot* is pure Wilder, energetic, humanistic, concerned very deeply with the relationship between risk and security, between death and identity. *Some Like It Hot* was not Wilder's first masterpiece. That honour, in my estimation, goes to *Double Indemnity*. Nor was it Wilder's last to date. All of Wilder's last three films—*The Private Life of Sherlock Holmes, Avanti!*, and *The Front Page*—qualify for that honour. But *Some Like It Hot* will always remain the definitive Wilder movie, however much it owes its inspiration or its language to Howard Hawks.

* * *

I take it to be self-evident by this point that Wilder is an under-valued and generally misunderstood figure in cinema history. And none of his films has been more consistently undervalued and misinterpreted than *Kiss Me, Stupid*. Even critics generally sympathe-tic to Wilder have felt compelled to condemn *Kiss Me, Stupid* for going too far (see Richard Corliss). But in the case of Axel Madsen, whose

Walter Matthau (as "Whiplash Willie" Gingrich), Billy Wilder, and Jack Lemmon (as Harry Hinkle) rehearse *The Fortune Cookie*.

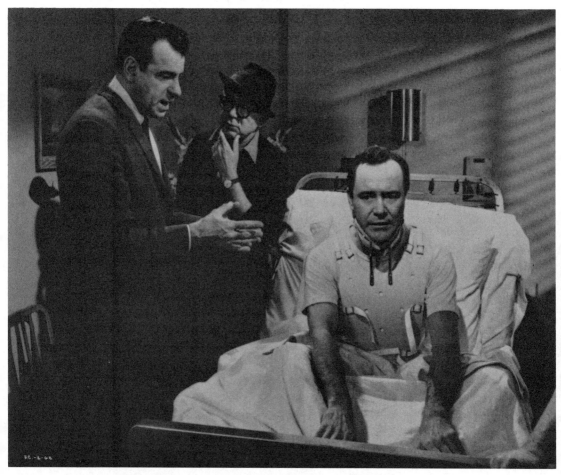

**Tom Ewell and
Marilyn Monroe
in *The Seven Year
Itch*.**

"Cinema One" monograph on Wilder is the only extended study of
the Wilder cinema to date, this distaste leads to serious descriptive
distortions that can only further damage the film's reputation.

Specifically, Madsen's description of the film gives the impression
that the film's central character, Orville J. Spooner (Ray Walston),
music teacher, jealous husband, church organist, and amateur song
writer, is a self-conscious con man of the Chuck Tatum *(Ace in the
Hole)* or Whiplash Willie *(The Fortune Cookie)* sort—and nothing could
be further from the truth. It is Spooner's song-writing cohort, Barney
Millsap (Cliff Osmond), the lyric-man who runs the Shell Station
across the street from Orville's homestead-cum-music studio, who
dreams up and orchestrates the scheme to keep Dino (Dean Martin)
in town over night in order to sell him on their tin pan alley
compositions. And even his motives for so doing cannot really be
described as vicious or sordid. Which therefore requires that Orville
be compared not to the Spats Columbo sort of villain but rather to
weaker Wilder characters, like Jerry in *Some Like It Hot,* Richard
Sherman (Tom Ewell) in *The Seven Year Itch,* or Harry Hinkle (Jack
Lemmon) in *The Fortune Cookie*—men who dream but who seldom act

out their dreams under normal circumstances. Indeed, as Richard Lippe points out in his excellent "Velvet Light Trap" piece on *Kiss Me, Stupid,* Orville Spooner is "a supreme fantasist."[15] And it's Orville's over-active imagination which makes him simultaneously frenetic, vulnerable, and intensely human—particularly when both his dream (the big break necessary to musical success) and his nightmare (losing his wife: Felicia Farr) seem to be coming true at once.

Orville's identity crisis can be understood to involve the interplay of two idealistic contexts—the financial and the sexual—both of which are central to Orville's sense of self and to the film in general. Thus, for example, the film begins in Las Vegas with a supperclub floorshow—Dino singing "That You Should Care for Me" while surrounded by two ranks of statuesque but scantily clad show girls, all of them looking quite bored and mechanical. So much so, in fact, that the song's lyrics—which embody a vision of romantic ecstasy and fulfillment—seem ridiculous in the night club context. Furthermore, Dino continually undercuts the lyric by periodically interrupting the song in order to tell jokes about sexual entrapment ("she was banging on my door for forty-five minutes—but I wouldn't let her out"), about motherhood (his 85-year-old mother "don't need glasses—she drinks right out of the bottle"), money (Crosby has "twenty-one million dollars—on him") and Santa Claus ("I don't care who you are, fat man . . ."). The entire performance appears crass, slick, and commercial—as Wilder no doubt intended it to appear—and Dino continues to be crass, slick, and mechanistic about sex (Dino must get laid every night or suffer headaches, or so he tells Orville) throughout the film.

The following scenes, which take place in Climax, Nevada, present alternatives to Dino's sort of "one for the road" sexuality. Thus we find Orville pacing his living room-cum-studio while young Johnnie Mulligan proceeds to mangle Beethoven on the piano. Zelda (Mrs. Spooner) then enters from the kitchen, motions to Orville, gropes under his Beethoven sweat shirt (Orville: "Please dear, not now"), and comes away with the pen from his shirt pocket: she has to write a note to the milkman. Orville is visibly torn at this point between affection (he assumes Zelda wants to make love) and the fear of infidelity (he spies through the kitchen door as Zelda writes her message and stuffs it in a milk bottle). But nothing happens so Orville returns to the living room where young Mulligan continues to "monkey around with Beethoven." His mind for the moment on the business at hand, Orville wonders aloud who ever told Johnnie to take up the piano.

Johnnie replies, "You did, sir." And Orville rejoins: "Well, I need the money—but what's your excuse?"

At this point the milk truck pulls up outside, and the ever suspicious Orville forgets all about money and young Mulligan in order to "follow" the milkman, moving melodramatically from window to window inside the house so as to keep the milkman in sight. Finally, after the milkman picks up Zelda's note, Orville gives in to temptation, runs out the front door, and confronts the milkman ("I know your type, sneaking around to back doors"), demanding that he turn over the incriminating missive. Again, it is nothing, simply a request for milk and eggs; and Orville, knowing full well how foolish he looks, sheepishly tells the milkman that Zelda forgot to order buttermilk.

Orville then returns to the house, waving the buttermilk bottle absentmindedly like a baton, as Mulligan continues to mangle the master—at which point Zelda again enters (Orville stashes the milk in the piano) and asks Orville to zip her up—she doesn't want to keep the dentist waiting (or so she says—though she is actually going out to buy a cake for their fifth anniversary). As Zelda turns back around to kiss Orville goodbye, however, he notices and inquires about the flowers she is wearing, a gift from young Mulligan, and no sooner does Zelda leave than Orville flies into a fit of jealous rage ("Pussyfooting around behind my back, bringing flowers to a married woman!"). Orville is so overwrought, indeed, that Johnnie is lucky to escape with his skin (Orville literally rips the shirt off his back). Orville wants no "teenage werewolf" taking lessons in his front room.

And the point to this detailed description of the first scene at the Spooner house is to demonstrate that Orville values Zelda far more than money. He would rather lose all of his pupils than lose his wife. And yet Orville's untoward jealousy can only be understood in the context of Orville's identity crisis and his identity crisis is in turn a function of financial expectation. As we eventually come to discover, Zelda's mother is a financial harpy who never forgave her daughter for marrying Orville when she could have married "the second most successful chiropractor in Carson City." At some level, then, Orville must agree with his mother-in-law however much he may despise her—and his jealousy clearly results from his self-image: he is a "no talent slob," as his mother-in-law put it, a rank amateur, buried in Climax, Nevada, teaching piano to talentless students, playing the occasional wedding or funeral, and it follows naturally that Zelda ought to leave him. Indeed, when Barney comes over to audition the lyric to "I'm a Poached Egg," Orville declares the whole song-writing routine "ridiculous" in terms indicative of his self-disgust: it's a foolish game and he's a fool for playing it. Yet the fact that Orville measures his self-worth in terms of financial success permits Barney—ever the more active and hopeful of the two—to appeal to Orville's sexual insecurity as a means of convincing Orville to keep at it. Every time Orville complains of the odds against success, Barney comes back with the name of a pop songwriter who beat the odds. And when Orville finally admits to his fear of infidelity, Barney comes back with the clincher: "All it takes is one hit. . . . You think Irving Berlin is afraid of losing his wife?"

It is not the case, however, that Barney takes unfair advantage of Orville, at least not until such time as Dino arrives unexpectedly in Climax. On the contrary, Barney's situation in Climax seems genuinely sterile, on balance far more negative than Orville's. Orville, at least, has Zelda, who appreciates Orville's better qualities and forgives him his failings: she married him despite her mother, after all. Barney, on the other hand, has nothing but his Shell Station, and even that offers little sense of social or personal purpose. So, for example, the first scene in Climax — which precedes the scene in the Spooner home and serves to define the level of purpose in Barney's everyday existence—finds a truck pulling into Barney's station. Barney asks the obligatory question—"Fill 'er up?"—and the truck driver holds out his cigarette lighter, which Barney dutifully fills. No wonder, then, that Barney's imagination seizes upon songwriting as vehicle for his hopes. And it is only natural that he and Orville should team up. Furthermore, it is significant that the songs Barney writes with Orville are almost always concerned with romantic love and sexual longing. "I'm a Poached Egg," for example, the first song we hear Barney sing, presents a series of images, each dealing with something absent or incomplete: "I'm a poached egg, without a piece of toast,/Yorkshire pudding, without a beef to roast,/I'm a haunted house, that hasn't got a ghost/When I'm without you." Of course, Barney seems too busy writing songs and urging Orville on to appear melancholy or neurotic. But his intense will to succeed seems motivated more by a desire for purpose in life, for some measure of success and recognition, some measure of affection, perhaps, than it is for mere money. As long as he works at songwriting he has something in common with Johnny Mercer and Richard Rodgers. Indeed, Barney has an encyclopedic memory for the trivia of top ten statistics, as if he were already an industry insider. It's all a dream, of course, but what else is there to do in Climax, Nevada but dream, particularly when everyone else is married and even the bar girls at the local road house are losers? In which case it is understandable that Barney should go to such great lengths—disabling Dino's car, suggesting that Dino spend the night at the Spooner's, arranging to bring a road house girl to play the Zelda role when Orville refuses to let the oversexed Dino get anywhere near his wife—in order to sell a song: it might very well be his one (and only) opportunity to escape the dreariness of life in Climax.

The importance of this "escape" motif is underlined by the character and presence of Polly the Pistol (Kim Novak), the bar girl that Barney hires to take Zelda's place as Mrs. Spooner. Polly had been a manicurist in New Jersey, had been saving towards opening her own beauty shop, but she fell in love with a travelling hula hoop salesman and her money had gone to buy a second-hand car and

Wilder and Kim Novak rehearse a scene from *Kiss Me, Stupid*.

trailer for the trip to a quickie wedding in Vegas. They had stopped overnight in Climax—and when morning came the guy was gone, the car was gone, and Polly was left with "six dozen plastic hula hoops." There being no demand for manicures in Climax, Polly had no choice but to sign on at the Belly Button. But, like Barney, she longs to escape her barren circumstances. Indeed, she takes the extra work, accepting propositions like Barney's, in the hope of earning enough money to purchase another second-hand car, believing that if she can just get out of Climax, out of the desert, she may be able to realise her ideal: she wants more than anything else to be a housewife, to do the dishes, to read "Ladies Home Journal," to hitch her trailer up to the right guy and leave the Polly the Pistol life behind. Otherwise she will always be "just somebody the bartender recommends."

It can hardly be said of *Kiss Me, Stupid,* then, that it is an immoral film or that its characters are devoid of virtue or feeling. On the contrary, with the exception of Dino, all of the major characters are committed to a vision of sexual/emotional fulfilment and marital integrity. Even Barney seeks success in terms which suggest that financial success is for the most part a means to more important emotional ends. The irony of it all, however, and perhaps the reason behind the film's extremely negative reception, is that Dino is the only character with the power and the money necessary for the realisation of those ends. Put another way, virtue and feeling are not portrayed as intrinsically self-sufficient, not in a culture that encourages Dino's sort of sexual exploitation. Indeed, it is arguable that Dino represents only a slightly exaggerated but completely logical extension of the sort of sexual/financial morality that motivates people like Zelda's mother who would sell their daughters in marriage for the sake of financial security.

And yet it is not the case that Orville *et al* are left totally in the comic lurch. It is rather the case, as it was in *The Major and the Minor* and *Some Like It Hot,* that Wilder admires characters such as Orville, Zelda, Polly, and Barney, admires them for their courage, for their will to survive, for their will to love and be loved, and he expresses that admiration by allowing them opportunity to be (or to become) their better selves in ways they had not thought possible. Thus Dino's presence in Climax serves a catalytic function. He is the dream come true, as it were, and facing up to Dino and what he represents requires Polly, Orville, Zelda, and Barney to face up to themselves. That they are the better for it in no way denies the legitimacy of the experience: they were basically right-headed to begin with and it is for their right-headedness that Wilder rewards them, not for the sinful specifics.

The film's central intrigue, involving all of the major characters, revolves around satisfying Dino's egocentric sexual demands. No sooner does he agree to stay overnight at the Spooner's than he asks Orville about the "action" in Climax. Orville mentions the bowling alley, and the colour television sets in the hardware store window, but Dino gets specific ("What's with the broads around here?") and Orville, catching on, suggests that Dino try the Belly Button ("They've got these cocktail waitresses. They're very friendly—at least, that's what I hear"). By this time, however, they have arrived in the guest room (Zelda's sewing room) and Dino's lecherous gaze has zeroed in on Zelda's full figured sewing dummy ("Must be a great girl, all around"). Dino's tendency to objectify women is perfectly reflected in the fact that he is aroused by Zelda's dress form. And Orville's tendency to be protective—overly so—is perfectly reflected by his response: he takes the dress form into the kitchen, covers it with his Beethoven sweatshirt (again, the metonymic association of music and sex), and stuffs it into the kitchen closet. The gesture is touching in its naïveté; but it also reflects Orville's increasingly fantastic state of mind, as if he genuinely believed that stuffing Zelda's dress form into the closet would somehow serve to protect Zelda from Dino (and it doesn't).

Already, then, Orville has come to embody the notion of "mad jealousy"—and this even before Barney suggests that a friendly hostess might be helpful in promoting their songs. But Orville's sense of mad panic only grows worse when he learns, soon thereafter, that Zelda had once had a high school crush on Dino. Just as Orville stuffs "Zelda" into the kitchen closet, the real Zelda returns from the "dentist." Orville then confronts her with the fact that she was not due to see the dentist for another three days or so, and Zelda confesses, after some further discussion of Orville's over-suspicious mind, that she had been at the bakery to pick up the anniversary cake. Indeed, she was delayed a bit when the baker gave her the wrong flavour cake and the delay gave her the chance to see Dino driving by in his car ("He wore sunglasses and he needed a shave but I recognized him"). As it turns out, Zelda had once been "crazy about" Dino, to the point of establishing the local Dino fan club, and the sight of Dino seems to have reawakened her enthusiasm (only with difficulty does Orville prevent her from playing a Dino album).

All of which only serves to drive Orville further into distraction and dissimulation. He cannot let Zelda go back into the sewing room—not with Dino back there, not when she is crazy about him—so Orville proposes a bit of love in the afternoon. Zelda agrees ("Orville, have you been reading 'Playboy' again?") and goes to take a shower. Orville, meanwhile, checks quickly in on Dino, only to find Dino standing in his underwear while examining the negligee that Zelda had been sewing as an anniversary surprise. It is more than Orville can take—and he runs outside to tell Barney the deal is off: "I don't care if I never sell a song. I'd rather starve first, because I love my wife, I adore her, I worship her." Barney counters by suggesting that they could get rid of Zelda for the evening rather than Dino. Orville replies that Dino won't stay the night without "action" and Barney proposes that they bring the action to Dino rather than let Dino go prowl for the action ("That'll keep him in the house"). Orville wonders how he will go about explaining the presence of a road house girl to Dino, and Barney replies by urging that Orville not bother to explain—he can simply introduce the girl as Zelda. Indeed, the scheme seems so perfect that Barney waxes rapturous at the splendor of it ("That's it, he's gonna get all the action he wants") and Orville, more deeply involved with every passing moment, expresses an equally intense distaste for the whole affair ("Barney, you're sick!"). Orville then plays his trump card, raising what seems to be one last and insur-mountable objection to Barney's scheme: how is he going to get rid of Zelda for the evening? And Barney has an answer: "That's the easiest part—hit her, start an argument, get her sore at you, shove a grapefruit in her face." Orville is horrified at the thought ("Do you want to louse up my marriage?") and Barney comes in once more with the clincher. Orville must do it for Zelda's sake: "It's for her own good."

There are several things to remark about this exchange between Orville and Barney. To begin with, the substance of the exchange—which deals with the particulars of satisfying Dino's sexual needs—is a function of Dino's egocentric personality. *He* is the one who demands "action." And it is only in response to that demand, a response conditioned by Barney's desire to sell a song and Orville's fear of losing Zelda, that they cook up their scheme to supply Dino with a Belly Button girl. Note, further, how quickly things escalate: one minute Orville tells Barney to forget it, the next he agrees to shove a grapefruit Cagney-fashion in Zelda's face. Once again Orville allows himself to be manipulated by the logic of insecurity—and the faster things go the less secure Orville becomes. Indeed, he can hardly stand still and the dialogue summarised above is punctuated by Orville's repeated and manic forays into the house to check on Zelda and Dino. The effect, therefore, is to emphasise Orville's ever increasing sense of desperation. His tenuous sense of self is so vulnerable that he literally risks destroying his marriage in order to save it—and in the process he almost destroys himself (he even talks of suicide). Before it is all over, Orville kicks Zelda out of the house, spends the evening dancing Saturnalian jigs with Polly—and then, at the depths of his madness, he reasserts himself by tossing Dino out of the house. At which point the whole scheme seems to have backfired.

But, of course, it does not all go for naught, and it is the measure of Orville's basic integrity and Wilder's comic benevolence that Barney's questionable con should fail precisely as it does. It is somehow appropriate that the bar girl Barney picks up is Polly the Pistol—and it serves Barney right that Polly's presence should revive Orville's sense of marital integrity. Polly would like nothing better than to be married to someone like Orville and she takes the Zelda role very seriously. No sooner does she put on Zelda's dress, for example, than she begins asking Orville about the specifics of their courtship ("in case it comes up"). And Orville obliges: he had first noticed her at choir practice (Zelda sang off key) and in order to ingratiate himself with Zelda's mother ("She never liked me much") he gave blood three times a week at the bloodbank where she worked (he snuck off to Silver City on the other two days to get transfusions). Polly is touched by Orville's dedication ("Boy, you must have been nuts about— uh—me") and she asks about the proposal. Orville replies: "I wrote this love song and one afternoon while I was tuning your piano I played it for you and that did it." So for the moment, at least, as evidenced by the ambiguous pronouns in the dialogue, Polly *is* Zelda—acting the wife role, setting the table while Orville gets the booze out of the liquour cabinet. It is all very domestic and yet it is all very privileged as well. Indeed, they even "get married" as Orville puts his own ring on her finger. No wonder then that Polly treats Dino like an intrudor when he makes his entrance a moment or two later. No wonder then that Polly eventually asks Orville to sing the song he wrote for "her" as a sort of last request before Orville leaves her alone with Dino for the evening. And no wonder that singing the song ("All the Live Long Day") serves as prologue to Orville's mad rampage. Song, in the world of *Kiss Me, Stupid,* serves as a repository of values and feelings. And it is by getting in tune with what he values most, his love for Zelda (his "one and all time"), that Orville is enabled to reclaim his self-image. Being loved by Zelda is enough. And therefore Orville takes monumental offence at the implication that people like Dino can just ride into town and take over: "Does he really think he can buy my wife for a song!"

Neither Polly nor Orville, it must be remarked, ever lose complete touch with reality. They come close, like Jerry in *Some Like It Hot,* but the agony of their situation is predicated on a continuing though occasionally submerged sense of reality. Were it otherwise, were Orville and Polly to have gone off the deep end, like Norma Desmond in *Sunset Boulevard,* the film would have ended (as *Sunset Boulevard* ends) at the moment when their madness became complete. But however much Polly and Orville might wish that Polly were Zelda, that all is right with the world, the pretence cannot be maintained. One cannot counter the charge that *Kiss Me, Stupid* condones adul-

"All the Livelong Day": Dino gets to go bowling while "Mr. and Mrs. Spooner"—Ray Walston and Kim Novak—reminisce.

tery, then, simply by asserting that Polly and Orville *are* Mr. and Mrs. Spooner when they go to bed together after Orville throws Dino out the door. Orville *says* they are, of course. But he says it very self-consciously, and primarily to counter Polly's sense of self disgust. She is not Polly "the pushover" and he is not "the bartender"—"not tonight" at least. And their going to bed, to the strains of "All the Live Long Day," is more elegiac than adulterous. Orville no doubt believes he has lost Zelda for good and he goes to bed with Polly to memorialise, as it were, his lost love. And, furthermore, he rewards Polly—who made it possible for Orville to regain his sense of integrity—by loving her for herself, as a woman of feeling and dignity. They may *not* be husband and wife in literal fact, but their love-making effectively celebrates the *real* value of marriage and marital relationships by celebrating the integrity of the heart.

And a similar logic ought to determine, it seems to me, our response to Zelda's adulterous liaison with Dino. Zelda had gone home to mother—only to be driven away by her mother's non-stop monologue to the effect that Zelda had made a "mess" of her life. Zelda then returns to the Spooner house, only to see Orville and Polly dancing around the love seat in the front room. Which would seem, then, to confirm Orville's assertion, made for the purpose of getting Zelda out of the house, that Orville was a frequent customer at the Belly Button. Outraged, Zelda then goes to the road house herself— to give Orville a dose of his own medicine, perhaps, or just to get good and corked. Her going there, however, is also thematically appropriate. That is, the road house represents a brand of exploitation not unlike Dino's, and it is therefore ironically appropriate that Orville's attempt to prevent Zelda's exploitation should result in her being treated like a road house whore. It is also appropriate to the degree that Zelda earns a comeuppance of her own. That is, she goes there believing that her mother was right about Orville after all—she even repeats parts of her mother's monologue—so that she too begins to buy the Dino sort of logic: she should have married that chiropractor. Thus it makes ironic sense that Zelda should wind up drunk in Polly's trailer, where she is mistaken for Polly when Dino, still on the prowl after being thrown out by Orville, comes to "shoot it out" with the "fastest draw in the west." Not only does she get what she deserves—in that her momentary allegiance to her mother's marital credo requires acceptance of Dino's crass vision of sex—but she is forced to see how crass it really is (Dino: "I prefer to eat out").

But Zelda doesn't go to bed with Dino (and, despite the re-shot scenes, she clearly does make love to Dino, even in the present release print) for reasons of despair. On the contrary, no sooner does Zelda recognise Dino than Dino tells the tale of Orville's sexually-loaded sales promotion ("Get the scene?"). At which point it becomes clear to Zelda that Orville still loves her after his scatterbrained fashion. Thus Zelda takes offence when Dino insults Orville's talent, and she begins a promotion of her own. That is, she tells Dino that he's "too old" for a song like "Sophia," the Italian number that Dino had pretended to buy from Orville before Orville gave him the boot, and bets him that the Singing Nun sells more records than he does. She thus challenges his musical potency in the hope that he will sing the song (and eventually record it) to prove her wrong. Indeed, he starts to sing, as one proof of potency, and it seems logical that he would want to prove another sort of potency before the night is over. At this point in the release print, Dino's back goes out of whack and we fade out as Zelda gives him a back rub. When we fade in the next morning, however, Dino has left the trailer, apparently in good spirits, no headache, Zelda is naked beneath the sheets, and there is $500 stuffed in the neck of a liquor bottle—so there can be little doubt as to what took place. But the point is not so much what Zelda did as her reason for doing it—for love of Orville, for having learned how far her crazy husband would go to prove himself for her sake. Indeed, it is a lesson she never would have learned had Dino not been detoured through Climax. That Zelda learns it at all is thus "fortunate" in the extreme. That is, it was only by chance that she did not see Dino in the front room with Orville and Polly (had she seen him there she would not have gone to the Belly Button) and had she not gone to the Belly Button she would never have had the opportunity to sell Dino on "Sophia."

It seems fairly clear, then, that Polly, Orville and Zelda really do earn the good fortune which befalls them, however bizarre it all may seem. Before the film is over Polly—who gets the $500 from Zelda in return for Orville's wedding ring—has her used car and is on her way out of Climax. She deserves better than Climax has to offer and Wilder grants her the chance to find it. Orville does not get off quite so easily as Polly. Zelda concocts a little scheme of her own—going through the motions of divorce proceedings—in order to bring home to Orville the value of their marriage (this recalls the Lubitsch of *That Uncertain Feeling*). But all ends well when Zelda gives the ring back in what amounts to a re-marriage ceremony outside of Pringle's Hardware. By this point, indeed, Orville's intense jealousy has been replaced by intense bewilderment. He knows nothing of Zelda's liaison with Dino, does not know how Zelda got his ring even if he remembers giving it to Polly, and he is amazed at the sight of multiple Dinos, one for each of the many television sets in Pringle's window, singing "Sophia" to a national audience. We can therefore reasonably assume, with Zelda, that Orville henceforth will be content with his marriage and himself as he had not been before. Zelda has forgiven him the worst of all possible transgressions, or so it seems to Orville, and there can be little doubt in his mind that Zelda loves him, imperfections and all. And furthermore, he is a song-writing somebody, at least for the moment.

But then again, so is Barney. And if the conclusion of *Kiss Me, Stupid* rankles, it rankles for allowing Barney—the least deserving of the four more sympathetic characters—to share in Orville's good fortune. It is not the case, it seems to me, that Barney deserves the sort of condemnation earned by Dino or by characters like Chuck Tatum (*Ace in the Hole*) or Col. von Scherbach (*Stalag 17*). And indeed Barney does redeem our sympathies before the film is over by accepting responsibility for Polly's presence at the Spooner house (he tells Zelda

Barney (Cliff Osmond) conspires with Zelda (Felicia Farr) to set Orville (Ray Walston) straight.

not to blame Orville: "The whole thing was my idea") and by aiding Zelda in her scheme to set Orville straight. Yet it remains the case that Barney's good fortune far exceeds in degree his good works.

Wilder's point, however—a point he makes with some frequency—is that human societies generally do not abide by principles of absolute justice. If anything, it takes an exceptional sort of comic fortune to insure the happiness of characters such as Orville Spooner who find their right-headedness at hazard in a wrong-headed culture. This was true in *The Major and the Minor* (Susan and Kirby are clearly exceptions to the rule, both in New York City and at Wallace Military) and it is true in *Kiss Me, Stupid* with Orville and Zelda: in a society that values money more than love they stand out for valuing love more than money. As a general rule, however, Wilder's vision of society is cynical to the extent that characters like Dino quite frequently prosper beyond all equity. No wonder, then, that Wilder extends a certain generous measure of sympathy to underdogs like Barney in *Kiss Me, Stupid,* or even to "Whiplash Willie" Gingrich (Walter Matthau) in *The Fortune Cookie:* both men scheme to get rich, both exploit the emotional instability of weaker characters, but neither goes to the extreme of murder (unlike Walter Neff in *Double Indemnity,* for example), and Barney, at least, does his belated best to help Zelda set things straight. Life may never be perfect in the world of Billy Wilder, but it is very often human. And if Wilder's humanism is inclusive enough to forgive characters like Barney Millsap their imperfections, then it would be ungenerous for us to be any less forgiving on our part, particularly when it is clear that Wilder's deeper sympathies are with those who have the courage to defy the way of the world.

The Lubitsch Principle:
Love in the Afternoon, The Apartment, The Private Life of Sherlock Holmes

There are very few Wilder films which do not bring to mind the legacy of Ernst Lubitsch. Lubitsch and Wilder worked together in harmony and accord on *Bluebeard's Eighth Wife* and *Ninotchka;* and Wilder continually refers back to these films, and to other Lubitsch movies, by repeating situations, themes, visuals, even lines of dialogue on occasion, which are to be found in the Lubitsch canon. In all of this, Wilder never ceases to be Wilder. He does not merely copy—he assimilates. Indeed, it seems an understatement to describe certain Wilder films, *A Foreign Affair, Irma La Douce, Avanti!,* as upholding the

Left, Ernst Lubitsch. Below, Gary Cooper, Edward Everett Horton, and Claudette Colbert in *Bluebeard's Eighth Wife* (directed by Ernst Lubitsch from the screenplay by Brackett and Wilder).

Lubitsch tradition.[16] Wilder's references to Lubitsch are not so much a matter of homage but principle: Lubitsch represents a set of humane values, worldly yet ever hopeful, that Wilder wholeheartedly shares.

Specifically, Wilder shares with Lubitsch a certain bitter-sweet vision of sexual/emotional relationships. Both film-makers, for example, tend quite often to juxtapose love and death. In *To Be or Not to Be* (as in *The Man I Killed*), Lubitsch demonstrates how interrelated the two can become: Joseph Tura's love of Poland requires that he risk his life in the service of his country, and his feelings for his wife increase the risk by decreasing his ability to act the role of the Gestapo Colonel. Similarly, in films like *The Merry Widow,* Lubitsch shows us how readily love can be transformed into hatred—a form of emotional death—even when the lovers are genuinely committed to each other. Wilder is likewise concerned with the realities of feeling and with the dangers implicit in the expression of love. Love of one sort or another leads to death in *Double Indemnity, Sunset Boulevard,* and *Witness for the Prosecution;* and conversely, death, or the threat of death, leads to love in, for example, *Sabrina, Some Like It Hot, Irma La Douce,* and *Avanti!*

In general, both film-makers portray characters who long very deeply for love and security. Such characters fear the risks involved, however, and their anxiety tends to pervert or prevent the love which they so anxiously seek (as in *Kiss Me, Stupid).* Wilder tends to be the more bitter of the two in that perversity, either social or personal, more frequently tends to triumph over legitimate feeling. Such is certainly the case in *Double Indemnity, Sunset Boulevard,* and *Ace in the Hole.* And the threat of perversity is always strong in Wilder, whether it is eventually overcome or not (as it is in *Avanti!,* for example). Nevertheless, the fact of love's perversion in Wilder, of its tenuous (and tenacious) existence in often loveless societies, serves to magnify the significance of those Lubitsch-like moments when love does find legitimate means of expression.

*   *   *

Love in the Afternoon recalls, in its structure, style, and concerns, the Lubitsch of *One Hour with You, The Merry Widow,* and *Cluny Brown* (not to mention the obvious though somewhat superficial similarities to *Bluebeard's Eighth Wife).* Like *One Hour with You, Love in the Afternoon* begins with the issue of love and love's proper place. Lubitsch shows us

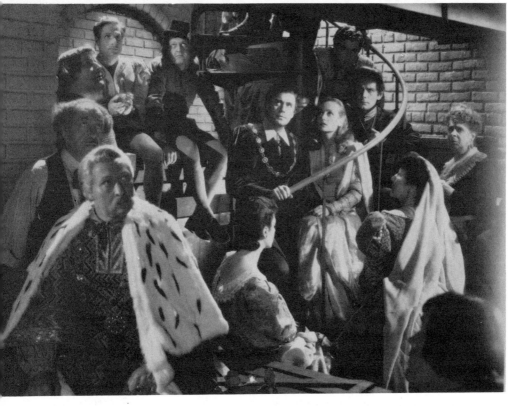

Above, Jack Benny and Carole Lombard (centre) in *To Be or Not to Be* (directed by Ernst Lubitsch). Below, Juliet Mills and Jack Lemmon in *Avanti!*

Love's proper place: Jeanette MacDonald and Maurice Chevalier in Ernst Lubitsch's *One Hour with You*.

lovers embracing in a Paris park; while Wilder, via his narrator, Maurice Chevalier, sets about to catalogue the varieties of love to be found in a post-war Paris ("Poodles do it, tourists do it, generals do it—once in a while even existentialists do it"). *Love in the Afternoon* also recalls *One Hour with You* in its relatively relaxed and intimate tone of voice. Indeed, it is the same voice, Chevalier's, speaking directly to us, in both cases. The mere fact of Chevalier's presence is enough to bring Lubitsch to mind; and *Love in the Afternoon* partakes of that easy grace which Chevalier came to embody through the course of his collaborations with Lubitsch. To be sure, by 1957 Chevalier was too old to play the philanderer role—so was Gary Cooper, for that matter—and in *Love in the Afternoon* Chevalier is less a participant in the game of love than an observer, "What you would call the 'private eye,' " as Claude Chevasse (Chevalier) himself puts it.

Cluny Brown: Jennifer Jones and Charles Boyer.

The film's love affair, between an ageing American playboy, Frank Flannagan (Gary Cooper), and a detective's blooming young daughter, Ariane Chevasse (Audrey Hepburn), recalls, by turns, *Cluny Brown* and *The Merry Widow.* Like Cluny Brown in her film, Ariane Chevasse is an unconventional girl longing to lead an unconventional life, despite the contrary wishes of her guardian. Cluny Brown (Jennifer Jones) longs to follow her uncle's trade—she wants to be a lady plumber who takes tea at the Ritz when the mood strikes her—but her uncle sends her into service as an upstairs maid, instead. Cluny is obliging but unhappy, does her best to fit into the sort of lower middle-class existence her position permits her (e.g., her genuine attempt to become interested in the local chemist); but she longs for something better, more genteel, more romantic—longs, in other words, for the sort of unconventional self-assertion embodied by Adam Belinski (Charles Boyer), an expatriate foreigner residing at the estate where Cluny is employed. Belinski represents a life of knowledge, sophistication, tolerance—and Cluny longs to share life with him, despite the obvious differences in their ages.

Ariane Chevasse leads a similar double life. On the one hand there is her "neat, normal" existence as the detective's daughter—pleasant, comfortable, but uneventful. Ariane watches her father's clients come and go (peeking through the transom window on occasion to do so), and spends the rest of her time rehearsing her cello, either at the conservatory or at home (or so her father would like to think). On the other hand, however, Ariane is as likely to have one of her father's case files on her music stand as a score. Indeed, Ariane considers her father's files a "private library," a treasure trove of romantic narratives which provide rich food for Ariane's somewhat thrill-starved adolescent imagination. She admits as much to her father, who is upset but not surprised. He has told her "a thousand times" to stay away from the files, wants to protect her from the "sordid matters" he has to deal with, but he reluctantly recognises the difference in their perspectives. As he puts it: "This is not a library, this is a sewer." And the give and take of the following conversation, which Ariane carries by weight of her enthusiasm, foretells the potentially dangerous direction subsequent events will take. Specifically, Ariane brings up the "sad and so beautiful" example of the English Duchess and the Alpine guide. It was, in her father's words, "a terrible scandal and it had to lead to a terrible end." But Ariane protests that "it was worth it—what woman could ask for more than to die together with her love, buried under an avalanche, locked in each other's arms, forever?"

The danger here is two-fold, reflecting the extremes of caution and foolhardiness, one leading inevitably to the other. That is, overmuch caution, overmuch concern that life follow predictable routine, not only results from, but inexorably leads to, overmuch romanticism. As Ariane tells us, her father secretly enjoys his cases, and would enjoy them even if he were not paid for his effort. He is romantic enough at heart to understand the attractions of sexual/emotional fantasy; but he is experienced enough to understand the risks romantics run. Accordingly, he tries to shield Ariane from life's dangers. He sends her to a conservatory, encourages her relationship with Michel, a fellow music student, and hopes she will marry into Michel's very respectable, very bourgeois family—a family which Chevasse has thoroughly investigated: "Father and two uncles work for the government; mother plays the harp; grandfather was a missionary in French Equatorial Africa; and there hasn't been a scandal in the family since 1822." It's not done oppressively. Chevasse sees the investigation not as an invasion of Ariane's privacy but as a gift: "If I were an Indian potentate, I'd shower you with diamonds. If I were a cobbler, I'd sew your shoe. But since I'm only a detective, all I can offer you is a detailed dossier." It is charming, touching, and leaves no doubt as to the essential harmony of father and daughter. But Chevasse knows himself—recognises something of his own romantic inclination in Ariane—and he wishes to save her from "disillusionment and heartbreak." To do so, however, is to unwittingly condemn Ariane to a life of mean expectations and vicarious pleasures. Michel is, as Ariane somewhat indirectly puts it, "conceited and clumsy and very unimaginative"—certainly no fit match for a girl of such vitality and drive. Indeed, Michel's greatest achievement is to sit in an opera box and "conduct" the orchestra by proxy, flipping through the Wagnerian score as if he really were wielding the baton. This sort of cautious, back-seat conducting is comfortable, without risk (Michel can hardly get bad reviews); but a life without risk is lifeless indeed, offering few dangers, and fewer rewards—and it is not good enough for Ariane.

Thus it is appropriate that Chevasse himself should be the one to bring Ariane and Frank Flannagan together. All of his caution, his order that Ariane not read his files, for example, only encourages her romanticism. Indeed, she becomes particularly fascinated by the Flannagan file. Chevasse is working on the Flannagan case at the film's beginning—Flannagan is romancing a married woman and the woman's "foolish husband," driven to distraction by the uncertainty

Ariane Chevasse (Audrey Hepburn) shows an interest in her detective father's most recent case—to the displeasure of Monsieur Chevasse (Maurice Chevalier).

of it all, has engaged Chevasse to untangle things. And Chevasse brings home a roll of incriminating film. Ariane, ever curious, wanders into the darkroom (there are many dark rooms in the film) and is immediately taken with Flannagan's image as the devil-may-care lothario. She has never seen his face in the files before, finds him "very attractive," and her interest is reinforced when Chevasse describes him as "very objectionable, quite immoral, utterly no good." Her curiosity is even further excited when the foolish husband arrives, and she overhears her father reporting on Flannagan's amatory activities. Flannagan is, it turns out, "American, very rich, oil, construction business, turbo jet engines, Pepsi Cola," and he has been romancing Madame X for "a week or so" by having her to dinner every night in his suite at the Ritz. Madame X is very discreet and punctual in all this: she always takes the service elevator, "always wears a veil" and arrives at Flannagan's hotel room every night at nine, where their meal is served to the accompaniment of a four piece gypsy orchestra—which always concludes its programme at five to ten by playing "Fascination."

Ariane is naturally wide-eyed at all this; but thus far Flannagan remains simply one more character in the running romance that her father keeps on file. Or he would have remained such a character had Chevasse taken a little less cautious, a little less callous attitude towards his work. The foolish husband, it turns out, is a man for all that. As was the case with Adolphe (Charlie Ruggles) in *One Hour with You,* the husband's passion is simultaneously ridiculous and genuine; and in his agony and anger he decides to shoot Mr. Flannagan. Chevasse attempts at first to dissuade him: "You do realise this is cold-blooded murder?" But the foolish husband will not be dissuaded, and Chevasse regretfully replies: "In that case, Monsieur, you leave me no choice—I must insist on being paid as of right now." As a perpetual spectator, it never occurs to Chevasse that he ought to warn Flannagan of the husband's intentions. Chevasse bears some measure of responsibility for the situation—but his sideline mentality, which governs his relationship with Ariane as well as with his customers, blinds him to the facts of the matter. Ariane, however, is all the more wide-eyed (we see her in close-up), instantly perceives the implications of it all, and she takes it upon herself to rescue Mr. Flannagan. Thus her father's caution, his general desire to avoid the "dirt" of life, requires his daughter to involve herself very directly in the sort of "fly-by-night" affair he so fears.

Chevasse clearly overreacts in all this, and we forgive him, as we forgive Henry Van Cleve's mother in *Heaven Can Wait,* because his intentions are basically right-headed and kind-hearted, even if his behaviour is somewhat self-destructive. Chevasse clearly wishes the best for Ariane, as Uncle Arn wishes the best for Cluny Brown; and Chevasse finally comes to understand that Ariane must be free to learn life's lessons on her own. She cannot learn them by proxy through him.

Furthermore, Ariane is quite anxious and able to learn. For Ariane, at least, there's a brave new world out there—and Frank Flannagan, the rich American playboy, represents a very interesting case study. There is little sense that Ariane sets out, in advance, to fall in love with Flannagan—she is never conniving or demanding, and their initial meeting, however melodramatic the circumstance, is a matter of rather practical necessity: either she warns him or the foolish husband will come in shooting. Once in Flannagan's presence, however,

Ariane is all the more fascinated, legitimately drawn not by some perverse or self-destructive urge but by a genuinely child-like sort of camaraderie. We do not get ultra-sophisticated dialogue of the sort that often serves to initiate sexual relationships in Lubitsch (in *Trouble in Paradise,* for example)—Cooper's Flannagan admits he's not much of a "talker"—but the feeling is very similar, a feeling of instant sympathy, reinforced by a sense of urgency. Ariane must get to the Ritz before the gypsy orchestra concludes the programme. Furthermore, Flannagan has only one more night in Paris, and if Ariane is going to learn from him she must learn quickly. And colouring it all is the more general issue of time. Flannagan is almost old enough to be her father (indeed, Cooper plays the Lothario role that Chevalier developed in his Lubitsch films) and he will soon be far too old to be her lover, should that eventuality develop (he is, we should note, very touchy about his age).

The relationship between Frank and Ariane develops at several levels and by definite stages, and recalls in its organisation, issues, and in its primary setting the Sonia/Danilo relationship in *The Merry Widow.* Thus their first meeting takes place in Flannagan's suite where Ariane watches Flannagan and Madame X dance through the room's dark shadows while the gypsy orchestra plays "Fascination." There is a *Merry Widow* elegance about it all, a ritualised sensuality recalling the "dining room" scene between Sonia and Danilo. But underlying the elegance—in both cases—we find genuinely pressing emotional issues, issues which threaten to become inelegant very quickly. In *Love in the Afternoon,* specifically, there is the issue of the foolish husband in the corridor, pacing up and down, waiting only for the orchestra's departure before staging his own melodramatic entrance. It is a matter of life and death, so serious that Ariane feels compelled to break in on the ritual seduction: she climbs in over the balcony and quite unexpectedly disrupts the proceedings (as Danilo in *The Merry Widow* climbs over the garden wall and disrupts Sonia's comfortable ritual of widowhood). It takes persistence on Ariane's part to break the romantic spell—she says "Mr. Flannagan" three times before getting his attention—but once the message is delivered another ritual of sorts begins: the deception of the foolish husband. Like Sonia, Ariane plays the woman of the world role—complete with black veil—and the couple that the foolish husband discovers upon entering is Ariane and Flannagan, embracing in the shadows.

Ariane thus begins her relationship with Flannagan by saving his life (a matter of consequence, as Flannagan slowly discovers), but she saves his life by enacting her fondest fantasy. She is a mystery woman, anonymous, possessed of uncanny knowledge, and Flannagan is genuinely fascinated by her combination of innocence and experience. She is obviously young—doesn't know the difference between Pepsi and champagne—and yet she knows the details of his love life and can quote "official figures" as to the frequency of illicit liaisons in Parisian hotels. Ariane does her best to seem the sophisticate while Cooper as Flannagan betrays a sort of Deedsian naïveté as he questions her ("Are you a religious fanatic, or something?") Yet the physical action of the scene makes it clear that Ariane, however self-possessed her lines, clearly fears for her emotions. Flannagan offers to recall the gypsies ("It's amazing what a couple of fiddles can do for ya"), but Ariane backs away, both physically and mentally: "Oh no, no, no, no gypsies, no 'Fascination.' " She is clearly unsure of herself, senses that she is getting in over her head, particularly when he asks her to dinner—and in her ambivalence she encourages him to believe that she is living with a man without the benefit of matrimony (i.e., with her father), while at the same time she lets Flannagan dance her against the wall. The intimacy between them thus finds its visual expression in a two-shot close-up; and at that distance Ariane is overwhelmed by Flannagan's charm. Both of them are romantics, after all, devotees of the passionate life, and Ariane's rapture finds expression in music: she hums "Fascination" on the way home (to Michel's chagrin) and she dances with her cello as she carries it in the front door.

Their second meeting, the next afternoon, continues this pattern of uncertain motives and emotional risks. Ariane arrives early—in order to tell Flannagan that she will not be coming at the appointed hour. It is a charming tactic, at once self-deceiving and self-expressive. She wants to be with Flannagan, but she fears what that may bring. She assumes a worldly stance ("I have another date"); but her worldliness is undercut by the visuals. She is a very little girl in a very large room (Wilder shows us this in long shot as Ariane enters)—and she rightly fears the possibility that her self-control will be overwhelmed by grand desire. She knows, from having read Flannagan's file, that other women have been overwhelmed by Flannagan's charm—one even to the point of suicide—and while she longs to lose her heart she does not want to lose her life.

A similar fear motivates Flannagan himself. At the scene's beginning he is recording a series of memos on a dictaphone, including a list of female companions for his upcoming New York sojourn. He

Upper class intimacy: Jeannette MacDonald and Maurice Chevalier in *The Merry Widow* (above) and Audrey Hepburn and Gary Cooper in *Love in the Afternoon* (below).

arranges his life in such a manner that he never stays in one place for long, nor does he ever devote concerted attention to any one woman, not for reasons of malice, but for fear of involvement. As he puts it to Ariane, as they sip champagne on the balcony of his suite: "He who loves and runs away lives to love another day." And thus his attraction to Ariane. She seems, on the surface, to share Flannagan's "no involvements, no complication, no danger" philosophy—she "lives" with one man, "plays" with another, and still finds time to dance with rich Americans when opportunity arises. And yet both clearly long for something more lasting, more genuine, something that will give real substance to the rituals of seduction. Flannagan admits as much when he grants the supposition that "most girls are sentimental about their first love." There are powerful emotions at work within the human heart, too powerful to be contained by Flannagan's "between planes" ethos, and Flannagan understands the danger involved. What he lacks, however, is sufficient understanding of the rewards that love can bring. A life of fly-by-night affairs is not calculated to develop such an awareness. On the contrary, such a life is designed specifically to avoid risks, and to avoid the sort of woman who might be worthy of risk taking. In Ariane, however, Flannagan has met his match, a girl of vitality, sincerity, and ingenuity, a girl who asks for nothing that money can buy. Her only keepsake when Flannagan leaves Paris is the flower from his lapel. Thus they part without tears—but not without pain, the very sort of pain that Flannagan would rather avoid.

The next stage in their relationship is marked by even greater urgency, greater risk, and increased determination on Ariane's part. Flannagan has been gone for a year, and Ariane meets him at the opera. Flannagan's presence at the opera, while fortuitous, is not inappropriate, and is a function not of sophistication but naïveté. He thought he was getting tickets to the Folies Bergères, but his poor French dictated otherwise. Ariane, on the other hand, while no less romantic at heart (the opera is "Tristan and Isolde"), has gained in sophistication. Her gown is elegant, and she carries herself with far more dignity than Flannagan's companion. She protests that she has "too many dates" to accept Flannagan's dinner invitation, but he insists they meet again. And his insistence requires Ariane to make a decision—either she gives him up altogether, or goes all out to win him once and for all.

Ariane decides upon the latter tactic, and she attempts, through the course of their next several meetings, to awaken his heart by arousing his jealousy. She attempts, in other words, to turn the sexual tables on him, to put him on the defensive, as Claudette Colbert puts Cooper on the defensive in *Bluebeard's Eighth Wife.* Ariane will not win Flannagan by pleading her own needs. But perhaps Flannagan can be made to feel the sting of disappointment, the ache of longing, the bewilderment of powerful emotion. Perhaps he can come to understand the pain of wanting someone who does not seem to want him. It is unfortunate that love requires such deception, such heartache, such risk—it is only the foolish husband's threat to kill Flannagan that rejuvenates the husband's marriage, for example—but people have a way of taking things for granted in Wilder, and it takes extraordinary measures, even in so comparatively relaxed a film as *Love in the Afternoon,* to bring people to their sexual/emotional senses.

And Ariane brings Flannagan to his senses by virtue of her quick wit and romantic imagination. Specifically, she draws upon the material in her father's files to create a very bizarre, though very detailed, and therefore very convincing list of previous and concurrent love affairs—complete with props, the ermine coat that her father had been keeping for a client, and an "anklet" improvised from a keychain. For once in his life Flannagan is given a taste of his own medicine—and he finds it "maddening." The thought of Ariane with Mr. Export/Import, or with the Alpine guide ("he had the most attractive knees—you know, they wear those short leather pants—so naturally one thing led to another"), or with the bullfighter (he gave her the anklet, or so Ariane tells the tale), or with the Canadian ice-hockey player ("very high scorer"), drives Flannagan to distraction. Suddenly it matters how many men she has known (he asks her point blank: "How many others were there?"); and it matters as well the sort of man she plays with (Flannagan: "I know how those jokers operate"). Flannagan's "love and run" ethic thus falls apart because Flannagan has finally found someone worth loving.

Flannagan's change of heart is evidenced not only by jealousy. Ariane's next visit to his hotel is prolonged when Flannagan hides her shoe (Danilo employed the identical gambit in *The Merry Widow);* and Flannagan seems genuinely embarrassed to get a phone call from the Swedish twins: he is no longer comfortable in the Lothario role. Furthermore, while Flannagan is on the phone, Ariane uses his dictaphone to record a long and detailed list of her "previous" love affairs. Flannagan finds the tape after Ariane leaves for the evening; and his reaction is doubly significant. He is not jealous, at least not in the overpossessive sense of the word. On the contrary, he seems

Wilder directs Audrey Hepburn in *Love in the Afternoon.*

immensely pleased just to hear her voice, even if it is on tape. He is so captivated that he leaves the water running in the bathtub: all that really matters is the sense of Ariane's presence. There is, however, a message on the tape, and that message carries certain implications. Flannagan had asked for the list, after all, much against his creed of non-involvement, and he thereby indicates the degree of his own seriousness. Ariane really does matter to him. And Ariane gives him the list in return, indicating seriousness on her part as well. And as Flannagan plays the tape over and over again, drinking all the while, accompanied by the similarly sloshed band of gypsies, it dawns on him that Ariane is a girl worth worrying about. Accordingly, he grabs his hat and coat and sets out, gypsies and all, for the local steambath. She seems to be getting under his skin—perhaps he can sweat the ambivalence and uncertainty out of his system. He has never had to sweat for a woman before; but now he is doubly troubled—just what sort of girl is she? Experienced, as *she* believes *him* to be, or genuinely innocent, as innocent as is Flannagan in his heart of hearts? And what sort of a man is he, that he should worry one way or the other?

The answers to these questions are self-evident, at least to the audience. But it is not what we know that matters at this point in the film. It is rather what we feel; and the primary emotion, for us as for Ariane and Flannagan, is anxiety. If anything, our anxiety is the greater for knowing how much they love each other and how difficult it will be for that love to find full expression. Their dilemma is maddeningly simple. Flannagan fears the uncertainty and vulnerability that love requires. In the past he sought certainty in flight, and there is increasingly the possibility that he might flee again. On the other hand, Ariane fears (mistakenly) that certain knowledge of her true identity will alienate Flannagan forever. How could a romantic playboy like Flannagan ever fall for such an everyday sort of a girl? The more she loves him, then, the more Ariane fosters Flannagan's uncertainty—and there seems no way that they can overcome this barrier on their own. The universe of *Love in the Afternoon*, however, like the universe of *Cluny Brown*, is essentially benevolent, and the necessary assistance is provided: Flannagan shares his steambath with, of all people, the foolish husband; and the latter, empathetic toward Flannagan's uncertainty, suggests that Flannagan consult

Claude Chevasse, "the very best man in Paris, very thorough, very discreet." Coincidence is thus compounded in Flannagan and Ariane's favour. Chevasse will no doubt make quick work of the investigation and Flannagan will finally be possessed of the truth.

But before Flannagan can be so informed, Chevasse himself must face the facts and their implications. It was his over-cautious attitude toward Ariane and her sexuality which effectively initiated her relationship with Flannagan. More specifically, it was Chevasse's tendency towards over-simplification and categorisation (his quite mistaken description of Flannagan as "utterly no good") which led him to believe that he could protect Ariane from life's unpleasantness. If evil can be readily identified, it can be readily avoided—or so Chevasse had thought. But attempts to avoid life's irritations tend also to preclude the experience of the joy that life and love can bring (a lesson that both Flannagan and Chevasse need to learn). Chevasse must therefore come to understand that his over-simple view of life is not in tune with reality—that, for example, the supposedly heartless Flannagan has a heart after all. And he must come to understand as well that he cannot order Ariane's emotional life to suit his own emotional ends. That is, he cannot tell her to stay away from Flannagan anymore than he could effectively order her to keep out of the files. The best he can hope to do is to cushion what he still (falsely) perceives to be the inevitable blow. Accordingly, when he delivers Ariane's one page "dossier" to Flannagan's hotel room, he begs Flannagan to give her a chance: "She's so helpless, such a little fish. Throw her back in the water." Again, he underestimates Ariane's abilities (she is not all that helpless), but Chevasse rightly perceives that whatever happens must happen between Flannagan and Ariane. If Chevasse's fault as a detective is that he avoids responsibility, his fault as a father is his attempt to assume too much responsibility, thus denying Ariane the right to make her own mistakes. It is as a father, however, that Chevasse begs Flannagan's kindness (Chevasse refuses payment for his professional services) and it is as a chastened and truly responsible father that Chevasse allows Ariane to go her own way.

A similar decision now faces Flannagan. The truth of his relationship with Ariane turns out to be far more profound and far more disturbing than he had anticipated. If anything, his worst fears are confirmed. Ariane is precisely the sort of woman he has spent a lifetime trying to avoid. The depth of her seriousness, indeed, is measured by the extremely elaborate measures she has taken to

arouse his jealousy. That is, Ariane's pretending not to care only
evidences how deeply Flannagan matters to her. And Flannagan,
knowing the truth, adopts a similar tactic. Ariane matters very much
to him—her happiness is everything—and Flannagan attempts to
insure her happiness by pretending not to care. That is, like Virgil
Smith in *The Emperor Waltz*, Flannagan pretends to be his worst self,
the callous, unthinking, insensitive American businessman, as a
means of protecting the woman he loves. Ariane will be better off
without him, or so Flannagan reasons, and when she arrives at his
hotel suite it is just in time to help him pack his bags ("Those Swedish
twins . . . you know how it is"). The point, however, is not Flannagan's
decision to leave but his motive for doing so. He does not run for fear
of commitment. He is not a "scared rabbit" at this point. On the
contrary, he fears not for himself but for Ariane. Like Chevasse,
Flannagan tries to act in Ariane's best interests; and Ariane's devotion
to him makes him keenly aware of his past failings. How could a sweet,
everyday girl like Ariane fall for someone so utterly no good as
Flannagan?

   Thus, once again, caution takes the upper hand. Flannagan's
caution, however, is undermined every step of the way by Ariane's
emotional determination. There is no doubt that she loves him very
deeply. Her love is evidenced by her expressions, by her tears, by the
entire history of their relationship. More important, however, is the
strength of emotional character that Ariane demonstrates at the
railway depot. Tears or no, she continues to enact the sophisticate
role: she loves Flannagan too deeply to let him know how much his
leaving hurts. She is not ashamed of her emotions. But the emotional
language of their relationship speaks by contraries. Thus Ariane's
apparent nonchalance ("We did have a good time, didn't we?") is
rightly understood by Flannagan (who now "speaks" the same
language) as devotion of the highest order. And as the train pulls
out, as the camera tracks back, as Wilder cuts from tracking close-ups
of Ariane to tracking close-ups of Flannagan, it becomes clear to
Flannagan that his caution is unfounded. Ariane is no emotional
weakling but a woman of strength and beauty. If anything, Flannagan
will hurt her more by leaving than by loving her, and he accordingly
throws caution to the wind and commits himself, sweeping Ariane up
in his arms and on to the train at the last minute. It is a gesture of the
most profound tenderness, the perfect expression of Wilder's
genuine romanticism. Indeed, by contrast with the equivalent scene
in *Cluny Brown* (Cluny bids Belinski farewell at the Friars Carmell

Sexual and emotional integrity: Ariane bids Flannagan farewell—only moments before he sweeps her up and takes her with him.

railway depot and he decides at the last minute to take her with him), Wilder's is the more moving, the more powerful moment. The comparison implies no slight to Lubitsch. Adam Belinski is more self-controlled a character than Flannagan, and accordingly it requires less anxious circumstances to move him to action. Differences aside, however, both films can be understood to celebrate the same sort of sexual/emotional integrity, and *Love in the Afternoon* speaks volumes to Wilder's credit.

* * *

The major difference between the American films of Ernst Lubitsch and those of Billy Wilder is one of milieu. Though working in Hollywood, Lubitsch still generally prefered to focus on a European world of the rich and fashionable. And even in those few Lubitsch films with an American setting (*Three Women, That Uncertain Feeling, Heaven Can Wait*), Lubitsch concerned himself primarily with characters of wealth and status. Partly this resulted from personal experience. As a highly successful European director, Lubitsch had ample opportunity to sample, to understand, and to appreciate the marvellous though doomed decadence of post First World War Europe: it was the right time and the right place to be rich. But there is also the matter of public response. American audiences seemed, particularly in the early Thirties, to appreciate the contrast between the drab quality of everyday Depression existence and the exhilarating stylishness of life in Lubitsch's somewhat imaginary Europe. When properly understood, however, Lubitsch can hardly be accused of manipulating public desires for personal profit. His films are very much *about* style, and are concerned both with the tyranny of social decorum (*The Student Prince*) and with the necessity for rejuvenating over-rigid social conventions (*The Love Parade*). But it is true that Lubitsch remains very Continental in his outlook. Indeed, Europe and its institutions provided Lubitsch with the ideal context for the exploration of civilisation and its rituals.

Wilder, on the other hand, is very American in his outlook and concerns. Hence the vast majority of his films either take place in America or are concerned with Americans abroad. Indeed, Wilder was not, like Lubitsch, an established talent upon his arrival in Hollywood (1934), and his growth as a film-maker coincides with his discovery of America. As a perpetual if self-aware romantic, Wilder very readily came to understand the romanticism at the heart of the American dream. Even capitalism comes to be seen, at times, as a romantic adventure. Only a romantic like Virgil Smith (the name itself embodies a sense of egalitarian heroism) would attempt to sell phonographs to a kingdom of violinists (*The Emperor Waltz*). Only a romantic industrialist like Linus Larrabee (Humphrey Bogart) can contemplate the creation of entire and entirely new industries *(Sabrina)*. Even the Lindbergh flight in *The Spirit of St. Louis* is portrayed as a sort of capitalist adventure: Lindbergh (James Stewart) works hand in hand with local bankers to underwrite the transatlantic crossing. Such adventures are not *a priori* suspect in Wilder. Even questionable cons of the Whiplash Willie sort earn some measure of

James Stewart as Charles Lindbergh in *The Spirit of St. Louis*.

Wilder's respect. But dreams by their very nature risk disappointment, and disappointment has a way of possessing the dreamer, as we
have seen in *Double Indemnity* and *Sunset Boulevard*. For Wilder, then,
there are two sides to any dream: fulfilment and frustration. And *The
Apartment*, like *Kiss Me, Stupid,* specifies the often antithetical and very
complex relationship between emotional/sexual frustration and
economic success.

In exploring these issues of emotional and financial security, *The
Apartment* locates itself midway between the urban paranoia of *The
Lost Weekend* and the middle-class comic humanism of Lubitsch's *The
Shop Around the Corner*. C.C. "Bud" Baxter (Jack Lemmon) is, like Don
Birnam, a frustrated romantic. He had fallen in love with his best
friend's wife; had attempted suicide to relieve the agony; had botched
the job, shooting himself in the knee; and he had moved to New York
City, to an apartment "in the West Sixties, just half a block from
Central Park" and to an accountant's job in the Ordinary Policy
Department of Consolidated Life, in order to start anew. By so doing
he embraces the sort of "quiet desperation" that Don Birnam so
feared in *The Lost Weekend*. Baxter's life, even under ordinary
circumstances, is drab and eventless. He spends most of his time at his
desk, one desk like every other desk in the sea of desks which
constitute the Premium Accounting Division of the Ordinary Policy
Department. And when not bent over his adding machine Baxter can
be found at the Arthur Murray studios, or seated before the television
set in his apartment, eating TV dinners while watching Dinah Shore.
It's a life of minimal expectations, minimal rewards, and minimal risks.

And Baxter seems content with the arrangement. He is, as he tells
us in voice-over at the film's beginning, "not overly ambitious." He
seems quite happy to be another statistic, another statistician. Indeed,
it's Baxter's desire to be one of the boys—not, it is important to point
out, an inordinate desire to get ahead—that results in Baxter's
dilemma. As Baxter tells J. D. Sheldrake (Fred MacMurray), the head
of Personnel, his apartment key began circulating among certain
fellow employees (all of them superior to Baxter in the pecking order)
because Baxter once allowed a guy in his department to use "the
apartment" one evening for the purpose of changing from work suit
to tuxedo before a banquet. The result of Baxter's kindness, however,
was that "all sorts of guys were suddenly going to banquets." And, as
Baxter puts it, "when you give the key to one guy you can't say no to
another."

Thus, by the point in time of the film's beginning, things have gotten "out of hand"—Baxter's apartment has become a short-order rendezvous for Baxter's less than ethical superiors—and Baxter literally finds himself spending nights in Central Park while Mr. Dobisch (Ray Walston) and "Marilyn Monroe" paint murals *après* Picasso on his apartment wall. And it is no longer a matter of Bud's willingness to help a friend. It is clear to us and to Bud that the price of his refusal would be dismissal from Consolidated Life. He chooses, however, to continue the "buddy boy" fiction, as if Dobisch and Kirkeby (David Lewis) and the rest of the boys were simply adolescent pranksters and Bud were simply one of the gang. He perceives no other choice. His dedication to his job is itself a tactic born of emotional desperation—and keeping the job is imperative.

Furthermore, Bud has no objections to getting ahead. Indeed, he catches advancement fever from Dobisch, who tempers his demand that Baxter vacate the apartment for forty-five minutes with promises of superior efficiency ratings. Bud even goes to the extreme of buying a bowler ("the junior executive model") as the thought of moving up (literally, from the 19th floor to the 27th) takes hold. It is also true that prior to the film's beginning no one (other than a coldprone Baxter) is hurt by the goings on in Bud's apartment: he does not profit at anyone else's expense. Thus Baxter's "good fortune" seems, from his point of view, only a slight inconvenience when measured against the likelihood of advancement. In addition, Bud rather enjoys the "iron man" reputation he acquires by virtue of the constant sexual activity in his flat. In his heart of hearts Bud would like to be a sexual success, although his manner and personality clearly preclude the sort of unfeeling sexuality practiced by Dobisch, Kirkeby, and Sheldrake. Indeed, Bud treats the elevator girl, Miss Kubelik (Shirley MacLaine), with an almost chivalric sort of courtesy. He calls her "Miss Kubelik" rather than Fran, and he always takes off his hat when he enters her elevator.

The film's issue is not, therefore, a simple matter of business ambition *vs.* sexual integrity. Bud's dedication to his job is, in a way, a form of sexual integrity—he prefers celibacy to insincerity of the Sheldrake sort. And Sheldrake, like Dobisch and Kirkeby *et al*, can hardly be seen as a business man. His only "work" involves his effort

The elevator girl and the insurance clerk: Shirley MacLaine and Jack Lemmon in *The Apartment*.

to maintain his off-hours relationship with Miss Kubelik—in which connection he pressures Bud for the key to the apartment. The greatest danger facing Bud Baxter, therefore, is the possibility that he might become another Sheldrake. That is, he could rise so high on the bureaucratic ladder that he would have nothing to do but indulge in heartless rituals of sexual gamesmanship. Sheldrake's motives are murky; his one attempt at explaining them to Miss Kubelik rings hollow ("Why does a man run around with a lot of girls? Because he's unhappy at home—because he's lonely"); and he continues to pursue Fran, not for love, but for the sake of pursuit. The point is clear: Sheldrake's managerial mind, so accustomed to manipulating the careers of those below him, so used to pulling strings, so used to stringing women along, takes a certain perverse locker-room delight in seeing how far he can push Fran before her string runs out. It is certainly difficult to imagine Baxter playing such a cynical role—but the danger is there. Miss Kubelik's expression when Bud shows her his new bowler at the office Christmas party indicates her fear that Bud will follow in Sheldrake's footsteps. And Baxter reinforces this fear by offering to get Miss Kubelik a "little promotion." As he tells her, "I have quite a bit of influence in Personnel"—*i.e.*, he has been letting Sheldrake use the apartment. To be sure, Bud's offer to pull strings is well motivated, by genuine affection and a desire to improve Miss Kubelik's lot in life; but string-pulling can become a nasty if not self-destructive habit, as Sheldrake demonstrates. And we (and Wilder) would be loath to see an essentially kind-hearted goof like Bud Baxter so corrupted.

The film's most basic issue, therefore, involves the opposition of self-centredness and compassion. To the extent that self-centredness seems naturally to consume those in positions of power—and to the extent that big business of the capitalist variety requires that some people exercise such power—we are correct to understand de-humanisation as a logical corollary of living in an advanced industrial society (and Consolidated Life, as Bud points out at the film's beginning, is a microcosm of that society: the home office has a greater population than Natchez, Miss.). And yet Wilder does not attempt in any concerted fashion to suggest a realistic alternative to the hierarchical social model embodied by "Consolidated Life." Like Lubitsch, Wilder takes society as a given, something to be regretted, to be comprehended, but something unlikely to change. American society in *The Apartment* is a post-romantic institution, lacking the sort of visionary excitement and vigour that characterised capitalists and capitalism in such films as *Stalag 17, Sabrina,* and *The Spirit of St. Louis.*

The issue in *The Apartment* is not, therefore, a social issue *per se.* Rather, in *The Apartment,* Wilder focuses not on society and its reformation but on characters who manage to come to appropriate terms, neither despairing nor acquiescent, with the reality of living under depressing though unalterable circumstances. And it is in arguing this positive case that Wilder recalls the somewhat atypical Lubitsch of *The Shop Around the Corner.* At a certain level, to be sure, *The Apartment* serves to parody the Lubitsch film. That is, in *The Apartment* Wilder specifically rejects the possibility that the employees of Consolidated Life can ever be "one big happy family," as Kirkeby sarcastically puts it. The difference is a matter of size. Matuschek & Co., the shop around the corner, is a small enterprise, in an old world setting, and the workers rightly come to look upon each other as members of a single family unit. Indeed, their problems are family problems, arising from an over abundance of feeling rather than from a lack of it. In *The Apartment,* on the other hand, pain generally arises not from conflicts of feeling but from the manipulation of compassion by calculation. Sheldrake is not motivated by emotional regard for Miss Kubelik. On the contrary, he cares very little what happens to her. Witness his lack of concern over her suicide attempt: he simply wants to avoid publicity. Wilder does not argue the impossibility of living a meaningful existence while working at Consolidated Life. As Bud tells Sheldrake, there are only a few rotten apples in the Consolidated Life barrel. But the actions of Sheldrake, and the power he wields by virtue of his position, make continued existence at C.L. a very sorry alternative for both Bud Baxter and Fran Kubelik.

Margaret Sullavan, Frank Morgan, and James Stewart in Lubitsch's The Shop Around the Corner.

At a deeper level, therefore—at the level where characters manage to assert their better selves despite their extraordinary (and extraordinarily precarious) middle class circumstances—*The Apartment* can be seen as Wilder's retelling and updating of *The Shop Around the Corner* story. Again we see ordinary white collar workers doing their best to find some sort of meaning in the midst of middle-class routine. Again we see problems of mistaken identity and self-deprecation obstructing the drive towards more fruitful human relationships. Again the theme of emotional renewal is specified as the creation of an emotional bond between a man and a woman. Again there are precarious financial circumstances which complicate matters. Again an attempted suicide serves to bring things into ethical and emotional focus. And once again we see a narrative structure which parallels a movement in time—both films take place primarily during the Christmas holidays—with a corresponding emotional movement through stages of despair to a hopeful yet self-aware resolution.

The primary focus of interest in *The Apartment* is the developing relationship between Bud Baxter and Fran Kubelik. It is a relationship built upon a foundation of shared desires, shared fears, and shared experiences. Both Bud and Fran, for example, attempt suicide at some point in life rather than accept the reality of an impossible love affair. Suicide in both cases, however, is symptomatic of more genuine and more general feelings of self-disgust. Thus Bud tells his neighbour, Mrs. Dreyfuss (the wife of the doctor who eventually pumps the sleeping pills from Fran's stomach), that there is nothing in his apartment that anyone would want to steal. The remark is intended to allay Mrs. Dreyfuss's fear that Bud's apartment has been burglarised. But Lemmon's casual yet hurried delivery of the line evidences a general tendency toward self-deprecation. And Fran shares this tendency. Her decision to cut her hair short, for example, while ostensibly a gesture of independence, an implicit rejection of Sheldrake, is equally a gesture of self-mutilation. Indeed, the whole relationship with Sheldrake has a masochistic strain to it: Fran argues that Sheldrake is a "taker," that she knows she is being "took," and that there's nothing she can do about it. But her willingness to continue the relationship evidences a certain measure of collaboration in her own disappointment. That is, she is used to the patsy role, literally considers herself a bad risk in love ("I just have this talent for falling in love with the wrong guy in the wrong place at the wrong time"), and she takes some comfort in the ugliness of it all: at least her situation matches up with her fractured self-image. By the same token, however, there is a certain resiliency to her personality. Her relationship with Sheldrake, after all, is the fifth such disaster in her life, and her perseverance in love, like Sugar Kane's perseverance in *Some Like It Hot*, indicates a continuing desire for something better than despair. Thus it seems arguable that Fran's suicide attempt is as much a cry for help as a genuine run at oblivion.

Both Fran and Bud are caught up, then, in cycles of defensive despair; and the cycles can only be broken by increased self-knowledge and self-esteem. Bud and Fran are therefore important to each other for being mirror images (as James Stewart and Margaret Sullavan are mirror images in *The Shop Around the Corner*). Bud sees something of himself in Fran from the very beginning. She is unassumingly kind (as he is); she appreciates his courtesy (as he appreciates hers); and she makes no effort to manipulate him (a welcome change from the C.L. routine). Thus it is all the more agonising for Bud to learn that Fran is Sheldrake's off-hours playmate—the one Sheldrake brings to Bud's apartment. Even here, however, Bud's anger is self-directed. That is, the degree of his disenchantment with Fran far exceeds the gravity of her offence. He had expected her to be different—and it turns out that she is very much like Bud himself, dissatisfied, self-deprecating, the sort of person who gets involved with people like Sheldrake. And what Bud must come to learn is that people like Fran (i.e., people like Bud) are capable of genuine feeling, genuine ethics, and genuine concern, however inept their expressions of concern may be.

Fran's suicide attempt is therefore important for several reasons. First of all, it clarifies for Baxter the nature of Fran's involvement with Sheldrake. However self-destructive, it was not a matter of casual heartlessness, at least not on her part. Secondly, it reinforces the sense of identity which exists between Fran and Bud. That is, Baxter comes to see Fran as repeating a familiar pattern of desire and desperation—and seeing it in her allows Bud the opportunity to place that sort of despair in the larger context of life. Thirdly, Fran's convalescence in Bud's apartment—the time they share together, the gin rummy games, the candlelight dinner ("It's a wonderful thing—dinner for two")—forces Bud to admit to the loneliness of his low-key bachelor existence. As he puts it to Fran: "You know, I used to live like Robinson Crusoe—shipwrecked among eight million people. Then one day I saw a footprint in the sand—and there you were." And finally, the confrontation between Bud and Fran's brother-in-law, which takes place when the brother-in-law comes to take Fran home and which concludes with a bloodied Baxter sprawled upon the floor, allows Fran to express her concern for Bud. He willingly took the punch as a means of protecting Fran's reputation, and Fran returns the kindness by tenderly calling him a "damn fool" and kissing him—gestures in their context of profound affection and respect.

Love thus leads naturally to self-respect (i.e., Bud's affection for Fran is equally an assertion of self-worth) and self-respect in turn leads to independence. Which explains, perhaps, Bud's continued deferential attitude towards Sheldrake even after Fran's suicide attempt. There is no doubt that Bud despises Sheldrake's arrogance, but Bud maintains, at least in Fran's presence, the fiction that Sheldrake is not so bad after all. On the one hand it is a gesture of kindness. If Fran really loves Sheldrake, then Bud's action can be understood as an attempt to grant Fran her wish. On the other hand, it is equally clear, to Bud and to ourselves, that Fran must declare her independence, if she is to declare it at all, without Bud's coaching. The point of the film is that people can cut loose from the past, can reject strategies of self-deprecation, and such action is to be understood as its own reward. Thus, when Bud finally tells Sheldrake near the film's conclusion that "the old payola won't work any more," he does so with no assurance that his action will bring Fran back. If anything, Bud believes just the contrary, that Fran will eventually marry Sheldrake now that Sheldrake has left his wife (in reality Sheldrake is "fired" when his secretary informs Mrs. Sheldrake of her husband's infidelity). And yet Bud makes no effort to dissuade Fran from her course. He merely refuses Sheldrake the use of the apartment.

But this gesture on Bud's part is not futile. By making it he becomes, in the words of Dr. Dreyfuss, a "mensch," a human being. He declares his independence—of Sheldrake, of Consolidated Life, even of the apartment itself. Furthermore, the gesture serves as a model for Fran. It is ironic but appropriate that Sheldrake should be the bearer of such glad tidings; but it is through Sheldrake, as he and Fran sit joylessly in their booth at the Chinese restaurant, that Fran learns of Bud's self-assertive action. As Sheldrake puts it to Fran, Baxter "just walked out on me—quit—threw that big fat job right in my face." The news brings a smile to Fran's face, and she decides to start the New Year by cutting loose from her desperate past. With Bud's example before her, Fran is able to leave Sheldrake behind; and the film concludes with the resumption of the gin rummy game that comes to symbolise the mutuality and continuity of the life that

"Shut up and deal."

Fran and Bud have shared and will share henceforth.

Like *The Shop Around the Corner*, then, *The Apartment* allows for the possibility of human renewal under the worst of circumstances. Neither film, we should note, takes place in a world of style and elegance. On the contrary, both films take place in a flat world of blacks and grays. On balance, Wilder paints the bleaker picture, both thematically and visually. Indeed, the panavision screen seems to magnify the harsh neon glare in Bud's 19th floor office, and it serves to emphasise as well the dark loneliness of Bud's evenings spent pacing the streets outside his brownstone walk up. Wilder's point, however, is that Bud need not acquire a wood panelled 27th floor office to assert his humanity. It is not circumstance which counts but integrity—and Bud's integrity finds sufficient context and legitimate reward in the closing two-shots of Bud and Fran playing cards in his now bare-walled apartment.

* * *

The Private Life of Sherlock Holmes has a grace and style beyond all power of description: it must be seen to be valued. And that it is not

seen, and was not much seen at the time of its release, is no small
indictment of the critical establishment.[17] Richard Corliss does his
belated best by the film in "Talking Pictures," but he gets rather
bogged down in a general discussion of twilight works by ageing
masters, so that *Sherlock Holmes* itself gets only a scant (though often
eloquent) four pages. And even Stephen Farber, in his lengthy defence
of Wilder in "Film Comment," does little more than express disappointment that Wilder became sidetracked (or so Farber argues) by
the conventional detective intrigue and accordingly backed away "from
the more disturbing [i.e., homosexual] aspects of the story" (p. 16).

My own respect for the film is so great that I hesitate to write about
it: just where does one begin to discuss a perfect work of cinema? And
furthermore, given the topical organisation of this essay, under which
heading are we to consider *The Private Life of Sherlock Holmes?* The film
is an almost inexhaustible lexicon of typical Wilder concerns and
motifs: again we have the flashback structure *(Sunset Boulevard, Stalag
17);* again we have the issue of the artist and the artist's reaction to
experience (like Don Birnam in *The Lost Weekend,* Dr. Watson deals
with the agony of existence by setting pen to paper); again we have the
detective figure (recalling Keyes in *Double Indemnity* and Chevasse in
Love in the Afternoon); again we have the partnership of male professionals (Joe and Jerry in *Some Like it Hot,* Orville and Barney in *Kiss Me
Stupid*); again we pay particular attention to physical location (the
Baker street digs shared by Holmes and Watson carry a symbolic
weight nearly equal to that of Bud Baxter's pad in *The Apartment*—in
both cases the flat serves as a retreat); again we see an ageing prima
donna who seeks a younger lover (Madame Petrova in *Sherlock Holmes*
recalls Norma Desmond in *Sunset Boulevard*); again we have international intrigue *(Ninotchka, Five Graves to Cairo, One, Two, Three);* again
we have a sexually fascinating German "actress" (Ilsa von
Hoffmanstall recalls Erika von Schluetow from *A Foreign Affair*);
again we see the use of a parasol as a particularly important symbol
(Five Graves to Cairo); again we have the issue of role playing (Ilsa is not
the only one who "acts a part" through the course of the film); again
we have the journey of personal discovery, complete with a railway
sleeping-car scene (recalling similar scenes in *The Major and the Minor*
and *Some Like It Hot*); and we could go on almost indefinitely.

Sherlock Holmes is most interesting, however, for the perspective it
provides on the rest of Wilder's career—and in this it recalls
Lubitsch's *The Student Prince.* Wilder and Lubitsch are both frequently

International intrigue—Lubitsch style: Greta Garbo and Melvyn Douglas in *Ninotchka*.

(though mistakenly) reputed to be cynics—and yet *The Student Prince* and *The Private Life of Sherlock Holmes* are like-minded expressions of a profound though elegiac romanticism. The point, however, in both films, is not merely the inevitability of disappointment but rather the value which is assigned to those moments of feeling and integrity which precede disappointment and which therefore lend the fact of regret the status of ethical assertion. In other words, to regret the loss of something (love in both cases) is implicitly to acknowledge and celebrate its value. And the values so celebrated, in Lubitsch and Wilder generally, in *The Student Prince* and *The Private Life of Sherlock Holmes* specifically, are remarkably similar in terms both of ethic and execution.

Thus, for example, *The Student Prince* and *The Private Life of Sherlock Holmes* can be seen to share a similar outline of action; and we can begin our analysis by attending to the structural analogies. Each film, first of all, opens with a prologue which is chronologically prior to and at some remove in time from the period encompassed by the film's major action. The connection between the prologue and the narrative in both cases follows a thematic rather than strictly cause and effect logic; but both prologues serve (1) to specify the dialectical terms of the action which follows and (2) to raise more general issues of time, age, and fate (in that the specifics of the major action are foreshadowed by events in the prologue: the overall effect is one of cloture or predestination).

Thus, in *The Student Prince*, to consider the specific issue raised by the prologue, we see Karl Heinrich (Ramon Novarro) as a child, brought against his will to a 19th century European capital, there to

Karl Heinrich (Ramon Novarro) signs the order for his royal marriage to Princess Ilsa in Ernst Lubitsch's *The Student Prince*.

become the ward and heir of his stern-faced authoritarian uncle, the King. The conflict between emotional integrity (the young lad's fearful reaction to the cannon salute) and the demands of social position (he must ride in parade) is quickly established. And this tension between private feelings and public duties remains central throughout the film. Similarly, the opening act of *Sherlock Holmes* focuses on the gap between the private life of the great sleuth (Robert Stephens), a life of suffocation, of Victorian elegance, of boredom, of London fog, of dust, of tobacco ash, of seemingly insignificant cases (missing midgets, for example) or uninteresting propositions (such as Madame Petrova's), of mournful violin solos, of cocaine—and his public life as it is portrayed in (or sensationalised by) Dr. Watson's "Strand Magazine" pieces.

Both films then shift setting, moving from the constraining city (Karlsberg/London) to a lush pastoral countryside (Heidelberg/Inverness), and in both instances this shift in setting is coincident with the development of a strong sexual attraction between the central character and a beautiful, innocent (or apparently innocent) woman. Thus the student prince falls in love with Kathi, the Heidelberg bar maid (Norma Shearer), while Sherlock Holmes becomes deeply involved with Ilsa von Hoffmanstall (Genevieve Page), known to Holmes as Gabriel Valladon. In each instance, however, the demands of state override the reality of private feelings: Karl must forswear his love of Kathi and assume his role as monarch, while Holmes must face the fact of Ilsa's deceit (and the fact that she bettered him in the battle of wits) and acquiesce to her expulsion from England. Indeed, Holmes becomes an active agent in her expulsion. Were it not for his suggestion that she be exchanged for a captured English agent she would have remained a prisoner in a damp English jail.

And finally, both films conclude with epilogues which serve to emphasise the cost, in human terms, of society's triumph. *The Student Prince,* specifically, ends with a wedding procession in celebration of Karl Heinrich's state marriage to Princess Ilsa: but Lubitsch never shows us the face of the bride. Rather, we see long shots of the royal carriage and the jubilant crowds, intercut with close medium shots of Karl Heinrich, his face joyless, his eyes staring grimly toward an equally joyless future. Likewise, *The Private Life of Sherlock Holmes* ends on a note of agony and resignation. Watson and Holmes are interrupted at breakfast by a letter from Sherlock's brother, Mycroft, informing Holmes of Ilsa's execution at the hands of the Japanese for spying on naval facilities in Yokahama harbor. It is more than Holmes can take, particularly as she had been living under the name of "Mrs. Ashdown" for the last months of her life (she and Holmes had travelled as husband and wife, Mr. and Mrs. Ashdown, in Scotland) and Holmes has no other recourse (or so it seems) than to ask Watson for the cocaine: and Watson, for once, willingly tells Holmes where to find it.

None of which is intended to imply that *The Private Life of Sherlock Holmes* is a re-make of *The Student Prince* in any literal sense of the word, although Wilder was clearly familiar with the film (Sabrina likens herself to Kathi in *Sabrina,* and Walter Burns implicitly likens Hildy Johnson to Karl Heinrich in *The Front Page*). But the similarity between the two films evidences once again the close affinity between Wilder and Lubitsch. Furthermore, as I have already argued, both films underscore the essentially romantic sensibilities of their respective directors. In this, of course, *Sherlock Holmes* is the far more complex work, raising issues of artifice and deception, and arguing the necessity of accepting life's contradictions. But the fact that Wilder can raise such issues, issues that he has raised in far more ironic terms elsewhere, and the fact that he can appropriate such themes to such an elegiac fable, evidences an astoundingly inclusive and paradoxically optimistic sense of value.

The central thematic antinomy in *Sherlock Holmes* involves the interplay of memory and action. The issue, of course, is implicit in the flashback structure: the film is, in effect, Watson's value-charged reflection upon an already completed series of events, as it is Wilder's reflection upon the value of a bygone era and its ethics. But the thematic conflict is clearly evident *within* the events set forth in

Watson's narrative, as well. Thus the first act of the film, as I have already noted, is imbued with a sense of suffocating futility, of inaction. But that futility, it eventually becomes clear, is a function of the Holmes character, and that character, in turn, is a function of past experience and primarily of past *sexual* experience. Of course, Holmes would rather *not* acknowledge that fact, publicly or privately, which accounts for the almost casual, piecemeal explication of the emotional situation. Indeed, during the "first act" Holmes is positively hostile to the suggestion that his sex life is anyone's business but his own: Watson is, he says, "presumptuous" for asking. It is only *after* Holmes becomes enchanted by "Gabrielle" that he begins slowly to reveal his emotional history. But that he does so at all indicates a longing on Holmes's part for something better: he is not just "a thinking machine incapable of any emotion," however much he might wish that were the case.

Like most of Wilder's "cynics," then—like Don Birnam in *The Lost Weekend,* like Sugar Kane in *Some Like It Hot,* like Bud Baxter in *The Apartment*—Sherlock Holmes is at heart a romantic. He may lament that "there are no great crimes anymore," he may admit that he distrusts women ("the twinkle in the eye, the arsenic in the soup"); but both his distrust of women and his mania for investigation, I would argue, are explicable as symptoms of a more profound emotional malaise and can be seen to have a common source in past experience, and specifically in a sexual experience of such emotional magnitude that Holmes spends most of his life, previous to accepting the case of Gabrielle Valladon and her "missing" husband, running away from the memory of it. As it turns out, Holmes had once been engaged to the daughter of his violin teacher. The invitations were out, Holmes was even being fitted for a tail coat, but "twenty-four hours before the wedding she died of influenza." Which proves, according to Holmes, the contention that "women are unreliable and not to be trusted." It is not womankind that Holmes distrusts, however. It is life itself which is unreliable and unpredictable. His fiancée did not betray his love—she simply died. And her death was more than Holmes could take. From that point forward even memory itself would be seen as a source of pain. As Holmes puts it, midway through investigating the Valladon case: "Some of us are cursed with memories like flypaper."

But, of course, consciousness is unavoidable, except, perhaps, in the depths of an occasional cocaine binge, and Holmes generally deals with life's uncertainties by attending to the minutia of existence—how far parsley can sink into butter on a hot day, for example, or by cataloguing the many varieties of tobacco ash. And furthermore, he follows a profession devoted to making neat and decorous sense of life's apparent contradictions and mysteries. In the world of consulting detectives, at least, it is possible to force life into the strait-jacket of logic and predictability. In addition, the world of Sherlock Holmes is almost consciously designed to exclude the opportunity for romantic attachment. Like Frank Flannagan in *Love in the Afternoon,* Holmes organises his life in such a fashion, alternately moving all over the map of Europe and retreating to the security of 221b Baker Street, that precludes the sort of social contact necessary to the development of sexual relationships. In other words, Holmes devotes himself to a specific sort of action in the world as a means of avoiding the memory of his sexual past. Indeed, his ostensible reason for accepting the Valladon case specifies this relationship between detection and sexuality: the sooner he solves the case of Gabrielle's missing husband the sooner he will be rid of her.

Paradoxically, however—as Corliss points out—we do not want Holmes to solve the case. To begin with, of course, we know in advance that Holmes is being used. We know from the credit sequence, for example, that Gabrielle Valladon is really Ilsa von Hoffmanstall (this is implied by the order in which the objects are removed from Watson's heretofore sealed dispatch box—the watch with her picture in it is immediately preceded by a musical composition by Sherlock Holmes, dedicated to "Ilsa von H.") Furthermore, it is clear from the beginning of Ilsa's contact with Holmes, when the cabby brings her wet and bedraggled to Baker Street, that Ilsa is not alone. Thus the cabby no sooner "delivers" Ilsa to Watson and Holmes than he turns the cab around and picks up Ilsa's confederate, who has been standing across the street all the while. And any doubt as to the confederate's role or Ilsa's complicity is erased after Holmes decides, contrary to Mycroft's orders, that he, Ilsa, and Watson must go to Scotland to pursue their only clues (the canaries, the three boxes, and the red runner): Ilsa communicates the information to that same accomplice by opening and closing her parasol while standing at the window of the Baker Street flat. Clearly, then, Gabrielle Valladon is not an innocent lady in distress, however much Holmes would like to think so, however much we would like to think so; and Wilder does not allow us to forget it—he cuts constantly to the accomplices as Holmes, Ilsa, and Watson travel through Scotland. Cracking the case, discovering Ilsa's duplicity, can only result, therefore, in further disillusionment for Holmes (or so it would seem).

Ramon Novarro   Norma Shearer

Celebrations of love: Ramon Novarro and Norma Shearer (right) in *The Student Prince* and Robert Stephens and Genevieve Page (below in *The Private Life of Sherlock Holmes*.

And yet we do not want Holmes to drop the case, either—not, as Corliss argues, merely because we enjoy watching Holmes at work, but because pursuing the case allows Holmes to continue his relationship with Ilsa. It is not a function of simple boy-gets-girl genre expectation, however, that we come to value their relationship above all else, above the inevitable and labyrinthian requirements of the intrigue plot, although that expectation is there (as it is, say, in *The 39 Steps*). It is rather the case that Wilder reinforces the expectation by motivating their relationship from *within* the fable. And specifically, Wilder makes it clear that Holmes *himself*, perhaps subconsciously, comes to assign great value to his strange yet marvellous relationship with "Gabrielle." It is clear, however, that Holmes is not genuinely disinterested in women even before he meets "Madame Valladon." Disinterest would not generate distrust nor could it account for the vehemence verging on cruelty with which Holmes first interrogates "Gabrielle." Indeed, as it becomes clear to Holmes that he will not be able to break through the veils "shrouding" her memory (Ilsa pretends to amnesia), he becomes angry to the point of shouting at her in school-book French (the labels in her clothes indicate that she is Belgian). His anger, however, only further evidences a fear of involvement—a fear clearly based on a subliminal desire to get involved. And the strength of that desire is measured that same evening.

Holmes stays up most of the night pondering the case of Gabrielle's "missing memory"—and he finally goes to Watson's bedroom to look in on his "client." He says nothing, merely opens the door, looks in, and leaves; but Gabrielle rises nude from her bed and follows him into *his* bedroom, as if Holmes were her long lost husband ("Emile, is that you, Emile?"). Holmes replies, "Yes, Gabrielle"; she runs to his arms; and they embrace as Gabrielle tells him of the expensive pink négligée she had purchased in anticipation of their reunion. She then backs away and beckons with her hands as she lies down, impassioned, on the bed ("Come here. Come here. Oh, please"). Holmes is visibly affected by her intensity (and Wilder emphasises that intensity by shooting the scene largely in close-up), but Holmes remains detective enough to ask her where she left the négligée (in her luggage) and where she left her luggage. Holmes then takes a mirror and holds it up to her right hand—at which point what had seemed to be smears of Thames-soaked ink are legible as numbers, their image once reversed. Cut then to the front room as Mrs. Hudson wakes Watson for breakfast (he slept the night on the couch)—and we then follow her to

Watson's bedroom, where she does *not* find Gabrielle. Watson, in a panic, then goes to wake Holmes, only to find Gabrielle asleep in Sherlock's bed. And the obvious deduction, for Watson and for us, is that Holmes must have made love to her. Indeed, given the ardour of her invitation it hardly seems possible that Ilsa could have let him leave the flat (he goes to Victoria station to claim her valise)—the numbers on her hand were from her luggage check—without requiring that he make love to her. To do otherwise would destroy the illusion of her delusion.

But it is not completely illusion for either one of them. Or, to put it another way, they both willingly enter into the husband-and-wife fiction, in this scene and throughout the film, until such time as Mycroft blows the whistle on Ilsa. Thus Holmes almost willingly overlooks the quite obvious fact that the sleepwalking Belgian wife speaks *English* to the man she "believes" to be her Belgian husband— and this even after the film has explicitly broken with the normal convention which allows anyone to speak English no matter what their mother tongue. At some level, then, it is clear that Holmes is willing to let his sexual interest in being Gabrielle's "husband" override his professional interest in deduction. Thus he ignores the most obvious clue where acknowledging it would require returning to the logic of distrust.

And Ilsa's willingness to play the role of Holmes's wife—physically in London, socially in Scotland—is more self-evident yet, even before she tells Holmes, near the film's conclusion, that she had passed over the Yokahama assignment for the opportunity to test her wits against the one man in the universe who could "match" her powers of intelligence. As she puts it: "I couldn't resist the challenge of coming up against the best." Indeed, the fact of her respect is evidenced from the very moment of her arrival at Baker Street. She knows she can win Holmes over only by taking the most elaborate risks—risks which respect his intelligence while trying to get the better of it. Thus Ilsa banks everything on the probability that Holmes will "read" the few and very esoteric clues that she provides. Holmes does. And were she not to take such risks she would neither fool Holmes nor earn his respect.

At the very least, then, the relationship between Holmes and Ilsa represents from the outset a willingness on both their parts to take emotional risks. Holmes risks disappointment by allowing himself to be attracted to Ilsa. And indeed his involvement grows ever deeper as the film progresses, so that Holmes eventually bares his soul to Ilsa as he never had to Watson. Thus it is to Ilsa, in their northbound sleeping car, that Holmes reveals his sexual history. And Ilsa risks capture and imprisonment to involve herself with Holmes. That is, she involves herself for private reasons, not for any particular political ideology. The point I wish to argue, however, is not merely that Holmes and Ilsa take risks but that their risk-taking, their willingness to hazard their feelings and their lives for the sake of genuine human involvement, is rewarded, however ironic the rewards might seem out of context.

Which returns us to the memory/action antinomy. The world of *The Private Life of Sherlock Holmes* may appear less hostile than, say, the *film noir* world of *Double Indemnity,* and we should not underestimate the iconographic value of Wilder's pastoral *mise-en-scène;* the marvellous long shots of the lush Highland countryside, for example, which provide an appropriate context for the developing Ilsa/Holmes relationship. But not even the Scottish countryside is safe refuge in a

storal *mise-en-scène* in *The Private Life of Sherlock Holmes*.

civilisation bent on self-destruction through the development of ever more sophisticated weapons systems, like submarines and dirigibles. Indeed, one of those picturesque Scottish castles turns out to be a secret naval shipyard where Mycroft and his associates are busy perfecting a prototype submersible, manned by a crew of midgets, powered by acid batteries and ventilated by the Valladon invented air-pump—which is the objective of Ilsa's mission: if Holmes can find Ilsa's "husband," the Germans will no doubt get either the air-pump or its inventor (or such is their line of reasoning). But, unfortunately for nearly everyone involved, life in *The Private Life* is never so predictable or benevolent as to allow the unhindered fruition of human hopes, either in love or espionage. Thus Holmes lost his first love to influenza. Thus M. Valladon and two midgets die when the submersible, the H.M.S. Jonah, bursts a seam while submerged. Thus Mycroft almost jubilantly informs Holmes that his "client" is not Madame Valladon but Ilsa von Hoffmanstall, one of Germany's most

Mycroft Holmes (Christopher Lee) turns the tables on his younger brother: "Madame Valladon", it turns out, is a German agent.

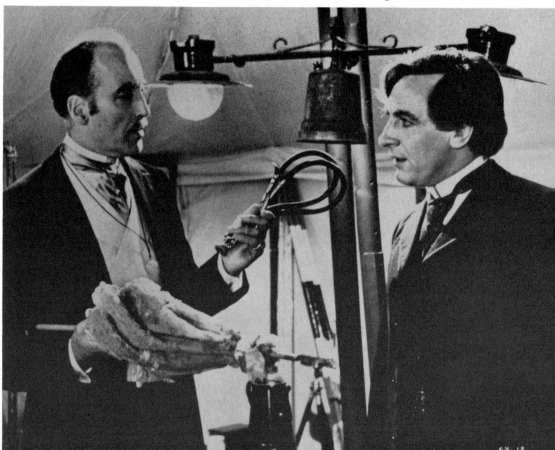

skilled agents. Thus Queen Victoria tells Mycroft to scuttle the boat, declaring it unsportsmanlike, un-English, and "in very poor taste." Thus Ilsa's accomplices, disguised as Trappist monks, drown when the submersible they have stolen from the castle once again takes water (Mycroft had the bolts loosened). And thus Sherlock's gesture of respect for Ilsa, convincing Mycroft to exchange her for a captured British agent, results ironically if indirectly in her death.

But Wilder's point, I would argue, is not that the world is a terrible and agonising place to be. That is rather a given, in *Sherlock Holmes* and in Wilder's flashback films generally. Terrible or not, it's the only world we've got. Wilder is concerned rather with personal strategies for dealing with the fact of life's capriciousness. One strategy, the strategy that Holmes follows at the film's beginning, is to let past disappointments delimit future action. By taking few risks one guarantees few failures. But, as Holmes demonstrates, such a life can be agonising in its own right. Holmes is totally at the mercy of circumstances—and, if cases do not present themselves, Holmes becomes a prisoner in his Baker Street digs, trapped quite literally by his unwillingness to take emotional chances. The alternative strategy—Ilsa's strategy, Holmes' strategy once Ilsa enters his life—is to accept risk, knowing that any risk involves hazards, both physical and emotional, but knowing that the greatest satisfaction awaits only those who take appropriately courageous actions. In other words, rewards of any sort are contingent upon risk-taking. One cannot require that life obey rules of simple justice.

One can, however, fight the tendency to despair at life's injustices. Indeed, while Ilsa never seriously considers the possibility of escaping her life as an undercover agent, she certainly seizes the opportunity to involve herself with Holmes. It could never be anything but a momentary break with the normal routine of her life—but even momentary liaisons can serve positive emotional ends (such is the case in *Avanti!* as well). For Ilsa, indeed, it's as if the confrontation with Holmes were a confrontation with the ultimate—and certainly his declaration, deeply felt and deeply moving, that Ilsa is "better than some consulting detectives," serves as the ultimate acknowledgement, not only of her abilities, but of her very existence. Thus, even after the game is up, she continues to memorialise the significance of her relationship with Holmes by using the "Ashdown" name.

And the ultimate reward for Holmes is likewise of a metaphysical sort. Of course, one could argue that Holmes is not rewarded at all, for anything. In which case Ilsa's involvement with him is not a reward in itself—only a provocation, particularly in light of the agony eventually engendered by her death. But it is fairly clear, for anyone with an adequate recollection, that Holmes does not close the door on Ilsa's memory when he takes the cocaine and retreats to his room at the film's conclusion. No, indeed. Holmes makes one final gesture— which we never see but always sense. He writes a violin concerto, "For Ilsa von H.," and thus he celebrates and memorialises the value of their relationship. Ilsa's "almost love," her willingness to risk imprisonment for his sake, gives him the courage to risk vulnerability for hers. So rather than deny or misinterpret the past, Holmes chooses to confront it through art. In which case memory no longer serves to imprison feeling but to liberate it. Indeed, this "feeling" for the value of the Ilsa/Holmes relationship is liberated at the film's beginning when the composition is removed from Watson's dispatch box. At the moment of its removal the piece is heard on the soundtrack—and from there on the courtship of Holmes and Ilsa is accompanied and coloured by the Miklos Rosza music. At every crucial juncture in their relationship the music serves to place that moment in context—to signify the value that we are to accord to it. So, for example, when Ilsa seduces Holmes, we know that the seduction leads to genuine feelings, and we are therefore little inclined to condemn Ilsa's duplicity. Furthermore, it is a "violin" concerto—and the violin is associated throughout the film with sexuality. Thus Holmes's first love was the daughter of his violin instructor. And Madame Petrova offers to pay for Holmes's sexual services with a Stradivarius. That Holmes speaks his love for Ilsa in music, with his violin, therefore indicates that her presence enabled him not only to know something like love once again, but that she also allowed him to retrieve some of the feeling lost with the death of his first love—something Holmes never dreamed would happen.

Ultimately, then, *The Private Life of Sherlock Holmes* can be understood as a celebration of memory and memory's power through art to retrieve and memorialise the value of past experience. One cannot change the facts of life. People die. Societies scheme to find more efficient methods for killing them. But in the midst of this inevitable suffering it is possible to enter into relationships, however transitory, which lend life some sense of personal meaning. Thus Holmes loves Ilsa and loving her allows him to achieve a necessary perspective on life, even after the fact of her death. No longer does he deny the past and we can reasonably assume that he will thereby be enabled to face the future with greater hope and courage. Similarly, it is clear that

Billy Wilder loved Ernst Lubitsch and by emulating the Lubitsch cinema, in *Sherlock Holmes* and elsewhere, Wilder is able to achieve a necessary perspective on his own role as a romantic film-maker in a very unromantic universe. Wilder knows that he cannot bring Lubitsch back, any more than Holmes can bring Ilsa back from the dead, and it is significant that *Sherlock Holmes* is no more a re-make of *The Student Prince* than *The Apartment* is a re-make of *The Shop Around the Corner.* But Wilder's ability to bring Lubitsch so thoroughly to mind in these two cases (and in many others) both evidences and celebrates the power of art to transcend the imperfections of existence. Such transcendence is ultimately the essence of Wilder's romanticism. And *The Private Life of Sherlock Holmes,* however ironic its presentation, is arguably the most genuinely and movingly romantic film in the Wilder canon.

Wilder on Wilder:
The Front Page

The critical response to Wilder's *The Front Page* has been, with the significant exception of Andrew Sarris's *Village Voice* piece, predictable.[18] At best it is a weary Wilderisation of the snappy Hecht/ MacArthur stage play. At worst it is just another cynical and opportunistic Wilder film, produced and cast with an eye for the current wave of nostalgia and for the post-Watergate fascination with the newspaper racket ("a movie conceived with indifference and made with disinterest," as Jay Cocks put it).[19] To be sure, few Hollywood directors can escape the charge of commercialism; nor should they, for without an enthusiastic populace we could hardly enjoy anything approaching a genuinely public art. And yet, as is quite often the case in the popular cinema, more went into the creation of *The Front Page* than the mere desire to make a buck. Indeed, I would suggest that *The Front Page* is one of the most completely personal films of Wilder's career, a film not unconcerned with its public (far from it), but a film very deeply concerned with its director, betraying right in its surface the dilemma of the popular artist and his strangely compulsive relationship with both his art and his audience.

The Front Page can thus be seen as an intensely retrospective self-examination of the Hollywood ethos. To begin with, of course, *The Front Page* is a re-make of at least two generally successful films

Hildy Johnson (Jack Lemmon) tells Walter Burns (Walter Matthau) what he can do with *The Front Page*.

based upon the same play—one of them, the Howard Hawks *His Girl Friday,* a definitive classic (reason enough, I might add, for Wilder to return to the original character alignment rather than follow Hawks in making Hildy Johnson a female reporter). Wilder clearly invites comparison of the two films, then, thereby invoking the spirit of an earlier, perhaps healthier, anarchy. But it would be a mistake, I believe, to measure Wilder's *The Front Page* solely against the *His Girl Friday* yardstick, particularly if by so doing we ignore less obvious though equally important parallels.

For example, Wilder joyfully resurrects the frenzied and satiric spectre of the Keystone Cops, their running-boarded squad cars rushing blindly and aimlessly after a nonexistent sort of justice. We even get a classic silent sight gag to underline the reference. After the Viennese psychiatrist (Madame Bovary, c'est moi?) is shot in the groin by the escaping Earl Williams, the shrink is trundled past wise-cracking reporters ("Hey, Doc, how do you like Chicago?") into a waiting ambulance, which then sets out, siren blaring, for the hospital. Unfortunately for the good doctor, however, other sirens blare as wave upon wave of black police sedans trail streams of flashing red light double-time through the dark city sky. The ambulance is caught in the midst of this motorised havoc, and comes to a screeching, jolting halt, just avoiding collision with a phalanx of police cars. And the doctor's four-wheeled stretcher flies out the back of the vehicle and down the street, carrying the mad professor into the darkness of a slapstick limbo. Here we have the classic Sennett situation, "people caught up in chaos," though it's a chaos ultimately if indirectly of their own making.[20]

And there are other, more obviously serious, parallels to the world of the early cinema. Sheriff Hartman's cops clearly demonstrate a sort of Keystonish ineptitude, but the threat they represent takes on a darker shading by implicit references to at least two other films, *Underworld* and *Scarface*—both, interestingly enough, based like *The Front Page* on Ben Hecht stories. We thus move from *film rire* to *film noir* as the police prepare to storm the headquarters of "The Friends of American Liberty." The heroics are as empty as the offices (Earl never left the courthouse), but the police assault recalls in its violence the overkill tactics of the police who besiege Bull Weed in *Underworld* and Tony Camonte in *Scarface:* the order of the day is "shoot to kill." Thus the *Front Page* cops bash down doors with fire axes, swarm up fire escapes, crash through windows with shotguns at the ready, wounding only water coolers and a deaf janitor in their mad rush for glory (and votes). And all for naught: their only suspect is a premature infant whose mother was traumatised into delivery by the police-inspired commotion.

Wilder thus conjures up a world on the brink of chaos, caught between Stalin and the Phantom of the Opera, between flapper opulence (recall references to Hearst costume parties and Marion Davies) and Depression decadence (Hildy's Edward G. Robinson impression), between the silent cinema (Peggy plays organ at a plush cinema palace) and the talkies (the newsreel short). Of course, as Sarris points out, there are anachronisms (Stalin's Red Army looks far too healthy for 1929), but Wilder's design, I believe, is to evoke the sense of an era in which the time (and just about everything else) is out of joint. Complaints that Wilder's timing is off only reinforce my point. Like *The Private Life of Sherlock Holmes*, *The Front Page* is a film *about* timing and mistiming, *about* the inability of human beings to keep time and life under neat and decorous control.

More importantly, however, *The Front Page* is a film about Billy Wilder: about his history, his time, his own 24-frame-a-second career. Wilder has always been an introspective film-maker, acutely aware of Hollywood and its traditions. And *The Front Page* continues in this vein by direct reference to *The Student Prince* (the love overcome by duty theme), and by implicit references to *Some Like It Hot* (Hildy scooped the other reporters on the St. Valentine's Day massacre), *Irma La Douce* (the whore-with-the-heart-of-gold theme), and through casting to films such as *The Apartment* and *The Fortune Cookie*. As Sarris points out, "Lemmon and Matthau are not options for Wilder, but imperatives" (p. 83). The use of Lemmon, in particular, recalls to mind a veritable rogues' gallery of lovable Wilder goofs, and his presence as Hildy Johnson in *The Front Page* only reinforces the introspective tone of the film.

The strongest evidence for my case, however, is not to be found in the occasional reference. Indeed, it is almost (though not quite) a

Jack Lemmon and Shirley MacLaine in *Irma La Douce*.

mistake to discuss *The Front Page* as a re-make of *His Girl Friday.* If *The Front Page* is a re-make of anything, it is a re-make of Wilder's only other examination of the journalism game, *Ace in the Hole (The Big Carnival),* arguably one of his most overtly cynical films, and certainly one of his most personal films prior to *The Front Page.*[21] Wilder began his writing career as a sports reporter in Vienna and then as a crime reporter in Berlin, and hence it requires little extrapolation to think of Chuck Tatum (Kirk Douglas) in *Ace in the Hole,* or of Walter Burns (Matthau) and Hildy Johnson (Lemmon) in *The Front Page,* as Wilder surrogates, symbolic stand-ins who allow Wilder the possibility of self-examination (see Madsen and Farber for biographical detail).

The parallels are amazingly precise in terms of plot, character, and theme. *Ace in the Hole* recounts the checkered career of ace reporter Chuck Tatum, a man whose self-image is ever on the verge of megalomania—hence his inability to keep his New York City jobs, and hence the necessity that he find work of any journalistic sort out in the sun-baked provinces. He winds up writing for an Albuquerque daily, but his eye is always open for the big story that will get him a wire service byline and national attention. Despite his assertion to the

e Law and The Press: Ray Teal and Kirk Douglas in *Ace in the Hole.*

contrary—"I don't make things happen, all I do is write about them"—Tatum is clearly looking for a tear-jerking opportunity to exploit, a real human interest blockbuster.

The film's initial issue, then, is whether or not Tatum will regain his stature as a big time reporter. Similarly, the issue in *The Front Page* concerns the efforts of Walter Burns to retrieve Hildy Johnson from the folly of matrimony and the advertising racket. In both films we see a reporter on the way out, and in each instance we see a concerted effort to bring either the reporter or his reputation back into the journalistic limelight.

Tatum's "ace in the hole" is Leo Minosa, a not too bright ex-GI who is trapped by a cave-in while hunting Indian artifacts deep within the crumbling bowels of the Mountain of the Seven Vultures (eight, if you count Tatum), a ghostly precinct sacred to the local tribe. Little, however, is sacred to Tatum, and he does not hesitate to risk the ancient curse and venture in to check Leo's condition. Tatum has to find out if this is the story he's been searching for. And neither does he hesitate to prolong Leo's agony or his imprisonment for the sake of headlines. Thus Tatum convinces the head of the rescue crew that the more time consuming rescue strategy, drilling an emergency shaft down from above, is the better, despite the foreman's belief that the quicker method, merely shoring up the old shaft, will do the job with greater speed and safety.

Tatum is aided in his colossal con-game by the local sheriff, a swaggering, self-important sadist (he keeps a pet rattlesnake) who understands the political wisdom of orchestrating a protracted rescue operation in cahoots with the mad Eastern reporter. As Tatum points out, free publicity is not to be scorned in an election year, and the Sheriff deputises Tatum to seal the bargain.

We see a similar though far less conscious collaboration between Walter Burns and Sheriff Hartman in *The Front Page*. Both men use the plight of Earl Williams for personal or political gain. For "Honest" Pete Hartman and the political regime Earl translates as votes, the votes of blacks (Earl's crime was the accidental shooting of a coloured cop), and the votes of Red-baiters (the Sheriff's campaign slogan: "Reform the Reds with a rope"). For Walter Burns, Earl Williams becomes a handle by which Burns can hold on to Hildy Johnson. The man who got the death-bed confession of Three Finger Banducci could never walk away from the Earl Williams story ("an outraged minnow battling against the tides of injustice"), wedding plans or no wedding plans, and Walter Burns knows it. Furthermore, Burns's desire to hold on to Hildy is reinforced by the power that Hildy represents, the power of that "old Johnson word magic" to influence public policy. The undisguised goal of "The Examiner's" attack on the mayor and the sheriff is the ouster of the *ancien régime* and its replacement by a Burns/Johnson administration. As Burns puts it in a fit of prophesy: "We'll crucify 'em . . . be running this town . . . They'll name streets after us."

Both films, therefore, raise the issue of the writer's responsibility to his subject and his audience. *Ace in the Hole,* seen in this light, is clearly a parable of the irresponsible artist. Tatum's self-seeking promotion stunt results not in his own rise to permanent power and prestige but in the death of Leo Minosa (Earl Williams is a similar pawn facing a similar fate). And while Leo slowly and agonisingly dies, driven to the verge of madness by the endless pounding of the drill bit, Tatum slowly becomes disgusted with (though more deeply involved in) his role as a demoniac Cecil B. DeMille. Tatum has always held his public in low esteem, and it's no small part of Wilder's social satire that the

The crowds gather in *Ace in the Hole*.

public proves so morbid so quickly (people argue over who was the first to arrive at the scene). It's clear, however, that it takes a media wizard of Tatum's calibre to bring out the morbidity of the mob (some members of the crowd, indeed, seem genuinely remorseful at Leo's death) and this responsibility weighs heavy upon Tatum's shoulders.

Thus it's significant and perfectly in keeping with Wilder's tragic moralism that Tatum should be stabbed by Leo's estranged, Monroesque wife, a woman whose self-disgust is only matched by her disgust for Tatum himself. And furthermore, he is stabbed at the point in the film when his cynic's revulsion for the sadistic crowds calls into question his own sadistic impulses. In other words, the stab wound provides a focal point for his otherwise subconscious sense of guilt. Thus, while he cannot save Leo, he can and does redeem himself to some extent by confessing his sins—and then he dies, the victim of his own exploitation, falling face forward into closeup on the city-room floor.

Ace in the Hole, like *Double Indemnity* and *Witness for the Prosecution,* thus redeems its cynicism by bringing its central character to some elementary sense of reckoning. Indeed, despite the overwhelmingly cynical, *film noir* tone of the film, it carries a self-sufficient moral critique right in its surface in the character of Tatum's Albuquerque editor, a man who admires Tatum's talents, but who is quick to understand the obsessive egomania, bordering even at the film's beginning on the psychotic, which powers Tatum's career. Thus it is morally appropriate that Tatum should fall dead at the editor's feet, as if to verify the editor's moral authority.

The Front Page differs from *Ace in the Hole* precisely to the extent that Walter Burns differs from Tatum's editor. In *Ace in the Hole* it's the reporter who goes berserk against the best advice of the editor. In *The Front Page,* on the other hand, the reporter, Hildy Johnson, is doing his level best to go straight—to go, literally, to Philadelphia. As Hildy puts it to his former press room colleagues, he does not want to end up a cynical courthouse reporter, a professional "buttinsky", forever peeking through keyholes, or stealing family photos from old ladies to illustrate juicy front page rape stories. "And for what? So a million shop girls and motormen's wives can get their jollies." Burns, on the other hand, thrives on this sort of muckraking obscenity. He gleefully schemes, for example, to photograph Earl Williams dangling from the gallows (although he personally prefers electrocution to hanging: "There's something you can sink your teeth into"), and he is determined that Hildy will write the Williams story and remain the top reporter on the "Examiner" staff. And by so doing, Burns represents a real threat to the sort of normalcy embodied in the Hildy Johnson/Peggy Grant relationship. Burns thus represents, in potential at least, a sort of self-seeking hucksterism very much akin to Tatum's in *Ace in the Hole.*

The threat represented by Burns, and the relationship between political and journalistic irresponsibility, is clarified when Burns makes the first of his many attempts to frighten Peggy away from Hildy. Burns finds her leading a follow-the-bouncing-ball sing-along ("Button up your overcoat . . . you belong to me") at a plush cinema house; and when the song is over and the newsreel starts up, he follows her backstage to her dressing room, where he poses as a probation officer and accuses Hildy of exhibitionism ("Button up your overcoat"). But before he gets to the dressing room, Burns stops in the shadows behind the screen and watches a few moments of newsreel. The first news item concerns the return of Admiral Byrd from Antarctica, and the second features the previously mentioned footage of Red Army troops parading before Stalin in Red Square.

There are three equations which concern us here. The first has to do with the relationship between journalism and cinema—both forms of mass media are joined together in the "Universal Newspaper Newsreel." Thus Wilder can make a film about journalism which in turn serves as a critique of his own practice as a film-maker. Both arts involve a certain degree of public manipulation and a corresponding degree of public responsibility. The second equation concerns the sorts of images projected: the hero, as embodied by Admiral Byrd, and the villain, as embodied by Stalin ("tame Reds with ropes"). The two men are different, of course, but the mass media can blow the human image up out of all humane proportion, so that Byrd and Stalin occupy very much the same space (the screen) in the public eye. And the third equation concerns the relationship of media to government. Both Admiral Byrd and Marshal Stalin are political entities, representatives of the ruling order, and their political prominence results to a large degree from the active co-operation of the mass media (as, for example, in the newsreel).

The point, then, is that neat distinctions between good guys and bad guys tend to blur when the art of power and the power of art come, as they inevitably seem to do, into alignment. There tends to be an unholy sort of attraction between the two, between those who revel in lawlessness for the sake of circulation or box office and those who decry lawlessness (while condoning it, or practising it) for the sake of votes. Both prey upon the fears and fantasies of the public, both owe their existence to the ability to stoke the fires of the public imagination, and both share, therefore, the responsibility for the failure of society to meet genuine human needs.

Such is a far more profoundly sceptical social vision than anything implied by *Ace in the Hole*. We have no straight-arrow editor to serve as our moral anchor. All of the people in power are corrupt to one degree or the other, Hildy included, though Hildy less than most. The only characters who manage to escape the film's general condemnation are such as Earl Williams, Mollie Malloy, Jenny the cleaning woman, and Peggy Grant—little people who seem, in context, to be divine innocents rather than worldly cynics. Those Capraesque characters aside, however, the film is populated by a gallery of intensely human if frequently perverse rogues, out to excel each other in the skills of manipulation and exploitation.

The film's basic plot conflict, therefore, is not between innocence and experience (Earl Williams *vs.* the establishment) but between various power blocks within the establishment itself, i.e., the press vs. the politicians, so that Earl Williams only represents a Langdon-like pawn in a larger and ongoing power game. Hence the film's real issue is one of escape. Can Earl escape execution (i.e., can any form of innocence survive?) and can Hildy escape his reporter's persona? Wilder's answers are contradictory—yes in one instance, no in the next—and together they reflect the film's larger sense of ambivalence.

Hildy Johnson is thus at the film's moral centre. He is the character who must choose: either to save himself, which means abandoning Earl to the sheriff and the rest of the bloodthirsty courthouse crew; or to fight for Earl's salvation, which means exposing the motives of those who are killing the little anarchist for their own political gain. The choice is not an easy one, surely, though Hildy somehow remains naïve enough to imagine he can escape the necessity of choosing. *The Front Page,* however, is a film about human limitations, about the necessity for accepting less than perfect solutions. So that however much Hildy wants to stop being Hildy, however much he wants to wed his cinema princess and live happily ever after, he must remain as he is, sublimating his energies, sexual and otherwise, in the service of the fourth estate. Such is his nature, his social role in a clearly berserk society, and he cannot escape it (no more than Lubitsch's Student Prince could escape his royal duties, however much he longed to marry his lovely Heidelberg bar-maid).

And, furthermore, there's a certain freedom within limitation.

A parable of human limitations: Jacobi (Cliff Osmond) puts the cuffs on Johnson and Burns in *The Front Page*.

Marriage to Peggy may seem ideal, healthy, heterosexual, eventless. But marriage to Walter Burns and to the journalism game provides a sort of perverse satisfaction: the only time Burns "gets it up" is when he "puts the paper to bed," and Hildy himself admits (though jokingly) that he finds bullets and sirens "stimulating . . . you know . . . sexually." No doubt most of us would prefer satisfyingly normal sex lives, but normalcy seems out of the question in *The Front Page*. The best one can hope for is some relatively harmless mode of sublimation (Bensinger and Keppler eventually open a gay antique shop on Cape Cod, for example).

All of which seems, by the boy-gets-girl standards of Wilder's more conventional comedies (*The Major and the Minor,* for example), cynical in the extreme, evidence once again of Wilder's basic lack of values. But *The Front Page* does not so much lack values as question them, and Wilder has the courage to raise what are clearly the central Hollywood issues. What sort of responsibility does the artist have to himself and his public and how might he best exercise that responsibility? The artist cannot avoid responsibility, any more than Hildy Johnson can escape being a newspaperman. Neither can the artist avoid wielding power, without ceasing his artistry, nor can he avoid rubbing shoulders with corruption. The world does not work that way. Artists can, on the other hand, be aware of the dangers they face, of the risks involved, and they can employ their power with a certain ruthlessness in the service of those more sinned against than sinning, as Burns and Johnson employ the power of the press to free Earl Williams, as Wilder employs the power of cinema to save us from our own complacent and conformist selves.

There are limits, then, to perfection, and *The Front Page* is to a certain extent a parable of failure, a parable of Hildy's failure to escape one sort of "rat race," a parable, perhaps, of Wilder's failure to escape another sort of rat race. Like it or not, Billy Wilder is a Hollywood film-maker. And yet once such limits are clearly (Wilder would say "realistically") defined, one can revel in the possibilities that remain. Thus Hildy enjoys the hell out of writing the Earl Williams story (it is, he tells Peggy, "the greatest thing that ever happened to me"), and there can be little doubt that Wilder enjoyed the hell out of making *The Front Page*. Indeed, the opening credit sequence is a parable within a parable, showing with loving and enthusiastic detail the creation of "The Examiner's" front page. We see typesetters, printers, pressmen, all working double time to crank out the next edition of the paper. The "front page" parallel is obvious. And when the plates are set in press, and when the press begins to roll at top speed, the credit flashes: "Directed by Billy Wilder." A byline to be proud of, a byline worth attending to. Wilder is thus an "examiner," of himself, his art, and his audience. And while his sense of life's limits and inequities remains as strong as ever, stronger perhaps in light of his recent lack of commercial success, there is no doubting the integrity, the intelligence, or the vigour of his film-making.

NOTES

1. Charles Higham, "Cast a Cold Eye: The Films of Billy Wilder," *Sight and Sound*, 32, No. 2 (1963), p. 84. See also Higham's "Meet Whiplash Wilder," *Sight and Sound*, 37, No. 1 (1968), pp. 21-23; Douglas McVay, "The Eye of a Cynic: A Monograph of Billy Wilder," *Films and Filming*, 6, No. 4 (1960), pp. 11-12, 34; Raymond Durgnat; "Wilder Still and Wilder," in *The Crazy Mirror: Hollywood Comedy and the American Image* (London: Faber, 1969; New York: Horizon Press, 1970); and Tim Onosko, "Billy Wilder," *The Velvet Light Trap*, No. 3 (1971), pp. 29-32.

2. John Simon, "Belt and Suspenders: The Art of Billy Wilder," *Theatre Arts*, 46, No. 7 (1962), p. 20.

3. John Simon, *Ingmar Bergman Directs* (New York: Harcourt, Brace, Jovanovich, 1974), p. 41.

4. Samuel Johnson, "Preface to Shakespeare" in *The Norton Anthology of English Literature*, I, Revised Edition, ed. M.H. Abrams et al (New York: W.W. Norton, 1968), p. 1851.

5. Joseph McBride and Michael Wilmington, "The Private Life of Billy Wilder," *Film Quarterly*, 23, No. 4 (1970), pp. 2-9; and Stephen Farber, "The Films of Billy Wilder," *Film Comment*, 7, No. 4 (1971), pp. 8-22. The best foreign language treatment of Wilder that I have seen is Michel Ciment's "Sept Réflexions sur Billy Wilder," *Positif*, No. 127 (1971), pp. 1-21. Gerald Mast discusses Wilder briefly in *The Comic Mind: Comedy and the Movies* (New York: Bobbs-Merrill, 1973), pp. 272-278. I should add that I completed writing the present study in July, 1976. Immediately thereafter Andrew Sarris's "Billy Wilder, Closet Romanticist" appeared in *Film Comment*, 12, No. 4 (1976), pp. 7-9. In the article Sarris recants on his earlier, mostly negative view of Wilder's career, and argues, however briefly, a position quite similar to my own. (See "Some Versions of Billy Wilder," *Cinemonkey*, No. 16 [1979] for my most recent thoughts on Wilder.)

6. James Agee, *Agee on Film* (New York: McDowell, Obolensky Inc., 1958), p. 182.

7. As reported in Axel Madsen, *Billy Wilder* (London: Thames and Hudson, 1968; Bloomington: Indiana University Press, 1969), p. 69.

8. Agee, p. 183: "The causes of Don Birnam's alcoholism were not thoroughly controlled or understood . . . in the novel. In the movie they hardly exist."

9. Charles Higham and Joel Greenberg, *Hollywood in the Forties* (London: Tantivy Press, 1968; New York: A.S. Barnes, 1968).

10. Richard Corliss, *Talking Pictures* (Woodstock, NY: Overlook Press, 1974). p. 146.

11. Billy Wilder, quoted in Richard Lemon, "Well, Nobody's Perfect," *Saturday Evening Post*, December 17, 1966, p. 37.

12. It is worth remarking that both *One, Two, Three* and *Pocketful of Miracles* were released (in the U.S.) in December of 1961.

13. Two articles, in addition to the career studies already cited, are of special interest in regards to *Double Indemnity*: Paul Jensen, "The Writer: Raymond Chandler and the World You Live In," *Film Comment*, 10, No. 6 (1974), pp. 18-26; and "Tough Guy," *Film Comment*, 12, No. 3 (1976), pp. 50-57, an interview with James Cain by Peter Brunette and Gerald Peary.

14. Andrew Sarris, *The American Cinema* (New York: E.P. Dutton, 1968), p. 166.

15. Richard Lippe, "Kiss Me, Stupid: A Comedy Dilemma," *The Velvet Light Trap*, No. 3 (1971), p. 34.

16. See Joseph McBride, "The Importance of Being Ernst," *Film Heritage* (Summer 1973), pp. 1-9. See also William Paul's review of *Avanti!* in *Rolling Stone*, January 18, 1973, p. 58; and Olivier Eyquem, "Le Rose et le Noir," *Positif*, No. 155 (1974), pp. 9-14.

17. On *The Private Life of Sherlock Holmes* see the review by Robert Mundy in *Cinema* (Los Angeles), 6, No. 3 (1971), pp. 49-50; and Louis Sequin, "La Finalité du Problème," *Positif*, No. 127 (1971), pp. 29-31.

18. Andrew Sarris, "The Front Page: Wilder and More Wistful," *The Village Voice*, December 23, 1974, pp. 83-85.

19. Jay Cocks, "Late, Late Edition," *Time*, December 23, 1974, p. 4.

20. Durgnat, op. cit., p. 69.

21. On *Ace in the Hole*, see Bernard F. Dick, "Serpents in the Desert," *Movietone News*, No. 41 (1975), pp. 21-24.

Billy Wilder Filmography

by Gary Hooper and Leland Poague

Samuel ("Billy") Wilder was born 22 June 1906 near Vienna. After completing studies at the Real Gymnasium, he was enrolled in the law curriculum at the University of Vienna, but quit after less than a year to become a reporter for the Viennese tabloid "Die Stunde." Moving to Berlin in the mid nineteen-twenties, Wilder eked out a living at a variety of jobs, including reporter and *eintänzer* (ballroom dancer/gigolo). In 1927, through fortuitous circumstances, he broke into the movies as a scriptwriter. (See Maurice Zolotow, "Billy Wilder in Hollywood" [New York: Putnam, London: W. H. Allen; 1977], which is rich in anecdotes and details about Wilder's early years.)*

I. WILDER IN EUROPE

From 1927 through 1929, Wilder learned the craft of screenwriting as a "ghostwriter" at UFA studios. It is esti-mated that during this period at least two hundred scenarios credited to such es-tablished writers as Franz Schulz and Robert Leibman (who in his heyday as the head of UFA's story department was contracted to write ten screenplays a *month*) were actually ghosted by Wilder. It was not until 1929 that Wilder received an official credit, as scenarist for *Der Teufelsreporter (The Devil's Reporter)*, a fable about a reporter who sells his soul to the devil (see Zolotow, p. 40).

MENSCHEN AM SONNTAG (PEOPLE ON SUNDAY) (1929). A semi-documentary fiction film about four lower middle-class people on Sun-day holidays. Notable for its use of non-professional actors and extensive loca-tion shooting in and around Berlin, it was the last important German silent film. *Dir:* Robert Siodmak. *Assts:* Edgar G. Ulmer, Fred Zinnemann. *Sc:* Billy Wilder (an idea by Curt Soidmak). *Ph:* Eugene Shuftan. *With* Brigitte Borchert, Christil Ehlers, Annie Scheyer,

---

*Steve Seidman's reference volume, "The Film Career of Billy Wilder" (Boston: G. K. Hall, 1977), appeared after we completed the present Wilder filmography. Seidman's book is essential to Wilder studies, particularly for its excellent bibliography and for the detailed plot synopses which are found in his filmog-raphy. Our filmography differs from Seid-man's primarily in format rather than detail. Indeed, despite independent research ef-forts, the two are remarkably in accord. Nevertheless, we have decided it would be false to our research to undertake the wholesale revision necessary to iron out every minor inconsistency of spelling or attribution or whatever between the two filmographies. Readers should therefore be advised that there are some differences (e.g., Seidman lists under "Other Film Related Activities" the 1973 television remake of *Double Indemnity* while we do not) but they can rest assured that in the main they are well served by either or both accounts of the facts of Wilder's career.

Wolfgang von Walterschausen, Erwin Splettstösser. *Prod:* Filmstudio. 59m.
DER KAMPF MIT DEM DRACHEN (HIS BATTLE WITH HIS DRAGON) (1930). Short fantasy about a tenant who murders his shrewish landlady. *Dir:* Robert Siodmak. *Sc:* from an idea by Billy Wilder (uncredited). *With* Felix Bressart. *Prod:* UFA. 12m. (See Zolotow, p. 43.)
SEITENSPRÜNGE (EXTRAMARITAL ESCAPADE) (1930). *Dir:* Stefan Szekely. *Sc:* Ludwig Biro, B. E. Luthge, Karl Note (from an idea by Billy Wilder).
DER MANN, DER SEINEN MÖRDER SUCHT (LOOKING FOR HIS MURDERER) (1931). When a despondent young man finds he lacks the courage to take his own life, he hires a burglar to kill him within twenty-four hours. After changing his mind, the young man finds that the burglar has sold the contract to a professional gunman. *Dir:* Robert Siodmak. *Sc:* Billy Wilder, Ludwig Hirschfeld, Curt Siodmak (a play by Ernst Neubach). *With* Heinz Rühmann. *Prod:* UFA. 82m.
IHRE HOHEIT BEFIEHLT (HER MAJESTY COMMANDS) (1931). A musical about a princess disguised as a manicurist who falls in love with a lieutenant disguised as a delicatessen clerk. *Dir:* Hans Schwarz. *Sc:* Billy Wilder, Paul Franck, Robert Liegmann. *Mus:* Werner R. Heymann. *With* Käthe von Nagy *(Princess Marie Christine)*, Willi Fritsch *(Lieutenant von Conradi)*, Reinhold Schünzel *(Prime Minister)*, Paul Hörbiger *(Pipac)*, Paul Heidemann

Emil and the Detectives.

(Prince von Leuchtenstein). *Prod:* UFA. 91m.
DER FALSCHE EHEMANN (THE COUNTERFEIT HUSBAND) (1931). A young man impersonates his twin brother and rejuvenates the brother's business *and* his marriage. *Dir:* Johannes Guter. *Sc:* Billy Wilder, Paul Franck. *With* Johannes Riemann, Maria Paudler, Gustav Waldau, Jessie Vihrog, Tibor von Halmay, Martha Ziegler, Frits Strehlen. *Prod:* UFA. 81m.
EMIL UND DIE DETEKTIVE (EMIL AND THE DETECTIVES) (1931). After being robbed, a young boy pursues the thief and eventually causes his arrest after enlisting the aid of a group of Berlin children. *Dir:* Gerhard Lamprecht. *Sc:* Billy Wilder (the novel by Erich Kästner). *Ph:* Werner Brandes. *Mus:* Allan Gray. *With* Rolf Wenkhaus *(Emil)*, Fritz Rasp *(the thief)*, and Inge Landgut, Hans Löhr, Hans Schaufuss, Hubert Schmitz, Hans Richter, Käthe Haack, Olga Engl. *Prod:* UFA. 80m.
ES WAR EINMAL EIN WALZER (ONCE UPON A TIME THERE WAS A WALTZ) (1932). Musical about a young Berliner who comes to Vienna to marry an heiress, only to discover that she is not rich and that she loves a poor musician. *Dir:* Viktor Janson. *Sc:* Billy Wilder. *Mus:* Franz Lehar. *With* Martha Eggerth, Rolf von Goth, Lizie Natzler, Ernst Verebes, Ida Wüst, Albert Paulig, Paul Hörbiger, Hermann Blasee. *Prod:* AAFA.
EIN BLONDER TRAUM (A BLOND DREAM) (1932). Musical about two young window cleaners in love with a dancer. *Dir:* Paul Martin. *Sc:* Billy Wilder, Walter Reisch. *Mus:* Werner R. Heymann. *With* Lilian Harvey, Willi Fritsch, Willi Forst. *Prod:* UFA.
EIN MÄDEL DER STRASSE (A GIRL OF THE STREET) (1932). Comedy-romance about an orphan girl who is forced to live in phone booths and do odd jobs, until she meets a destitute banker who recoups his fortune and marries the girl. *Dir:* Hans Steinhoff. *Sc:* Billy Wilder, Max Kolpe (a play by Dario Nicomedi). *With* Dolly Haas, Carl L. Diehl, Oscar Sima, Paul Hörbiger, Hed-

wig Bleibtreu. *Prod:* Lothar Stark. 96m.
DAS BLAUE VOM HIMMEL (THE BLUE FROM HEAVEN) (1932). Musical comedy about a pretty underground ticket agent, with the stationmaster, an aviator and a businessman all vying for her attention. *Dir:* Viktor Janson. *Sc:* Billy Wilder, Max Kolpe. *With* Martha Eggerth, Hermann Thimmig, Margarette Schlegel, Ernst Verebes, Fritz Kampers, Jakob Tiedtke, Margarette Kupfer, Hans Richter, Walter Steinbeck. *Prod:* AAFA.
MADAME WUNSCHT KEINE KINDER (MADAME DESIRES NO CHILDREN) (1933). The wife of a child specialist is too devoted to athletics to want children of her own. After comic and romantic mix-ups, a reconciliation is finally achieved. *Dir:* Hans Steinhoff. *Sc:* Billy Wilder, Max Kolpe (a novel by Clément Vautel). *With* Liane Haid, Georg Alexander, Lucie Mannheim, Otto Walburg, Erika Glässner, Willi Stettner, Hans Moser. *Prod:* Lothar Stark.
WAS FRAUEN TRÄUMEN (WHAT WOMEN DREAM) (1933). Described by "The New York Times" (2 July 1933) as "a criminal comedy [which] moves forward with the solemnity of a problem play." *Dir:* Geza von Bolvary. *Sc:* Billy Wilder, Franz Schulz. *With* Nora Gregor, Gustav Fröhlich, Kurt Horwitz, Peter Lorre. 99m.

Soon after Hitler assumed power, Wilder fled from Berlin to Paris. His final writing job for UFA was an unproduced screenplay (co-authored with Walter Reisch) entitled *Der Frack mit Chrysanthemum (Tailcoat with Flower)*, an episodic account of the peregrinations of a suit from owner to owner. Years later the script served as the basis (uncredited) for *Tales of Manhattan*, directed by Julien Duvivier (1942). (See Zolotow, p. 45.) In Paris, Wilder joined with other exiles to write and produce an independent film. Lack of funds forced Wilder into a director's chair for the first time.

MAUVAISE GRAINE (BAD SEED) (1933). A semi-documentary fiction film about the brief, violent life of a gang of juvenile car thieves. *Dir:* Alexander Esway, Billy Wilder. *Sc:* Alexander Esway, Max Kolpe, H. G. Lustig (a story by Billy Wilder). *Mus:* Franz Waxman. *With* Danielle Darrieux, Pierre Mingand, Raymonde Galle, Paul Velsa, Jean Wall, Michel Duran, Maupi, Paul Escoffier. *Prod:* General Edouard Corniglion — Molinier (Compagnie Nouvelle Commerciale). 80m.

Joe May, an expatriate German director working in Hollywood, sold a Wilder story to Columbia Pictures. The film, a musical entitled *Pam-Pam*, was never produced, but the promise of a Hollywood contract encouraged Wilder to fulfil his longstanding dream of emigrating to America.

II. WILDER IN AMERICA

ADORABLE (1933). A musical re-make of the German *Ihre Hoheit Befiehlt* (1931). *Dir:* William Dieterle. *Sc:* George Marion Jr., Jane Storm (a screenplay by Billy Wilder and Paul Franck). *Mus and Lyrics:* Werner R. Heymann, Richard A. Whiting, George Marion Jr. *With* Janet Gaynor (*Princess Marie Christine*), Harry Garat (*Karl Conradi*), C. Aubrey Smith (*Von Heynitz*), Herbert Mundin (*Pipac*), Blanche Frederici (*The Countess*), Hans von Twardowski (*The Prince*). *Prod:* Fox. 88m.

MUSIC IN THE AIR (1934). Musical about a composer and a prima donna who quarrel and who nearly break up the romance of a young country couple before things are straightened out. *Dir:* Joe

C. Aubrey Smith, Janet Gaynor, and Henry Garat in *Adorable*.

Gloria Swanson and Reginald Owen in Music in the Air.

May. *Sc:* Howard I. Young, Billy Wilder (the operetta by Jerome Kern and Oscar Hammerstein II). *With* Gloria Swanson *(Frieda)*, John Boles *(Bruno)*, Douglass Montgomery *(Karl)*, June Lang *(Sieglinde)*, Al Shean *(Dr. Lessing)*, Reginald Owen *(Weber)*, Joseph Cawthorn *(Uppmann)*, Hobart Bosworth *(Cornelius)*, Sara Haden *(Martha)*, Marjorie Main *(Anna)*, Roger Imhof *(Burgomaster)*, Jed Prouty *(Kirschner)*, Christian Rub *(Zipfelhuber)*, Fuzzy Knight *(Nick)*. *Prod:* Erich Pommer for Fox. 85m.

ONE EXCITING ADVENTURE (1934). A re-make of the German *Was Frauen Träumen* (1933). *Dir:* Ernest L. Frank. *Sc:* William Hurlbut, Samuel Ornitz (a story by Billy Wilder and Franz Schultz). *With:* Neil Hamilton, Binnie Barnes. *Prod:* Universal.

LOTTERY LOVER (1935). *Dir:* William Thiele. *Sc:* Billy Wilder, Franz Schulz. *With* Lew Ayres. *Prod:* Fox Film Corp. (See Seidman.)

Gladys Swarthout and Fred MacMurray in Champagne Waltz.

CHAMPAGNE WALTZ (1937). In Vienna, a jazz cafe threatens to drive a waltz palace out of business. Meanwhile, the leader of the jazz band romances the palace owner's daughter. *Dir:* A. Edward Sutherland. *Sc:* Don Hartman, Frank Butler (a story by Billy Wilder and H. S. Kraft). *Mus and lyrics:* Burton Lane, Ralph Fried, Sam Coslow, Frederick Hollander, Leo Robin, William Daly, and Ann Ronnell. *With* Gladys Swarthout *(Elsa Strauss)*, Fred MacMurray *(Buzzy Bellew)*, Jack Oakie *(Harpy Gallagher)*, Veloz and Yolanda *(Larry and Anna)*, Herman Bing *(Max Snellinek)*, Vivienne Osborne *(The Countess)*, Frank Forest *(Karl Lieberlich)*, Benny Baker *(Flip)*, Ernest Cossart *(Waiter)*, Fritz Leiber *(Franz Strauss)*, James Burke *(Mr. Scribner)*, Maude Eburne *(Mrs. Scribner)*, Michael Visaroff *(Ivanovich)*, Guy Bates Poest *(Lumvedder)*, Maurice Cass *(Hugo)*. *Prod:* Harlan Thompson for Paramount.

In addition to his official credits, Wilder was forced to do more ghostwriting, and formed a brief collaboration with scenarist Oliver H. P. Garrett. The partnership was dissolved when Pioneer Pictures, to whom they were contracted, went defunct before any Garrett and Wilder screenplays could be produced. After four less than spectacular years in Hollywood, Wilder was teamed with another frustrated Paramount writer, Charles Brackett. Their first assignment was to write a script for Ernst Lubitsch.

BLUEBEARD'S EIGHTH WIFE (1938). An oft-married American's latest wife is determined that she will be his last. Her machinations to prove her point (she feigns adultery; sues for divorce) eventually drive her sometimes husband to the sanitorium, where things are finally set straight. *Dir:* Ernst Lubitsch. *Sc:* Charles Brackett, Billy Wilder (a play by Alfred Savoir). *Adapt:* Charlton Andrews. *Ph:* Leo Tover. *Art dir:* Hans Dreier, Robert Usher. *Ed:* William Shea. *Sp. eff:* Farciot Edouart. *Cos:* Travis Banton. *Mus:* Werner R. Heymann. *With* Claudette Colbert *(Nicole de Loiselle)*, Gary Cooper *(Michael Brandon)*, Edward Everett Horton *(Marquis de Loiselle)*,

Claudette Colbert in *Blue-beard's Eighth Wife.*

David Niven *(Albert de Regnier)*, Elizabeth Patterson *(Aunt Hedwige)*, Herman Bing *(Pepinard)*, Warren Heymer *(Kid Mulligan)*, Franklin Pangborn *(Asst. Hotel Manager)*, Armand Cortes *(Asst. Hotel Manager)*, Rolfe Sedan *(Floorwalker)*, Lawrence Grant *(Prof. Urganzeff)*, Lionel Pape *(Potin)*, Tyler Brooke *(Clerk)*, Tom Richetts *(Uncle André)*, Barlow Borland *(Uncle Fernandel)*, and Charles Halton, Sacha Guitry. *Prod:* Ernst Lubitsch for Paramount. 80m.

MIDNIGHT (1939). Down on her luck in Paris, a gold-digging American chorus girl is hired by a wealthy gentleman to divert the attentions of his wife's lover. Meanwhile, the chorus girl is pursued by a romantic and persistent taxi driver. *Dir:* Mitchell Leisen. *Sc:* Charles Brackett, Billy Wilder (a story by Edwin Justus Mayer and Franz Schulz). *Ph:* Charles Lang Jr. *Art dir:* Hans Dreier, Robert Usher. *Ed:* Doane Harrison. *Spec eff:* Farciot Edouart. *Cos:* Irene. *Mus:* Frederick Hollander. *With* Claudette Colbert *(Eve Peabody)*, Don Ameche *(Tibor Czerny)*, John Barrymore *(Georges Flammarion)*, Francis Lederer *(Jacques Picot)*, Mary Astor *(Helene Flammarion)*, Elaine Barrie *(Simone)*, Hedda Hopper *(Stephanie)*, Rex O'Malley *(Marcel)*, Monty Woolley *(Judge)*, Armand Kaliz *(Lebon)*, Lionel Pape *(Edouart)*, Ferdinand Munier and Gennaro Curci *(Major Domos)*, Leander De Cordova, William Eddritt, Michael Visaroff, and Joseph Romantini *(Footmen)*, Carlos De Valdez *(Butler)*, Joseph De Stefani *(Head Porter)*, Arno Frey *(Room Clerk)*, Eugene Borden and Paul Bryar *(Porters)*, Leonard Sues *(Bellboy)*, Robert Graves *(Doorman)*, Eddy Conrad *(Prince Potopienko)*, Elspeth Dudgeon *(Dowager)*, Helen St. Raynor *(Coloratura)*, Billy Daniels *(Roger)*, Bryant Washburn *(Guest)*, Max Luckey *(Lawyer)*, Alexander Leftwich *(Court Clerk)*, Donald Reed *(Ferdinand)*, Louis Mercier *(Leon)*, Nestor Paiva *(Woman's Escort)*, Harry Semels *(Policeman)*, Harry Vejar *(Garage man)*. *Prod:* Arthur Hornblow Jr. for Paramount. 92m.

WHAT A LIFE (1939). Film version of the popular stage play that introduced trouble-prone teenager Henry Aldrich. *Dir:* Jay Theodore Reed. *Sc:* Charles Brackett, Billy Wilder (the play by Clifford Goldsmith): *With* Jackie Cooper *(Henry Aldrich)*, Betty Field *(Barbara Pearson)*, John Howard *(Mr. Nelson)*, Janice Logan *(Miss Shea)*, Lionel Stander *(Ferguson)*, Hedda Hopper *(Mrs. Aldrich)*, Vaughan Glaser *(Mr. Bradley)*, James Corner *(George Bigelow)*, Dorothy Stickney *(Miss Wheeler)*, Kathleen Lockhart *(Miss Pike)*, Lucien Littlefield *(Mr. Patterson)*, Sidney Miller *(Pinkie Peters)*, Andrew Tombes *(Prof. Abernathy)*, George Guhl *(Janitor)*, Arthur Aylesworth *(MacGowan)*, Wilda Bennett *(Miss Dolittle)*, Bennie Bartlett *(Butch Williams)*, Kay Stewart *(Marjorie)*, Leonard Sues *(Harold)*, Eddie Bryan *(Don Bray)*, Janet Waldo *(Gwen)*, Betty McLaughlin *(Jessie)*, Douglas Fahy *(Tony Milligan)*, Robert Smith *(Gertie)*, Nora Cecil *(Miss Eggleston)*. *Prod:* Paramount. 75m.

NINOTCHKA (1939). Sent to Paris on a diplomatic mission, a cold-blooded Communist meets a fast-talking capitalist gigolo who depends for his livelihood on the favours of an exiled Russian Grand Duchess. When the envoy and the playboy fall in love, Ninotchka learns how to laugh and her lover becomes his own man. *Dir:* Ernst Lubitsch. *Sc:* Charles Brackett, Billy Wilder, Walter Reisch (a story by Melchior Lengyel). *Ph:* William Daniels. *Art dir:* Cedric Gibbons, Randall Duel, Edwin B. Willis. *Ed:* Gene Ruggiero. *Cos:* Adrian. *Mus:* Werner R. Heymann. *With* Greta Garbo *(Ninotchka)*,

Melvyn Douglas *(Leon)*, Ina Clair *(Swana)*, Bela Lugosi *(Razinin)*, Felix Bressart *(Buljanoff)*, Alexander Granach *(Kopalski)*, Sig Ruman *(Iranoff)*, Gregory Gay *(Rakonin)*, Rolfe Sedan *(Hotel Manager)*, Edwin Maxwell *(Mercier)*, Richard Carle *(Gaston)*, and George Tobias, Paul Ellis, Dorothy Adams, Peggy Moran. *Prod:* Ernst Lubitsch for M-G-M. 110m.

ARISE MY LOVE (1940). Posing as the prisoner's wife, a female news correspondent rescues an adventurer from a Spanish jail. While their romance develops, the course of events—by turns farcical and melodramatic—take them across a Europe drawing ever closer to war. *Dir:* Mitchell Leisen. *Sc:* Charles Brackett, Billy Wilder, (a story by Benjamin Glazer and John S. Toldy). *Adapt:* Jacques Théry. *Ph:* Charles Lang Jr. *Art dir:* Hans Dreier, Robert Usher. *Ed:* Doane Harrison. *Cos:* Irene. *Mus:* Victor Young. *With* Claudette Colbert *(Augusta Nash)*, Ray Milland *(Tom Martin)*, Dennis O'Keefe *(Shep)*, Walter Abel *(Phillips)*, Dick Purcell *(Pink)*, George Zucco *(Prison Governor)*, Frank Puglia *(Father Jacinto)*, Esther Dale *(Susie)*, Paul Leyssac *(Bresson)*, Ann Codee *(Mme. Bresson)*, Stanley Logan *(Col. Tubbs-Brown)*, Lionel Pape *(Lord Kettlebrook)*, Aubrey Mather *(Achille)*, Cliff Nazarro *(Botzleberg)*, Michael Mark *(Botzleberg's Asst.)*, Jesus Topete *(Guard)*, Nestor Paiva *(Uniformed Clerk)*, Fred Malatesta *(Mechanic)*, Juan Duval *(Spanish Driver)*, Paul Bryar *(Desk Clerk)*, George Davis *(Porter)*, Alan Davis *(Cameraman)*, Jean Del Val *(Conductor)*,

Jon Easton, Jean de Briac and Eugene Borden *(Waiters)*, Sarah Edwards and Fern Emmett *(Spinsters)*, Jacques Vanaire, Olaf Hytten, Louis Mercier and Guy Repp *(Employees)*, Paul Everton *(Husband)*, Mrs. Wilfred North *(Wife)*, Maurice Maurice, Marcel de la Brosse and François Richier *(French Newsboys)*, Douglas Kennedy *(College Boy)*, Charles de Ravenne *(Bellboy)*, Charles Bastin *(Elevator Boy)*, Nadia Petrova, Blanca Vischer and Irene Colman *(Girls at Maxim's)*, Poppy Wilde *(Hungarian Girl)*, Mme. Louise Colombet *(Flowerwoman)*, Armand Kaliz *(Orchestra Leader)*, Gregory Golubeff *(First Violin)*, Mayor Fred Farrell *(Cab Driver)*, George Bunny *(Fiacre Driver)*, Knud Kreuger *(German Sentry)*, Reginald Sheffield *(Steward)*, David Thursby *(Irish Fisherman)*, Tempe Pigott *(Woman in Irish pub)*, Ellis Irving, *(RAF Corporal)*, Sigfrid Tor *(German Captain)*, Douglas Grant *(German Lieutenant)*, Hans Furberg *(German Sentry)*, Robert O. Davis *(Prussian Officer)*, Frank Bruno, Alphonse Martell, Anthony Nace, Sherry Hall, Anthony Merlo and Leyland Hodgson *(Correspondents)*. *Prod:* Arthur Hornblow Jr. for Paramount. 100m.

RHYTHM ON THE RIVER (1940). Two musicians, a young man and a young woman, ghostwriters for a popular composer, meet, compose their own hit song, and fall in love. *Dir:* Victor Schertzinger. *Sc:* Dwight Taylor (a story by Billy Wilder and Jacques Théry). *With* Bing Crosby *(Bob Summers)*, Mary Martin *(Cherry Lane)*, Basil Rathbone *(Oliver Courtney)*, Oscar Levant *(Starbuck)*, Oscar Shaw *(Charlie Goodrich)*, Charlie Grapewin *(Uncle Caleb)*, Lillian Cornell *(Millie)*, William Frawley *(Westlake)*, John Scott Trotter *(himself)*, Phyllis Kennedy *(Patsy Flick)*, Jeanne Cagney *(Country Cousin)*, Wingy Mannone *(Woody)*, Brandon Hurst *(Bates)*, Charles Lane *(Mr. Schwartz)*, Pierre Watkin *(Uncle)*. *Prod:* William LeBaron for Paramount.

HOLD BACK THE DAWN (1941). Stranded in Mexico, a European refugee marries a naive schoolteacher in order to enter the United States. After discover-

audette Colbert and Ray Milland
Arise, My Love.

ing his motives, she is injured in an auto wreck, and he risks arrest and deportation by entering the U.S. illegally to see her in the hospital. *Dir:* Mitchell Leisen. *Sc:* Charles Brackett, Billy Wilder (a story by Ketti Frings). *Ph:* Leo Tover. *Art dir:* Robert Usher. *Ed:* Doane Harrison. *Cos:* Edith Head. *Mus:* Victor Young. *With* Charles Boyer *(Georges Iscovescu)*, Olivia De Havilland *(Emmy Brown)*, Paulette Goddard *(Anita Dixon)*, Victor Francen *(Van Den Leucken)*, Walter Abel *(Inspector Hammock)*, Curt Bois *(Bonbois)*, Rosemary DeCamp *(Berta Kurz)*, Eric Feldary *(Josef Kurz)*, Nestor Paiva *(Flores)*, Eva Puig *(Lupita)*, Micheline Cheirel *(Christine)*, Madeleine Le Beau *(Anni)*, Billy Lee *(Tony)*, Mikhail Rasumny *(Mechanic)*, Mitchell Leisen *(Mr. Saxon)*, Brian Donlevy, Richard Webb, and Veronica Lake *(actors in Saxon's film)*, Sonny Boy Williams *(Sam)*, Edward Fielding *(American Consul)*, Don Douglas *(Joe)*, Gertrude Astor *(Young Woman at Climax Bar)*, Jesus Topete and Tony Roux *(Mechanics)*, Francisco Maran *(Mexican Doctor)*, Carlos Villarias *(Mexican Judge)*, Arthur Loft *(Mr. Elvestad)*, June Pickrell *(Mrs. Brown)*, Buddy Messinger *(Elevator Boy)*, George Anderson *(Emmy's Doctor)*, Pauline Wagner *(Nurse)*, Charles Arnt *(Mr. MacAdams)*, Harry T. Shannon *(American Immigration Official)*, William Fraralla *(Asst. Director)*, Henry Roquemore *(Driver)*, Ella Neal *(Bride)*, Antonio Filauri *(Mexican Priest)*, Placido Sigueros *(Old Peon)*, Ray Mala *(Young Mexican Bridegroom)*, Soledad Jimenez *(Old Peon's Wife)*, Daniel Rea *(Ox-Cart Driver)*, Russ Clark and Alden Chase *(Cops in Patrol Car)*, Katherine Booth and Jean Phillips *(Girls at Desk)*, June Wilkins *(Vivienne Worthington)*, Harold F. Lannon *(Studio Guide)*, Norman Ainsley *(Waiter)*, Frank E. Dae, Mrs. Wilfrid North and Mitchell Ingraham *(Members of Kiwanis Group)*, Leon Belasco *(Mr. Spitzler)*, John Hamilton *(Mac)*, Kitty Kelly *(American Lady at Bullring)*, James Flavin and Gordon DeMain *(Immigration Guards)*, Martin Faust *(Gas Station Attendant)*, Chester Clute *(Man at Climax Bar)*. *Prod:* Arthur Hornblow Jr. for Paramount. 115m. It is worth remark-

ing in connection with *Hold Back the Dawn* that Wilder had his own troubles with the U. S. Immigration Service after arriving in the states and he had to leave the country, residing briefly in Mexico, before things were straightened out.

BALL OF FIRE (1941). An English professor, one of a group of encyclopaedists, enlists the aid of several people to help with research on slang. Among the recruits is a night club singer who uses the opportunity to hide from the authorities, who want to question her about her gangster boyfriend. To protect herself and her mobster, the singer feigns affection for the English professor, even to the extent of accepting his proposal of marriage. Her change of heart and Cooper's haymaker hook save the day. *Dir:* Howard Hawks. *Sc:* Charles Brackett, Billy Wilder (a story by Wilder and Thomas Monroe). *Ph:* Gregg Toland. *Art dir:* Perry Ferguson. *Ed:* Daniel Mandell. *Mus:* Alfred Newman. *With* Gary Cooper *(Prof. Bertram Potts)*, Barbara Stanwyck *(Sugarpuss O'Shea)*, Oscar Homolka *(Prof. Gurgakoff)*, Henry Travers *(Prof. Jerome)*, S. Z. Sakall *(Prof. Magenbruch)*, Tully Marshall *(Prof. Robinson)*, Leonid Kinsky *(Prof. Quintana)*, Richard Haydn *(Prof. Oddly)*, Aubrey Mather *(Prof. Peagram)*, Allen Jenkins *(Garbagemen)*, Dana Andrews *(Joe Lilac)*, Dan Duryea *(Duke Pastrami)*, Ralph Peters *(Asthma Anderson)*, Kathleen Howard *(Mrs. Bragg)*, Mary Field *(Miss Totten)*, Charles Lane *(Larsen)*, Charles Arnt *(McNeary)*, Elisha Cook *(Waiter)*, Alan Rhoin *(Horseface)*, Eddie

Gary Cooper and Barbara Stanwyck in *Ball of Fire*.

he British advance in *Five Graves to Cairo*.

Foster *(Pinstripe)*, Aldrich Bowker *(Justice of the Peace)*, Addison Richards *(District Attorney)*, Pat West *(Bum)*, Kenneth Howell *(College Boy)*, Tommy Ryan *(Newsboy)*, Tim Ryan *(Motorcycle Cop)*, Will Lee *(Benny the Creep)*, Gene Krupa and His Orchestra, Otto Hoffman *(Stage Doorman)*, Pat Flaherty and George Sherwood *(Deputies)*, Geraldine Fissette *(Hula Dancer)*. *Prod:* Samuel Goldwyn for Goldwyn Productions. *Rel:* RKO. 111m.

THE MAJOR AND THE MINOR (1942). To save the train fare, the heroine disguises herself as a twelve-year old. Complications arise when she meets an officer from a boy's military school who is engaged to the commandant's daughter. *Dir:* Billy Wilder. *Sc:* Charles Brackett, Billy Wilder (suggested by the play "Connie Goes Home" by Edward Childs Carpenter and the story "Sunny Goes Home" by Fannie Kilbourne). *Ph:* Leo Tover. *Ed:* Doane Harrison. *Art dir:* Hans Dreier, Roland Anderson. *Mus:* Robert Emmett Dolan. *Cos:* Edith Head. *Sound:* Harold Lewis, Don Johnson. *Asst dir:* C.C. Coleman Jr. *With* Ginger Rogers *(Susan Applegate)*, Ray Milland *(Major Kirby)*, Rita Johnson *(Pamela Hill)*, Robert Benchley *(Mr. Osborne)*, Diana Lynn *(Lucy Hill)*, Edward Fielding *(Colonel Hill)*, Frankie Thomas *(Cadet Osborne)*, Raymond Roe *(Cadet Wigton)*, Charles Smith *(Cadet Korner)*, Larry Nunn *(Cadet Babcock)*, Billy Dawson *(Cadet Miller)*, Lela Rogers *(Mrs. Applegate)*, Aldrich Bowker *(Rev. Doyle)*, Boyd Irwin *(Major Griscom)*, Byron Shores *(Capt. Durand)*, Richard Fiske *(Will Duffy)*, Norma Varden *(Mrs. Osborne)*, Gretl Dupont *(Mrs. Shackleford)*, and Stanley Desmond, Billy Ray, Marie Blake, Mary Field. *Prod:* Arthur Hornblow Jr. for Paramount. 100m.

The Major and the Minor was Wilder's first self-directed American film. Unless otherwise noted, all subsequent films are directed by Wilder.

FIVE GRAVES TO CAIRO (1943). The lone survivor of a British tank crew takes refuge in a desert hotel where he assumes the identity of a dead servant, who had been, he soon discovers, a German spy. Aided somewhat reluctantly by the hotel's owner and a servant girl, he discovers the whereabouts of Field-Marshal Rommel's secret caches of military supplies. *Sc:* Charles Brackett, Billy Wilder (a play by Lajos Biro). *Ph:* John F. Seitz. *Ed:* Doane Harrison. *Art dir:* Hans Dreier, Ernst Fegté. *Set dec:* Bertram Granger. *Mus:* Miklos Rozsa. *Cos:* Edith Head. *Sound:* Ferol Redd, Philip Wisdom. *Asst dir:* C.C. Coleman Jr. *With* Franchot Tone *(Bramble)*, Anne Baxter *(Mouche)*, Akim Tamiroff *(Farid)*, Fortunio Bonanova *(General Sebastiano)*, Peter Van Eyck *(Lt. Schwegler)*, Erich von Stroheim *(Field-Marshal Erwin Rommel)*, Konstantin Shayne *(Major von Buelow)*, Fred Nurney *(Major Lamprecht)*, Miles Mander *(Colonel Fitzhume)*, Ian Keith *(Captain St. Bride)*. *Prod:* Charles Brackett for Paramount. 96m.

DOUBLE INDEMNITY (1944). A scheming woman draws an insurance salesman into a plot to murder her husband. The insurance company's chief investigator tries to prove homicide, but the tangled relationship of the murderers brings about their downfall. *Sc:* Billy Wilder, Raymond Chandler (the story by James M. Cain). *Ph:* John F. Seitz. *Ed:* Doane Harrison. *Art dir:* Hans Dreier, Hal Pereira. *Set dec:* Bertram Granger. *Mus:* Miklos Rozsa; and Symphony in D minor by César Franck. *Sound:* Stanley Cooley. *Asst dir:* C.C. Coleman Jr. *With* Fred MacMurray *(Walter Neff),* Barbara Stanwyck *(Phyllis Dietrichson),* Edward G. Robinson *(Barton Keyes),* Porter Hall *(Mr. Jackson),* Jean Heather *(Lola Dietrichson),* Tom Powers *(Mr. Dietrichson),* Byron Barr *(Nino Zachette),* Richard Gaines *(Mr. Norton),* Fortunio Bonanova *(Sam Gorlopis),* John Philliber *(Joe Pete),* and Betty Farrington. *Prod:* Joseph Sistrom for Paramount. 107m.

Wilder and Ray Milland on the set of *The Lost Weekend.*

THE LOST WEEKEND (1945). An alcoholic writer, prompted by his fiancée and his brother, struggles to give up drinking. But his weakness drives him into a hell of petty thievery, delirium tremens, and the horrors of an alcoholic ward. *Sc:* Charles Brackett, Billy Wilder (the novel by Charles Jackson). *Ph:* John F. Seitz. *Sp eff:* Farciot Edouart, Gordon Jennings. *Ed:* Doane Harrison. *Art dir:* Hans Dreier, Earl Hedrick. *Set dec:* Bertram Granger. *Mus:* Miklos Rozsa; and overture, opening aria, and "Libiamo" from "La Traviata" by Verdi. *Mus dir:* Victor Young. *Sound:* Stanley Cooley. *Medical advisor:* Dr. George N. Thompson. *Asst dir:* C.C. Coleman Jr. *With* Ray Milland *(Don Birnam),* Jane Wyman *(Helen St. James),* Howard da Silva *(Nat),* Philip Terry *(Wick Birnam),* Doris Dowling *(Gloria),* Frank Faylen *(Bim),* Mary Young *(Mrs. Deveridge),* Lillian Fontaine *(Mrs. St. James),* Anita Bolster *(Mrs. Foley),* Lewis L. Russell *(Charles St. James),* Helen Dickson *(Mrs. Frink),* David Clyde *(Dave),* Eddie Laughton *(Mr. Brophy),* and Frank Orth, Clarence Muse. *Prod:* Charles Brackett for Paramount. 99m.

THE EMPEROR WALTZ (1948). At the turn of the century, an itinerant American phonograph salesman becomes involved in the politics of the Austro-Hungarian Empire when he falls for a beautiful countess. *Sc:* Charles Brackett, Billy Wilder. *Ph:* George Barnes (Technicolor). *Sp eff:* Farciot Edouart, Gordon Jennings. *Ed:* Doane Harrison. *Art dir:* Hans Dreier, Franz Bachelin. *Set dec:* Sam Comer, Paul Huldschinsky. *Mus:* Victor Young. *Songs:* "The Emperor Waltz," melody based on music by Johann Strauss, lyrics by Johnny Burke; "Friendly Mountains," melody based on Swiss airs, lyrics by Johnny Burke; "Get Yourself a Phonograph" by James Van Heusen and Johnny Burke; "A Kiss in Your Eyes" by Richard Heuberger and Johnny Burke; "I Kiss Your Hand, Madame" by Ralph Erwin and Fritz Rottier; "The Whistler and His Dog" by Arthur Pryor. *Vocal arrangements:* Joseph J. Lilley. *Cos:* Edith Head, Gile Steele. *Chor:* Billy Daniels. *Sound:* Stanley Cooley, John Cope. *Asst dir:* C.C. Coleman Jr. *Prod mgr:* Hugh Brown. *With* Bing Crosby *(Virgil Smith),* Joan Fontaine *(Johanna),* Roland Culver *(Baron Holenia),* Lucile Watson *(Princess Bitotska),* Richard Haydn *(Emperor Franz Josef),* Harold Vermilyea *(The Chancellor),* Sig Ruman *(Dr. Semmelgries),* Bert Prival *(Chauffeur),* Alma Macrorie *(Proprietress of Tyrolean Inn),* Roberta Jonay *(Anita),* John Goldsworthy *(Obersthofmeister),* Gerald Mohr *(Marques Alonso),* Harry

Allen *(Gamekeeper)*, Paul De Corday *(Prince Istvan)*, and Julia Dean. *Prod:* Charles Brackett for Paramount. 106m.

A FOREIGN AFFAIR (1948). In postwar Berlin, a prudish Congresswoman crusades to improve G.I. morale and morals by discouraging fraternisation. However, her own morale and morals begin to crumble when she falls for an opportunistic soldier who deals in the black market and keeps a German cabaret singer for a mistress. *Sc:* Charles Brackett, Billy Wilder, Richard L. Breen (an original story by David Shaw). *Adapt:* Robert Harari. *Ph:* Charles B. Lang Jr. *Sp eff:* Farciot Edouart, Dewey Wrigley, Gordon Jennings. *Ed:* Doane Harrison. *Art dir:* Hans Dreier, Walter Tyler. *Set dec:* Sam Comer, Ross Dowd. *Mus:* Frederick Hollander. *Songs:* "Black Market," "Illusions," "The Ruins of Berlin," "Iowa Corn Song," "Meadowland," by Frederick Hollander. *Cos:* Edith Head. *Sound:* Hugo Grenzbach, Walter Oberst. *Asst dir:* C.C. Coleman Jr. *Prod mgr:* Hugh Brown. *With* Jean Arthur *(Phoebe Frost)*, Marlene Dietrich *(Erika von Schluetow)*, John Lund *(Capt. John Pringle)*, Millard Mitchell *(Col. Rufus J. Plummer)*, Bill Murphy *(Joe)*, Stanley Prager *(Mike)*, Peter von Zernech *(Hans Otto Birgel)*, Raymond Bond *(Pennecott)*, Boyd Davis *(Griffen)*, Robert Malcolm *(Krauss)*, Charles Meredith *(Yandell)*, Michael Raffeto *(Salvatore)*, James Larmore *(Lt. Hornby)*, Damian O'Flynn *(Lt.-Colonel)*, Frank Fenton *(Major)*, William Neff *(Lt. Lee Thompson)*, Harland Tucker *(Gen. McAndrew)*, George Carleton *(Gen. Finney)*, Gordon Jones and Freddie Steel *(M.P.s)*. *Prod:* Charles Brackett for Paramount. 116m.

A SONG IS BORN (1948). A musical remake of *Ball of Fire* (1941), featuring Danny Kaye as a musicologist researching jazz. *Dir:* Howard Hawks. *Sc:* Harry Tugend (a story by Wilder and Thomas Monroe, and the screenplay by Charles Brackett and Billy Wilder). *Ph:* Gregg Toland (Technicolor). *Mus:* Emil Newman, Hugo Friedhofer. *With* Danny Kaye *(Prof. Hobart Frisbee)*, Virginia Mayo *(Honey Swanson)*, Benny Goodman

(Prof. Magenbruch), Hugh Herbert *(Prof. Twingle)*, Steve Cochran *(Tony Crow)*, J. Edward Bromberg *(Dr. Elfini)*, Felix Bressart *(Prof. Gerkikoff)*, Ludwig Stossel *(Prof. Traumer)*, O. Z. Whitehead *(Prof. Oddly)*, Esther Dale *(Miss Bragg)*, Mary Field *(Miss Totten)*, Howland Chamberlin *(Mr. Setter)*, and Tommy Dorsey, Louis Armstrong, Lionel Hampton, Charlie Barnet, Mel Powell, Buck and Bubbles, The Page Cavanaugh Trio, The Golden Gate Quartet, Russo and the Samba Kings. *Prod:* Samuel Goldwyn. *Rel:* RKO Radio, 113m.

SUNSET BOULEVARD (1950). On the run from creditors, a scriptwriter takes refuge on the decaying estate of an ageing and grandly psychotic silent film star. By mutual consent, she "keeps" him, but eventually murders him when he tries to return to the "real" world. The story is told in flashback, from the point of view of the dead writer. *Sc:* Charles Brackett, Billy Wilder, D. M. Marshman Jr. *Ph:* John F. Seitz. *Sp eff:* Farciot Edouart, Gordon Jennings. *Ed:* Doane Harrison, Arthur Schmidt. *Art dir:* Hans Dreier, John Meehan. *Set dec:* Sam Comer, Ray Moyer. *Mus:* Franz Waxman; and "The Dance of the Seven Veils" by Richard Strauss. *Song:* "The Paramount-Don't-Want-Me-Blues" by Jay Livingston and Ray Evans. *Sound:* Harry Lindgren, John Cope. *Asst dir:* C. C. Coleman Jr. *With* Gloria Swanson *(Norma Desmond)*, William Holden *(Joe Gillis)*, Erich von Stroheim *(Max von Mayerling)*, Nancy Olson *(Betty Schaefer)*, Fred Clark *(Sheldrake)*, Jack Webb *(Artie Green)*, Lloyd Gough *(Morion)*, Cecil B. DeMille, Hedda Hopper, Buster Keaton, H. B. Warner, Ray Evans, Jay Livingston, and Anna Q. Nilsson *(Themselves)*, Franklyn Farnum *(Undertaker)*, Larry Blake *(First Finance Man)*, Charles Dayton *(Second Finance Man)*, and E. Mason Hopper, Virginia Randolph, Gertrude Astor, Eva Novak, Creighton Hale, Ralph Montgomery. *Prod:* Charles Brackett for Paramount. 111m.

ACE IN THE HOLE [THE BIG CARNIVAL] (1951). A down-and-out newspaperman sees his chance to get back into big time reporting when a man is trapped by a cave-in. By prolonging rescue operations, in order to build up the story, the reporter is responsible for the death of the cave-in victim. *Sc:* Billy Wilder, Lesser Samuels, Walter Newman. *Ph:* Charles B. Lang Jr. *Ed:* Doane Harrison, Arthur Schmidt. *Art dir:* Hal Pereira, Earl Hedrick. *Mus:* Hugo Friedhofer. *Song:* "We're Coming, Leo" by Ray Evans and Jay Livingston. *Professional Advisors (Journalists):* Agnes Underwood, Harold Hubbard, Wayne Scott, Dan Burroughs, Will Harrison. *Sound:* Harold Lewis, John Cope. *Asst dir:* C. C. Coleman Jr. *Assoc prod:* William Schorr. *With* Kirk Douglas *(Charles Tatum)*, Jan Sterling *(Lorraine)*, Bob Arthur *(Herbie Cook)*, Porter Hall *(Jacob Q. Boot)*, Frank Cady *(Mr. Federber)*, Richard Benedict *(Leo Minosa)*, Ray Teal *(Sheriff)*, Lewis Martin *(McCardle)*, John Berkes *(Papa Minosa)*, Frances Dominguez *(Mama Minosa)*, Gene Evans *(Deputy Sheriff)*, Frank Jaquet *(Smollett)*, Harry Harvey *(Dr. Hilton)*, Bob Bumpus *(Radio Announcer)*, Geraldine Hall *(Mrs. Federber)*, Richard Gaines *(Nagel)*. *Prod:* Billy Wilder for Paramount. 111m.

STALAG 17 (1953). During World War Two, an opportunistic American POW is suspected of being a collaborator by his prison mates. In the end he uncovers the real collaborator and aids in the escape of a prisoner wanted by the Gestapo. *Sc:* Billy Wilder, Edwin Blum (the play by Donald Bevan and Edmund Trzcinski). *Ph:* Ernest Laszlo. *Sp eff:* Gordon Jennings. *Ed:* Doane Harrison, George Tomasini. *Art dir:* Hal Pereira, Franz Bachelin. *Mus:* Franz Waxman. *Sound:* Harold Lewis, Gene Garvin. *Asst dir:* C. C. Coleman Jr. *Assoc prod:* William Schorr. *With* William Holden *(Sefton)*, Don Taylor *(Dunbar)*, Robert Strauss *(Stosh)*, Harvey Lembeck *(Harry)*, Neville Brand *(Duke)*, Richard Erdman *(Hoffy)*, Otto Preminger *(Oberst von Scherbach)*, Peter Graves *(Price)*, Gil Stratton Jr. *(Cookie)*, Jay Lawrence *(Bagradian)*, Sig Ruman *(Schulz)*, Michael Moore *(Manfredi)*, Peter Baldwin *(Johnson)*, Robinson Stone *(Joey)*, Robert Shawley *(Blondie)*, William Pierson *(Marko)*, Edmund Trzcinski *(Triz)*, and Erwin Kalser, Herbert Street, Rod-

Audrey Hepburn and William Holden in *Sabrina*.

ric Beckham, Jerry Gerber, William Mulcany, Russell Grower, Donald Cameron, James Dabney Jr., Ralph Gaston. *Prod:* Billy Wilder for Paramount. 121m.

SABRINA (G.B.: SABRINA FAIR) (1954). A chauffeur's daughter falls in love with a wealthy playboy but she ends up with the playboy's conservative older brother. *Sc:* Billy Wilder, Samuel Taylor, Ernest Lehman, (the play "Sabrina Fair" by Samuel Taylor). *Ph:* Charles Lang Jr. *Ed:* Doane Harrison, Arthur Schmidt. *Art dir:* Hal Pereira, Walter Tyler. *Set dec:* Sam Comer, Ray Moyer. *Mus:* Frederick Hollander. *Songs:* "Sabrina" by William Stone, "Isn't It Romantic" by Richard Rogers and Lorenz Hart. *Sound:* Harold Lewis, John Cope. *Asst dir:* C. C. Coleman Jr. *With* Humphrey Bogart *(Linus Larrabee)*, Audrey Hepburn *(Sabrina Fairchild)*, William Holden *(David Larrabee)*, John Williams *(Thomas Fairchild)*, Walter Hampden *(Oliver Larrabee)*, Martha Hyer *(Elizabeth Tyson)*, Joan Vohs *(Gretchen van Horn)*, Marcel Dalio *(Baron)*, Marcel Hillaire *(The Professor)*, Nella Walker *(Maude Larrabee)*, Francis X. Bushman *(Mr. Ty-*

Robert Strauss, Tom Ewell, and Marilyn Monroe in *The Seven Year Itch.*

son), Ellen Corby *(Miss McCardle),* and Rand Harper. *Prod:* Billy Wilder for Paramount. 114m.

THE SEVEN YEAR ITCH (1955). After seven years of marriage, a middle-aged husband is left on his own and becomes imaginatively, if not actually, entangled with the kooky blonde who lives upstairs. *Sc:* Billy Wilder, George Axelrod (the play by George Axelrod). *Ph:* Milton Krasner (CinemaScope, DeLuxe colour). *Spec eff:* Ray Kellogg. *Ed:* Hugh S. Fowler. *Art dir:* Lyle Wheeler, George W. Davis. *Set dec:* Walter M. Scott, Stuart A. Reiss. *Mus:* Alfred Newman; and Piano Concerto No. 2 by Rachmaninoff. *Titles:* Saul Bass. *Sound:* E. Clayton Ward, Harry M. Leonard. *Asst dir:* Joseph E. Rickards. *Assoc prod:* Doane Harrison. *Wtih* Marilyn Monroe *(The Girl),* Tom Ewell *(Richard Sherman),* Evelyn Keyes *(Helen Sherman),* Sonny Tufts *(Tom McKenzie),* Robert Strauss *(Kruhulik),* Oscar Homolka *(Dr. Brubaker),* Roxanne *(Elaine),* Donald MacBride *(Mr. Brady),* Carolyn Jones *(Miss Finch),* Doro Merande *(Waitress),* Butch Bernard *(Ricky),* Dorothy Ford *(Girl). Prod:* Charles K. Feldman, Billy Wilder for 20th Century-Fox. 105m.

THE SPIRIT OF ST. LOUIS (1957). A period-piece account of Charles Lindbergh's solo flight across the Atlantic, with flashbacks to his earlier life as a barnstormer and mail pilot. *Sc:* Billy Wilder, Wendell Mayes (the book by Charles A. Lindbergh). *Adapt:* Charles Lederer. *Ph:* Robert Burks, J. Peverell Marley (CinemaScope, WarnerColor). *Tech ph advisor:* Ted McCord. *Aerial ph:* Thomas Tutwiler. *Aerial supervisor:* Paul Mantz. *Sp eff:* H. F. Koenenkamp, Louis Lichtenfield. *Ed:* Arthur P. Schmidt. *Art dir:* Art Loel, William L. Kuehl. *Mus:* Franz Waxman. *Sound:* M. A. Merrick. *Tech advisors:* Maj.-Gen. Victor Bertrandias, USAF (Ret.), Harlan A. Gurney. *Asst dir:* Charles C. Coleman Jr., Don Page. *Assoc prod:* Doane Harrison. *With* James Stewart *(Charles A. Lindbergh),* Murray Hamilton *(Bob Gurney),* Patricia Smith *(Mirror Girl),* Bartlett Robinson *(B. F. Mahoney),* Marc Connelly *(Father Hussman),* Arthur Space *(Donald Hall),* Charles Watts *(O. W. Schultz),* and Robert Cornthwaite, David Orrick, Robert Burton, James Robertson Jr., Maurice Manson, James O'Rear, Carleton Young, Harlan Warde, Dabs Greer, Paul Birch, David McMahon, Herb Lytton. *Prod:* Leland Hayward for Warner Bros. 135m.

LOVE IN THE AFTERNOON (1957). In Paris, a young girl falls in love with an ageing American playboy. While the young lady seeks his love, her father, a private detective, seeks to discover the identity of the playboy's latest conquest—none other than his own beloved daughter. *Sc:* Billy Wilder, I. A. L. Diamond (the novel "Ariane" by Claude Arnet). *Ph:* William Mellor. *Ed:* Leonid Azar. *Art dir:* Alexander Trauner. *Mus:* Franz Waxman. *Songs:* "Fascination" by F. D. Marchetti and Maurice de Feraudy; "L'Ames des Poètes" by Charles Trent; "C'est Si Bon" by Henri Betti and André Hornez; "Love in the Afternoon," "Ariane," "Hot Paprika" by Matty Malneck. *Sound:* Del Harris, Jo De Bretagne. *Asst dir:* Paul Feyder. *Assoc prod:* William Schorr, Doane Harrison. *With* Gary Cooper *(Frank Flannagan),* Audrey Hepburn *(Ariane Chevasse),* Maurice Chevalier *(Claude Chevasse),* Van Doude *(Michel),* John McGiver *(Monsieur X),* Lise Bourdin *(Madame X),* Bonifas *(Commissioner of Police),* Audrey Wilder *(Brunette),* Gyula Kokas, Michel Kokas, George Cocos and Victor Gazzoli *(Four Gypsies),* Olga Valéry *(Lady with dog),* Leila Croft and Valerie Croft *(Swedish Twins),* Charles Bouillard *(Valet at Ritz),* Minerva

Pious *(Maid at Ritz)*, Filo *(Flannagan's Chauffeur)*, André Priez and Gaidon *(Porters at Ritz)*, Gregory Gromoff *(Doorman at Ritz)*, Janine Dard and Claude Ariel *(Existentialists)*, François Moustache *(Butcher)*, Gloria France *(Client at Butcher's)*, Jean Sylvain *(Baker)*, Annie Roudier, Jeanne Charblay and Odette Charblay *(Clients at Baker's)*, Gilbert Constant and Monique Saintey *(Lovers on Left Bank)*, Jacques Préboist and Anne Laurent *(Lovers near Seine)*, Jacques Ary and Simone Vanlancker *(Lovers on Right Bank)*, Richard Flagy *(Husband)*, Jeanne Papir *(Wife)*, Marcelle Broc *(First Rich Woman)*, Marcelle Praince *(Second Rich Woman)*, Guy Delorme *(Gigolo)*, Olivia Chevalier *(Little Girl in Gardens)*, Solon Smith *(Little Boy in Gardens)*, Eve Marley and Jean Rieubon *(Tandemists)*, Christian Lude, Charles Lemontier and Emilye Mylos *(Generals)*, Alexander Trauner *(Artist)*, Betty Schneider, Georges Perrault, Vera Boccadoro and Marc Aurian *(Couples under Water Wagon)*, Bernard Musson *(Undertaker)*, Michèle Selignac *(Widow)*. *Prod:* Billy Wilder for Allied Artists. 125m.

SILK STOCKINGS (1957). Film version of the stage musical based on *Ninotchka* (1939). *Dir:* Rouben Mamoulian: *Sc:* Leonard Gershe, Leonard Spigelgass (the play by George S. Kaufman, Leueen McGrath and Abe Burrows based on the screenplay by Charles Brackett, Billy Wilder and Walter Reisch and the story by Melchior Langyel. *Ph:* Robert Bronner (CinemaScope, Met-rocolor). *Art dir:* William A. Horning, Randall Deull. *Set dec:* Edwin B. Willis, Hugh Hunt. *Ed:* Harold F. Kress. *Cos:* Helen Rose. *Mus and lyrics:* Cole Porter. *Mus dir:* Andre Previn. *Choreo:* Hermes Pan, Eugene Loring. *With* Fred Astaire *(Steve Canfield)*, Cyd Charisse *(Ninotchka)*, Janis Paige *(Peggy Dainton)*, Peter Lorre *(Brankov)*, Jules Munshin *(Babinski)*, Joseph Buloff *(Ivanov)*, George Tobias *(Commissar)*, Wim Sonneveld *(Peter Ilyitch Boroff)*, Belita *(Dancer)*, Ivan Triesault *(Russian Embassy Official)*, Betty Utti, Tybee Afra and Barrie Chase *(Dancers)*. *Prod:* Arthur Freed for M.G.M. 117m.

WITNESS FOR THE PROSECUTION (1958). An eccentric barrister defends a seemingly sincere young man on trial for murder. The trial is all the more intriguing and complicated due to the fact that the prosecution's chief witness is the young man's wife. *Sc:* Billy Wilder, Harry Kurnitz (the story and play by Agatha Christie). *Adapt:* Larry Marcus. *Ph:* Russell Harlan. *Ed:* Daniel Mandell. *Art dir:* Alexander Trauner, Howard Bristol. *Mus:* Matty Malneck. *Song:* "I Never Go There Anymore" by Ralph Arthur Roberts and Jack Brooks. *Sound:* Fred Lau. *Asst dir:* Emmett Emerson. *With* Tyrone Power *(Leonard Vole)*, Marlene Dietrich *(Christine Vole)*, Charles Laughton *(Sir Wilfrid Robarts)*, Elsa Lanchester *(Miss Plimsoll)*, John Williams *(Brogan-Moore)*, Henry Daniell *(Mayhew)*, Ian Wolfe *(Carter)*, Una O'Connor *(Janet McKenzie)*, Torin Thatcher *(Mr. Meyers)*,

Tyrone Power (in the dock) and Marlene Dietrich (right) in *Witness for the Prosecution.*

Francis Compton (*Judge*), Norma Varden(*Mrs. French*), Philip Tonge(*Inspector Hearne*), Ruth Lee (*Diana*), Molly Roden (*Miss McHugh*), Ottola Nesmith (*Miss Johnson*), Marjorie Eaton (*Miss O'Brien*). *Prod:* Arthur Hornblow Jr. for Theme Pictures (Edward Small). *Rel:* United Artists. 116m.

SOME LIKE IT HOT (1959). After witnessing the St. Valentine's Day Massacre, two male musicians are forced to flee Chicago as members of an "all girl" orchestra. At film's end they are still on the run, but they are joined in their flight by a blonde torch singer and an eccentric playboy. *Sc:* Billy Wilder, I. A. L. Diamond (a story by R. Thoeren and M. Logan). *Ph:* Charles Lang Jr. *Ed:* Arthur Schmidt. *Art dir:* Ted Haworth, Edward G. Boyle. *Mus:* Adolph Deutsch. *Songs:* "Running Wild" by A. H. Gibbs and Leo Wood; "I Want to be Loved by You" by Herbert Stothart and Bert Kalmar; "I'm Through with Love" by Matty Malneck and Gus Kahn. *Cos:* Orry Kelly. *Sound:* Fred Lau. *Asst dir:* Sam Nelson. *Assoc prod:* Doane Harrison, I. A. L. Diamond. *With* Marilyn Monroe(*Sugar Kane*), Tony Curtis (*Joe*), Jack Lemmon (*Jerry*), George Raft(*Spats Columbo*), Pat O'Brien (*Mulligan*), Joe E. Brown (*Osgood Fielding*), Nehemiah Persoff(*Bonaparte*), Joan Shawlee (*Sue*), Billy Gray (*Poliakoff*), George E. Stone(*Toothpick Charlie*), Dave Barry (*Beinstock*), Mike Mazurki and Harry Wilson(*Spats's Henchmen*), Beverly Wills (*Dolores*), Barbara Drew (*Nellie*), Edward G. Robinson Jr.(*Paradise*). *Prod:* Billy Wilder for the Mirisch Company. *Rel:* United Artists. 121m.

THE APARTMENT (1960). To get ahead in the company, an insurance clerk lets his executive betters use his apartment for extra-marital affairs. His illusions are shattered when he finds out that the girl he secretly loves is the mistress of the Director of Personnel. *Sc:* Billy Wilder, I. A. L. Diamond. *Ph:* Joseph La Shelle (Panavision). *Sp eff:* Milton Rice. *Ed:* Daniel Mandell. *Art dir:* Alexander Trauner, Edward G. Boyle. *Sound:* Fred Lau. *Asst dir:* Hal Polaire. *Assoc prod:* Doane Harrison, I. A. L. Diamond. *With* Jack Lemmon (*C. C. Baxter*), Shirley MacLaine (*Fran Kubelik*), Fred MacMurray (*J. D. Sheldrake*), Ray Walston (*Dobisch*), David Lewis (*Kirkeby*), Jack Kruschen(*Dr. Dreyfuss*), Joan Shawlee (*Sylvia*), Edie Adams (*Miss Olsen*), Hope Holiday (*Margie MacDougall*), Johnny Seven (*Karl Matuschka*), Naomi Stevens (*Mrs. Dreyfuss*), Frances Weintraub Lax (*Mrs. Lieberman*), Joyce Jameson (*The Blonde*), Willard Waterman (*Vanderhof*), David White (*Eichelberger*), Benny Burt (*Bartender*), Hal Smith (*The Santa Claus*). *Prod:* Billy Wilder for the Mirisch Company. *Rel:* United Artists 125m. Screenplays of *The Apartment* and *The Fortune Cookie* were published by Praeger (New York) in 1971.

ONE, TWO, THREE (1961). A short-tempered executive's plans to conquer Russia for Coca-Cola are complicated when his boss's daughter, in Berlin on a visit, promptly marries a militant young Communist from the Eastern sector. *Sc:* Billy Wilder, I. A. L. Diamond (a play by Ferenc Molnar). *Ph:* Daniel Fapp (Panavision). *Sp eff:* Milton Rice. *Art dir:* Alexander Trauner. *Mus:* Andre Previn. *Sound:* Basil Fenton-Smith. *Asst dir:* Tom Pevsner. *Assoc prod:* I. A. L. Diamond, Doane Harrison. *With* James Cagney (*C. R. MacNamara*), Horst Buchholz (*Otto Ludwig Piffl*), Pamela Tiffin (*Scarlett Hazeltine*), Arlene Francis (*Mrs. MacNamara*), Lilo Pulver (*Ingeborg*), Howard St. John (*Hazeltine*), Hanns Lothar (*Schlemmer*), Leon Askin (*Peripetchikoff*), Peter Cappell (*Mishkin*), Ralf Wolther (*Borodenko*), Karl Lieffen (*Fritz*), Henning Schluter (*Dr. Bauer*), Herbert von Meyerinck (*Count von Droste-Schattenburg*), Lois Bolton (*Mrs. Hazeltine*), Tile Kiwe (*Newspaperman*), Karl Ludwig Lindt(*Zeidlitz*), Red Buttons(*M. P. Sergeant*), John Allen (*Tommy MacNamara*), Christine Allen (*Cindy MacNamara*), Rose Renee Roth (*Bertha*), Ivan Arnold (*M. P. Corporal*), Helmud Schmidt (*East German Police Corporal*), Otto Friebel (*East German Interrogator*), Werner Buttler (*East German Police Sergeant*), Klaus Becker and Siegfried Dornbusch (*Policemen*), Paul Bos (*Krause*), Max Buschbaum (*Tailor*), Jaspar von Oertzen (*Haberdasher*), Inga de

Toro *(Stewardess)*, Jacques Chevalier *(Pierre)*, Werner Hassenland *(Shoeman)*, and Abi Von Hasse. *Prod:* Billy Wilder for the Mirisch Company. *Rel:* United Artists. 115m.

IRMA LA DOUCE (1963). When an idealistic young ex-policeman turned pimp falls in love with his girl, he impersonates an eccentric and wealthy Englishman, thus to monopolise her time and to keep her "faithful" to him. His scheme backfires, however, when he becomes his own worst rival—and only a miracle can save the day. *Sc:* Billy Wilder, I. A. L. Diamond (the play by Alexandre Breffort). *Ph:* Joseph LaShelle (Panavision, Technicolor). *Sp eff:* Milton Rice. *Ed:* Daniel Mandell. *Art dir:* Alexander Trauner. *Set dec:* Edward G. Boyle, Maurice Barnathan. *Mus:* Andre Previn; adapted from the score for the original stage musical by Marguerite Monnot. *Cos:* Orry Kelly. *Sound:* Robert Martin. *Tech adv:* Christian Ferry, Maurice Barnathan. *Asst dir:* Hal Polaire. *Assoc prod:* I. A. L. Diamond, Doane Harrison. *With* Jack Lemmon *(Nestor)*, Shirley MacLaine *(Irma La Douce)*, Lou Jacobi *(Moustache)*, Bruce Yarnell *(Hippolyte)*, Herschel Bernardi *(Lefevre)*, Hope Holiday *(Lolita)*, Joan Shawlee *(Amazon Annie)*, Grace Lee Whitney *(Kiki the Cossack)*, Tura Santana *(Suzette Wong)*, Harriet Young *(Mimi the Maumau)*, Paul Dubov *(André)*, Howard McNear *(Concierge)*, Cliff Osmond *(Police Sergeant)*, Diki Lerner *(Jojo)*, Herb Jones *(Casablanca Charlie)*, Ruth and Jane Earl *(Zebra Twins)*, Lou Krugman *(First Customer)*, John Alvin *(Second Customer)*, James Brown *(Customer from Texas)*, Bill Bixby *(Tattooed Sailor)*, Susan Woods *(Poule with Balcony)*, Sheryl Deauville *(Carmen)*, Billy Beck *(Officer Dupont)*, Jack Sahakian *(Jack)*, Don Diamond *(Man with Samples)*, Edgar Barrier *(General Lafayette)*, Richard Peel *(Englishman)*, Joe Palma *(Prison Guard)*. *Prod:* Billy Wilder for the Mirisch Company. *Rel:* United Artists. 147m.

KISS ME, STUPID (1964). A pair of amateur songwriters scheme to sell their stuff to "Dino" when the famous entertainer passes through their out-of-the-way Nevada town. Complications involve Dino's sexual appetites, the tunesmith's wife, his mother in law, and a local party girl. *Sc:* Billy Wilder, I.A.L. Diamond, (suggested by the play "L'Ora della Fantasia" by Anna Bonacci). *Ph:* Daniel Mandell. *Art dir:* ·Alexander Trauner, Robert Luthardt. *Set dec:* Edward G. Boyle. *Mus:* Andre Previn. *Songs:* "Sophia," "I'm a Poached Egg," "All the Livelong Day" by George and Ira Gershwin. *Choreo:* Wally Green. *Sound:* Robert Martin. *Asst dir:* C. C. Coleman Jr. *Assoc prod:* Doane Harrison, I.A.L. Diamond. *With* Dean Martin *(Dino)*, Kim Novak *(Polly the Pistol)*, Ray Walston *(Orville J. Spooner)*, Felicia Farr *(Zelda Spooner)*, Cliff Osmond *(Barney Millsap)*, Barbara Pepper *(Big Bertha)*, Doro Merande *(Mrs. Pettibone)*, Howard McNear *(Mr. Pettibone)*, Henry Gibson *(Smith)*, Alan Dexter *(Wesson)*, Tommy Nolan *(Johnnie Mulligan)*, Alice Pierce *(Mrs. Mulligan)*, John Fiedler *(Rev. Carruthers)*, Arlen Stuart *(Rosalie Schultz)*, Cliff Norton *(Mack Gray)*, James Ward *(Milkman)*, Mel Blanc *(Dr. Sheldrake)*, Bobo Lewis *(Waitress)*, Bern Hoffman *(Bartender)*, Susan Weddell and Eileen O'Neill *(Showgirls)*, Gene Darfler *(Nevada State Trooper)*, Henry Beckman *(Truck Driver)*, and Laurie Fontaine, Mary Jane Saunders and Kathy Garber. *Prod:* Billy Wilder for the Mirisch Company. 124m.

THE FORTUNE COOKIE (G. B.: MEET WHIPLASH WILLIE) (1966). Injured during a football game, a television cameraman is persuaded by his shyster-lawyer brother-in-law to fake paralysis and sue the National Football League. *Sc:* Billy Wilder, I.A.L. Diamond. *Ph:* Joseph LaShelle (Panavision). *Sp eff:* Sass Bedig. *Ed:* Daniel Mandell. *Art dir:* Robert Luthardt, Edward G. Boyle. *Mus:* Andre Previn. *Sound:* Robert Martin. *Asst dir:* Jack Reddish. *Assoc prod:* I.A.L. Diamond, Doane Harrison. *With* Jack Lemmon *(Harry Hinkle)*, Walter Matthau *(Willie Gingrich)*, Ron Rich *(Boom-Boom Jackson)*, Cliff Osmond *(Mr. Purkey)*, Judi West *(Sandy Hinkle)*, Laurene Tuttle *(Mother Hinkle)*, Harry Holcombe *(O'Brien)*, Les Tremayne *(Thompson)*, Marge Redmond

(Charlotte Gingrich), Noam Pitlik *(Max)*, Harry Davis *(Dr. Krugman)*, Ann Shoemaker *(Sister Veronica)*, Maryesther Denver *(Ferret-Faced Nurse)*, Lauren Gilbert *(Kincaid)*, Ned Glass *(Doc Schindler)*, Sig Ruman *(Prof. Winterhalter)*, Archie Moore *(Mr. Jackson)*, Howard McNear *(Mr. Cimoli)*, Bill Christopher *(Intern)*, Bartlett Robinson, Robert P. Lieb, Martin Blaine and Ben Wright *(The Specialists)*, Dodie Heath *(Nun)*, Herbie Faye *(Maury)*, Judy Pace *(Elvira)*, Billy Beck *(Locker-room Attendant)*, Helen Kleeb *(Receptionist)*, Lisa Jill *(Ginger)*, John Todd Roberts *(Jeffrey)*, Keith Jackson *(Announcer)*, Herb Ellis *(Television Director)*, Don Reed *(Newscaster)*, Louise Vienna *(Girl in Commercial)*, Bob Dogin *(Man in Bar)*. *Prod:* Billy Wilder for the Mirisch Company. *Rel:* United Artists. 126m.

THE PRIVATE LIFE OF SHERLOCK HOLMES (1970). A case which Holmes does *not* solve, involving a missing husband, the Loch Ness monster, and Holmes's attraction for the distraught "wife." *Sc:* Billy Wilder, I.A.L. Diamond (based on characters created by Sir Arthur Conan Doyle). *Ph:* Christoper Challis (Panavision, DeLuxe Colour). *Ed:* Ernest Walter. *Art dir:* Alexander Trauner, Tony Inglis. *Mus:* Miklos Rosza. *With* Robert Stephens *(Sherlock Holmes)*, Colin Blakely *(Dr. Watson)*, Irene Handl *(Mrs. Hudson)*, Stanley Holloway *(Gravedigger)*, Christoper Lee *(Mycroft Holmes)*, Genevieve Page *(Ilsa von Hoffmanstall, alias "Gabrielle Valadon")*, Clive Revill *(Rogozhin)*, Tamara Toumanova *(Petrova)*, George Benson *(Inspector Lestrade)*, Catherine Lacey *(Old Woman)*, Mollie Maureen *(Queen Victoria)*, and Peter Madden, Robert Cawdron, Michael Elwyn, Michael Balfour, Frank Thornton, James Copeland, Alex McCrindle, Kenneth Benda, Graham Armitage, Eric Francis, John Garrie, Godfrey James, Ina De La Haye, Ismet Hassan, Charlie Young Atom, Teddy Kiss Atom, Willie Shearer, Daphne Riggs, John Gatrell, Martin Carroll, John Scott, Philip Anthony, Philip Ross, and Annette Kerr. *Prod:* Billy Wilder for the Mirisch Company. *Rel:* United Artists. 125m.

AVANTI! (1972) An American executive and a working class British girl arrive simultaneously in an Italian resort town to claim the bodies of his father and her mother—who had died together in an auto wreck. Problems arise when the executive discovers his father's infidelity and escalate when opportunistic peasants kidnap the bodies as security against a damage claim: the car wreck had ruined their grape vines. *Sc:* Billy Wilder, I.A.L. Diamond, (the play by Samuel Taylor). *Ph:* Luigi Kuveiller (DeLuxe Colour). *Ed:* Ralph E. Winters. *Mus:* Carlo Rustichelli. *With* Jack Lemmon *(Wendell Armbruster)*, Juliet Mills *(Pamela Piggot)*, Clive Revill *(Carlo Carlucci)*, Edward Andrews *(J. J. Blodgett)*, Gianfranco Barra *(Bruno)*, Franco Angrisano *(Arnold Trotta)*, Pippo Franco *(Mattarazzo)*, Giselda Castrini *(Anna)*, and Raffaele Mottola, Lino Coletta, Harry Ray, Guidarino Guidi, Giacomo Rizzo, Antonio Faa'di Bruno, Yanti Sommer, Janet Agren, Maria Rosa Sclauzero, Melu'valente and Aldo Rendine. *Prod:* Billy Wilder for the Mirisch Company. *Rel:* United Artists. 144m.

THE FRONT PAGE (1974). A reporter wants to quit newspaper work and settle down to a "normal" life. Meanwhile, Chicago awaits the execution of an anarchist and the editor schemes to keep his star protege on the paper. *Sc:* Billy Wilder, I.A.L. Diamond (from the play by Ben Hecht and Charles MacArthur). *Ph:* Jordan S. Cronenweth (Panavision, Technicolor). *Sp eff:* Nick Carey. *Ed:* Ralph E. Winters. *Art dir:* Henry Bumstead, Henry Larrecy. *Mus:* Billy May. *Song:* "Button Up Your Overcoat" by B. G. DeSylva, Lew Brown and Ray Henderson. *Asst dir:* Howard G. Kazanjian, Charles E. Dismukes and Jack Saunders. *Second unit dir:* Carey Loftin. *Exec prod:* Jennings Lang. *With* Jack Lemmon *(Hildy Johnson)*, Walter Matthau *(Walter Burns)*, Carol Burnett *(Mollie Malloy)*, Allen Garfield *(Kruger)*, David Wayne *(Bensinger)*, Vincent Gardenia *(Sheriff)*, Herbert Edelman *(Schwartz)*, Charles Durning *(Murphy)*, Susan Sarandon *(Peggy Grant)*, Austin Pendleton *(Earl Williams)*, John Furlong

(Duffy), Harold Gould *(Mayor)*, Noam Pitlik *(Wilson)*, Martin Gabel *(Dr. Egglehofer)*, Cliff Osmond *(Jacobi)*, Dick O'Neil *(McHugh)*, Jon Korkes *(Rudy Keppler)*, Lou Frizzell *(Endicott)*, Paul Benedict *(Plunkett)*, Doro Merande *(Jennie)*, Joshua Shelley *(Cab Driver)*, Allen Jenkins *(Telegrapher)*, Biff Elliot *(Police Dispatcher)*, Barbara Davis *(Myrtle)*, Leonard Bremen *(Butch)*. *Prod:* Paul Monash for Universal. 105m.

FEDORA (1978). Described by Seidman as a "Grand Guignol chiller about a legendary movie actress à la Garbo and Dietrich who has an unusual secret for perpetual beauty" (p. 16). *Sc:* Billy Wilder, I.A.L. Diamond (the Thomas Tryon novella published in his "Crowned Heads"). *Ph:* Gerry Fisher (colour). *Ed:* Stefan Arnsten. *Art dir:* Alexander Trauner, Robert André. *Mus:* Miklos Rozsa. *With* William Holden *(Barry Detweiler)*, Marthe Keller *(Fedora/Antonia)*, Jose Ferrer *(Dr. Vando)*, Frances Sternhagen *(Miss Balfour)*, Mario Adorf *(Hotel manager)*, Hans Jaray *(Sobryanski)*, Gottfried John *(Kritos)*, Michael York *(Michael York)*, Henry Fonda *(President of the Academy of Motion Picture Arts and Sciences)*, Panos Papadopulos *(Barkeeper)*, Elma Karlowa *(Maid)*, Christoph Künzer *(Clerk)*, Stephen Collins *(Barry aged 25 years)*, Hildegarde Knef *(Countess/Fedora)*. *Prod:* Billy Wilder, Helmut Jedele for Bavaria Atelier/NG Geria II. 110m.

LEO McCAREY

Moments, Meanings, and McCarey:
Going My Way

It is no slight to Leo McCarey to remark that he remains an enigmatic figure in film history, a man respected by his peers (Renoir, Hawks, Capra and Ford among them), defended on occasion by scholars such as Charles Silver and Robin Wood, but a director generally ignored, even by the ever growing cadre of young (and some now not so young) *auteur* critics.[1] His most revived film is *Duck Soup,* revived for reasons having little to do with McCarey; and his most notorious film is *My Son John,* attacked in print by Robert Warshow and on the screen by Peter Davis (in his anti-fascist documentary, *Hearts and Minds*).[2] Indeed, *Duck Soup* and *My Son John* represent, at least on the surface, such opposing points of view, one anarchistic, the other authoritarian, that McCarey's status as an *auteur* is called into question. Hence, perhaps, the general lack of scholarship: how are we to discover and describe a thread of authorial continuity strong enough to bind such disparate films together into a single career without misrepresenting the films in question?

Some critics, most notably Andrew Sarris and Jeffrey Richards, have answered that question not in terms of specific films but in terms of privileged moments. As Sarris put it: "After enough great moments are assembled . . . a personal style must be assumed even though it is difficult to describe."[3] Sarris is certainly correct in remarking that certain McCarey moments stand out. And he is correct as well to express a measure of scholarly humility—clearly a critic's inability to describe an authorial viewpoint is insufficient proof that such a viewpoint does not exist. Indeed, one might better argue on principle, with George Morris, that " 'great moments' cannot exist in a vacuum."[4] Put another way, it is far more likely the case that the moments that Sarris mentions as outstanding *are* outstanding, not because they transcend or contradict their films, but because they manage to crystallise the themes, feelings, images and issues which lend those films a real sense of import and significance. And we can

lay the "great moments/bad movies" theory to rest by demonstrating
that such is indeed the case.

Consider, for example, the closing scene in *Going My Way*. In visual
terms the sequence is neither self-conscious nor spectacular. McCarey
is clearly content to record rather than to comment, and he employs a
minimal number of shots and set ups. We begin (1) with a two-shot of
Father O'Dowd (Frank McHugh) and Father Fitzgibbon (Barry
Fitzgerald) as they assume their places before the altar of St.
Dominic's church. We cut then to a full shot (2) of the pews and the
people who have gathered to bid farewell to Father O'Malley (Bing
Crosby). We return to the two-shot (3) of the two priests as Father
Fitzgibbon begins to speak of Father O'Malley's contributions to the
parish and its parishioners. Cut next to a two-shot (4) of Genevieve
Linden (Rise Stevens), star of the Metropolitan Opera and a close
friend to Father O'Malley, as she stands with Father Fitzgibbon's
91-year-old Irish mother in the dark courtyard outside the sanctuary.
Father O'Malley enters from screen right and remarks that he has
heard "so much" about Mrs. Fitzgibbon and is pleased to see her. We
then return to a shot of the pews (5), but we focus on three figures in
the foreground; Mr. Haines (Gene Lockhart), the man who holds the
mortgage on the church, his daughter-in-law Carol (Jean Heather),
and his son Ted (James Brown). Resume, then, on a tight medium
shot (waist up) of Father Fitzgibbon (6) as he continues his praise of
Father O'Malley's selflessness ("He was always thinking of others, and
as you know, it can make life very beautiful"). At this point Father
Fitzgibbon is interrupted by "An Irish Lullaby," sung by the St.
Dominic's boys' choir. Cut briefly to the choir (7), seen from Father
Fitzgibbon's point of view, then back to Father Fitzgibbon (8) as he
slowly looks off, screen left. We get a two-shot of Miss Linden and
Mrs. Fitzgibbon (9); a tight medium shot of Father Fitzgibbon (10) as
he turns to face his mother, swallowing almost imperceptively, as if to
stifle a sob; a medium shot of Mrs. Fitzgibbon (11), the camera
tracking left-to-right as she walks, haltingly, her hands shaking,
towards her son; and then a closeup of Father Fitzgibbon (12), the
camera tracking right-to-left as he walks towards his mother, and
stopping as they embrace in a close-up two-shot, his head down upon
her shoulder (as if to hide from the camera).

Clearly, the most single significant concern in this sequence (and
throughout the film) involves the issue of character relationships,
both spatial and emotional. Thus the first shot in the sequence, the
two-shot of Father O'Dowd and Father Fitzgibbon, is expressive of

is first day at St. Dominic's: Barry
tzgerald (right) shows Bing Crosby
e rectory garden in *Going My Way*.

the unity between them. Of course, it is not *a priori* the case that a
two-shot expresses unity, but this shot clearly does, and does so for
echoing an earlier two-shot, before another altar, of Father Fitzgibbon and Father O'Malley. In the earlier shot, however, the unity is
only tenuous, and that sense of tenuousness is expressed by physical
detail. Thus, in the earlier shot, Father O'Malley is *not* wearing his
own regulation priestly garb, as Father O'Dowd does in the later shot
(Father O'Malley's only black suit had been drenched by a passing
street-cleaning truck—shades of Hal Roach—in the opening sequence). Rather, O'Malley wears a black suit coat, belonging to Father
Fitzgibbon, which the Father had given O'Malley in the immediately
preceding scene to cover O'Malley's St. Louis Browns sweat shirt
(although, clearly, it was less the sweat shirt itself than the "see no evil"
monkies emblazoned on the back of it that sparked Father Fitzgibbon's displeasure). Despite the fact, then, that the two men strike a
truce of sorts—Father O'Malley lights two candles and sets them side
by side, thus signifying his desire to work together with Father
Fitzgibbon for the good of St. Dominic's parish—the coat and the

sweat shirt both remain visibly prominent in the shot, and they effectively evidence Father Fitzgibbon's tendency to overvalue surface propriety. Furthermore, after Father O'Malley lights the candles, the ever independent Father Fitzgibbon offers to pay for them himself, although he rather studiously delays pulling his coin purse from his pocket, thus allowing Father O'Malley, in his generosity, to pay for the both of them. And the point, once again, is to emphasise the nature of Father Fitzgibbon's dilemma: he has built St. Dominic's almost singlehandedly in his forty-five year ministry to the parish (hence his sense of independence) but his single-minded sense of purpose and propriety has made it almost impossible for the church to continue as an active and vital force in the community (hence the falling attendance, the falling collections, and hence St. Dominic's financial difficulties).

The two-shot of Father O'Dowd and Father Fitzgibbon in the final sequence evidences, then, the emotional distance that Father Fitzgibbon has travelled. The very fact that Father O'Dowd is in the shot signifies the fact that Father O'Malley is leaving (St. Dominic's is revived, and Father O'Malley has been transfered to another distressed parish) and the fact of Father Fitzgibbon's presence, specifically for the purpose of bidding Father O'Malley a heartfelt farewell, signifies his recognition that men are (and must be) dependent upon one another, particularly in times of trouble, whether that trouble involve parish finances or world-wide hostilities. To think otherwise, to rely solely upon one's self and one's untested and convention-bound sense of the world, is to invite disaster, as Father Fitzgibbon almost demonstrates.

The nature of that disaster is clarfied in shots two, five, and seven of the final sequence; and once again it is a matter of spatial and emotional relationships. Shots two and seven, for example, are relatively deep focus shots of the choir, now led by Tony Scaponi (Stanley Clements). The first time we see the boys it is in a similar deep focus shot, but they are not singing. On the contrary, they have hijacked a poultry truck and are doing their best to abscond with their fine feathered booty. Two of the boys, indeed—Tony and Herman (Alfalfa Switzer)—decide to escape via the churchyard—where they encounter Father Fitzgibbon. And the only possible explanation they can offer for their presence and their cargo is that they have won the bird in a raffle and have come to donate the bird for the rectory table, a prospect which has Father Fitzgibbon rubbing his hands in gleeful anticipation ("That's a fine, fat bird you have there").

From Father Fitzgibbon's point of view, then, Tony is as fine a lad as there is in the parish, the son of "a fine, upstanding Catholic family." Father O'Malley knows differently, however. The first shot of Tony and the boys at work on the turkey cages is taken from Father O'Malley's point of view—so that he clearly knows, as Father Fitzgibbon does not, that Tony (who comes on like a minor league James Cagney) and his gang are "terrorising" the whole neighbourhood. Father Fitzgibbon, however, refuses to agree with Father O'Malley's assertion that the boys are likely "to wind up in a reform school." Father Fitzgibbon replies that Father O'Malley has "been listening to Patrick McCarthy," the local cop on the beat, and a man who has not been to mass "in the last ten years." As far as Father Fitzgibbon is concerned, then, the fact of McCarthy's poor church attendance makes him an unreliable source of information, even if it is information that ought to be of vital concern to the local priest. And the point is that Father Fitzgibbon here allows his narrow preconceptions to blind him to the gravity of the situation. If the young of the parish end up in prison, there will be no parish left to serve.

Thus the presence of Tony and the gang in the final sequence is significant of Father O'Malley's success in re-establishing the relationship between the boys and the church. And it is a relationship which we see and experience very directly in the sequence under consideration. The shots of the boys—who have become the church choir under Father O'Malley's musical and spiritual direction—are taken from Father Fitzgibbon's point of view. And while it is true that we do not see them together in the same shot, it is clear that they occupy the same space, both physically (the half-rebuilt sanctuary of St. Dominic's) and emotionally (the boys express their regard for Father Fitzgibbon by singing "An Irish Lullaby").

A similar thematic situation is mirrored in the fifth shot of the concluding scene, the three-shot of Mr. Haines, Carol Haines, and Ted Haines. Two important sets of relationships are involved here. The first has to do with the relationship between the elder Haines and his son. We first see them in the film's opening scene, as the elder Haines pressures Father Fitzgibbon to make the overdue payments on the church mortgage (as Haines half-jokingly puts it to Father Fitzgibbon, "The Lord loveth a cheerful giver"). The fact that Ted tags along on such errands is a clear indication that the elder Haines intends his son to follow in his own financial footsteps. Indeed, we eventually see young Ted attempting without much conviction to evict the parish gossip from her flat for falling behind on her rent. To an important degree, then, this relationship prefigures and mirrors the relationship between Father Fitzgibbon and Father O'Malley: in both instances the elder man expects the younger to toe the line, and in both instances such expectations are destructive of the institution (the family/the church) that they are intended to protect. In other words, Haines is, as he himself admits, a "heel"—and to insist that Ted follow his example is to destroy the vitality of the family.

The second set of relationships brought to the foreground by the fifth shot of the concluding scene are those which revolve around Carol Haines. We first see her as a rebellious eighteen-year-old, on the run from oppressive parents who seek to stifle her sexuality. As Carol puts it to Father O'Malley, after officer McCarthy delivers her to St. Dominic's, she and her parents "don't agree on anything," and particularly not on the way she does her hair, her make-up, the kinds of clothes she wears, or the hours she keeps ("No matter how early I get in—too late"). Here again we see the conflict of youth and age, and once again youth, and the sexual and social vitality that youth represents, is endangered by the overcautious exercise of authority. Indeed, Carol no sooner has the chance to explain herself and her plans (she hopes to find work as a singer) to Father O'Malley than Father Fitzgibbon enters to underline the point. Upon learning of Carol's situation he offers to get her a housekeeping job. Carol, predictably enough, turns it down, and Father Fitzgibbon, in a fit of Irish huff, tells her "to go home and stay home until the right man comes along." Once again, Father Fitzgibbon relies upon a rigidly formulaic response, and that response is clearly to be disapproved of. First of all, McCarey makes it clear, by the presence and character of Genevieve Linden, that "being a good wife and a mother" is not the only possible path a girl might follow in life: Carol might very well become, like Miss Linden, a successful singer. Furthermore, Father Fitzgibbon's advice is likely to backfire even were Carol to take it. That is, given what we know about Carol's parents, it is unlikely that the right man will ever come near her house (to paraphrase Carol's own reply). In other words, she has to leave home if her energies, sexual and otherwise, are to find legitimate personal and social expression.

The three-shot of Mr. Haines, Carol, and Ted therefore carries multiple meanings. First of all, the very fact of their presence indicates that the financial and emotional conflicts between the church and the Haines family have been resolved. Mr. Haines has clearly cancelled plans to tear the church down in order to build a parking lot in its place. Indeed, as we discover in the previous scene, he has agreed to write a new mortgage and forgive the remaining debt on the old one. Similarly, Carol's presence is indicative of the fact that she too has come to terms with Father Fitzgibbon—although in her case it was Father Fitzgibbon who had to come around. Furthermore, it is significant that Carol is in the middle of the frame. The first time we see all three characters (Mr. Haines, Carol, and Ted) together is after Carol and Ted have been married. As far as Mr. Haines is concerned, then, Carol has come between himself and his son. And to a degree the visual/spatial treatment of this "recognition" scene seems to underline the point: throughout most of the scene Carol *is* between them. But before the scene is over we discover, as Carol and Mr. Haines discover, that the effect of her presence is to bind all of them far more closely together. Carol's influence on Ted has allowed him to see that some things are more important than money: hence his decisions to marry and to join the Army Air Corps. And the fact that his son is set to ship out to the combat zone brings the same lesson home to Mr. Haines himself. Suddenly mortgages and foreclosures and the financial pages seem insignificant—and Mr. Haines seems far less a heel. Thus Carol's presence between the two of them in the final sequence is indicative of the central role she plays in their lives. Indeed, like Father O'Malley, Carol is a catalyst, in this case a catalyst which brings both Ted and Mr. Haines back to their humane senses.

One final set of character relationships remains to be considered before moving on to matters of music and setting. With the exception of Carol Haines, most of the characters we have so far considered are male, so that most of the shots are populated predominantly though not exclusively by men or boys. In two shots of the final sequence, however, shots four and nine, the reverse holds true. In shot four we see Genevieve Linden, Mrs. Fitzgibbon, and, after his entrance from off screen, Father O'Malley; and in shot nine we see only Miss Linden and Mrs. Fitzgibbon. And the issue raised has to do with the relationship of sex, sacrifice and society. That is, both shots bring to mind the emotional price that men like Father O'Malley and Father Fitzgibbon have to pay for the privilege of dedicating their lives to the service of others. In Father Fitzgibbon's case there has been a double sacrifice: by taking the vow of chastity he guarantees that no woman can be more important to him than his mother, and by ministering to the parish of St. Dominic he is almost forced to give up that relationship as well. As Father Fitzgibbon wistfully puts it to Father O'Malley, "I always planned that as soon as we got a few dollars ahead I'd go back to the old country and see my mother—would you believe it, that was forty-five years ago?" And Father O'Malley makes a similar sacrifice. It is clear from the conversation between Genevieve Linden and Father O'Malley, before she becomes aware of his vocation, that their relationship had been a sexually serious one: on the one hand she scolds him for not writing, and on the other she is so glad to see him that her scolding has the ring of endearment to it. But when she enters from her dressing room to see Father O'Malley, his priestly garb no longer hidden beneath his overcoat, her only slightly hesitant reaction ("Where's your parish, father?") indicates the rightness of Father O'Malley's decision. She had loved him for his selflessness (he was the first to encourage her singing and her singing lead to their separation) and that selflessness finds its logical expression in the priesthood.

Thus far we have considered the iconographic values of the characters who appear in the closing moments of *Going My Way*, but other factors work as well in determining the scene's impact and significance. Consider the issue of music. In general terms, music and song serve throughout the film as contexts for the expression of powerful feelings and aspirations. Indeed, song provides a sort of licence, allowing people to express themselves musically where they could not express themselves within the conventions of conversation. Thus when we first see Carol the conversation between her and Father O'Malley tends to focus on the negative aspects of her relationship with her parents. When she lets it be known that she plans a singing career, however, Father O'Malley suggests that she audition for him, and the song she sings ("The Day After Forever") allows the expression of a more positive vision of life. Of course, Carol does overdo the hand gestures as she sings (another marvellous McCarey sight gag), but her heart is clearly in the right place.

And Carol is not alone in finding music a more meaningful form of communication—nor is she the film's only singer. Most obviously there is Genevieve Linden, the international opera star. Of course, one could argue, in the context of Hollywood's often hostile treatment of opera (e.g., in *Mr. Deeds Goes to Town*—although Capra's satire is aimed at the board of directors), that opera singing is seldom allowed the sort of personal significance that we associate with Carol's singing in *Going My Way*. And it is true that there is some light-hearted satire of the opera crowd in the film (note Fortunio Bonanova's portrayal of the conductor). But in Miss Linden's case it is clear that her singing is expressive of her personality. Indeed, there is a certain poignant irony to the fact that Miss Linden sings the seductive lead in

"Carmen" only moments after her discovery of Father O'Malley's vocation. And yet the fact of her singing allows safe expression of the sexuality that Father O'Malley's priestly vows otherwise prohibit. It is not a matter of simple sublimation, however. Singing is itself a sensuous act—and through the course of the film Father O'Malley and Miss Linden effectively consummate their love by means of musical collaboration.

Thus Father O'Malley's music is central to his sense of self and his sense of mission. Like Carol and Miss Linden, Father O'Malley finds a freedom in music that allows the expression of his most deeply felt convictions. He would prefer, indeed, to sing his sermons; and it is by selling a song that Father O'Malley hopes to revive the fiscal fortunes of St. Dominic's. His songs, however, are not just commercial product. Rather they embody certain basic thematic antinomies—hope vs. hopelessness ("Going My Way") and nature vs. culture ("Swinging on a Star")—central to Father O'Malley's ministry and to the film in general. The latter song, indeed, takes on particular significance when understood in the context of the war years (recall that Ted Haines is in uniform in the final sequence). Underlying the issue of the revival of St. Dominic's is the more general issue of civilisation and its continuity (the issue is treated far more explicitly in *Once Upon a Honeymoon* which takes place in a Nazi-dominated Europe) and it is essential for that continuity that people the world over have faith in their ability to "be better off than [they] are." The alternative is a zoo-world of mules, fish, and monkeys. In which context, then, the presence of song in the final sequence can be understood in general terms as an assertion of faith in the efficacy and continuity of human relationships. Indeed, the song effectively embraces four generations of that continuity: the boys, Father O'Malley (the choir leader), Father Fitzgibbon, and Mrs. Fitzgibbon.

More specifically, the song "An Irish Lullaby" is a pointed celebration of Father Fitzgibbon's resurgent, selfless, ever hopeful humanity. We first hear it after the Father comes in from the rain. He had left the rectory in a childish huff, a little boy run away from home, after Father O'Malley confirmed his intuitive guess that the younger man is to assume control of parish affairs. Father Fitzgibbon finally returns to the rectory, accompanied appropriately enough by Officer McCarthy, and after a hearty meal Father O'Malley suggests "a little something" to warm the elder man's rain-drenched spirits. At first Father Fitzgibbon is reluctant to admit to the possession of alcohol, but he soon breaks down and instructs Father O'Malley to "look

Telling tales of Old Ireland: Father O'Malley and Father Fitzgibbon reminisce in *Going My Way*.

yonder in the bookcase." Father O'Malley then pulls a music box from behind "The Life of General Grant" and upon opening the box he discovers "a bit of old Ireland"—both the music ("An Irish Lullaby") and the bottle (a yearly Christmas present from Father Fitzgibbon's mother). Father Fitzgibbon then pours each of them a generous drink and tells Father O'Malley of his oft-postponed plans to visit Ireland and his mother.

The association here of music with honesty and childhood is clear enough. Indeed, Father O'Malley sings Father Fitzgibbon to sleep as if Father Fitzgibbon were a child. But Father Fitzgibbon's childishness, and Father O'Malley's willingness to acknowledge that childishness by singing a lullaby, is indicative of the fact that together they have taken the first and proper step towards reviving Father Fitzgibbon and with him the fortunes of St. Dominic's. Father Fitzgibbon has grown too old, too settled in his ways, too sure of himself, and it is therefore important that he acknowledge his own mortality and dependency by recalling his past and his childhood: and "An Irish Lullaby" serves as a vehicle for that recollection.

We hear the song for the second time only moments before the final sequence. Father O'Malley has packed his bags and is ready to leave. Before beginning the public farewell ceremony, however, Father

Fitzgibbon comes to Father O'Malley's room to bid him a private farewell by toasting their friendship. But he does not just walk in to the room. Rather, he is preceded by the music box strains of "An Irish Lullaby." By so doing he recalls the earlier "Irish Lullaby" scene, and he proceeds to commemorate the significance of that scene, with its implicit recognition of time and mortality, by holding up his bottle. It is almost empty. Christmas is near. Time passes. And Father Fitzgibbon has found a new humility in the face of its passage. Indeed, recognizing his mortality has made him "ten years younger," able to carry on without Father O'Malley (though not without the less talented Father O'Dowd). The song thus serves both to mark the passage of time (its repetition implies such a passage) and to specify the proper response to the fact of time's passage: one must embrace time and by so doing embrace humanity.

By the time of its third occurence, then, in the film's final sequence, "An Irish Lullaby" has accumulated a wealth of significant associations. It stands for a genuine depth of feeling; for an extraordinary openness to the facts of time and mortality; for emotional integrity; for rejuvenation; for the continuity and significance of human relationships. This would be true even were Mrs. Fitzgibbon not actually present—but her presence serves to emphasise and validate our sense of the song's import. She *is* the continuity of human civilisation, at least metaphorically, and yet she is first and foremost Mother Fitzgibbon. Thus we feel a genuinely motivated sense of privilege for being present at the reunion of mother and son. And "An Irish Lullaby" lingers in the imagination as a vivid reminder of that privileged moment.

Another factor determining the significance of (and hence our response to) the closing scene of *Going My Way* has to do with the matter of setting. For the most part, *Going My Way* is restricted to a few locales within the parish of St. Dominic. We do go to the opera on two occasions, once to the golf course, but the predominant location for the film's action is the rectory and sanctuary of St. Dominic's. This is clearly appropriate given the metonymic equation of Father Fitzgibbon and the parish, and it allows McCarey the opportunity to reflect upon the relationship between institutions (the church) and individuals. Briefly, the point McCarey makes is that the identity between institutions and individuals can become too strong, as it does for Father Fitzgibbon. He becomes St. Dominic's to such a degree that he cannot perceive or respond to the changes taking place in the lives of his parishioners. It is therefore necessary rather than coincidental that St. Dominic's should burn to the ground at the very moment when it seems that Father Fitzgibbon's troubles are over. Stasis in *Going My Way* is equivalent to death. And while the gutting of St. Dominic's represents to Father Fitzgibbon the destruction of his dream it represents in truth the resurrection of his hopes: life once again has a purpose. Thus it is appropriate that nearly every shot in the final sequence has in the background the partially rebuilt sanctuary of St. Dominic's. The relationship between place and person is therefore reasserted, but that relationship is now a matter of creativity rather than rigidity. Life is never certain. Parishioners come and go. Churches rise, decay, and are rebuilt. It is the process of living that matters, the process of loving and celebrating that love, and the set in the film's closing moment is an iconographic reminder of life's ebb and flow.

One final shot, raising one final issue, remains to be considered. After Father Fitzgibbon and his mother embrace, McCarey cuts to a

The artist at work: Father O'Malley greets Mother Fitzgibbon while Genevieve Linden (Risë Stevens) looks on.

medium shot of Father O'Malley standing outside the sanctuary. And his presence *outside* the sanctuary is significant. In effect, Father O'Malley is the director of the scene we have been considering, forever outside the action, but implicit in that action nevertheless. It was Father O'Malley who orchestrated the reunion of Father Fitzgibbon and Mother Fitzgibbon, and his selflessness is evidenced by the fact that the reunion of mother and son interrupts and supercedes the more formal and public farewell ceremony. In other words, Father O'Malley once again puts the needs and feelings of others first, even if by so doing he once again upsets parish routine.

Indeed, Father O'Malley represents the spirit of improvisation—and the issues of improvisation and artifice are central to McCarey's vision, both in *Going My Way* and elsewhere. Thus it is perfectly in keeping with Father O'Malley's basic sense of moral values that he accedes to and collaborates in the occasional low-key deception as long as those deceptions serve legitimate and humane purposes. Thus, for example, he pretends to be merely the curate of St. Dominic's, despite the fact that the bishop has made him responsible for the parish. Thus he suborns Father O'Dowd's white lie when that lie (in the form of a pun) is intended to spare Father Fitzgibbon's feelings. And thus on the golf course he assists Father O'Dowd to give Father Fitzgibbon the impression that his chip shot has holed out. In every case, however, the fictions are benevolent, and are intended either (1) to spare people's feelings where doing otherwise would be counterproductive, (2) to loosen people up to the point where they can take productive and responsive action in the world.

Thus *Going My Way* concludes with the image of the invisible but responsible artist; and by so doing Leo McCarey asserts one final though implicit equation. In their function and method, at least, Father O'Malley and Leo McCarey are identical. Both of them are improvisational artists, and art for both is a means of insuring life's continuity by celebrating and encouraging the revitalisation of human relationships and institutions. Our response to the closing moments of *Going My Way* is therefore an implicit recognition of McCarey's success. The moment "means" because McCarey has orchestrated its meaning. It is significant for the perspective it provides on the film's larger issues and concerns. The closing moments of *Going My Way* are memorable precisely because they bring together all that has gone before in the film; and the film, in turn, finds its proper conclusion by not concluding. Put another way, the final shot of *Going My Way*, Father O'Malley closing the sanctuary door and walking away across the snowy churchyard, validates the emotional character of the reunion scene between Father Fitzgibbon and his mother. Their reunion does not solve a problem, or resolve the plot, but is expressive, rather, of a timeless sense of value. This timeless value, however, resides in the significance of *Going My Way*, in its meaning, not merely in images divorced from context. Indeed, the timeless significance of the embrace between mother and son depends for its impact upon our recognition that life is transitory, time-bound, and therefore precious. Father O'Malley's departure reinforces our sense of time's passage by recalling his arrival at the film's beginning. The film ends, therefore, not merely with an embrace but with an implicit sense of temporal/emotional context which allows value and significance to what would otherwise be a mundane gesture. Context thus redeems significance. Art thus redeems life.

McCarey and the Clowns:
Putting Pants on Philip, Duck Soup, Six of a Kind

Categorisation is a basic tool of scholarship, in film studies no less than elsewhere, and categories are useful to the extent that they provide a conceptual framework for discussion and debate. In the case of Leo McCarey, however, it seems clear that the generally accepted chronological categories, which purport to describe his career in developmental terms, tend to blur or background certain important continuities. Thus McCarey's career is usually discussed in terms which suggest three chronological categories: the apprentice period, which covers the years from 1923 (or so?) through 1934, years in which McCarey was occupied primarily as the director of comic actor/*auteurs* such as Charley Chase, Laurel and Hardy, the Marx Brothers, Eddie Cantor, Mae West, and W. C. Fields, among others; the masterwork period, which Charles Silver characterises as running from Marx (the brothers) to McCarthy (Joe), and which includes the great screwball comedies, *The Awful Truth* and *Love Affair,* as well as *Ruggles of Red Gap* and *Make Way for Tomorrow;* and finally there is the McCarthyite period, during which McCarey's characteristically light touch became heavy-handed and moralistic. The latter period, indeed, at least as Jeffrey Richards explicitly describes it, was the period of McCarey's single greatest popular success, *Going My Way* (1944), though it began with *Once Upon a Honeymoon* (1942) and reflected in

e eccentric personality: Cary
nt and Deborah Kerr (center
right) in *An Affair to Remember*.

its uncertainties and its villains the emotional sterility of the Cold War
years.[5]

In general, the categories work—at least to the extent that they
serve roughly to chart the rise and fall of McCarey's commercial
fortunes. But it is important to remark that McCarey did not undergo
a sea-change between 1934 *(Belle of the Nineties)* and 1935 *(Ruggles of
Red Gap)*. The notion implicit in the first two categories is that during
his apprentice period McCarey's expressive sensibilities were subser-
vient to those of the great clowns that he worked with. His masterwork period, therefore, would be characterised by the increasing
domination of the director over his actors. Such a picture is plausible,
of course, and in the case of someone like Frank Capra, who began his
career directing films for Harry Langdon, it might even be accurate.
But in McCarey's case the antithesis between actor and director
seldom, if ever, existed. Indeed, one could argue that McCarey's
fascination for the eccentric personality found its greatest expression
in his Cary Grant films *(The Awful Truth, Once Upon a Honeymoon,* and
An Affair to Remember, all of which were made after 1935) rather than
in, say, *Duck Soup* or *The Kid from Spain.* Thus it would be a grievous
mistake to overlook the stylistic/thematic continuities which bridge
the gaps between the period categories. Indeed, some such oversight

may very well account for the degree of critical neglect of McCarey: too much attention has been devoted to attacking the politics of *My Son John* and too little has been devoted to describing McCarey's basic narrative/thematic project.

We can best begin to characterise that project by briefly comparing *Putting Pants on Philip* (1928), one of the earliest of the McCarey-supervised Laurel and Hardy films, with *Going My Way*. On the surface, of course, the two films appear to have little in common and, even after all possible analogies are remarked upon, it will remain the case that the two films are separate entities. And yet they share certain narrative devices, certain character types, and certain essential themes, which are striking in their consistency. Both films, for example, begin with the arrival of a wide-eyed outsider, a kilt-clad Philip (Stan Laurel) in one case, Father O'Malley, complete with his St. Louis Browns sweat shirt, in the other. In each film the young man comes into conflict with an elder man, Piedmont Mumblethunder (Oliver Hardy) in *Putting Pants on Philip*, and Father Fitzgibbon in *Going My Way*. And in each case that conflict focuses on issues of social decorum, surface propriety, and youthful (or sexual) energy.

We have already considered *Going My Way* in some detail, and we need not comment further except to remark that the effect of Father O'Malley's unconventional presence at St. Dominic's is to bring Father Fitzgibbon back to his humane senses. In other words, Father O'Malley is a catalyst, and he serves to shake Father Fitzgibbon out of his self-destructive and somewhat self-centered pattern of behaviour and belief. And a similar sort of conflict is at work in *Putting Pants on Philip*. Like Father Fitzgibbon, Piedmont Mumblethunder is a re-spected member of the community, "influential, dignified, proud, a credit to society." And like Father Fitzgibbon, Mumblethunder sets too great a value on maintaining the facade of respectability. Indeed, in the case of Mumblethunder, respectability and sexuality are set in direct opposition (as they are for Father Fitzgibbon when he tries to advise Carol in *Going My Way*). As it turns out, young master Philip is Mumblethunder's Scotch nephew, and Mumblethunder has been enjoined to "guard him well" lest Philip indulge his one weakness: "at the sight of a pretty girl he has spots before his eyes."

Like Father Fitzgibbon, Mumblethunder would rather be quit of the whole affair. When it becomes clear that the foolish fellow in the kilt is the nephew he has come to meet, Mumblethunder attempts to melt into the dockside crowd; and even after Philip identifies him, Mumblethunder continues to insist that his nephew follow only at a

**Laurel and Oliver Hardy: a
duction still from *Putting
ts on Philip*.**

distance, so that Mumblethunder can feign ignorance of Philip's
presence. Philip, however, is far too energetic and curious to be
ignored, and though he does his best to obey his uncle's self-
important instructions, Philip invariably catches up and takes his
uncle by the arm. Which is embarrassing enough from Mumblethunder's point of view, particularly as they are being followed by a group
of curious bystanders, but nowhere near so embarrassing as what is to
follow.

Merely strolling the streets, we discover, is clearly insufficient outlet
for Philip's energetic self; and he soon finds a better method of
self-expression. A glamorous flapper whom he had seen briefly on
the dock continually crosses Philip's path, and at each sighting Philip
leaps into the air, kicks out his legs, and sets off in hot-blooded, Harpo
Marx pursuit, which in turn sets off a recurrent pattern of social
action. In each instance, Mumblethunder tries to avoid crowds so as to
avoid embarrassment. And every time he turns to admonish his

unwelcomed audience, telling them in so many gestures to get lost, Philip sets off in pursuit of his dream girl (just as, thirty-four years later, Siu-Lan sets off in pursuit of her prince charming in *Satan Never Sleeps*). Thus the effect of Mumblethunder's efforts to disperse the crowd is the creation of an ever larger crowd as people flock to witness the confrontation of Philip and the flapper. Indeed, the camera set-ups tend to emphasise the ever greater measure of Mumblethunder's frustration by repeating the visual pattern: close-up of an incredulous Mumblethunder, long shot of the crowd converging in the distance, long shot of the well-fed Mumblethunder running spasmodically from foreground to background in a determined attempt to reassert some measure of control and decorum.

As we have already remarked, the central issue in *Putting Pants on Philip*, as it often is elsewhere in McCarey, involves the continual dialectic between sexuality and society. That issue is not foreign to *Going My Way*, although the sexuality of the young man character finds its expression in the encouragment of sexuality in others (as Father O'Malley encourages and consecrates the union of Ted and Carol). For the most part, however, the sexuality theme in *Going My Way* is only a variation on the larger issue of social rigidity. In *Putting Pants on Philip*, however, sexuality is the over-riding issue. Thus Philip draws crowds precisely because he seems a sexual anomaly—a woman chaser in skirts. There is even a hint of androgyny in the Philip character. But that adrogyny is less a function of the character himself than it is of the society that surrounds him. On one occasion he is referred to as a "dame;" on another a man tips his hat as if Philip were a lady—but Philip never really acts effeminate. Except, perhaps, in the tailor shop when he refuses to let the tailor take an inseam measurement. Even here, however, the gestures are a function of the clothing (Philip pushes his kilt down), and the fact that such gestures carry androgynous overtones is clearly socially conditioned. In other words, Philip represents a direct challenge to the simplistic and over-rigid notion that skirts equal women. And thus Mumblethunder's tactic for dealing with the situation—his promise to "put pants on Philip"—must be understood as a gesture of sexual repression.

The strength of sexual taboos in the society of *Putting Pants on Philip* is evidenced in the marvellous air-vent routine which follows Philip's first attempt at seducing the flapper. Mumblethunder and Philip walk down the sidewalk, followed once again by a fairly large crowd, and as Philip passes over an air-vent his kilt flies up (thus anticipating the famous bit with Marilyn Monroe in *The Seven Year Itch*). This happens twice before Mumblethunder in his embarrassment turns to the crowd and lectures them. Meanwhile Philip takes a pinch of snuff, sneezes, his drawers fall to his ankles, and Mumblethunder pushes him along, walking him right out of his underwear, before Philip can recover. We track back as Philip and Mumblethunder approach the next air-vent, and cut to the crowd at just the moment when the air-vent must be doing its job. Women faint. Men revive them by waving their hats. And the point is clear: sex is to be feared (hence the fainting at the sight of an exposed male) but fear always makes for a powerful attraction (hence the crowd's presence in the first place).

The film's narrative device, and the source of most of its humour, is thus the injection of an unconventional character (Philip) into an overly conventional or conventionalised social situation, a situation personified by someone in a position of authority (Mumblethunder). In *Putting Pants on Philip*, then, the purpose of the humour is to loosen up the society by requiring that it face up to the issue presented by the outsider. Indeed, before the film is over, Mumblethunder's sense of propriety is completely destroyed. He relies on surface appearance once too often and finds himself ignominiously submerged in a mud puddle.

We see this question/response pattern repeatedly in McCarey—in *Going My Way*, as we have shown here, and also in such disparate films as *The Kid from Spain*, *Ruggles of Red Gap*, *The Bells of St. Mary's* and *My Son John*. An important variant or complement of this pattern focuses not on the outsider but on the character or characters who feel victimised by the intrusion of some external influence on their lives (we see this in many of the McCarey-directed Charley Chase comedies). And the effect is one of testing: how do people respond to situations which call their sense of reality into question? This variant is clearly implicit in the basic pattern we describe—but some films, such as *Let's Go Native* with its castaways, *The Milky Way* with its milkman turned middleweight, *Once Upon a Honeymoon* with its unwelcomed Nazis, or *Rally Round the Flag, Boys!*, with its unwelcomed army base, bear down on it more than others.

The point I would make, however, before going on to discuss two of McCarey's better known and still available "clown films," is that the pattern of structure and theme discernible in *Putting Pants on Philip* is clearly indicative of and applicable to McCarey's entire canon. Thus McCarey tends to focus on extreme or extremely eccentric character types (the unconventional and the overconventional) who find themselves in bizarre or unusual circumstances. And the humour as well as

Left, an early McCarey feature:
Sally O'Neil and Eddie Quillan in
The Sophomore. Right, Eddie Cantor
in *The Kid from Spain*.

the significance of the films derives from McCarey's patient though acute observation of the mayhem which generally ensues. Which is not to say that McCarey merely watches the world go by with no regard for the expression of a personal viewpoint. It says, rather, that McCarey's style of film-making is distinguished by the characters and situations that he chooses to observe: hence his propensity for long takes and eye-level set-ups, and hence as well his tendency to improvise by immersing his somewhat unconventional self into the often over-conventional situation implicit in shooting schedules and Hollywood studios.

* * *

Duck Soup is a classic though marvellously complicated example of the pattern we have been describing. Again we have quite unconventional characters (the Marx Brothers) injected into a highly conventional situation. The conventionality, however, is not totally a matter of the internal social milieu, as it is in *Putting Pants on Philip*—although Freedonian society certainly is over-rigid in its ceremonies and proprieties, and the Marx Brothers do play havoc with both. The situation is more complex than that and has to do with the generic component of the film as well as with the society that the film depicts.

Duck Soup can best be understood, I would suggest, as a parody—to the second power. In the first place *Duck Soup* is a musical comedy. And musical comedies, no matter how conventional their form, tend themselves to be parodies of conventional social behaviour. Thus, in musical comedy, characters are free to dance and sing whenever the mood strikes them, whenever it serves to express their sense of self. They are not constrained to sing only in the shower and dance only on the dance floor. Furthermore, musical comedy often gravitates toward political parody, simply by virtue of the fact that political protocol offers a strong set of conventions to be subverted. And, to the extent that *Duck Soup* does parody conventional sexual and social behaviour, it remains true to the tradition of musical comedy developed at Paramount by Ernst Lubitsch in films like *The Love Parade* and *One Hour with You* (indeed, we hear a few bars of "One Hour with You" when Harpo interrupts his midnight ride to indulge his taste for women).

Secondly, however, *Duck Soup* turns back upon its own artifice, for it consistently provides an implicit critique of the very musical comedy genre of which it is an example: hence the film's tendency towards the anachronistic and the artificial. Freedonia, for example, is a curious *mélange* of the Old World (fanfares, depleted treasuries, outrageously befuddled ministers) and the New (peanut vendors, baseball

The Lubitsch musical: Mariam Hopkins and Maurice Chevalier in *The Smiling Lieutenant*.

games, Paul Revere, American Civil War uniforms)—and the effect is one that both emphasises and undercuts the artifice and conventionality of the work. Indeed, on occasion, McCarey goes his script one better in this regard by consciously disregarding the continuity between shots. And this is important for providing a context in which actions signify in themselves rather than for their consequences. Thus, when Groucho machine-guns his own troops, we are not inclined to condemn him as we might were this a Peckinpah film. Rather, we are aware that *Duck Soup* is a movie, and a movie of such a style that Groucho's villainy matters only to the degree that it contributes to the film's parodistic theme. Thus, as Allen Eyles points out, Groucho subverts the notion of authority from within by enacting the Rufus T. Firefly role.[6] Firefly is unabashedly unscrupulous and self-serving ("If you think this country is bad off now,/just wait till I get through with it"); and yet it is true that we are little inclined to condemn him for his actions.

My last sentence, indeed, with its ambiguous pronoun (his/ Groucho's vs. his/Firefly's), gets directly to the thematic heart of *Duck Soup*. To a degree, it is true that *Duck Soup* parodies politics by setting two Ruritanian republics against one another in territorial struggle. Thus the plot intrigue focuses on Trentino (Louis Calhern), the Sylvanian ambassador, and his attempt to conquer Freedonia, either by winning the hand of Mrs. Teasdale (Margaret Dumont), the merry and well-off widow who bank-rolls the Freedonian treasury, or by military conquest if the marriage gambit fails (hence his concern that Chicolini and Pinky—Chico and Harpo—steal the Freedonian war plans from Mrs. Teasdale's safe). And yet the fact of the matter is that Groucho, Chico, and Harpo seem only marginally concerned with the specifics of politics or political intrigue. On the contrary, they seem only concerned to be their anarchic, unfettered, unconventional selves to the nth degree, and only on occasion do they revert to their ostensible character roles.

Thus the Marx Brothers effectively undercut the film's already parodistic intrigue by refusing to take it seriously. We see this disregard for plots and politics very clearly in two of the film's first three sequences. The film opens with Mrs. Teasdale's declaration that Freedonia needs a "new leader," a "progressive, fearless fighter, a man like Rufus T. Firefly." And in the next scene Groucho proceeds to make a fool of Mrs. Teasdale (and just about everybody else) by making a marvellous shambles of the elaborate welcoming reception she has arranged. He arrives late, enters via a fire pole rather than by

Body politics in *Duck Soup:*
Sylvanian agents (Chico and Harpo)
report to their superior in espionage
(Louis Calhern).

the grand and flower-bestrewn staircase, and he lines up with the
guard of honour, his cigar raised in mock salute to himself—etc., etc.
And, in the second sequence, Chico and Harpo (as Chicolini and
Pinky) report their surveillance activities to Trentino by playing
games (baseball, skeet shooting) and by telling jokes, both verbal
(Chico's "shadowday" routine) and visual (Harpo's mousetrap
gag)—and they have nothing at all to report on Firefly. Indeed, all
three of them—Groucho, Chico, and Harpo (I exclude the prosaic
Zeppo)—are ready at a moment's notice to drop pretence altogether
for the sake of game-playing.

Thus the two "slow-burn" routines, each pitting Edgar Kennedy as
a lemonade vendor against the craziness of Chico and/or Harpo,
ought not to be seen merely as McCarey inspired silent set-pieces, as
great moments unrelated to the film's developing theme. On the
contrary, in both instances, Kennedy's insistence on territorial integrity (he objects that Chico and Harpo are driving away his customers)

provides McCarey with an opportunity to parody the film's political intrigue (statesmen = peanut vendors) and at the same time Chico and Harpo have the chance to indulge their taste for inspired outrageousness. Thus their running battle with Kennedy—the kicks, the hat tricks, Harpo's leg routine, the lemonade-in-the-horn bit— escalates into a ballet of anarchic self-expression. Indeed, when the first skirmish is all over, after Harpo has finally burned Kennedy's hat to a crisp in his peanut roaster, Chico comments, "Oh, 'at'sa good, eh?" And it is clear that being "good" at being their game-playing selves is their primary and most legitimate concern.

We see this tendency toward game playing in the film's dialogue as well. Thus Chico's trial for treason quickly degenerates into a sequence of marvellous puns and *non sequiturs* as Chico and Groucho compete to go each other and the judge one better. The point, however, is not, as some would argue, to destroy language as a mode of civilised communication.[7] Indeed, Chico and Groucho would cease to be funny were their speech total nonsense. In fact, Groucho and Chico are the far more civilised characters for understanding and exploiting the opportunities that language allows, and their word games do make marvellous sense for expressing delight in the

Kindred spirits: the Marx Brothers in *Duck Soup*.

exercise of mind and imagination. Again, as Chico puts it to Groucho after a particularly nimble pun, "Hey, boss, I'm goin' good, eh?"

The sense of identity among the brothers, their shared delight in game playing for its own sake, is best imaged in another McCarey inspired bit of comic business—the marvellous mirror sequence. In order to steal the Freedonian war plans, Chico and Harpo disguise themselves as Groucho: grease-paint moustaches, cigars, night-shirts and night-caps. Groucho quickly catches on, however, and a chase ensues. Harpo in his panic crashes into a wall mirror, smashing it to bits, and he recovers in time to pose as Groucho's image when Groucho arrives on the scene. There are two things to notice here. First is the fact that all three brothers look remarkably alike: Harpo and Groucho (and Chico, when he turns up at the end of the scene) are clearly "kindred" spirits. And secondly, there is the fact that Groucho is not fooled for long. He quickly catches on to Harpo's strategem. But that does not really matter. Rather, he is intrigued by the game itself, and he allows Harpo a lapse or two—even to the point of handing Harpo his hat when Harpo inadvertently drops it—for the sake of playing the game to conclusion. It is only when Chico shows up on Harpo's side of the "mirror" that the spell is broken— Groucho can't have two images—and Chico's sin is not treason so much as breaking the rules and spoiling Groucho's fun.

All of which allows us to account for the fact that *Duck Soup* is a tremendously up-beat film, far more so than its reputation as a black comedy would seem to allow. As a family of clowns, the Marx Brothers represent, as Raymond Durgnat points out, a refreshingly absolute, "scathingly alive" sort of mental and emotional integrity.[8] They never fool themselves; they never fool us; and therefore we are inclined to join them in celebrating the virtues of honesty, however unconventional that honesty might seem in context. By being themselves, the Marx Brothers tend to overwhelm the stock-figure villains that seek to limit or deny them their freedom. We simply cannot take fools like Trentino seriously when they are set against the marvellous and self-aware folly of Groucho, Chico, and Harpo.

Thus it is appropriate that the film should conclude with the complete rejection of musical comedy politics. At the moment when Freedonia's defeat seems most certain, Chico and Harpo manage to catch Trentino's head in the door of Mrs. Teasdale's villa, and Trentino, ever the opportunist, surrenders. Surrender, however, has nothing to do with the game at hand. The Brothers Marx have a table full of fruit to throw and they'll hear nothing of surrender till they have had their fun. And neither will they hear of victory. No sooner does Mrs. Teasdale begin singing "Hail Freedonia" than the Marx Brothers begin throwing their green-garden missiles in her direction. Nothing is more sacred to the Marx Brothers than their own unconventional integrity. And neither we nor McCarey would have it any other way.

*   *   *

Duck Soup, like *Putting Pants on Philip,* tends to side with the unconventional character (or characters) who struggle to retain personal integrity in the face of social rigidity. *Six of a Kind,* however, shows us the other side of McCarey's comic coin, for it focuses on characters who are tested by the intrusion of the unconventional into their otherwise overconventional lives.

Of course, the film's title, *Six of a Kind,* and its credit sequence, which cuts between close-ups of six playing-cards (all jokers) and two-shots of, respectively, (1) Charlie Ruggles and Mary Boland, (2) W.C. Fields and Alison Skipworth, and (3) George Burns and Gracie Allen, implies a certain identity among the six major characters. But that identity has to do with a rather general sort of eccentricity. Within this eccentric context, however, the J. Pinkham Winneys, Pinky (Ruggles) and Flora (Boland), are exceedingly, to the point of being dangerously, conventional. And it is their conventionality which motivates the film's intrigue.

Six of a Kind begins on a note of domestic discord. The Whinneys are packing in preparation for their long-awaited second honeymoon, and Flora expresses surprise when Pinky manages to close a suitcase without her assistance. He is, she says, "so helpless around the house." Pinky is, naturally enough, offended by the inference that he "can't even pack a suitcase," and Flora replies by offering to cancel the honeymoon trip right then and there: "Just for that I won't go." The rapidity of the quarrel, its quick progress from insult to hurt silence (they wind up sitting at opposite ends of the front room sofa), evidences already, then, a certain tendency towards ritual: Flora and Pinky are clearly old hands at insulting one another. And yet there remains a large measure of concern and affection. Thus Pinky rightly points out the necessity for a vacation. They have not had two weeks alone since their honeymoon over twenty years ago. And indeed, at the mere mention of the Bristol Hotel, of Niagara Falls, of the bellboy with the icewater, Pinky and Flora break into animated laughter. A second honeymoon, then, is clearly what they need to restore vitality and civility to their marriage.

Unfortunately, however, and despite their determination to abandon their conventional roles—she as a homemaker, he as a bank clerk—Flora and Pinky seem unable to get fully into the "gypsy interlude" spirit of the trip. Pinky, for example, as if to prove his ability to do things right, plans their itinerary in such detail that it becomes a running joke at the bank. Everyone knows that Pinky will depart straight from work, and that the Whinneys' first stop will be the "Glen Falls Hotel in Glen Falls." It is hardly the gypsy thing to do, and it backfires when one of Pinky's colleagues, a ferret-like fellow named Ferguson, exploits Pinky's *naïveté* to smuggle $50,000 out of the bank. He figures he can catch up with the Whinneys in Glen Falls and switch suitcases.

Unbeknownst to Ferguson, however, Flora—ever the penny-pinching housewife—has advertised for a couple to share expenses on the trip. She plans to use the money thus saved to redecorate her middle-class nest. Her nesting instinct, indeed, may account for the fact that the Whinneys have not taken a vacation in twenty years. As Ferguson makes clear, a clerk's salary does not go very far (hence his felonious scheme). In any case, Flora's ad is answered by George Edwards (George Burns) and Grace ("Gracie for short") Devore (Gracie Allen). And one effect of their presence is to throw Pinky's plans all out of kilter. With George and Gracie and Rang Tang Tang (her gigantic "bird dog") along for the ride, there is no telling where the Whinneys will wind up next.

Another effect of the presence of George and Gracie is to deny all privacy to Flora and Pinky. This too, however, is a function of conventionality. To begin with, it never occurred to Flora that an unmarried couple would answer her ad; and secondly, once the Whinneys discover that George and Gracie are not man and wife, it never occurs to them to let George and Gracie fend for themselves. Rather, much against their will, and certainly in contradiction of their original intentions, Flora and Pinky agree to sleep dormitory style, Pinky with George, Flora with Gracie, for the remainder of the westward journey. Thus, where Pinky and Flora had been concerned originally to find two weeks of shared solitude, the presence of Gracie and George eventually forces Pinky and Flora to think in terms of the odd quarter hour.

For Pinky and Flora, then, conventionality is its own comeuppance. They discover that their plans to escape the bondage of routine only serve to bind them more tightly than ever into a self-destructive pattern of behaviour. And yet it is clearly the case that Flora and Pinky get more trouble than they deserve. If conventionality leads to petty quarrels and domestic discord, unconventionality carried to Gracie's extreme can lead to surreal nightmares. Thus Gracie lives in a world where people routinely have three feet (her niece "has grown another foot"), see with their mouths (her aunt "sees if the soup is hot"), and where "bird dogs" sleep in the trees. Thus it is not at all surprising, after Gracie rewrites the genetic history of mankind by astounding feats of literalmindedness, that she should seek her fortune as stage mother to an equally eccentric mastiff (he'll only sit in the front seat). Nor for that matter is it terribly surprising that Gracie takes it into her head to remake Flora in her own image by placing a reluctant Mrs. Whinney ("I felt fine till you met me") on a weight-reducing programme.

The latter enterprise, indeed, is prologue to one of the film's great gag routines. The "gypsies" have arrived at the Grand Canyon, and Gracie poses Mrs. Whinney for a "before" picture in order to document the progress of her weight loss (*Gracie:* "Your husband will never know you." *Flora:* "That's what I'm afraid of"). Gracie poses Flora on the Canyon rim; and it is indicative of the relationship between the two women that Gracie and her camera remain fixed while Flora is forced to back away in order to bring things into focus. Predictably enough, Flora gets more than a photo for her trouble— she backs right off the edge. And it is only by comic chance that she comes to perch in the only tree growing anywhere on the face of the cliff. Of course, it is all in good fun; it is shot against hyper-obvious backdrops which emphasise the artificiality of the situation; but the metaphor is clear, both for Flora and later for Pinky, who finds himself hung up in the same tree only moments after Flora is rescued (an over-exuberant Rang Tang Tang shoves him off the cliff). You can go too far (literally "out on a limb") in accommodating yourself to convention (having your picture taken), and if you go far enough your very life may be endangered.

The film's last act takes place in Nuggetville, Nevada. By the time of their arrival the Whinneys have been reduced, through accident (the cliff routine) and thievery (they are held up by hoboes who get a little help from crazy Gracie), to what is for them a very unconventional and unwelcomed state of affairs—they are exhausted and penniless. Their "gypsy interlude" has become almost a trial by combat, and their troubles are not over yet. By wiring the bank for money,

Whinney alerts both the authorities and Ferguson to his where-abouts—and the race is on. Fortunately for the Whinneys, how-ever, Nuggetville is not a very racy town, and while their trials are not yet ended—Whinney will be arrested and Flora will momentarily think him guilty of adultery on the evidence of the negligée that Ferguson had packed for his girl friend—events are set in motion that will eventually result in the vindication of Pinky and the deliverance of the Whinneys from the bondage of over-much eccentricity.

Those events, however, are a function of place and personality. To begin with, Nuggetville is so far removed from civilisation that it will take both Ferguson and the bank detectives some time to arrive on the scene. More importantly, Nuggetville is typified by a congenial blend of the conventional and the unconventional. Conventionality is personified by the proprietress of the local hotel. The Duchess (Alison Skipworth) is gruff and blustery, particularly with the local gin-sot sheriff, Honest John Hoxley (W. C. Fields), but she always loans him enough to keep him in drink, despite her ostensible disapproval. On the other hand, however, she is leery of penniless strangers, and she locks the Whinneys' luggage away as security against their bill. And later, upon examining that luggage, she is conventional and right-headed enough to know that something is afoot when she finds the $50,000, and to seek out proper authority to deal with the situation. Honest John is neither honest enough nor sober enough to be trusted with the investigation.

And yet Honest John's contribution to the salvation of Flora and Pinky is equally crucial. He is a most unconventional sheriff, more likely to pack a flask than a pistol, and not above stealing a nickle or two from the hotel pay phone. Most importantly, Honest John is irredeemably himself, sly of tongue, slow of speech, and slower yet at completing specific tasks. Thus it takes him a good five minutes to pick out a pool cue, to chalk it up, to establish a suitable grip and, finally, after much marvellous Fieldsian pantomime, to poke spas-modically at the cue ball, only to have it rebound off the far cushion and clunk him on the head. And thus, when he gets the message to arrest Pinky, it takes him an eternity of running back and forth before he ever gets around to asking Pinky about the money. As a result, Ferguson, who has arrived in advance of the detectives, is detained (indeed, John accidently locks him into the hotel luggage cage) and therefore everything falls into place when the Duchess returns with the bank detectives: the money is recovered, Ferguson is arrested, and Pinky is cleared. And in addition, while John hems and haws at

The unconventional sheriff: W.C. Fields (center left) interrogates Mary Boland (center right) while Gracie Allen and George Burns look on in *Six of a Kind*.

the top of his voice, George and Gracie decide that there must be a better way to get to Hollywood.

In *Six of a Kind*, then, as in *Putting Pants on Philip*, McCarey reflects upon the necessary relationship between conventional and unconventional behaviour. Either sort of behaviour, carried to extremes, can be dangerous, as the Whinneys demonstrate, as Gracie demonstrates. And each sort of behaviour is necessary to balance and humanise the other. Thus it is appropriate that the film concludes in Nuggetville, a place where conventionality and eccentricity exist in harmony, and where neither represents a genuine threat to continued existence. In fact, it is the balance of normality and eccentricity that makes life interesting in McCarey, and *Six of a Kind* is no less a McCarey film for the presence of strong clown characters. On the contrary, actors like W.C. Fields and Charlie Ruggles, and actresses like Gracie Allen and Mary Boland, allowed McCarey splendid opportunity to explore the marvellous range of human behaviour. We could hardly ask for more.

The Social Mythos of Leo McCarey:
Ruggles of Red Gap

It is important in any extended discussion of the McCarey cinema
to emphasise the significance of context in determining the specific
value of certain motifs. Thus in *Duck Soup* we are little inclined to
condemn Groucho Marx when he machine-guns his own troops and
this disinclination is a function of the film's artificial and farcical style.
In *My Son John*, on the other hand, John Jefferson is machine-gunned
to death gangland fashion, and we are clearly inclined to read the
scene "realistically"—the act of murder is here to be condemned, as it
was not in *Duck Soup*.

I raise the issue because there is a tendency when dealing with
McCarey to mistake metaphor for meaning—to assume, for example,
that McCarey's primary concern in *Going My Way* is to promote
Catholicism. We could hardly describe the film as anti-Catholic, but it
seems clear that in *Going My Way* the parish of St. Dominic serves a
metaphoric function. It is a microcosmic "community," a civilisation
in little, and McCarey uses it to make far more general and far more
profound assertions about the nature of social freedom and social
responsibility than would have been possible had the film been mere
propaganda for a particular religious ideology.

Something similar, it seems to me, needs to be said about McCarey's
use of political metaphors as well. McCarey is frequently characterised, for example, as a defender of bourgeois/capitalist American
democracy. And, to the extent that "democracy" serves in McCarey as
a powerful metaphor for social tolerance and flexibility, this is
certainly true. But it is clearly the case that "America," as a metaphoric
social entity, is hardly immune in McCarey from those dangers of
rigidity and complacency which beset and threaten St. Dominic's (and
hence civilisation) in *Going My Way*. Witness, for example, *Putting
Pants on Philip*, where Piedmont Mumblethunder's over-developed
sense of bourgeois self-importance is called into question by the
European vitality of young Philip. Or consider the conflict between
free enterprise and Christian charity in *Good Sam:* bourgeois
capitalism (in the person of the owner of the department store where
Sam works) hardly escapes unscathed. Indeed, as evidenced by *Six of a
Kind, The Milky Way* and *Make Way for Tomorrow,* the economic aspect
of American democracy is generally presented by McCarey as being
rigidly dedicated to the service of self-interest, and self-interest of any
sort is anathema in McCarey when it conflicts with the rights and

Lionel Stander and Harold Lloyd in
The Milky Way.

wellbeing of others. McCarey is thus *for* individuals. But individuals inevitably have social and familial responsibilities which disallow mere self-indulgence. Indeed, McCarey's characters are often most truly themselves when they willingly put themselves at hazard (as in *Once Upon a Honeymoon*).

All of which is relevant to *Ruggles of Red Gap* because *Ruggles* is arguably McCarey's most *personal,* most *social,* and most *idealistic* film. Put another way, in *Ruggles of Red Gap* McCarey explores the relationship between personality and society and does so in an idealistic literary context which asserts the essential (and necessary) identity of personal and social imperatives.

The overall movement of *Ruggles of Red Gap* is from bondage to freedom, from servitude to selfhood, from social discord to social harmony. Thus, at the film's beginning, McCarey cuts back and forth between two very conventionalised social/personal relationships, each of which embodies a somewhat discordant balance of social and personal priorities—and the contrast between the two relationships serves to specify the film's central issue. The first such relationship is that of master and servant, and involves the Earl of Burnstead (Roland Young) and his valet, Marmaduke Ruggles (Charles Laughton). On the surface, their relationship is congenial. We first see the Earl in his bed, hung over after playing poker all night with rich American tourists. And while the Earl comes slowly to his senses Ruggles sets quite efficiently and enthusiastically about the morning routine, opening curtains, setting out a light grey suit ("There is something in the air this morning which calls for light grey"), asking after his lordship's evening in terms which indicate a strong distaste for things provincial. His preference for the continental life is such, indeed, that when Lord Burnstead finally breaks the news—he lost Ruggles to the Americans in the poker game—Ruggles cringes at the thought of going to Britain's former colonies. America is, as a pained Ruggles puts it, a "country of slavery." The Earl assures Ruggles that "some fellow named Pocahontas or something" took care of the matter. But McCarey's point is clear: to a certain extent, at least, the obvious pleasure that Ruggles derives from his position results from an almost wilful ignorance of alternative social models. (And it is this sort of naiveté which guarantees that Ruggles *will* go to America, like it or not.) Thus the relationship between the Earl and Ruggles is personal to a degree. It is personal to the extent that Ruggles takes pride (perhaps too much pride) in his ability to satisfy his lordship's every need with style and grace; and personal to the extent that Ruggles and the Earl share their enthusiasm for upper class pursuits (their discussion of the Spanish dancer betrays a sort of conspiratorial camaraderie). But their relationship is impersonal to the extent that Ruggles submerges his personality into his role as valet (note his mask-like expression, all pomade and stiff upper lip); and impersonal to the degree that both Ruggles and the Earl assume that a valet is something to be wagered (and lost) in a card game. It never occurs to either of them that even a gentleman's gentleman has individual rights.

The second relationship is that of husband and wife, and involves Effie (Mary Boland) and Egbert (Charlie Ruggles) Floud of Red Gap, Washington, U.S.A. There are several things to remark about their marriage and their function in the film. To begin with, their marital bickering serves to emphasise and clarify the negative aspects of the Ruggles/Burnstead relationship. Thus the tendency to let social decorum devalue human rights, a tendency evidenced to a certain degree by the behaviour of Ruggles and his about-to-be-ex-master, is taken to its absurdly comic extreme by Effie Floud. Of course, Effie is *nouveau riche* in the worst way, and she lusts after Ruggles in the general hope that he will lend "tone" and "joy da vee" to the social life of Red Gap upon their eventual return home from Paris. But Effie is particularly interested in making a gentleman of her eccentric husband and she insists that Egbert—who won Ruggles in the poker game—collect his winnings. An English valet is just what Egbert needs to set him straight. And, indeed, Ruggles initially acquiesces to Effie's scheme. Even at their first meeting, when Egbert comes to collect him, Ruggles is taken aback by Egbert's elaborate handle-bar moustache, his ten gallon hat, and his loud check suit. And through the course of the next few scenes Ruggles collaborates in Effie's effort to "smart up" Egbert. Which means, in practical terms, that Egbert must be, as Ruggles puts it, "well turned out"—morning coat, spats, top hat, the whole works. They even resort to trickery to trim Egbert's much-loved moustache. And the point once again is clear: if Effie has her way, Egbert "will look like a different man"—he will cease to be

Egalitarianism in action: Egbert Floud (Charlie Ruggles) drags a reluctant Ruggles (Charles Laughton) to a sidewalk café where they eventually get good and corked together in *Ruggles of Red Gap*.

himself. In which case, it would seem that personal freedom and social decorum are irrevocably at odds.

But in the final analysis such is not the case. For all of Effie's machinations, Egbert generally remains Egbert, outspoken, outrageous, egalitarian in the best sense of the word. He may let Effie push him around on occasion—to the point where we admire his patience—but only because she represents little genuine threat to his sense of self. If anything, Effie's scheming only serves to demonstrate how ridiculous her pretensions are: she is the butt of her own joke. It is therefore one measure of McCarey's idealist belief in the efficacy of responsible individualism that, despite Effie's intentions, Egbert changes Ruggles far more (and far more profoundly) than Ruggles changes Egbert. No sooner does Effie leave to go shopping, for example, than Egbert hustles "Bill" off to a sidewalk café where he insists that the reluctant "Col. Ruggles" sit down and drink a beer with him. Ruggles objects: "It just doesn't do for a gentleman's servant to sit with his superiors." But Egbert will have none of Ruggles' continental logic: "Superior, nothing. You're as good as I am and I'm as good as you are." Ruggles has no choice but to sit down—which proves to be an important move in the right direction. Thus the immediate result of Egbert's egalitarian equation is that Ruggles gets thoroughly drunk. So drunk, indeed, that, upon returning to the hotel with Egbert and Egbert's Red Gap cohort, he winds up wrestling on the floor with a befuddled Mrs. Floud, his stern face and mumbled "milords" replaced by a wide grin and uncontrollable laughter. And the ultimate result of Egbert's influence on Ruggles is that Ruggles finally gets up off the floor and learns to stand on his own two feet—as one free man among many.

But again, however, it is not a simple matter of preferring individuality to community or American eccentricity to European manners. To begin with, the relatively consistent tone of the film—which is almost equally light-hearted whether the action takes place in Paris or in Red Gap—disallows easy distinctions. It is important to remark in this regard that the "distance" which matters most in the film is a function of time rather than space. That is, *Ruggles of Red Gap* takes place in the past, in the turn of the century era that McCarey first explored with Mae West in *Belle of the Nineties,* and by setting his fable in such an idylic, pastoral context McCarey acknowledges the mythic or "should be" quality of his point. Indeed, our understanding of the film's pastoral quality allows us to account for the fact that the film moves from Europe to America, and to do so without necessarily

**Mae West, Katherine DeMille, and
John Miljan in** *Belle of the Nineties.*

asserting that McCarey is being simple-mindedly jingoistic. In the
context of romantic comedy it is completely appropriate to shift from
a city setting to a country setting. Red Gap is, after a fashion, a comic
"green world," akin to the Forest of Arden in Shakespeare's "As You
Like It" and to Nuggetville in McCarey's *Six of a Kind,* and in all these
cases the green world is a place where over-rigid social roles can be
loosened up or let go. Indeed, no sooner do the Flouds arrive home in
Red Gap than Egbert takes Ruggles to Nell Kenna's (Leila Hyams)
place—Nell is the "hostess" of the local "house"—and he orders
Ruggles to go on in and "mix." As Egbert's friend, Ruggles is
enthusiastically welcomed, and before long Ruggles finds himself
drinking and dancing and having a fine old time. He is no longer a
butler or a valet. On the contrary, he is treated as a celebrity of sorts, is
introduced by Egbert as "Col. Ruggles," and he rather enjoys the
novelty of social esteem.

And yet Red Gap—while looser in general than the Paris of the
film's opening section—cannot be described as a perfect picture of
social health. If anything, Red Gap's "looseness" leaves it vulnerable
to the whims of irresponsible egocentricity. Thus Effie, whose

foolishness seems self-evident and relatively harmless in the midst of
Parisian sophistication, becomes a genuine social lion upon returning
home. She has a new Parisian wardrobe, a new valet for her husband,
a cart-load of new names to drop—and a new mandate, as it were, to
"civilise" Red Gap, a mandate she shares with her fortune-hunting
brother-in-law, Charles Belknap-Jackson (Lucien Littlefield) of the
Boston Belknap-Jacksons, who came west upon learning of the oil
strike that made Effie's Ma a rich woman, and who brought with him a
precise knowledge of those things in life which "really matter," such
as doilies and finger bowls and the like. But Effie and her crew are less
a cause of social illness than a symptom. The greatest threat to the
continued social health of the Red Gap community is not Effie and
others like her but a more general sense of social complacency—
complacency of the sort that grants Effie and Belknap-Jackson social
authority, for example; complacency of the sort that permits ignorance of the struggle necessary to the maintenance of open societies
(no one but Ruggles can recall what Lincoln said at Gettysburg); or
complacency of the sort displayed by Ruggles' lady love, Mrs. Judson
(ZaSu Pitts), when she tells Ruggles that he's "not a man" unless he
renounces all loyalty to Lord Burnstead. It never occurs to her until
after the fact (i.e., after she tells Ruggles to go jump in the river) that
individuality and community are interdependent, that the concern
which Ruggles shows for Lord Burnstead and for tradition is that
very quality which makes him a genuinely interesting, considerate,
and humane individual.

So what McCarey holds out for in *Ruggles of Red Gap* is a proper
balance of social and personal concerns—and he achieves that
balance by allowing things to get momentarily but benevolently out of
hand. It would seem, for instance, only another example of social
imbalance that Ruggles should be accorded instantaneous status as a
visiting British celebrity. To do so is clearly to place too great an
emphasis on superficial and incidental characteristics, Ruggles' accent, his dress, etc., exactly as Effie (and Father Fitzgibbon in *Going
My Way*) place too great an emphasis on the superficial aspects of
"civility." The resulting tendency is for the more profound aspects of
civility to be overlooked and undervalued: there is more to civilisation
than finger bowls and doilies.

Yet again, in the idealistic context of the film, it is ironic but
appropriate that this misplaced emphasis on incidentals should
actually turn out for the better. To begin with, Effie finds it impossible
to fire Ruggles after Ruggles delivers Belknap-Jackson a well de-

Individuality and community: ZaSu Pitts, Charles Laughton, Charlie Ruggles, and Maude Eburne in *Ruggles of Red Gap*.

served kick in the pants. Ruggles is already the talk of Red Gap society and Effie is too social an animal to let him go. But, by thus keeping Ruggles in Red Gap, Effie allows him opportunity both to read the classic texts of democracy—particularly Lincoln's Gettysburg Address —and to practice a sort of sexual democracy in his personal life. For once Ruggles gets to go courting (he had always been the sexual onlooker while serving his lordship) and his courtship of Mrs. Judson (in contrast to the Floud relationship) is remarkable in its reciprocity: Ruggles teaches her to brew tea while she teaches him to make coffee. And secondly, *after* Ruggles has had the chance to live as a social equal for a while, it is Belknap-Jackson's socially motivated envy (Ruggles is getting all the mail at the Floud mansion) that results in the dismissal of Ruggles—at which point Ruggles is both free (for having been fired) and able (for having educated himself) to follow his own path in life.

The path he eventually chooses to follow, however, is neither idiosyncratic nor selfish. On the contrary, Ruggles' declaration of personal independence—his deeply felt and deeply moving recitation of the Gettysburg Address—is simultaneously a *personal* and a *social* act. McCarey's *mise-en-scène* emphasises this duality. Intense close-ups of Ruggles underscore the personal nature of the recitation. In the words of Robin Wood, it's as if Ruggles were finally "coming to *understand* a text long known by heart."[9] And yet those close-ups are set within a context of shot/reverse shot and reaction shots which firmly embed Ruggles within the society of his audience. Indeed, by the time Ruggles concludes his recitation, his own intensity has been generalised and everyone present has come to a new and more profound understanding of the relationship between social consciousness and individual liberty. Ruggles thus serves as an invaluable social model. To Red Gap in general—symbolised by the crew at the Silver Dollar Saloon—he brings a new sense of the value of personal freedom. It cannot be taken for granted or people like Effie and Belknap-Jackson will end up running the show (as happens, at least momentarily, in the Europe of *Once Upon a Honeymoon*). More specifically, Ruggles gives Egbert the encouragement and the vocabulary necessary to defy Effie to her face (and by this point Effie richly deserves Egbert's open defiance). Ruggles even shows his lordship, who had come to America for reasons of loyalty to rescue Ruggles from the Flouds, that America really is a land of opportunity rather than savagery: if Ruggles can leave a heritage of service to set himself up in trade, there is no reason why the Earl of Burnstead should not cast aside social caution and marry the melodious Nell Kenna—and indeed at the film's end the earl and Nell are engaged.

The film concludes, then, on a strongly egalitarian yet strongly social note. It is opening night at Ruggles' "Anglo-American Grill"—the very name implies a union of continental gentility and colonial energy—and the whole of Red Gap society turns out. Indeed, it is the first time in the film when the entire cast appears together. It was previously the case in every Red Gap scene that some important segment of local society was missing: Effie and her "circle of cats" never show themselves at Nell Kenna's place or at the Silver Dollar and, conversely, Nell and those who frequent her place are seldom if ever seen in the haunts of Red Gap high society. In the film's closing moments, however, everyone joins together to celebrate the opening of Ruggles' new establishment. Furthermore, and despite the proletarian implications of the word "grill" (as opposed, say, to "café" or "restaurant"), everyone is in formal dress: Effie, naturally enough, wears a Parisian formal; Egbert wears a cutaway and a top hat; even

Lord Burnstead (Roland Young) and Neil Kenna (Leila Hyams) announce their engagement in *Ruggles of Red Gap* while Egbert (Charlie Ruggles), Effie (Mary Boland), and Ruggles himself (Charles Laughton) look on.

Ma Pettingill (Maude Eburne) trades her buckskins for an evening gown. And clearly the wearing of formal attire here connotes not the suffocation of personality—as it does *vis-à-vis* Egbert in the Paris section of the film—but it rather connotes a playful and self-aware appreciation of social convention. It is a positive social gesture, made to honour Ruggles and Lord Burnstead, and it does not serve to squelch individuality. Of course, individuality can go too far—as the envy-stung Belknap-Jackson goes too far when he calls Nell a "cheap dancer" and Ruggles "a low, common shiner of boots"—but social convention now clearly disallows such incivility and Ruggles quite courteously and properly, as befits his position as proprietor, tosses Belknap-Jackson out by the seat of his pants.

Even in an idealistic film like *Ruggles of Red Gap*, then, McCarey evidently feels it necessary to qualify his myth-making by allowing for the possibility that the mythos won't "take." There will always be, or so McCarey implies, people like Belknap-Jackson, people unable to loosen up and be their better selves no matter how conducive a particular social context might be for such personal betterment. Indeed, after tossing Belknap-Jackson out the door, Ruggles himself fears that the integrity of his gesture will be the ruin of his hopes and he retires to the kitchen where Mrs. Judson does her homiletic best to assure him that "it's always darkest just before the dawn and every cloud has a silver lining." In this particular instance, at least, the cliché proves true enough. Ruggles has brought a new sense of life to Red Gap—and Red Gap salutes his contribution by declaring communally, in song, that Ruggles is indeed "a jolly good fellow"—Belknap-Jackson or no Belknap-Jackson.

Of course, Egbert has to drag Ruggles out of the kitchen, and Ruggles is shocked to learn that *he* is the jolly good fellow (*Egbert:* "Why, ya old plate of soup, they're singing it for you"). But nobody, and certainly not Leo McCarey, can deny the look of joy that comes to Ruggles' face as the song is repeated one last time. And the joy is not Ruggles' alone. McCarey alternates close-ups of Ruggles with close-ups of every other major character (excepting Belknap-Jackson) and by so doing he underscores the fact that personal and social imperatives are (or ought to be) indivisible. Everyone is granted the opportunity to express their strongly felt appreciation for the unity which Ruggles has brought about; but they do so as individuals, bound together not by ritual alone but by the bonds of personal loyalty which make those rituals socially and personally viable. Such viability is not easily arrived at—not in *Ruggles of Red Gap*, certainly not in later films like *My Son John*—but it is clearly the case that McCarey recognises the difficulties involved. And if he remains, in some sense of the word, an "apologist" for American democracy, he is far less naive and far more profound an apologist than some would have us believe.

Parents and Children:
Make Way for Tomorrow

It is curious but indicative of the continuity of McCarey's concerns that *Make Way for Tomorrow,* arguably the bleakest and most poignant of McCarey's films, should recall in several respects *Six of a Kind.* Both films focus on lovers who are well past their prime, Pinky and Flora Winney in *Six of a Kind,* Lucy (Beulah Bondi) and Barkley (Victor Moore) Cooper in *Make Way for Tomorrow.* In both cases the central couple find themselves at hazard in situations imposed upon them by what seem to be external forces (and in both cases those external forces are partly financial, e.g., the greedy bank-clerk in *Six of a Kind,* the bank manager who forecloses on the Cooper mortgage in *Make Way for Tomorrow*). In both films the situation is one which serves to separate husband and wife (Pinky and Flora must sleep apart, while Lucy and Bark each go to live with a different offspring). And in each film the resolution involves the re-assertion of marital identities by recalling the sense of adventure and hopefulness that marked the beginning of the marital relationship.

The films differ, then, not so much in terms of structure and theme but rather in terms of style and emphasis. Generically speaking, *Six of a Kind* is a knockabout comedy which focuses on the capacity of its characters to recover from the reversals which serve to call them or their lifestyle into question. Pinky and Flora may let conventionalized habits of mind get the better of them from time to time, but we never genuinely doubt their ability to muddle through no matter how

Gathering the clan in *Make Way for Tomorrow*: Beulah Bondi, Victor Moore, and Thomas Mitchell.

woebegone or frustrated they get to be on occasion. *Make Way for Tomorrow,* on the other hand, is far more tragic than comic, far more concerned with the fact that people are often incapable of recovery, are unable to react creatively and humanely enough to the difficulties which befall them. Indeed, *Make Way for Tomorrow* seems the far more realistic film (as tragedies generally seem more "realistic") for implicitly confronting the one reversal from which no one can recover—death. In metaphoric terms, however, *Make Way for Tomorrow* is concerned with something larger and more significant than the fact that Lucy and Barkley Cooper are old people who have reached the end of the line. *Make Way for Tomorrow* is concerned not only with the physical decline of Lucy and Barkley Cooper but with the emotional decline of the entire Cooper family in the face of a crisis that cannot be dealt with.

The nature and severity of the problem is evidenced in the film's opening scene. The first shot after the "Honour Thy Father and Thy Mother" prologue shows us an idealised, Norman Rockwell homestead, the yard deep in snow, smoke pouring comfortingly from the chimney of the house: all in all, a conventional picture of familial security. This conventionality is further emphasized when George Cooper (Thomas Mitchell), the eldest son, arrives at the door where he is greeted by his mother. They embrace, comment upon each other's health, and Mother Cooper asks about "the baby" as she shows a rather curious George ("Say, what is this gathering of the clan?") into the front room where they join the rest of the family.

The room itself, it is worth remarking, is also very conventional, both in terms of *décor* (the upright piano, the nick-nack shelves, the portrait over the fireplace) and in terms of the spatial relationships that seem implicit in that *décor*. After George and his mother enter the room, for example, George crosses the room to greet his father, who sits in the far corner, enthroned in "the same old" overstuffed chair. George then moves away from his parents, literally turning his back on them, as he greets his sisters, Nellie (Minna Gombell) and Cora (Elisabeth Risdon), who sit on the side of the room opposite their father.

Already, then, there are intimations of disharmony. The very fact of the family gathering, which we understand, by virtue of the greetings exchanged, to be a very infrequent occurrence ("I haven't seen you since . . ."), is itself unusual and foreboding. Some of those greetings, furthermore, tend to be forced in their enthusiasm. Indeed, Nellie's nervous reaction to younger brother Robert's toast

("Here's to our house, through sunshine or showers—be it ever so humble, by golly, it's ours") evidences a certain *nouveau riche* disgust with her "ever so humble" beginnings: she would rather not be there at all. In addition, the spatial relationships tend, particularly after Barkley informs Robert that the last line of his toast "don't make sense" (the house isn't theirs), to enforce a literal "gap" between parents and children. Thus Lucy stands beside Barkley's chair on one side of the room, while the kids seat themselves in a well ordered row opposite and quite far removed from their parents.

The scene then continues as Barkley explains the circumstances, his four year lack of work and income, the call from the bank, his chat with the bank manager (who had been a rival for Lucy's hand), etc., etc. McCarey cuts from the parents to reaction shots of the children as the significance of Father Cooper's recitation sinks in. They are relieved when he mentions a six-month grace period, but near panic when he informs them laconically that the six months are up next Tuesday. On the surface, of course, their reactions are normal—concern on the one hand and surprise on the other that they had not been informed of the problem sooner. George, indeed, is so concerned that he cannot sit still. Instead he paces the room, his back once again to his parents, and takes stock of the possibilities: Nellie cannot help because her husband's business is doing poorly; Cora's husband is unemployed and they haven't room to take both Father and Mother together; Robert, apparently, is resourceless (George just passes over the possibility that Robert might help out); Addie has never even sent an orange from California and it seems unlikely that she would be inclined to help out now; and George himself had been planning to send his daughter, Rhoda (no longer a "baby"), to college. It is finally decided, therefore, that Lucy will move in with George, taking the extra bed in Rhoda's room, and that Barkley will sleep on the couch in Cora's front room—but only until Nellie can make good her promise, made more to save face than to be helpful, to bring Lucy and Barkley "together again" within three months.

And the point to this relatively detailed description of the opening scene is to demonstrate that there are two sets of conventions at work—and often at cross purposes. On the one hand there is the picture postcard vision of rural American life, egg-nog, tiffany lamps, warm family gatherings, parental affection and mutual respect, family unity in the face of adversity. And, on the other hand, there are the conventionalised habits of mind and behaviour that characterise family relations among the Coopers. Thus, for example, we get the almost formulaic exchange of insults between Robert and Nellie, which Barkley only pretends to referee. Of course, the Coopers would all like to think that they embody the first set of traditional values—but the facade of family harmony quickly breaks down under pressure, as we have already demonstrated. Indeed, the degree of anxiety evident even before Barkley's formal announcement of disaster indicates that family cohesion has never been strongly motivated, except perhaps by external convention: it would not look right if Nellie did not make some gesture to help her parents, however insincere or meaningless that gesture might be. And even George, the most concerned of the children, hedges his bet by describing Lucy's impending stay as a "visit," as if she had some place else to go.

The temptation, therefore, is to blame everything on the kids. And there is, indeed, a strong current of anti-child sentiment in the film. The opening scene raises questions about the Cooper kids. The first scene in George's New York City apartment, furthermore, finds Rhoda surreptitiously removing her grandfather's portrait from the wall in her bedroom: as she tells Anita, her mother, she has grandmother in her room and "that's enough." And the first scene with Barkley in the small town where he lives with Cora is conspicuous for the degree to which children are portrayed not as angels but as parasites. Thus Mr. Ruben, who owns the local magazine and newspaper shop, makes it a point to frisk the kid who comes in to buy a stick of gum. And when a mother comes in to pick up the latest issue of "Sincere Confessions," Mr. Ruben very pointedly asks the lady's son whether he will be nice to his mother when he grows up. The lad is dumbstruck until his mother prods him, at which point he pleads no contest: "What should I say?" In neither instance, of course, is Mr. Ruben intentionally oppressive or overly cynical. He turns the frisk into a tickle, and his response to the young boy's reluctant reply is a bemused shrug of the shoulders. The point, however, is that Ruben and Barkley Cooper are both inclined to agree that the world is full of "schlemiels"—"And somebody," Barkley points out, "has to raise them."

Note, however, that Barkley thus manages to avoid all responsibility for the behaviour of his children. If kids are schlemiels, as he argues, then those who have the unfortunate duty of raising those kids are to be seen as victims rather than as agents. This, clearly, is how Barkley would like to see himself at this point in the film. We must remark, however, that the Cooper kids cannot be held totally responsible for the plight of their parents. On the contrary, there are many factors involved, some of them genuinely beyond the control of the children.

To begin with, of course, there are the economic factors. The bank has foreclosed on the mortgage and the kids can hardly be blamed for that. And furthermore, once the bank has foreclosed, it is generally the case that no one child alone (excepting, perhaps, Nellie) has the resources or the room to take both parents together—at least not right away. All of which amounts to a clear if not very pointed critique of society and its economic institutions: a social system that makes no adequate provision for its elders can hardly be described as humane. This anti-materialist attitude, we should also remark, is typical of McCarey, and *Make Way for Tomorrow* represents no exception in this regard. McCarey's attitude toward capitalism, as I remarked in connection with *Ruggles of Red Gap,* is frequently ambivalent and often downright hostile. On occasion, granted, we have establishments like the Anglo-American Grill, which are acceptable for being such clear expressions of responsible personalities. But, for the most part, McCarey portrays business, at best, as humorously absurd (as it is in the Laurel-and-Hardy *Big Business* which metaphorically equates capitalism with total destruction) and, at worst, as a genuine threat to human life and human ethics. Thus Ace Le Mont, music hall owner and fight promoter, both keeps a mistress (as does Ken in *Love Affair* and *An Affair to Remember*) and attempts to murder her in *Belle of the Nineties.* Indeed, one of McCarey's best characters—Good Sam—is a lousy businessman, and lousy precisely because he cares (perhaps too much) about other human beings. The only "business" which routinely has McCarey's approval is art: many of his independent women are independent by virtue of their ability as singers (Ruby Carter in *Belle of the Nineties,* Terry McKay in *Love Affair,* Genevieve Linden in *Going My Way*); and Nickie Ferrante in *An Affair to Remember,* like his predecessor in *Love Affair,* gains independence by virtue of his skill as a painter.

But economic factors alone cannot account for the situation of Lucy and Barkley Cooper in *Make Way for Tomorrow.* On the contrary, the economic facts of the matter are far less significant than how people choose to face or not face the facts at hand. Clearly, then, the single most important factor contributing to the plight of Lucy and Barkley is their naive but characteristic decision not to level with their children. As Lucy puts it, in response to Nellie's question: "Your father and I were hoping that something would turn up and we wouldn't have to tell you at all." Clearly the entire dilemma could have been avoided had Lucy and Barkley come right out and admitted that they could not continue making house payments after Barkley lost his job. Indeed, one rather suspects that even Nellie would have willingly contributed to an effort to keep the family homestead if by so doing she could avoid the trauma that would surely and foreseeably result from the loss of the house.

Of course, we might reasonably wonder why the children did not put two and two together, did not understand the likelihood that Barkley's unemployment would lead to foreclosure. But the issue is not defined by any one particular failure of foresight, except to the degree that these particular failures, Lucy and Barkley's failure to be straightforward with their children, the children's failure to foresee financial disaster, are indicative of a general pattern of irresponsible behavior. To put it bluntly, all the members of the Cooper family, both parents and children (and grandchildren as well), are addicted to the fantasy that they can avoid facing facts.

Such is clearly the case with Lucy and Barkley. By waiting for "something" to "turn up," they only guarantee the likelihood that they will be separated. A similar unwillingness to face facts likewise leads George and Anita to put Lucy in a home for aged women. Of course, Lucy "volunteers" to go to the home, in order to save George the agony of asking her to go, but that she goes at all, under whatever circumstance, is indicative of the fact that George and Anita, however genuine their agony, are agonised over a false issue, just as Lucy and Barkley were agonised over the equally false issue of whether or not to tell the kids about the impending foreclosure. The issue is not one of to tell or not to tell (or at least it shouldn't be). The issue is to leave each other or not to leave. And clearly the latter issue is the more significant. Likewise, George and Anita perceive the issue as Mother vs. Rhoda. But by so doing they fail to account for the fact that Rhoda will soon be leaving home no matter what—and so she should. The only probable solution to the parent problem, once the house is lost, would be to let Rhoda go her own way (perhaps to college, as originally planned) and to move Lucy and Barkley together into the room that Rhoda vacates. Together they would have companionship and neither would be troublesome or embarrassing. Apart, however, they tend toward quarrelsomeness and self-pity. But this solution never occurs to George or Anita because they are incapable of imagining a day when their eighteen-year-old daughter might go her own way. For that matter, nothing similar ever occurs to any of the other children. To the contrary, Nellie washes her hands of the whole affair early on. Robert, for all of his apparent insightfulness, never proposes any sort of solution. And Cora's lot is so difficult, her husband unemployed, her father a genuine embarrassment, that her only concern is to get out from under it all. She therefore welcomes the fact of Barkley's cold as excuse for shipping him off to California to stay with the last daughter.

Thus Lucy, Barkley, and the entire Cooper clan are both literally and figuratively torn apart by their lack of insight and responsibility. Assigning blame for this lack, however, is a difficult matter. If nothing else, *Make Way for Tomorrow* demonstrates how readily conventionalised habits of mind are passed from one generation to the next. However likeable, Barkley and Lucy must have offered very poor examples of responsible familial behaviour. Barkley, we eventually discover, was very seldom home. He was always the good time jokester, spent most of his free time at the barbershop with the boys, but he was never a genuine parent. Even in the opening scene he only pretends to authority. Indeed, Barkley forfeited all parental authority to Lucy early on—and she represents Barkley's mirror image. Where Barkley avoids responsibility, Lucy accepts too much. Thus when Robert offers her a cup of egg-nog in the opening scene, she rejects it in terms which indicate the degree of her dedication to motherhood: "That don't go with standing over a hot stove." But she clearly did more than just cook. She gave herself over totally to the task of homemaking: thus her insistence on playing the homemaker role even after she moves in with George and Anita; and thus as well Cora's angry response when Mr. Ruben brings her father the chicken soup (Cora takes the gesture as criticism of her own homemaking abilities: like mother, like daughter).

And the result of such parental behaviour is the clear implication that parent/child relationships are a one way street: Barkley gives nothing of himself, Lucy gives everything—and neither parent gives the children opportunity to contribute to the family. It is not at all insignificant, therefore, that we only see one Cooper grandchild. As a group the Cooper children have been lead to believe that parenthood means an almost unhealthy sort of self-sacrifice (hence Lucy's presence and Barkley's absence), and only George and Cora are willing to take the necessary risk in their turn (and we never see Cora's kids). Even George, however, runs afoul of the basic family logic: Rhoda seems just as spoiled as her aunt Nellie. In other words, parents in the Cooper clan tend toward extremes of selfishness or self-abnegation.

And Cooper children, of whatever generation, tend therefore to be alienated from and irresponsible toward their parents. No wonder, then, that the family cannot cope with the situation.

The total effect of all this is to generalise blame. Thus we understand the reasons behind Rhoda's irresponsible behaviour, and we are led to believe that similar factors contributed to the behaviour of Lucy and Barkley. In a sense, what happens is inevitable—given who these people are and the particular circumstances which envelop them. Hence the film's genuine sense of poignancy and fatalism. As a family, the Coopers seem almost incapable of breaking out of the roles which define them. Robin Wood, indeed, has argued that McCarey seems uncomfortable with and uncommitted to families in general. And he argues, specifically, that "the whole movement of *Make Way for Tomorrow* is toward an affirmation of marriage and a denigration of the family."[10]

Wood is clearly (and uncharacteristically) wrong in this. Families are terribly important to McCarey, and important for embodying the most basic McCarey issue in its most elemental and agonising form: if the original McCarey sin is mindless over-conventionality, then families are problematic for encouraging just that sort of behaviour: like parent, like child. And yet, at the same time, McCarey realises and acknowledges the necessity for families: they are basic to the continuation of life and society. Were there no families there would be no society to worry about. Thus the most basic social institution is simultaneously the most dangerous. This dilemma accounts for the sense of urgency that we see in McCarey's "family films"—*Make Way for Tomorrow, My Son John, Good Sam,* and *Satan Never Sleeps.* If these films are uncomfortable and controversial, it is partly because McCarey has had the courage to confront one of life's most basic problems head on. And furthermore, McCarey's sense of family dynamics allows us to account for the importance he generally assigns to priests in his films. Priests are unconventional to the degree that they have opted out of the family system, and as outsiders they can often provide the insight and knowledge required to save families from themselves (witness Father O'Malley's good works in this regard in *Going My Way* and *The Bells of St. Mary's*). Unfortunately for the Coopers, however, there is no such helpful outsider in *Make Way for Tomorrow.*

None of which is intended to describe *Make Way for Tomorrow* as a sombre parable of futility. To do so would be to wilfully ignore the generosity and even-handedness of McCarey's direction. Thus, while we slowly come to recognise and understand the behaviour patterns which characterise and constrict the Coopers, we are never allowed to overlook their humanity. On the contrary, McCarey's sense of space, both physical and psychological, grants everyone—even Nellie—their moment, their place, and their worth.

Perhaps the best example of this comes in the scene when Lucy receives a long distance phone call from Barkley. Lucy has just returned with Rhoda from the cinema (Rhoda had ducked out of the theatre to keep a date, however) and McCarey shoots the scene in a deep focus shot, Lucy and Rhoda in the background, Anita and the members of her bridge class in the foreground. Lucy is clearly out of place—neither her garb nor her diction is up to the tie-and-tux standards of Anita's very posh pupils—and Anita literally cringes when Lucy decides that she can stay up and socialise for a while longer. At this point the phone rings and Anita answers it. We cut

Lucy (Beulah Bondi) talks long-distance with Barkley while Anita's bridge pupils look on in *Make Way for Tomorrow*.

then to a medium shot of Lucy, with the bridge class in the background, as she takes the receiver from Anita.

It is clear already that Anita would rather Lucy did not talk (she had "forgotten" to tell Lucy that Barkley had called earlier) and Anita's fears are realised when Lucy raises her voice to speak: everyone in the background turns around as if to express disapproval of Lucy's less than elegant manners (how dare she interrupt their game?). McCarey holds on the medium shot for a moment as Lucy exchanges small talk with Barkley and then cuts to a deep focus shot with Lucy in the background, so as to emphasise the embarrassed discomfort of the bridge players. At this point, however, it is clear that the dynamics of space have been modified: Lucy no longer "intrudes" on the bridge players but rather the bridge players feel embarrassed for intruding on Lucy's privacy, and all the more embarrassed when Lucy describes them as "lovely people." Then McCarey again reverses his shot, Lucy now in the foreground as she asks about Cora and Bill and whether "everything" is going all right. Apparently things are not going well for Barkley, and Lucy offers comfort, both by assuring him that "three months isn't so long" and by shifting from the subject of "everything" to the less sensitive matter of the weather ("If it rains, don't go out at all"). At this, the bridge players in the background smile—it is indeed charming and touching—but as yet the real import of the situation has not impressed itself upon Lucy's audience. That changes very quickly, however, and McCarey underlines the change by individualising (and humanising) Lucy's audience. That is, he breaks the shot/reverse-shot pattern thus far established and cuts to reaction shots of small groups of bridge players as Lucy tells Barkley they'll "soon be together, for always." At this, people (including George and Anita) slowly lower their heads in recognition of the fact that Lucy's feelings for Bark far exceed in importance the specifics of bridge-table manners. In other words, they demonstrate their own humanity and worth by acknowledging Lucy's.

In this scene as elsewhere, then, McCarey "faces facts"—and forces us to "face facts"—by refusing to patronise his characters: none are perfect, all are human. Indeed, the movement of *Make Way for Tomorrow* generally is toward the recognition of reality. Again, however, McCarey's realism is not in any sense nihilistic. On the contrary, while it is true that the characters in *Make Way for Tomorrow* cannot escape the consequences of their past actions (by film's end there seems no chance that Lucy and Barkley will ever be permanently reunited), they are capable, almost despite expectation, of escaping the habits of mind which determined past action. In other words, Rhoda is right when she tells Lucy to "face facts"—and Lucy's reply ("When you're seventy ... about all the fun you have left is pretending there aren't any facts to face"), however quaint and poignant, serves to demonstrate both the legitimacy of Rhoda's advice (had Lucy and Bark faced facts they would not have lost the house) and the possibility that Lucy and Barkley will be able to transcend their history (the self-consciousness implicit in Lucy's remark holds hope for future action).

The positive tone of the film's final sequence—Lucy and Bark sharing a few hours together in New York City before he catches the train to California—reflects the fact, therefore, that something both positive and unconventional takes place. To put it briefly, Lucy and Barkley slowly but openly face the hard facts for the first time in fifty years: Barkley admits the insufficiency of his jokester's approach to life, and Lucy remarks, as they rest for a moment on a Central Park bench, that "you don't sew wheat and reap ashes." In other words, through the course of a few brief hours they both accept a real measure of responsibility for the fate that overwhelms them. Of course, that does not change the facts of the situation—Bark will still be leaving for California on the next train—but it does allow Lucy and Barkley to recapture a sense of vitality and to celebrate the fact of their love despite their circumstances. To a certain degree they have failed as parents—witness Barkley's somewhat hostile remark to the hotel manager on the subject of the joys of parenthood—but the fact of their failure does not cancel out the worth of their feelings for each other. In fact, their failure to deal creatively with the responsibilities of child-rearing only serves to emphasise the strength and value of their relationship. That they can still call each other "sweetheart" after all they have been through is eloquent testimony to the resiliency of the human spirit. Indeed, even the children come somewhat to their senses and are responsible enough to allow Lucy and Barkley their privacy in their final hours together.

It would be a mistake, therefore, to read the conclusion of *Make Way for Tomorrow* as a denigration of the family. In the context of the film any such denigration must extend to include Lucy and Barkley among those to be condemned, for they clearly share responsibility for the family's failure. If they had been less rigid as parents, the family might very well have survived the crisis. If Barkley had only told Nellie years earlier what she could do with her roast, things might very well have turned out otherwise. If Lucy had taken a drink or two

**a the town: Beulah Bondi and
ctor Moore are invited to take a
in in *Make Way for Tomorrow*.**

somewhere along the line, she might have devoted more time to dancing and less time to spoiling her children. But the past cannot be relived. The Hotel Vogard has been totally made over since Lucy and Barkley first honeymooned there. And all that Lucy and Barkley have left to them is the knowledge that their love has survived their failings. The closing moments of *Make Way for Tomorrow,* however, are not very much concerned with the family as a whole. On the contrary, more than anything else, the final shot of *Make Way for Tomorrow* is a celebration of courage in the face of life's inevitable disappointments. It took courage for "the man and the maid" to begin life together, not knowing what life would bring. It takes courage for Lucy and Barkley to say farewell to one another, both knowing too well what life remains to be lived. Indeed, there is no more powerful image of courage in the history of cinema than the simple and heart-rending close-up of Lucy Cooper on the railway platform as she watches her husband's train pull away ("Let me call you sweetheart, I'm in love with you . . ."). And it testifies to McCarey's artistic integrity that he fought so hard to make the film.

The Art of Human Relationships:
Theme and Structure in *The Awful Truth*

In retrospect it is arguable that *The Awful Truth* was something of a transition film for McCarey. To begin with, it was the first film he made after his departure from Paramount. *Make Way for Tomorrow* had not been a financial success for the studio and, after leaving, McCarey may have felt it necessary to re-establish his credentials as a bankable director: hence his move to Columbia and his return to comedy. More important, however, is the fact that *The Awful Truth* marks, as Charles Silver points out, something of a synthesis between McCarey's slapstick beginnings and his increasingly mature and increasingly serious romanticism. Here again, of course, we must be careful not to overgeneralise. *The Awful Truth* is hardly atypical McCarey. But the sense persists that *The Awful Truth* represents, at least to a certain degree, a new alignment of style and subject matter.

We have already remarked upon the thematic similarities evidenced by *Six of a Kind* and *Make Way for Tomorrow:* both films are very deeply concerned with the vitality and viability of sexual relationships, however much the films may differ in terms of overall style. *The Awful Truth* evidences a similar concern for the values and dynamics of the marital estate, and can be understood as a middle term between the earlier two films. Thus McCarey takes what appears to be a conventional slapstick couple, recalling in several respects the Whinneys from *Six of a Kind* (and played by Cary Grant and Irene Dunne, the two premier comic actors of the late Thirties), and pilots them through some of the fast talk and pratfalls characteristic of the screwball genre. But McCarey does not cast *The Awful Truth* altogether in the strongly slapstick mould of *Six of a Kind.* McCarey is careful to retain a relatively strong, though unobtrusive, sense of "reality," and hence of negative consequences—after all, Lucy and Jerry Warriner are working against the calendar and the clock to find a new foundation for their marriage (their divorce decree becomes final in ninety days). In *The Awful Truth,* we have no hyper-obvious backdrops, such as the Grand Canyon set in *Six of a Kind,* to maintain a certain comedic distance and to insure a positive outcome. The *mise-en-scène* of *The Awful Truth* more nearly resembles that of *Make Way for Tomorrow* in its careful attention to the details of the world the characters inhabit. It is this surface realism, I believe, that keynotes the underlying seriousness of McCarey's comic theme, and signals *The Awful Truth* as a prologue of sorts to the subsequent series of romantic comedies written and/or directed by McCarey, all of which focus to a large degree on the ethics of human sexuality.

Earlier I suggested that the central thematic antinomy in McCarey is the opposition of the conventional and the unconventional, particularly in regard to sexuality and society. Some films bear down more on society than sex (e.g., *Ruggles of Red Gap*), others more on sex than society (e.g., *Indiscreet*). But the series of sexual comedies beginning with *The Awful Truth* (1937) and including *The Cowboy and the Lady* (1938), *Love Affair* (1939), *My Favorite Wife* (1940), *Once Upon a Honeymoon* (1942), *Good Sam* (1948), *An Affair to Remember* (1957) and *Rally Round the Flag, Boys!* (1958), makes it clear that sexuality and society are ultimately inseparable concerns in McCarey's universe. Accordingly, McCarey's sex comedies generally tend to focus on various conventionalised social/sexual attitudes and situations which stand in the way of genuine sexuality and genuine sexual civility. In every case there is a central couple, partners who display an obvious unity of personal style and emotional purpose. In each instance their unity is threatened or called into question. And in each case the threat serves to clarify the emotional value to be found in sexual union.

The threat which tests this unity can originate (at least in part)

ly McCarey: Maude Eburne
t), Gloria Swanson (center
, and Ben Lyon (far right) in
screet.

outside the characters: witness the hostile social environment of European fascism in *Once Upon a Honeymoon*, or the extraordinary but benign accidents of *My Favorite Wife* where the legally deceased title character is rescued from her desert island. More commonly, the threat originates within the characters. Thus it is misguided romantic sentiment that separates the lovers in both *Affair* films and precipitates the disaster which delays their reunion. But in most of McCarey's films it is a combination of social circumstances and personal attitudes which endangers sexual integrity. The central couple in *The Cowboy and the Lady,* for example, has two obstacles to overcome. The first is a matter of mistaken identity. Stretch Willoughby (Gary Cooper) believes that Mary Smith (Merle Oberon) is a lady's maid, not the lady herself. And the second involves Stretch's dogmatic distrust of the wealthy. Stretch had once had his fill of the upper classes while working on a dude ranch, and he refuses to accept the proposition that rich people can be human too. Thus it is all the more difficult for Mary to reveal her true identity, even after their ship-board wedding. Likewise, in *Rally Round the Flag, Boys!,* the political issue raised when a small town becomes the site of an army missile base is complicated by the domestic squabbles of Grace (Joanne Woodward) and Harry (Paul Newman) Bannerman: as a notorious do-gooder she is chosen to be spokesperson for the town in its attempt to stop the base while he becomes a military public relations officer when he is called back into active duty.

**Merle Oberon and Gary Cooper
in *The Cowboy and the Lady.***

Seen within the general context of McCarey's sex comedies, the transition status of *The Awful Truth* is re-affirmed. That is, in most respects the film accords with the model I have proposed. There is a central couple, their relationship is tested, and in surviving the test the relationship is strengthened. But all things considered, *The Awful Truth* is the most positive film of the group (standing in relation to the sex comedies as *Ruggles of Red Gap* stands in relation to the more political films); and positive primarily because the partners almost knowingly collaborate in bringing the test upon themselves. The test thus becomes a self-conscious tactic for renewing and improving their marital relationship. That the relationship in some sense *needs* improvement is typical of McCarey's sex comedies; that improving it involves an increased capacity for social improvisation and a heightened degree of self-awareness is likewise typical. But that the characters should demonstrate their capacities for improvement from the very beginning by initiating the test voluntarily *is* rather unusual and sets the film somewhat apart from those that follow.

*   *   *

We may characterise the structural logic of *The Awful Truth* by two terms: "inferential" and "referential." The "inferential" quality of the narrative derives from the fact that McCarey maximises action and minimises exposition. We are thus left to infer motives for the behaviour of characters from the behaviour itself, with a minimum of directorial comment. Partly, as I have already suggested, this focus on action is a function of the fact that the central characters are basically right-headed to begin with: thus there is no great necessity to focus on motives, not as far as a simple comprehension of the "plot" is concerned. On the other hand, however, it is precisely this ability to "read" motives from action that the film is concerned, among others things, to celebrate and to encourage. Indeed, to "read" people in this fashion is, almost by definition, to be empathetic; and empathy is a cardinal virtue in the world view of Leo McCarey.

We see this "inferential" style at work all through the film—but its workings are particularly evident and noteworthy in the opening section, where the film's basic issues are set forth. We can describe the "denotative" value of the opening four scenes fairly briefly. The first takes place at Jerry's Manhattan athletic club. Jerry is under the sun lamp, determined to get a "Florida tan if it takes all afternoon," and he implies, without ever really admitting it, that he had not been anywhere near Florida. As Jerry puts it to one of his athletic club buddies: "What wives don't know won't hurt them." After which, on the spur of the moment, Jerry invites the gang over to the house for egg-nogs and a late breakfast.

The second (and the longest) scene of the opening section takes place at the Warriner estate. Jerry and his guests arrive, Jerry bearing gifts, a dog-toy for the pet terrier, Mr. Smith, a basket of "Florida" citrus fruit for Lucy. But Lucy is not there. Indeed, it is possible, as one of Jerry's guests points out, that Lucy has not been home for several days: there are several unopened letters from Jerry to Lucy on the desk. Jerry remarks that Lucy is probably at her Aunt Patsy's and goes on to express the enlightened opinion that Lucy *should* go out and "get some fun for herself." At this point Aunt Patsy enters, looking for Lucy, and then Lucy herself makes a breathless entrance, followed soon thereafter by her European voice teacher, Armand Duvalle. Lucy explains that their car had broken down the night before and they had been forced to stay the evening at the "nastiest little inn you ever saw." One of Jerry's guests, a woman, then wonders aloud at Jerry's equanimity ("Now if I stayed out all night . . .") and Lucy protests that "you can't have a happily married life if you're always going to be suspicious." At this point, the guests and Aunt Patsy beat a decorous retreat and the conversation continues for a few moments with Jerry, Lucy, and Armand—and then Armand departs, leaving Jerry and Lucy to themselves. Jerry expresses disbelief regarding the broken down car ("People stopped believing that one before cars started breaking down") and Lucy retorts that "there can't be any doubt in marriage: the whole thing's built on faith." Jerry agrees that the loss of faith means that the marriage is "washed up"—at which point they agree to call their lawyer.

The third scene is very brief: we see the lawyer, on the telephone, alternately assuring Lucy that "marriage is a beautiful thing" and telling his nagging wife to shut her "big mouth."

The fourth scene, in Chancery Court, then concludes the film's opening section. The judge grants an interlocutory decree, which will become final in ninety days, and is about to conclude the proceedings when Jerry's lawyer raises the still unsettled matter of Mr. Smith. At this point Jerry and Lucy engage in a bit of comically rhetorical oneupmanship ("He's mine"/"He's not") and the judge, in exasperation, asks Lucy to explain her claim to the dog. Lucy does a somewhat scatterbrained job of it, complete with asides on his honour's taste in pets, and the judge finally decides to let Mr. Smith himself make the

(Irene Dunne) and Jerry (Cary
t) Warriner vie for custody of
Smith in *The Awful Truth* (a
uction still).

choice. Then follows another slapstick shouting match, Jerry and
Lucy both calling the dog, which concludes when Lucy surreptitiously
offers the dog-toy to Mr. Smith: the dog goes to Lucy and Jerry is left
begging the judge for visitation rights.

There are several remarkable things to note about the sequence
just described. Most remarkable of them all, no doubt, is the fact that
the grounds for the divorce are never made explicit. They are never
mentioned in the courtroom scene; and the sequence of events in the
first two scenes can hardly be said to specify the reasons for the
breakup—at least not in anything approaching a straightforward
manner. For example, we never do find out where Jerry went if he did
not go to Florida. McCarey just leaves it hanging, as if it did not
matter. It matters so little, indeed, that Lucy herself never presses the
point, not when Jerry insinuates that she had been cheating on him
with Duvalle, not even at the end of the film when the final
reconciliation takes place, despite her knowledge that Jerry never

went to Florida (the oranges are from California and Jerry's tan does not square with the Florida rainstorms that had been in the news). Thus the quarrel, when it erupts, comes not over the issue of Jerry's fidelity or whereabouts but over the issue of Lucy's relationship with Armand. Here there *is* a plausible explanation—Armand is Lucy's voice-teacher, and they had accepted the invitation of another of his students to attend a junior prom—but Lucy never persists in defending herself or the purity of her motives. If anything, Lucy's seemingly inappropriate *double entendres* ("That's right, Armand, no one could ever accuse you of being a great lover") are perfectly timed to speed the quarrel to its apparently foregone conclusion. It is as if the both of them were convinced at some level, intuitive or otherwise, that their relationship is too valuable to trust to the normal course of marital events, so they almost self-consciously employ the rituals of infidelity and outrage, complete with correspondents (Duvalle) and witnesses (Jerry's friends), in order to test the marriage while it is still strong enough to withstand the test and be tempered by it.

And we know the strength is there: witness the fact that Lucy and Jerry seem intuitively aware of each other's motives. There is little sense that they consciously conspired in advance to set up the confrontation scene—but together they take immediate advantage of the relatively minor coincidence of the broken down car and Lucy's ill—or well—timed entrance to enact their almost parodistically civilised version of the washed-up marriage scene. In this context, indeed, all that talk about the necessity of faith in marriage becomes somewhat ironic. It is not a lack of faith that destroys the marriage but an abundance of faith in each other and in the value of their relationship which requires them to risk divorce. Thus Lucy and Jerry really are two of a kind, as Pinky and Flora Whinney are two of a kind, and the marvellous reciprocity of their give-and-take repartee, in the confrontation scene, in the courtroom scene, and throughout the film, constantly evidences that fact. The evidence is so strong, indeed, that even Dan Leeson (Ralph Bellamy), Lucy's ever honest but slow-witted and oil-rich Oklahoma suitor, remarks in the film's second section that Jerry and Lucy remind him of the red rooster and the little brown hen: "They fight all the time, too, but every once in a while they make up again and they're right friendly."

But why bother with all that fighting if the relationship is basically sound to begin with? What logic can possibly be invoked to justify the pain of physical separation if the fact of emotional unity is apparent for all to see? Put another way, what dangers are to be avoided by risking divorce such that the risk is necessary? Briefly, there are two such dangers, each related to the other, and both of them are set forth in the opening section of the film.

The first threat to the Jerry/Lucy relationship is specified in the very brief third scene of the opening sequence. As I have already noted, Jerry and Lucy agree to divorce and they call their lawyer. We then see the lawyer on the telephone, his 'wife in the background screen right, and the emotional/thematic focus of the scene shifts from foreground to background as the lawyer, on the one hand, assures Lucy of the beauty of marriage and, on the other hand, condemns his wife for nagging him that his supper is getting cold. Again, there is a certain dissociation of contexts, a contrast between marital fiction and marital fact, a contrast recalling that which we have already observed in the Jerry/Lucy confrontation scene (the fact of their love is evidenced by the fiction of their distrust). But here, in the third scene, the contrast is negative. Where Jerry and Lucy *use* the rituals of marriage, the lawyer and his wife are *bound* by them. And the implicit danger, recalling that which threatens the relationship of Lucy and Barkley Cooper in *Make Way for Tomorrow,* involves the deadening effect of mindless repetition. The quarrel between the lawyer and his wife is obviously a long-standing one, so deeply embedded in the history of their relationship that the lawyer can praise the beauty of marriage without ever perceiving the contradiction between his platitudinous words and his malevolent marital actions. History blindly repeated thus gives rise to negative, dehumanised conventions—and it is this very sort of dehumanisation that Jerry and Lucy intuitively fear and seek to avoid. Again, there is little sense of calculation. Jerry and Lucy never sit down and discuss this particular marital pitfall. But McCarey makes it clear that the danger is there by inserting the otherwise unnecessary lawyer/wife scene in the narrative: the scene could be dropped without consequence to the plot (indeed, the lawyer does not say a single word in the courtroom sequence) and we must therefore conclude that the scene bears particularly on the theme of the film.

The second threat to the Warriners is similar to the first, in that it has to do with the relationship of past and present, but the problem is a matter of "too little" rather than "too much." Where the lawyer and his wife are *too bound* by the past, too caught up in daily rituals of retribution, the Warriners are *not bound enough* by personal history, at least not at the film's beginning. Their courtship, for example, was instantaneous and involved little real effort or energy. As Lucy describes it to the judge in the courtroom scene, she and Jerry met when both of them tried to buy Mr. Smith at a petshop. "And things began to happen rather swiftly, and finally I said I think we better get married and we did and that way we were able to give Mr. Smith a better home and live happily ever after—until now." Of course, Lucy's frivolous tone of voice is partly an act (one suspects, for example, that Jerry was interested in more than just the dog) but the frivolousness of her recitation corresponds to (and comments on) the brevity of their wooing: it was too fast, too easy, and the memory of it is therefore unlikely to prepare them for or sustain them during real crises. Hence the necessity of inventing a crisis that can temper the relationship and fill the gap in the history of their love affair before something really crippling happens.

Note, then, that we are not talking about absolute threats, or of absolutely opposite threats, to human relationships. The two problems are interrelated in a very complex fashion. For example, to break with the conventional view of marriage as a "beautiful, happily-ever-after thing" (to paraphrase Lucy and the lawyer) is one way to *create* a history of personal adversity that can temper and validate sexual/emotional unity. By the same token, however, the act of creating a personal history can lead without difficulty into historical bondage of the very sort that constrains the lawyer and his wife. Indeed, before *The Awful Truth* concludes, Jerry is given evidence (an innocent phone call from Armand to Lucy at one point, Armand hiding in Lucy's bedroom at another) which tends to confirm *as fact* the *fiction* of Lucy's infidelity.

So the problem in *The Awful Truth* is not a matter of either/or, of accepting one view of marriage, say, and rejecting another. The problem involves maintaining a balance between two interrelated tendencies, either one of which, carried to extremes, is destructive. Thus one can be too spontaneous: that is, one can act rashly, without sufficient knowledge or experience; and one can be too conventional: that is, one can be frozen into patterns of action which deny knowledge. Either course of action is destructive. And the quality which enables people to maintain that balance, or so McCarey argues in *The Awful Truth*, is "consciousness" or "awareness"—of self, of others, and of society. And it's Jerry and Lucy Warriner who serve to prove the case. Thus Lucy and Jerry can be seen, as early in the film as the end of the opening sequence, to be both intuitively aware, of themselves, of each other, and of the social pitfalls that can destroy their relationship; and creatively (rather than destructively) spontaneous: that is, they act in accord with awareness while action is still possible. In which instance the greater part of the film can then be read as a series of variations on this basic awareness/spontaneity theme.

Gerald Mast complains, for example, that the "potential lovers that [Lucy and Jerry] dig up—a dumb, vulgar Southern belle for Cary Grant; a plodding, stupid Oklahoma millionaire for Irene Dunne—cannot be seen as serious, credible threats to their relationship"—as if this supposed lack of credibility reveals a failure of conception or expression on McCarey's part.[11] It seems fairly clear, however, that neither "potential lover" was *ever* intended as a credible rival. Dixie Belle Lee, for instance, only appears *once* in the film, in the nightclub scene, and she is in the club because she works there, not because she is out with Jerry. In which case Jerry's sharing a drink with her can hardly be called a courtship. Indeed, his mind is obviously elsewhere during the minute or two that they talk.

Likewise, Dan Leeson, while far less doltish than Mast describes him, can hardly be said to capture Lucy's imagination or admiration. Patsy brings him home to the townhouse apartment she shares with Lucy for the sole reason that he is the only man around and Lucy has

Part Time Wife, a forerunner of *The Awful Truth,* featuring Leila Hyams as the golf-addicted wife and Edmund Lowe as her exasperated husband.

not gone out for thirty days. It is not until Jerry shows up to visit Mr. Smith that Lucy seems at all inclined to go out with Dan. The next morning she talks a desperate blue-streak in a half-hearted attempt to generate and justify some enthusiasm for Dan's courtesy and consideration—but Patsy, who has been through it before, rightly points out that love on the "rebound" is "the bunk." As Patsy phrases it: "There's the first bounce, the second bounce; well, look at me—you wind up like an old tennis ball." And during the nightclub scene Lucy has to remind herself to call Leeson by his first name, despite the fact that they are engaged. Indeed, once Jerry invites himself and Dixie Belle Lee to sit down at their table, Lucy's general response to Dan and the prospect of life in Oklahoma is one of visible discomfort and embarrassment—which McCarey emphasises by reaction shots of Lucy. Given the clear fact that Lucy and Jerry are a matched sexual set—evidenced most remarkably in the nightclub scene by the fact that Dixie and Dan speak with heavy southern accents while Lucy and Jerry speak with lightly British accents—Lucy's engagement to Dan cannot be credible: it is, rather, ridiculous, and that's the point. As Jerry puts it to Lucy towards the end of the film, her engagement to Dan Leeson "doesn't even make sense." Lucy's relationship with Dan is therefore significant only as it bears on her relationship with Jerry: Dan's credibility as a suitor hardly matters.

Furthermore, it is arguable that Dixie Belle Lee and Dan Leeson (even their names are similar) function primarily as variations on the film's general spontaneity/awareness theme—again, their credibility as suitors is beside the point. Thus Dixie Belle Lee's southern accent, for example, is quite literally part of her act. As she tells Jerry: "I got wise to the fact that it helps me in my work." Dixie, like so many independent women in McCarey, is a singer—and to an important degree her nightclub act is to be seen as a form of socially-aware improvisation. On the other hand, the specifics of her act have to be taken as evidence of social/sexual rigidity. Indeed, the specifics hark back to *Putting Pants on Philip*. She sings a tongue-in-cheek torch song, about romantic hopes that have "gone with the wind," but the song is punctuated by air jets which blow her filmy skirts repeatedly skyward. She clearly knows what she is doing and why; but that she has to do it to survive is a clear indictment of society's sexual/financial ethics.

It is worth remarking in this connection that, while Jerry and Lucy seem genuinely embarrassed for Dixie, Dan Leeson seems to enjoy her act. Partly, he's being polite. But there seems to be no irony in his voice when he remarks that her act "would go great out west." And that there is no irony in his voice clearly sets him apart from Jerry and Lucy, who are almost always attuned to life's ironic possibilities. Thematically considered, then, Dan represents a literal-minded sort of social rigidity—very similar to the rigidity evidenced by the lawyer and his wife. Of course, Dan is not married; but his mother plays the "wife" role well enough: both the lawyer's wife and Dan's mother are apostles of regularity and repression. Thus the lawyer's wife constantly berates her husband's lack of punctuality: he's always late for dinner (and the lawyer, McCarey evenhandedly points out, is always complaining about cold food). Likewise, when we first see Mrs. Leeson she is complaining about Dan's lack of punctuality (he was out all night with Lucy and Patsy) and goes on to upbraid him for his lack of sexual caution. Thus she tells him to keep his mind off of women (*Dan:* "I can't, Ma"/*Mrs. Leeson:* "That's what your father always said"); and she is thoroughly convinced, without ever having met her, that Lucy has something to hide (she assumes Lucy's name is an alias). Indeed, it takes only a little extrapolation to conclude that Mrs. Leeson's fears are financially as well as sexually motivated: she doesn't want to share her son or their money.

And to a certain degree it can truly be said of Dan that he shares his mother's financial and sexual attitudes. McCarey is careful, as Charles Silver points out, never to poke fun at Dan in a cruel-hearted or condescending manner. After all, Dan makes his best effort to break away from his mother's influence. He does leave Oklahoma for New York City; he does take a rather expert turn on the dance floor; and he does his best to sing duets with Lucy: all three activities are clearly positive attempts at self-expression (as they are repeatedly in McCarey). Perhaps most in his favour is the fact that Dan is genuinely attracted to Lucy. But, despite his best efforts and honest intentions, he cannot break entirely with those habits of mind most encouraged by his mother. Thus he always talks in platitudes ("New York's all right for a visit but I wouldn't want to live here") and he apparently never considers the possibility of marrying without Ma's approval. As Dan puts it, after watching Jerry chase Duvalle from Lucy's apartment: "I guess a man's best friend is his mother."

This contrast between rigidity and improvisation is memorably evidenced midway through the film when Dan, Lucy, and Jerry meet to discuss the matter of the coal mine that Jerry and Lucy own together. The sequence begins with Lucy and Dan singing their famous, ill-tuned "Home on the Range" duet. Jerry then enters, ostensibly to sell "his interest" (Lucy's phrase) in the coal mine; but by rhetorical sleight-of-hand Jerry shifts the discussion from coal mines—through stocking drawers, marriage certificates, and hotel clerks—to the topic of Jerry and Lucy's honeymoon ("Gosh, we didn't want ice water"). The trick, however improvised, has its effect. Jerry's recitation begins in a three-shot, Jerry screen left, Dan screen centre, with his arm around Lucy, screen right. When the recitation ends the whole group shifts to the left, in order to sit down and talk business, but as they move Lucy walks away from Dan, around behind Jerry, so that the next stationary camera set-up has Lucy sitting tensely on the arm of a chair, screen left, while the two men are seated on the sofa, Jerry screen centre and Dan screen right. Thus, what had been intended as a civilised "transaction"—Jerry selling his interest, literally, in the mine, and metaphorically, in Lucy—hardly gets underway before Jerry upsets the ritual by refusing to observe propriety. Of

Ralph Bellamy (center) plays the rival, momentarily, in *The Awful Truth*.

course, the "unity" of Lucy and Dan was tenuous to begin with (as their duet indicates); but the effect of Jerry's ad-lib is, quite literally, to break Lucy and Dan apart by recalling to Lucy's mind the bonds of shared experience which link her, more properly, with Jerry. Things are still tense, to be sure, as evidenced by Lucy's refusal to sit down; but Jerry's willingness to subvert convention in the service of feeling confirms the fact of his affection and Lucy is visibly "moved."

To this point in the scene, McCarey has focused primarily on Jerry's ability to take spontaneous advantage of the situation: Jerry uses Dan and Dan's inability to break with convention (Dan doesn't interrupt—he just lets Jerry go on) in order to assert his unity with Lucy. At this point Dan's mother enters, and, for the moment at least, the focus of the scene shifts to Mrs. Leeson's rigid sense of social decorum. *Why* Mrs. Leeson does her best to call Lucy's integrity into question is unclear. Perhaps the prospect of a financial union between her son and Lucy is at the heart of it (again, the sex/money equation). But her actions speak eloquently of her general attitude towards her son's sexuality: no woman (save herself) is good enough for Dan. Thus she rattles on at length, citing tea-party gossip, to raise the issue of Lucy's fitness for marriage ("You do sing divinely, dear, but I'd never realised till this afternoon that you'd had a teacher").

At this point Jerry suddenly decides to talk business; and his attending to the topic of coal mines only serves to emphasise the fact that a new topic has become the centre of attention. After a moment's awkwardness, Lucy points out that "the gal's name needs clearin', partner"; and Jerry, taking the hint from Lucy, launches into an extended catalogue of romantic clichés ("She's as pure as the driven snow, as faithful as she is fair"). Again, we see the unity of Jerry and Lucy, in that both display an awareness of the sort of behavioural/conceptual rigidity that characterises the Leesons, and they answer that rigidity in kind, by parody. Of course, Jerry never does speak specifically to Mrs. Leeson's original question—about the music teacher—and it is even possible that Mrs. Leeson recognises Jerry's recitation of clichés as an attack on her sense of propriety. But Mrs. Leeson seems unaffected by Jerry's testimonial. Hence, after Jerry's melodramatic departure, she persists in her doubt; and Lucy, after taking a good long look at mother and son, asserts her unity with Jerry by following him out the door. As the disappointed Dan Leeson puts it: "Ah, Ma!"

All of which said, it would be inaccurate to leave the impression that Jerry and Lucy are totally immune from the dangers of rigidity.

Compared to the Leesons, Jerry and Lucy are remarkably flexible
and self-aware. But their "divorce" is itself based on a reasonable fear
that rigidity can overcome *any* relationship: hence the necessity that
Jerry and Lucy feel to loosen things up a bit as a means of testing their
marriage. They are clearly right in this—and their rightness is
emphasised, paradoxically, by their own behaviour during the separation. Thus Lucy involves herself in a ridiculous relationship with
Dan Leeson. It is hard to believe that she would ever go through with
marrying Dan (she doesn't); it seems likely that her primary motive is,
at least subconsciously, to arouse Jerry's jealousy; but her actions are
ambiguous enough, at least from Jerry's point of view, to call her
flexibility into question. Likewise, Jerry allows himself to be caught up
in the wronged-husband role, and he proceeds, through the last
several scenes of the film's second section, to make a genuine fool of
himself.

At one point, for example, soon after they leave the Leeson
apartment, Jerry and Lucy are standing in the entrance-way of her
apartment. Dan comes over to apologise for his mother's "old
fashioned" behaviour, and to recite a love poem he has written for
Lucy ("To you, my little prairie flower/I'm thinking of you every
hour"). In the middle of his recitation Lucy's phone rings. It is
Armand. Lucy does her best to get rid of Dan; she even gives him a
quick kiss in the hallway. And while she is busy with Leeson, Jerry,
who has been hiding all the while behind the door, picks up the phone
long enough to recognise Armand's voice. Lucy then returns and
Jerry asks who was on the phone. By this point, Lucy is obviously
hoping to get back together with Jerry; and rather than rekindle the
original fiction of her relationship with Duvalle, she tells a white lie: it
was her masseuse on the other end of the line. Her lie only serves,
however, to reinforce Jerry's fear ("Now I've heard everything") and
he leaves, vowing to get himself some popcorn and lemonade ("I've
just seen a three ring circus").

His leave-taking, however, is not the end of his foolishness. Indeed,
in his suspicion he goes Mrs. Leeson one better, and the following
sequence finds Jerry crashing Lucy's vocal recital (which had oc-
casioned Armand's phone call in the first place). Thus, after a quick
bout of slapstick ju-jitsu with Duvalle's Japanese butler, Jerry bursts in
on the recital, fully expecting to find Lucy and Duvalle in a clinch. He
is confronted, instead, by a crowd of very proper music lovers—and
Lucy and Duvalle perform nothing more than a duet for voice and
piano. Jerry does his best to regain his composure, but it is obvious that

for once he has gone too far: hence he no sooner takes a seat than his chair collapses from under him, and Jerry is reduced to an Oliver Hardy tangle of elbows, chair legs, and side tables—the perfect visual image of rigidity gone berserk.

Earlier, I referred to the film's "inferential/referential" structure —by which I implied that *The Awful Truth* could be understood, in one respect, to present a sequence of sketchily motivated actions, so that the process of "reading" the film is a process of "inference," of positing motives on the evidence of behaviour. In which case it is perfectly appropriate that McCarey should provide examples of both right-way and wrong-way inference—and he does just that. Mrs. Leeson and Jerry, for instance, are both clearly wrong to infer adultery as the motive for Lucy's largely perfunctory and professional relationship with Duvalle. And both are made to look foolish for their suspicions. In this respect, indeed, Jerry comes off as the more foolish of the two: he ought to know better (and at some level he probably does). Conversely, we are shown the right sort of inference when Lucy, having apologised to Armand for Jerry's behaviour at the recital, goes on to remark that Jerry's foolishness proves his sincerity: "I'm convinced he must care about me or he wouldn't do the funny things he does."

An alternative way of looking at the narrative structure of *The Awful Truth*, however, is in terms of repetition.[12] From this point of view the film is an elaborate series of cross-references, of repeated actions, issues, motifs, lines, etc.—and in large part it is this "referential" quality of the film that makes the drawing of proper inferences possible. For example, no reading of *The Awful Truth* could be complete without accounting for the presence and significance of Dan Leeson and his mother—and accounting for their significance, as I have already suggested, depends in large part on connecting them to the lawyer and his wife: each pair of characters fulfils basically the same thematic function, the lawyer and his wife in part one, Dan and his mother in part two. Likewise, parts one and two of *The Awful Truth* share a similar pattern of action. Each begins by isolating on one of the major characters, Jerry in part one, Lucy in part two. Each character then becomes involved in a social situation of some sort, the breakfast party for Jerry, the first meeting with Dan Leeson for Lucy; and in each instance the spouse then enters. Succeeding scenes involve some variety of sexual rivalry (the rivalry in both cases is more fictitious than real—Lucy is no more genuinely interested in Duvalle than in Dan Leeson). There is a "trial scene," literally in part one, effectively in part two when Mrs. Leeson grills Lucy and Jerry on the matter of Lucy's music teacher. In each case the trial scene is immediately associated with some recollection of Jerry and Lucy's marital past (Lucy explains her claim to Mr. Smith, which becomes an explanation of her courtship with Jerry; Jerry begins discussing coal mines but quickly shifts to the topic of the honeymoon he shared with Lucy—at which point Mrs. Leeson enters). We also find public displays of foolishness on the part of one or both major characters (part one: Lucy plays the scatterbrain with the judge, and she and Jerry have their dog-calling contest; part two: Jerry crashes the recital, and Lucy shuffles callers—Armand, Jerry, the Leesons—and derbies). And both sections end with a break up, Lucy walking out of the courtroom in part one, Jerry chasing Duvalle out of Lucy's apartment in part two.

The implications of this extensive series of repeated actions are various, and have to do, once again, with matters of convention, equilibrium, and awareness. The first section is remarkable for the manner in which Jerry and Lucy take mutual advantage of marital/ legal conventions, exploiting them in the service of a genuine sexual earnestness—however silly their actions may seem on the surface. Thus, despite the fact that Lucy and Jerry trade certain roles or functions from part one to part two, the emphasis in part one is on mutuality, on the intuitive togetherness of their actions. In which instance part one can be seen as a prologue of sorts—defining the issues and setting up the problem that the rest of the film must solve: given the fact that the divorce is a necessary and positive step towards insuring the health of the Warriner marriage, how, or under what conditions, is the ultimate fact of divorce to be avoided?

Caught in the middle: Cary Grant, with Gail Patrick and Irene Dunne, in *My Favorite Wife*.

The second section can largely be understood, then, as illustrating the conditions under which the reconciliation *cannot* be effected. To be sure, certain characters in part two do serve as positive examples (Dixie Belle Lee, Lucy near the end of the section), and the opposition between rigidity and flexibility is put repeatedly before us (Jerry is constantly improvising to intervene between Lucy and Leeson). But by and large it is rigidity that defines most of the action in part two. In structural terms, the first section repeats nothing, is therefore not bound by the past, and action within it is appropriately loose and relatively unconventional (in that Lucy and Jerry use divorce for positive ends). The second section, however, repeats a good many things, and the action within it is appropriately tight, somewhat tense, and relatively too conventional. Thus Lucy gets foolishly caught up with Dan Leeson while Jerry gets just as foolishly caught up in the wronged-husband role. Of course, Jerry's foolishness has its positive aspect—to the degree that it helps Lucy to overcome her own momentary fit of sexual folly—but Lucy's good sense, her acknowledgment that she's "still in love with that crazy lunatic," is not enough when set against Jerry's lunacy at its worst. Thus, despite her best intentions, Lucy is unable to allay Jerry's fears. In this respect, indeed, circumstances conspire against her (or so it seems), and when Jerry comes to her apartment to apologise for crashing the recital it is only to find the wrong hat on his head and the wrong man in Lucy's bedroom (Duvalle had come to accept Lucy's apology for Jerry and had hidden in the bedroom when Jerry appeared unexpectedly).

Two things happen in the second part of *The Awful Truth* which make possible the satisfactory and satisfying resolution of the film's issues. To begin with, Lucy learns (or has re-affirmed) a number of things: that she loves Jerry, that Jerry in some sense still loves her (hence his strange behaviour), and that improvisation (both within and against convention) is possible, as Dixie and Jerry demonstrate. Secondly, McCarey quite obtrusively short-circuits the reconciliation scene at the end of part two—with a little help from Mr. Smith and the Leesons (the dog finds Duvalle's hat, thus detaining Jerry; and the arrival of Dan and his mother forces Jerry into the bedroom where he finds Duvalle) and McCarey does so because Lucy needs an opportunity to put her awareness to work. Only if Lucy demonstrates her own awareness through action can Jerry be given the example and the affirmation he needs to act properly in his turn.

The third and concluding section of *The Awful Truth* is concerned, then, to re-assert a proper balance of action and awareness, of conventionality and spontaneity, of past and present, of male (Jerry) and female (Lucy). Hence, one reason for having a third section (rather than allow for reconciliation at the end of part two) is to enforce a sense of equality: Jerry has the chance to play the fool and prove his love in part two—and Lucy gets the same chance to play the fool and prove her love in part three. In this respect, parts two and three repeat each other—but the repetitions are of such a nature that they foster a very positive and self-aware sense of convention rather than promote a rigidly time-blind sense of probability and propriety. Thus, while the major elements of the third section are largely familiar, the section as a whole represents, both in structure and import, a significant variation on the pattern established in the film's first two sections.

In section three, specifically, McCarey telescopes (and thereby de-emphasises) certain actions and functions while expanding others. The introduction of the rival, for example, is rather perfunctorily accomplished, via newspapers (which Lucy and Patsy read in the bedroom of their apartment, and wherein Lucy learns of Jerry's impending marriage to a "mad-cap heiress") and by means of time-lapse montage (a "three ring circus" sequence of sporting events and fancy dress balls). We then jump immediately to the "recollection scene," which, in its general movement and significance, harks back to the "transaction scene" in part two and the courtroom scene in part one. Thus Lucy hunts Jerry down, ostensibly to wish him good luck on the occasion of their divorce (the decree becomes final at midnight). And, as in the earlier scenes, we again see the manipulation of convention in the service of genuine feeling. For instance, Lucy comments, without prompting, on the newspaper headlines announcing the wedding of Jerry and Barbara Vance (" 'Off with the old love' ") but she shifts her cliché in mid-sentence in order to call the viability of Jerry's relationship with Barbara into question ("I thought 'out of the frying pan' might have been better"). Lucy has been through "love on the rebound" with Dan and she can see, even if Jerry cannot, that his attachment to Barbara is of the rebound variety. Furthermore, when Jerry proposes a toast, Lucy uses the opportunity to recall an earlier toast, offered by Jerry on the occasion of their first drink together. Even Jerry Warriner, it turns out, once had a poetic streak—and Lucy's bringing that fact back to mind by reciting his "till death do us part" love lyric has a visible effect on both of them. Suddenly the prospect of separation seems genuinely frightening, all the more frightening for being so unnecessary, and McCarey underlines the significance of the moment by the use of background music—which is hardly used at all elsewhere in the film. The major point to be made, however, is that the unity of Jerry and Lucy is being re-affirmed here by the action and context of the scene, even if the ostensible "subject" of the scene is the dissolution of that unity. Lucy's tactics in the scene quite self-consciously mirror Jerry's tactics earlier: both shuffle clichés and recall the past. And by re-enacting the earlier scene Lucy both asserts her sense of marital identity and gives Jerry the glass wherein he can truly see himself.

Indeed, it is obviously the case at this point in the film that Jerry and Lucy are two of a kind and know it: witness the pain that both of them feel at the prospect of perpetual separation. And McCarey underlines the probability and rightness of their eventual reunion by downplaying the credibility of the rival. Barbara Vance gets far less screen time than Dan Leeson and we can infer from this that she is even less credible a rival to Lucy than Leeson was to Jerry. Furthermore, McCarey employs repetition to equate Barbara with Armand Duvalle. After the "transaction scene" in part two, Jerry and Lucy converse for a few moments in her apartment. Jerry is then about to leave when Leeson shows up at the door to recite his poem. The phone then rings, Lucy answers it, puts the receiver down for a moment while she finishes with Dan, and Jerry picks it up long enough to hear Armand's voice. All of which serves as prologue to and occasion for the following scene, in which Jerry crashes Lucy's recital, expecting to catch Lucy and Armand in the act. A somewhat similar sequence of events takes place only moments after Lucy recites Jerry's love lyric in part three of the film. The phone rings; Lucy answers it quite openly and hands it to Jerry; and Jerry, like Lucy in the earlier scene, tells a lie in order to avoid contention: he tells Barbara that the woman who answered the phone is his sister, newly returned from Paris. There are several things to be remarked on here—the fact, for example, that Lucy quite openly and instinctively picks up the phone (this contrasts with Jerry's behind-the-door eavesdropping) and she does so without malice or doubt (contrast this with Jerry who is obviously fishing for evidence that would confirm his suspicions). But in the present context the point to make is that the caller, in each case, is a rival only in potential—not in fact. And repeating the sequence reinforces the sense that Barbara will not get Jerry. She is no more a threat to the Warriner marriage than Armand Duvalle. If anything, Barbara functions as an "opportunity"—her engagement to Jerry provides the context within which Lucy can demonstrate her sincerity (just as Duvalle provides a context in which Jerry can prove his—by making a fool of himself). And Barbara's jealousy—she is not at all fooled by Jerry's uncharacteristically maladroit deception—serves, ironically, to provide Lucy with the forum she needs: Barbara urges Jerry to bring his "sister" along to the Vance estate as a means of calling Jerry's bluff.

The following sequence thus recalls several earlier scenes. We begin with an abbreviated sort of "trial scene"—Barbara and her parents grill Jerry about his sister and his father ("a Princeton man?") while Jerry self-consciously and ironically chides Barbara for her suspicions ("There can't be any doubts in marriage")—but the interrogation is cut short by the arrival of "Lola Warriner," at which point two additional contexts are invoked. In general, as I have already noted, Lucy's "Lola" routine is the structural equivalent of Jerry's chair number—again, public folly proves the fact of private feelings. Thus Lucy performs a marvellously extended series of purposeful social *faux pas*—flapping her scarf hither and yon, asking point blank for a drink ("I had three or four before I got here but they're beginning to wear off and you know how that is"), and downing it in one pull (it's really ginger ale); implying in so many words that Jerry is the alcoholic, gold-digging son of a college grounds keeper out to wed a rich if ugly duckling; wedging herself between Barbara and Jerry on the love seat; burping; accusing everyone present of stealing her purse, etc., etc. But the centrepiece of her performance is modelled on and recalls Dixie Belle Lee's "Gone With the Wind" number. Lucy is dressed for the occasion, all fringe and fingerless gloves, and she steers the conversation around to her work at the "Virginia Club." Once again Barbara falls prey to curiosity, and before Lucy can be stopped she picks a record for the victrola and does her improvised, slapstick best to emulate Dixie's act. Everyone except Jerry is, predictably enough, outraged. But Jerry knows what she is up to—we know Jerry knows by virtue of reaction shots—and we understand, as Jerry understands, that the motive for her action is love, however foolish the action itself may seem.

The point to make, however, and it applies to the entire third part of the film, is not merely that Lucy loves Jerry. It is rather that repetition, when it occurs in part three, is motivated largely by knowledge rather than ignorance. Lucy's visit to Jerry and her performance at the Vance place are both clear-cut attempts to convince Jerry of her sincerity, and both communicate that sincerity by the conscious use of convention—which consciousness is mirrored and emphasised for us by the fact of repetition. By telescoping the references, by piling convention (intrinsic, generic, and otherwise) atop convention, as McCarey repeats and telescopes aspects of several earlier scenes in the single sequence at the Vance estate, we are led to a heightened sense of "conventionality"—we have seen this and this and this before. McCarey thus "foregrounds" convention and by so doing allows for the creative use of it. Jerry and Lucy are no longer *bound* by the rigidity of an unconsciously ritualised past. Rather, the past serves as inspiration for the future—and Lucy re-affirms her future with Jerry by employing the past for her present purposes. It is clear, of course, that there is something special about it all. Not everyone can break creatively with past habits by recognising them *as* habits. The Vance family demonstrates this inability by their cross-examination of Jerry and by their reaction to "Lola." But at least during part three of *The Awful Truth* McCarey allows *us* the privilege of recognition: we know what goes on and why—and it's great fun.

The rewards of creativity and awareness are then evidenced in the film's final two sequences. Thus far in part three, every sequence has had some relationship to a previously witnessed (rather than recounted) action. The last two scenes are remarkable, then, because they *do not* mimic in any precise or rigid fashion the pattern of incident established in parts one and two. On the contrary, both scenes break with that pattern by completing actions which were either suppressed or hindered by the previously rigid progress of the narrative. Thus, for example, Lucy continues to play the drunken floozie role even after Jerry escorts her from the Vance townhouse (e.g., she turns the car radio on full blast and tosses away the knob) and by so doing she allows Jerry the opportunity to get into the car with her: he can't let Lucy drive a car in that condition. Of course, Jerry knows it's an act—but by playing along, by manipulating the etiquette of motoring, he gets to take Lucy for the head-clearing drive in the country which he had himself proposed in part two, when he came to apologise for crashing the recital, but which had been aborted when Jerry found Duvalle in Lucy's bedroom. Even here, of course, we do not totally leave the past behind. No sooner do they hit the road than Jerry starts talking nervously about borrowing the car to return to the city once he has dropped Lucy off at Aunt Patsy's cabin. And, furthermore, Jerry chooses to compare their country drive not to the one he had proposed earlier, but rather to the one that Lucy and Armand had been on when their car broke down. Jerry fears that his presence overnight at Patsy's cabin would give Lucy the chance to

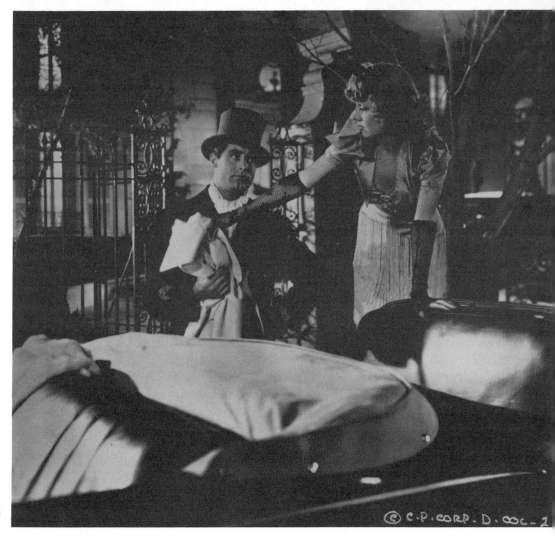

Lucy plays the drunken floozie in
The Awful Truth.

demonstrate "exactly how innocent a night in the country could be."
Note, however, that he does not fear being wrong about Lucy's
supposed infidelity. It is rather the case that an "innocent" night will
seal the divorce: they can only vacate the decree by making love (or
such is the implication). This circumstance accounts for Jerry's
quarrelsomeness, even if he expresses his fear in the language of
jealousy. And it accounts as well for the fact that Lucy, moments later,
takes advantage of a malfunctioning radio and some motorcycle cops
to cut off Jerry's retreat. As soon as they are pulled over, Lucy implies
that Jerry has been drinking, and while Jerry proves his sobriety by
walking the centre stripe Lucy releases the emergency brake and
sabotages the vehicle. Now Jerry can't go back. Thus, despite the fact

that the country drive has its antecedents (in the recounted "junior prom" episode and the proposed but aborted drive that Jerry suggests), and despite the fact that it depends for its success on the positive manipulation of convention (in that Lucy uses the laws of the road to her advantage), the overall movement of the scene effectively transcends the past, both by "re-writing" it (this country drive "replaces" the "junior prom" journey) and by exceeding it (this drive is the first drive that we actually *see*). In which case the drive can be said to "open up" the film. The very presence of the scene breaks the pattern of action and incident which had previously dominated. It is the *structural* expression of the freedom from rigidity that Jerry and Lucy have sought all along. And that freedom finds appropriate *visual* expression in the image of Jerry and Lucy riding wind-blown down the highway on the handlebars of police motorcycles.

It is significant, however, that the film does *not* end there. On the plot level, an endless ride would serve to dissolve the Warriner marriage rather than renew it. They have to get off the highway and down to love-making before midnight or else that divorce decree will take effect. Secondarily, there is still the somewhat superficial matter of that "awful truth" to clear up. Lucy will hardly have the chance to reassure Jerry that his suspicions regarding herself and Duvalle are (and always had been)groundless—not if they ride down the road with police sirens blaring full blast. But there is a good deal else going on in the film's closing moments which cannot be accounted for if the scene is read by simple cause-effect logic of the "Jerry now believes Lucy and therefore the marriage is saved" sort. As I have already remarked, and as Jerry quite obviously understands, the whole matter of fidelity is for the most part a superficial issue, be it a matter of Jerry's fidelity to Lucy (she does not care where he was if he wasn't in Florida) or of Lucy's to Jerry (by the film's end he is not all that worried about Duvalle). The genuine significance of the film's closing scene is to be understood, I would suggest, not merely in terms of its ostensible plot function, but in the context of the film's structure and of the closing scene's *place* in that structure. In which context, the scene serves several important thematic functions.

Like the immediately preceding scene, the cabin sequence repre- sents a break of sorts with the past: it completes a movement from marital fiction (the fiction of distrust) to marital fact that had begun earlier—but it does so in a way which gets to the real facts. That is, the closing scene, more than any other scene in the film, bears down on and emphasises the genuine mutuality of Jerry and Lucy, a mutuality which finds its initial expression in the fact that Jerry and Lucy risk fictionalising their relationship in order to strengthen it, yet a mutuality which finds its fullest expression in the fact that Jerry and Lucy can overcome their own quite real mistakes and can do so with a genuine measure of confidence—in themselves, in each other, and in the viability of their love affair.

In structural terms, the cabin scene is to be compared to the end of the courtroom scene in part one (wherein Lucy takes the dog and leaves Jerry with the judge) and to the aborted reconciliation scene in part two (wherein Jerry runs away from Lucy while in hot pursuit of Armand): each scene concludes a major section of the film and each marks a definite stage in the progress of the Warriner relationship. In this context, the final scene—which concludes with Jerry locking himself into Lucy's bedroom, at her suggestion, using yet another chair as an impromptu barricade—represents a significant and positive variation on the pattern of departures previously established: love-making thus replaces leave-taking and we certainly welcome the change. And yet the earlier break-ups, at least as I read the film, cannot really be seen as negative events. Both break-ups serve positive ends, in that they allow Jerry and Lucy to strengthen their relationship by testing it. So it is not breaking-up that represents the danger but repeatedly and mindlessly breaking-up. Thus what Jerry and Lucy must avoid is the strait-jacket of over-conventionality: they can't let the ritual of divorce become the reality of their relationship.

The most remarkable aspect of the film's closing scene, then, is the way Jerry and Lucy play "around" and "with" convention. In the generic terms of comedy we expect that the film will end with a reconciliation and McCarey musters the visual iconography of screwball romance to reinforce the expectation. The adjoining bedrooms and the lockless door, for example, recall in visual/spatial terms the twin beds and blanket "Wall of Jericho" in Capra's *It Happened One Night* (both *The Awful Truth* and *It Happened One Night* were filmed at Columbia and were photographed in the same intimate, back-lit style by Joseph Walker). But in the context of *The Awful Truth,* reconciliation is a very unconventional thing to do (it only happens once) and Jerry and Lucy do it with a certain style and grace which is also unconventional when set against the sexually graceless society seen elsewhere in the film.

Thus Jerry and Lucy do not simply reconcile. They have forty-five minutes left before the midnight deadline and they put that time to good use. Specifically, Jerry and Lucy effectively "re-marry" in an impromptu "ceremony of equality." Lucy takes the opportunity provided by that free swinging door to assure Jerry that "things could be the same if they were different"; and moments later Jerry repeats the action, again taking advantage of the breeze-blown door, by urging the proposition that "things could be the same again, only a little different." In denotative terms, to be sure, the exchange amounts to little more than an agreement to pick up the marriage where it left off. But neither partner seems content with expressing that agreement in a conventional manner. Rather, they both employ extended, relatively quick-spoken and extremely self-conscious monologues which effectively transcend denotation by using and re-using the "same/different" antinomy. Before they finish, "same" and "different" are not opposites but complements—as Jerry and Lucy are no longer (and never have been) opposites but complements—and they celebrate their "complementarity" by establishing a "private" convention (the monologue) which lends real validity to the more "public" conventions embodied in marriage certificates and divorce decrees. To be sure, Jerry and Lucy have some help along the line. They are not totally responsible for the fact that their divorce gambit proves a successful tactic for renewing their relationship. On the contrary, they have a good deal of assistance, provided by an obliging fox-terrier, by a string of propitious coincidences, by a fortuitously bumpy road and a malfunctioning radio, by an obliging pair of motorcycle cops, by a breezy evening and a swinging door, etc., etc. Clearly the universe is on their side (such is generally the comic case). But then again, Jerry and Lucy clearly *earn* their success, by knowing how and when to take advantage of life's accidents, and by having the courage to do so. Life is seldom neat and easy in McCarey—even an up-beat film like *The Awful Truth* demonstrates that fact—but it can be incredibly rewarding for those characters who face the awful truth head on. In which case the awful truth is something less than awful and a hell of a lot more fun.

Continuity and Community:
Love Affair and *Once Upon a Honeymoon*,
McCarey in the Forties, *The Bells of St. Mary's*

Among those few critics and reviewers who have bothered to concern themselves with Leo McCarey, there is a general agreement that McCarey's talent as a film-maker deserted him somewhere along the line. Jeffrey Richards is kinder than most in limiting his displeasure to

Once Upon a Honeymoon, My Son John, Rally Round the Flag, Boys!, and *Satan Never Sleeps*—all of them (except *Rally Round*) "serious message pictures" which encouraged McCarey's penchant for preaching. As Richards puts it, the films "don't come off" because "the essential and charming fragility of McCarey's talent is smothered by the elephantine demands of dogma" (p. 43). For James Agee and Richard Corliss, McCarey's failure has less to do with politics than with commerce: from their perspective, McCarey fell from grace when he tried to "repeat the unrepeatable" by making *The Bells of St. Mary's* immediately after *Going My Way*. Corliss is more rabid than Agee in condemning the later film (according to Corliss, *The Bells of St. Mary's* not only "chokes on its own calculated treacle, but almost manage[s] to cast suspicions on its genuinely appealing predecessor"); but both critics take McCarey's willingness to repeat himself as evidence that his inspiration had failed him, only to be replaced by a cynical brand of commercial sentimentalism.[13] Charles Silver, to take yet another critic, while genuinely sincere in praising McCarey's work during the Thirties, effectively extends the Richards critique to cover all of McCarey's post-Thirties films: now it is the second half of *Love Affair* that gives us the first taste of McCarey's "heavy handed religiosity" and that evidences, therefore, McCarey's inevitable capitulation to didacticism.[14] Finally and most recently, there is Gerald Mast, who saw fit largely to ignore McCarey in "The Comic Mind." From Mast's point of view, McCarey was a second rater who fell apart as soon as he began self-consciously "yearning for significance."[15] In which case, we can mark McCarey's decline as beginning with *Ruggles of Red Gap* ("McCarey striving to be Capra without Capra's feeling for human warmth and spontaneity").[16]

There are several false assumptions in all of this which require refutation for presenting a demonstrably inaccurate picture of McCarey's concerns and development. Thus Mast's notion that McCarey's early work in his "pre-self-conscious salad days" (p. 284) is both dissimilar and superior to his later work ignores the fact that McCarey was *always* self-conscious, as *Duck Soup* and *Six of a Kind* both demonstrate. Furthermore, to assert, as Mast does, that self-consciousness and spontaneity are at odds in McCarey is obvious foolishness. As *The Awful Truth* makes clear, self-consciousness and spontaneity are not opposites at all in McCarey: rather, they are complements, each depending for survival and significance on the other.

Another false notion at work here involves the strict equation of

The self-conscious image: Charles Boyer, Irene Dunne, and Maria Ouspenskaya (above) in *Love Affair* and Deborah Kerr, Cary Grant, and Cathleen Nesbitt (below) in *An Affair to Remember*.

originality, sincerity, and aesthetic validity. The charge against *The Bells of St. Mary's,* for example, comes to little more than this: the film repeats, in several obvious respects, *Going My Way.* Again we have Bing Crosby in the Father O'Malley role; again Father O'Malley is sent to minister to a troubled religious institution, a parochial school in this instance; again he deals with various personal and institutional problems; and again the film concludes with a heart-rending, heart-warming "recognition/departure" scene. In which case, *The Bells of St. Mary's* must be described as lacking a necessary measure of "originality." Not being "original," the film's sole *raison d'être* can only be the insincere exploitation of the previously tried and true. And, because it exploits the tried and true, *The Bells of St. Mary's* must be adjudged an aesthetic failure.

The logic here depends entirely on a single axiom: art = originality. But the criterion of originality is demonstrably secondary if it is relevant at all. The first casualty of serious study in any branch of aesthetics or art history is the concept of originality. There is no such thing as a totally original work of art. At best, a work can strike us as original for being constructed within traditions and conventions which are foreign to us or for combining familiar conventions in unfamiliar configurations (Picasso's "Demoiselles d'Avignon" is a paradigm case here). In which instance, the concept of "originality" ceases to be of much critical use. To praise originality in absolute terms is only to reveal ignorance. If the word is to have any legitimate meaning, it can only refer to variations within and against convention. Thus my discussion of *The Awful Truth,* for example, focused on just that sort of "originality," on the extent to which *The Awful Truth* extends and combines those elements of style and theme which may be said to constitute the cinema of Leo McCarey. And, as I have already demonstrated, those elements of style and theme are far more constant across the McCarey canon than most critics would have us believe. The elements themselves need not be (cannot be) original. As Robin Wood points out, McCarey is no more responsible for the classical Hollywood narrative film than Pope is for the heroic couplet. Yet both Pope and McCarey employ conventional aesthetic forms to express genuinely personal and sincere visions of experience—and such visions, as we "re-experience" them through the works in question, are what count. Thus, if we are going to condemn the ethos embodied in *Going My Way* and *The Bells of St. Mary's,* we had better be prepared, with Gerald Mast, to toss *Ruggles of Red Gap* and *The Awful Truth* out the window as well.

None of which is intended to deny that *shifts* of emphasis are evident in McCarey's films. But we must assign proper weight to those shifts, for being relative rather than absolute matters, and we certainly cannot employ those shifts as *a priori* arguments in a case against McCarey. We can agree, for example, that a certain shift in emphasis takes place between, say, *Love Affair* (1939) and *Once Upon a Honeymoon* (1942). The trial-tested lovers in the former film suffer largely from their own mistakes (the Irene Dunne character races across a busy city street without looking where she's going, while the Charles Boyer character assumes, history and memory notwithstanding, that Dunne has heartlessly stood him up when she fails to keep her appointment with him) and accordingly *Love Affair* can be read as a "private" or "personal" comedy (things do eventually work out).

Once Upon a Honeymoon, on the other hand, despite its title, is in many respects a strikingly "public" or "political" comedy. Hitler and various other high-ranking Nazis appear as characters in the film; the action takes place across the whole of war-time Europe; and the fate of democratic civilisation is a central and clear-cut issue, as it is repeatedly in McCarey's later films.

And yet, putting it that way, as if *Love Affair* and *Once Upon a Honeymoon* were to be located at opposite ends of the McCarey continuum, is not only to agree in some respects with accepted critical opinion, the Richards/Mast notion that McCarey went bad when his films became "socially conscious," but it is also to overlook several significant similarities which exist between the two films and between McCarey's work in the Thirties and Forties generally—similarities which serve to qualify whatever we might say about the differences involved. It is far more a matter of degree than kind.

Both *Love Affair* and *Once Upon a Honeymoon,* for example, begin on a strongly social note, and in each case the love affair at the film's centre is to be understood in relationship to the social background. In *Love Affair* the social background is fairly all-inclusive (we begin with radio news broadcasts from New York, London, and Rome) and basically negative (all three broadcasters report approvingly of the engagement of Michel Marnay [Charles Boyer] to a rich heiress, "Lois Clark and her twenty million snappers"—as if the sex-for-money trade off were something to be admired or emulated). And the central characters cannot at first be described as immune to this sort of sexual/social cynicism. Michel is engaged to his heiress, after all; and Irene Dunne's Terry McKay, we learn soon thereafter, as she and Michel exchange ship-board biographies, is the kept woman of a wealthy entrepreneur. In the case of both characters, however, it is clear that the cynicism is only a pose: both want (or wanted) something better. Michel, as his grandmother Janou eventually tells Terry, wants a perfect world, a world where "wishing will make it so." And Terry had sought self-expression and independence in show business. Both face disappointment. Michel is never satisfied with reality because "things come too easy for him." He is "always allured," as Janou puts it, "by the art he is not practising, the places he hasn't been, the girl he hasn't met." Terry's disappointment is less abstract but no less real. Her first singing engagement soon became an after-hours rat race as the manager chased her around the night club; and Terry gladly seized the opportunity to escape, even if escape meant becoming a kept woman. Disappointment for both thus leads to an acceptance of society's sexual/financial value system—but their ship-board meeting, their visit to Janou's hill-top garden, their obvious rightness for each other, their still strong desire not to accept the way of the world, prompts them to take one more chance.

It is a step in the right McCarey direction. But the step as Michel and Terry take it involves a potentially debilitating blend of financial realism and romantic naïveté. Love gives each of them the courage to seek financial independence—he as a painter, she as a singer—but their vision of love is still obscured by the all-or-nothing habit of mind that made them cynics in the first place. Thus they foolishly set the exact time, date, and place for their eventual rendezvous/reunion— six months later, 5 p.m., the observation floor of the Empire State Building ("The nearest thing to heaven that we have in New York")—as if the world were ever perfect or predictable enough to allow for such precision; and their heartbreak results directly from their folly. Terry is so busy looking heavenward that she gets run over; and Michel goes on a month-long bender to drown his sorrow at being stood up. Even at this juncture, of course, they are better off than before. Terry finds work as a music teacher at an orphanage and Michel continues painting despite his agony (one of his paintings eventually serves to bring them together again). And yet their heartbreak could readily have been avoided had they been capable at the time of acknowledging life for what it is: imperfect, inexact, and unpredictable.

And it is that very sort of imperfection which Michel and Terry acknowledge in the film's final scene. Terry acknowledges her folly by acknowledging her handicap. Her determination to avoid going to Michel until she could "run" to him thus collapses when she sees his side of the matter: her insistence on physical perfection had been a form of cruelty rather than kindness. Likewise, Michel acknowledges *his* folly, his more general tendency to insist on temporal perfection, by giving Janou's shawl to Terry. People die—even if they don't die on schedule (Janou had planned on dying at age seventy-five but didn't)—yet life goes on nevertheless (the scene takes place on Christmas Day, the day of Jesus's birth). The shawl can therefore be passed down in good faith. It is simultaneously a legacy and a birthday present, equally emblematic both of mutability and continuity—and, by giving it to Terry, Michel signifies his ability to accept life on its own terms.

In which context we can understand the appropriateness and significance of the film's closing image—Michel and Terry embracing in her modest first floor flat. In spatial terms both Michel and Terry have come, quite literally, "down to earth". By so doing they reject the "sky high" notion of love represented by the Empire State Building.

ming "down to earth": the clos-
 scene of *Love Affair*.

That kind of thinking had not served to unite them. It rather served to keep them apart. And in retrospect we must "re-read" the moment when Michel and Terry promise to meet in six months' time. The moment's *mise-en-scène* sets Michel and Terry, standing at the rail of the ocean liner, against the background of the New York City skyline, which is dominated by the Empire State Building. The building thus occupies the centre of the frame. At the time, we see the structure as Michel and Terry see it—as an emblem of romantic perfection. But the course of events makes it clear that the building's phallic thrust through space represents a false sort of potency—financial rather than emotional. It is, quite literally, a barrier to love rather than an emblem of it, separating the lovers into private spaces, he screen left, she screen right, and it is this sort of privacy, carried to extremes, that Michel and Terry reject and transcend with their embrace. Love need not be "heavenly" to be worthwhile. That conclusion is not easily arrived at, particularly in a world where the worth of love is usually measured in dollars and cents, but "personal" knowledge is possible, however impersonal the sexual ethics of society in general might be. The point to make in the present context, however, is not that personal knowledge is possible. It is rather that this sort of personal or interpersonal understanding gains in significance for being set against the fact of general public folly. Only against a background of social ignorance can the act of individual understanding be fully imagined and fully appreciated.[17]

A similar interplay of foreground and background, involving similar characters in similar situations, is at work in *Once Upon a Honeymoon*. Again, we begin on a strongly social note: we cut from a calendar and a clock ("Timetable by A. Hitler") to documentary footage of a Nazi-dominated Vienna. Cut then to what is obviously a high-class hotel room; a maid answers the phone; she calls her mistress—at which point Ginger Rogers enters and dismisses the maid in her best British-accented English; the maid then leaves; and "Katherine Butte-Smith" drops the accent and the vocabulary ("Hello, Mama") to break the good news: she is going to marry the sole heir of a wealthy and noble Austrian family. The parallel is fairly clear and fairly ominous: National Socialism and Katherine Butte-Smith have both come to "conquer" Austria—and in both cases the motive is greed, for money, for power. Of course, Katie O'Hara ("Miss Butte-Smith") is obviously less dangerous to Austria than Adolph Hitler; her greed is mostly focused on clothing and jewelry and is basically a response to the fact that she had once made a living as a striptease artist (she now prefers to wear her clothes rather than doff them); but her willingness to surrender her sexual integrity for the sake of financial security is just as sterile in its context (she will become a *Baron*ess) as Michel Marnay's willingness to surrender his freedom for the sake of financial security in *Love Affair* (his fiancée is also a member of the nobility—the "industrial nobility"). In which case, it is clear that both films are concerned with the way public pressures—in both cases, the pressure to sell out selfhood—can have private ramifications.

Furthermore, the selves in both films are remarkably alike, in their temperaments as characters and in their alignment within the thematic matrix of their respective films as well. I have already remarked upon the similarity of Katie O'Hara and Michel Marnay: both are engaged to wealthy fiancés, Baron von Luber (Walter Slezak) and Lois Clarke (Astrid Allwyn) respectively, and for both the engagement represents a capitulation to the way of the world. Indeed, in Katie O'Hara's case it represents a capitulation to the "new order": her intended is an advance man for Hitler and their honeymoon is really a business trip—their arrival in any country (Austria, Czechoslovakia, Poland) inevitably precedes by only a few days that country's capitulation or surrender to Hitler. It seems fairly clear, in fact, that the Baron's primary motive for marrying "Katherine Butte-Smith of Philadelphia" is her American citizenship: the Baron is an expert on U.S. passport laws and the last stop on his itinerary, though he never arrives at his destination, is the United States. In both cases, however, the sympathetic character is clearly ill-suited to the role of cynic—and in both instances their genuine desire for something better is evidenced by a character from the past—Janou in Michel's case, Mama O'Hara in Katie's—who serves as a link to childhood innocence, and by the appearance of an appropriate sexual partner who represents the promise of a vital sexual future.

In both films, moreover, the sexual partner represents something of a mirror image for the protagonist. Michel and Terry are *both* engaged to rich suitors—although Terry's relationship is complicated by the fact that she "works" for her fiancé (in something having to do with the fashion business?). And by seeing themselves in each other, both positively and negatively, they gain the courage and determination to break with society and its value system. Likewise, Katie O'Hara and Patrick O'Toole (Cary Grant) are mirror images of one another. Katie sells out, at least momentarily, to the Baron; while O'Toole's apparent political idealism (he complains that Austria has been sold

Once Upon a Honeymoon: **Cary Grant takes the measure of Ginger Rogers in the famous fitter scene.**

out to the Nazis without the question being put to a vote of the people) is undercut by the fact that he accepts the von Luber assignment, despite his determined assertion that he's a "news commentator, not a leg man," only *after* his boss assures him that getting the von Luber story will insure O'Toole's status as a broadcaster ("They'll *give* you a broadcasting station"). Furthermore, once on the story, it is fairly clear that O'Toole's primary motive is (like Katie's) sexual rather than political. Thus, when they meet in the hotel in Warsaw, O'Toole raises the emotional issue first ("If you are really in love with your husband, I'll stop right now") before he goes on to give her the political scoop. Partly, the gesture bespeaks a respect for Katie's emotional integrity. But by admitting that she "can still be curious," Katie makes it clear that she *does not* love von Luber and that she *is* interested in O'Toole—at which point O'Toole's personal and political motives fall into rough alignment: getting the story on von Luber will also get him Katie O'Hara. It is clear, however, that O'Toole, like Katie herself at the film's beginning, places personal requirements first, even if those requirements, his desire to woo and wed Katherine, are preferable to Katie's desires for clothes and jewelry. Thus he would rather save Katie than save America. In political terms, Katherine would be far more useful (though more greatly endangered) as a spy. Indeed, as soon as O'Toole and O'Hara arrive in Paris, the American Embassy proposes just that. Katie hasn't the heart to tell O'Toole right off—not during their romantic, open-air, candle-light supper in the moon-cast shadow of the Eiffel Tower (another false symbol of potency?); particularly not after he refuses to hear what she has to say ("What I don't know won't hurt me")—but when he does learn of it he is outraged ("I don't mind giving up coffee and sugar, but when it comes to . . .").

It can hardly be argued, then, that O'Toole is to be seen as an unquestioned or unquestionable example of democratic potency, even if genre/star expectations might lead toward that conclusion. In O'Toole's case, democracy and potency come into conflict—and it is rather Katie, who realises her social duty and does it, who leads the way. She is the one who trades passports with the Jewish maid (in this respect O'Toole does nothing more than approve her action). She is the one who agrees to get the goods on von Luber (in which case she "replaces" O'Toole as reporter). And she is the one, ultimately, who shoves the Baron overboard. Even here, however, Katie demonstrates her genuine concern for the lives and happiness of others (compare her to O'Toole or to Michel in *Love Affair;* each tends to measure everything in terms of his own contentment). That is, Katie is genuinely shocked and distraught at having shoved von Luber overboard, even if it was a clear-cut matter of self-defence. She is so upset, in fact, that it takes her quite a while to tell O'Toole what happened, and her hesitation spells the death of the Baron: he cannot swim. Baron von Luber thus earns his death because he does not value enough the lives of others; and he comes to die, ironically but appropriately, because Katie *does* value the lives of others—even von Luber's.

That, indeed, is the point of both films: to value life fully is to assume a responsible personal stance *vis-à-vis* both sex and society. In *Love Affair,* responsibility is defined as "empathy"—Michel for Terry, Terry for Michel—and its opposites are sexual/financial "exploitation" (a "social" relation of self to others) and "self pity" (a "personal" relation of self to self). In *Once Upon a Honeymoon,* responsibility extends beyond "empathy" to "democracy," the latter being the public and political expression of the former, and again the opposites are "exploitation" (von Luber's exploitation of Katie's ignorance in the service of fascism) and "self pity" (O'Toole's self pity when Katherine quite self-consciously chooses to spy on her husband). In which case, we must say that the values celebrated in *Love Affair* and *Once Upon a Honeymoon* are nearly identical. They are both McCarey films. It will hardly do, therefore, to praise one movie at the expense of the other. Both films are "serious." Both films are "socially conscious." And no statement of personal preference can change the facts. The most we can do is to observe the degree to which *Once Upon a Honeymoon* "extends" the ideological premises underlying both films—and doing so should serve to warn us against facile overgeneralisations, particularly when the generalisations purport (quite falsely) to explain a supposed failure of vision on McCarey's part.

*   *   *

All of which said, there *are* some interesting generalisations to be made regarding McCarey's Forties films. The first of these, which we have already remarked upon in connection with *Once Upon a Honeymoon,* involves McCarey's increasing concern with "society." It is hardly the case, as anything but the most cursory glance at films like *Ruggles of Red Gap* and *The Awful Truth* would indicate, that McCarey *ever* lacked concern for society and its conventions. Furthermore, to say that McCarey came to focus increasing attention on society is in no way to agree that McCarey suddenly got "serious" or "preachy" after *Love Affair.* We can be less subjective and more precise than such complaints would seem to allow. What distinguishes McCarey in the Forties from McCarey in the Thirties is the increasing heterogeneity of the societies he pictures. That is, McCarey's Forties films, with the possible exception of *Once Upon a Honeymoon,* tend to focus on communities which serve as microcosms of society. Thus the real protagonist of *Going My Way* is not Father O'Malley but rather the parish of St. Dominic—all of its parishioners, from the cop on the beat to the local gossip, are seen as essential components of the social whole. Likewise *The Bells of St. Mary's* involves a parochial school and its environs, and is concerned, in an often quite literal way, with the "health" of the community: the school is run down, Sister Benedict (Ingrid Bergman) has tuberculosis without knowing it, and various parishioners suffer from a variety of spiritual ills. In *Good Sam,* the community is a small city, large enough to need a big department store (where Sam works) but small enough for "Good Sam" to have a genuine and personal impact on his neighbours, and Sam serves the same exemplary function in his film that Father O'Malley serves in *Going My Way.* Both are unconventional, for being so unselfish, and each serves as a catalyst, helping families to get started, giving institutions (a bank in Sam's case) the opportunity to loosen up, etc., etc. The only exception to this generalisation is, as I have already remarked, *Once Upon a Honeymoon*—and here the generalisation breaks down because the microcosm is so large. We are dealing with an entire continent, not with a city or a parish. But putting it that way demonstrates the continuity of McCarey's concern. Europe *is* a civilisation; St. Dominic's parish *stands for* civilisation: the issue is constant. In this respect, we could see the Europe/America antinomy in *Honeymoon* as giving us a two-sided metaphor for society. "Europe" with its "new order" is the negative image while "America," which the film defines as a heterogenous collection of various, mostly European ethnic groups, is the positive image: the relationship is almost one of parent (Europe) to child (America).

At which point we can offer another generalisation. Concomitant with McCarey's focus on social microcosms is a focus on children. Again, children *per se* are nothing new in McCarey. We can point out the importance of children in *Love Affair* to demonstrate that children were not foreign to McCarey's Thirties films. Indeed, both Michel and Terry have to return in some sense to their childhood before they can really grow up, Michel by means of his painting, Terry by means of her broken leg (she tells a little boy on board ship that she herself had once had a broken leg, as a little girl; and breaking it again results in her working at an orphanage). But the great number of children who populate McCarey's Forties films is striking nevertheless. Again, *Once Upon a Honeymoon* is the odd man out in that children as characters are rather secondary. The only children we see are the

The *Honeymoon* becomes a nightmare: O'Hara and O'Toole at the mercy of the Gestapo.

children of the Jewish maid—and they are important dramatically for providing Katie the opportunity to step outside of herself and show concern. Thematically, however, children serve as a focal point of the film's life vs. death, fertility vs. sterility conflict. Thus Hitler's greatest crime is not military conquest but sterilisation (the issue is raised at the detention camp where O'Toole and O'Hara are taken when the only passport they can produce belongs to the Jewish maid). By proposing to decide who can and cannot bear children, Hitler usurps the power of God to give or take life; and by usurping that power Hitler denies people any prospect of a hopeful, fruitful future.

The issue of procreation is also central to *Good Sam*. In many respects, *Good Sam* can be grouped with the sex comedies. Again we attend to a central couple, Sam (Gary Cooper) and Lu (Ann Sheridan) Clayton, and once again the progress of their relationship is charted against the backdrop of conventional social attitudes towards money. At the film's beginning, it appears that Good Sam is *too good:* he lends

The Clayton clan in *Good Sam:* Gary
Cooper, Louise Beavers, Lora Lee
Michel, Ann Sheridan, and Bobby
Dolan, Jr.

his car to a nearly blind neighbour; he opens his home to a variety of
ne'er do wells, including a suicidal young girl, a sales clerk in the
music department of the department store where Sam works, and his
wife's wise-cracking, pool-shooting, on-probation younger brother;
and, beyond that, Sam is constantly involved in various charities,
official (the church charity bazaar, the annual Christmas charity
dinner) and otherwise (Sam lends money to a young couple who want
to start a business and start a family).

All of which is problematic enough for Sam, and for his family. But
two consequences in particular follow from Sam's spontaneous
generosity which seem to call that generosity into question. First is the
fact that the presence of Lu's brother forces the family to sleep
dormitory style, males in one room, females in another. Thus, like
Pinky and Flora Whinney in *Six of a Kind,* Sam and Lu Clayton are
forced to sleep apart—and that clearly endangers the vitality of their
relationship. Secondly, there is the matter of Lu's dream house. On

the practical level, a new house would solve the sleeping problem—and that would do much to revitalise the Clayton marriage. But Lu talks about the house in terms which indicate a greater emotional investment than practicality would seem to dictate. Thus when she sees the house they eventually decide to buy she declares: "This is paradise." And the film's climactic scene comes at the moment when Sam has to tell Lu that he loaned the house fund money to Joe Adams and his wife—to finance their filling station and, more importantly, to finance their soon-to-be-born child. Sam points out that the young couple would not be having a baby if it were not for the loan ("You do believe that babies should be born, don't you?"); and Lu is reduced to pounding the bed in frustration ("Why can't people stand on their own two feet and have babies?").

It testifies to the basic strength of the Clayton marriage that it survives the blow-up over the house money; and it testifies to the basic rightness of Sam's actions that things eventually work out. Mr. and Mrs. Adams sell their service station at a profit, which allows them to repay Sam with interest and to purchase another station, and they are also blessed with an eight pound baby boy. Lu's brother, in turn, gets a job (working for Joe Adams), moves out, and marries the sales girl (thus solving the Clayton's sleeping problem). Even the bank manager loosens up a bit and loans Sam the down payment for Lu's dream house after Sam loses the house money to muggers. The point to be made here, however, is that Sam's actions are clearly predicated on a faith both in people *and* in the future—so that it is completely appropriate that the film's central issue should eventually be defined as an opposition between procreation (as Sam puts it to Lu: "It seemed so right to tell them they must have the baby") and convention (Lu's desire that her own married life should be just exactly what mother told her it would be). To believe in children is to believe in both the immediate reality of life and the imminent reality of a hopeful future. In which context all else is secondary.

Children play a similar thematic function in both *Going My Way* and *The Bells of St Mary's*. In *Going My Way* in particular, children are seen as the hope of the parish. Father Fitzgibbon's greatest failing is less a matter of dwindling collections than of his inability to empathise with the youth of the parish. He assumes things are normal when they are not (Tony Scaponi and his sidekicks are well down the road to reform school); and he assumes things are abnormal when they are just the contrary (he cannot see that Carol's leaving home and her show biz ambitions are necessary and acceptable, given her family

cCarey and the kids on the set of
e Bells of St. Mary's.

situation). It is only when the younger Father O'Malley comes along that Father Fitzgibbon slowly awakens to the situation—and before the film concludes it is the boys' choir that earns the money to rebuild St. Dominic's. In *The Bells of St. Mary's,* the situation is somewhat different in that the school is implicitly dedicated to its students and their future. There is no question that Sister Benedict and the other nuns are concerned about and attentive to the needs of their pupils, even if Sister Benedict and Father O'Malley disagree occasionally over matters of educational policy. The issue, then, at least as regards the school, is not whether the nuns who teach at St. Mary's *will* show their concern but whether or not they can *continue* to do so. There is more to it than that (i.e., the necessity to keep St. Mary's going needs to be placed in a certain ethical/experiential perspective) but the value both of schools and children is never called into question.

One further generalisation is well worth making in connection with McCarey's post-Thirties films. We have already remarked on the fact that McCarey's Forties films show increased concern both for society, as symbolised by various microcosmic communities, and children.

The logical relationship is fairly clear: children provide society with the opportunity both to perpetuate and renew itself. What is surprising, then, is the fact that McCarey apparently found it impossible to provide a complete or completely satisfying image of the family —a social unit which could serve as a mediating institution between children and civilisation. It is not that McCarey denigrates the concept of the family; nor is it that his Forties films lack family relationships. Katie O'Hara has her mother in *Once Upon a Honeymoon,* where we also see the Jewish maid and her kids; there is the Haines family in *Going My Way,* not to mention Mrs. Fitzgibbon; *The Bells of St. Mary's* has a major subplot which involves the reunion of a family; and *Good Sam* has several families, the Claytons themselves, the Adams family, the Nelsons, the Butlers, etc., etc. But in nearly every case there is something missing. We know nothing of Katie's father. Mrs. Haines is never seen and is only mentioned once—in the past tense. We hear nothing of Father Fitzgibbon's father. And all that we know about Father O'Malley's parents is that his mother died when he was quite young. In *The Bells of St. Mary's,* Patsy's parents are separated and it takes Father O'Malley to bring the family back together again. And in *Good Sam* the kids—with the exception of Lu's brother—are too young to be the cause of much trouble. What we *never* see in a positive light in McCarey is a *whole* family that has managed to *grow* together. If the family works, the kids are young, as we see in *My Favorite Wife* and *Good Sam,* or else the family is in some sense incomplete for lacking a parent. And if the kids are grown, the family tends not to work (see *Make Way for Tomorrow* and *My Son John*). Thus the only healthy young adults or teenagers in McCarey are those who manage to run away from home (Carol in *Going My Way,* Siu-Lan in *Satan Never Sleeps*) or those who live with only one parent (Ted Haines in *Going My Way,* Comfort Goodpasture in *Rally Round the Flag, Boys!*).

There are two relevant explanations for the fact that families in McCarey seldom manage to transcend the generation gap intact. In negative terms, family breakdowns evidence the destructive power of habit and convention. As we have already remarked in connection with *Make Way for Tomorrow,* families by virtue of their structure and longevity tend to foster conventions of behaviour and belief—and any convention, carried unselfconsciously to extremes, can be dangerous in McCarey (as *The Awful Truth* and *Love Affair* both demonstrate). Thus those films where families do in some sense stay together—even if "togetherness" is defined as a debilitating relationship of dependency—tend to be tragedies of rigidity. I have no doubts that McCarey would have preferred to live in a world where parents and children always got along; yet he was honest enough to his own sense of human reality not to force the issue in his films.

We can see family breakdowns in McCarey in more positive terms, however, as metaphors for opportunity. The breakdown of a family in McCarey inevitably leaves a vacuum to be filled. Suddenly it is necessary to create new families, to establish new relationships, to bring a new generation into the world. And, as we have already demonstrated, children remain symbols of hope in McCarey, despite the fact that those kids often find growing up to be no easy task. Every so often a Chuck O'Malley or a Sam Clayton is born: it is enough to keep hope alive. The point, after all, is *not* that *particular* families must survive. Particular families cannot because family members inevitably die (as Janou dies in *Love Affair*). The point, rather, is that we need not despair at our failings. It is even possible to learn from them. Thus what looks to be a negative circumstance in McCarey often becomes an opportunity for growth and change—and it's that creative process of growing and changing that McCarey celebrates.

* * *

I began this discussion of McCarey in the Forties by arguing against the criterion of originality. It is no adequate criticism of *The Bells of St. Mary's* to say that it repeats in certain respects *Going My Way*. Critics who operate on the assumption that their primary task is to praise originality are often more concerned with demonstrating their own critical superiority or independence than with elucidating the texts in question. What does their kind of praise ever tell us about a film? It seems clear, in fact, that searching for the strikingly "original" aspects of a given movie leads more often than not to genuinely false descriptions of the film in question. And *The Bells of St. Mary's*, we can see in retrospect, has been particularly victimised by this sort of superficial critical thinking. Some further remarks in defence of the film are therefore in order.

Critics who berate *The Bells of St. Mary's* often focus their attention on the relationship between the Bogardus character (Henry Travers) and the St. Mary's staff. Bogardus is the childless capitalist who wants to buy out St. Mary's and use the land as a parking lot for his almost finished and long cherished office building; while the nuns of St. Mary's hope (and/or scheme?) to get Bogardus to donate the structure as a replacement for St. Mary's dilapidated classroom buildings. Richard Corliss, for example, has described the film's central thematic issue, in broadly allegorical terms, as the "struggle between Church and Capital" (p. 233). And yet even the most cursory glance at the film will make it clear that the Bogardus plot is only one of several plot threads—important, surely, but not the whole movie. Thus the Catholicism/Capitalism antinomy cannot be used as the ruling thematic paradigm—not unless all other plot conflicts in the film also involve capitalists of one sort or another.

A far more fruitful approach—for being more accurate, both to McCarey's concerns in general and to those of *The Bells of St. Mary's*—is to read the film as a reflection on the interplay between rigidity and flexibility, particularly as that interplay is personified in the film's two central characters, Sister Benedict (Ingrid Bergman) and Father O'Malley (Bing Crosby). The film's very first scene sets up the expectation that the two will be at odds with one another. Mrs. Breen, the rectory housekeeper, welcomes Father O'Malley to St. Mary's; and as he is led to his room Father O'Malley asks about his predecessor, Father Fogarty. Mrs. Breen informs him rather cryptically that Father Fogarty was taken away the day previous and she expresses sympathy for the "poor man's" plight—carefully avoiding an explanation of that plight lest Father O'Malley be relieved of the necessity for asking further questions: she is obviously an old hand at the gossip game and wants to exploit O'Malley's naïveté for all it is worth. O'Malley takes the bait, asks what the mystery is all about, and he is finally informed, after some further detour and delay, that Father Fogarty left St. Mary's for Shady Rest, in a wheel chair, "mumblin' to himself," driven to distraction by the nuns. As Mrs. Breen finally puts it: "You see, he had very definite ideas about running this school, about the raising and education of children—and so did they."

The equation of rigidity with madness here is clear enough (that equation is the *central* issue in *My Son John*). And there is little reason to question the basic facts of Mrs. Breen's account. But it is worth remarking that Mrs. Breen's habit of mind, her well-developed willingness to exaggerate for rhetorical effect, is also a form of rigidity, a far more concrete and specific rigidity, for being *enacted* rather than recounted; and it is a rigidity that will have (as it turns out) a real and largely negative effect on the future course of events. Her exaggeration may thus seem harmless, even humorous. Yet it is a similar tendency to exaggerate and to overdramatise on the part of several different characters that the film is concerned, among other

McCarey (centre) and Ingrid Bergman (right) take time out for a song.

things, to discredit. If Father O'Malley takes Mrs. Breen too seriously (as in part he does) there is no doubt that his stay at St. Mary's will be maddening for everyone involed.

The film's second scene, however, goes a long way towards lessening Father O'Malley's fears. The issue of rigidity remains front and centre; but the action of the scene makes it clear that the nuns of St. Mary's are not totally incapable of recognising rigidity when they see it—or of laughing at it. Thus Father O'Malley's attempts to observe propriety become laughable as he rises mechanically and repeatedly out of his chair to greet each and every nun in turn. And while the nuns do their best *not* to laugh, out of deference to Father O'Malley, they cannot refrain from laughter when Father O'Malley's straw hat starts to dance, seemingly of its own accord, along the mantelpiece behind him. Even Sister Benedict the most rigidly authoritarian nun of the group by virtue of her position as Sister Superior, is amused by the slapstick contrast between Father O'Malley's obviously well rehearsed speech and the improvised hat dance performed by one of the school's more rumbustious kittens. Rigidity thus remains the issue—immediately after his speech to the nuns, for example, O'Malley speaks to the students and declares an instant holiday, much to

Sister Benedict's chagrin—but rigidity is now seen more as a source of amusement than madness. Indeed, before the film concludes almost all the film's characters are invited, in one way or another, to laugh at themselves. And their capacity generally to do so evidences precisely that sort of self-awareness which typifies McCarey characters at their best.

The emotional conflict between Father O'Malley and Sister Benedict takes place for the most part in two separate though thematically related contexts. The first of these, already referred to, is the Bogardus plot. Bogardus is chairman of the city council and he uses his position to put the squeeze on St. Mary's. He wants the land to build an office building, has already acquired a piece of it, a piece that had once been the school playground and which the nuns had been forced to sell in order to finance city-council mandated improvements on the classroom buildings, and Bogardus wants the rest of the St. Mary's property so that he can provide parking space for the employees who will occupy his office building. Such is the situation when Father O'Malley takes over as school pastor.

Now, as Richard Corliss and Jeffrey Richards have it, the intrusion of Father O'Malley into the Bogardus plot initiates an unsavoury scheme, apparently hatched in concert by Father O'Malley and the nuns, to swindle Mr. Bogardus out of his building. But this description is obviously and demonstrably false. Sister Benedict and the nuns, for example, are quite incapable of scheming. Indeed, their inability to deal creatively with the rigidly single-minded Bogardus is a contributing factor in their dilemma. If anyone schemes, it is Bogardus himself—and the nuns adopt a detached and altogether doctrinaire tactic for dealing with his schemes: they do their best to keep St. Mary's in minimal repair, and in the meanwhile they pray that Bogardus will just up and give them his building.

By contrast, Father O'Malley's handling of Bogardus is far more practical, though hardly inhumane. If Father O'Malley "does" anything, it is simply that he takes the trouble to get acquainted with Bogardus. Indeed, it is Father O'Malley's relationship with Bogardus that gives us the chance to understand the circumstances which eventually lead Bogardus to donate his building to St. Mary's. The very first time we see Bogardus it is from O'Malley's point of view—and by his actions in the scene that follows Bogardus demonstrates how great an "emotional" investment he has made in the building. That is, he chases the St. Mary's kids off the property himself. We thus get the strong impression that the building is something more than a business venture, something far more personal—and that impression is reinforced by Bogardus's willingness to use his political influence to force the property issue, by his *un*willingness to talk about the fact that he is childless, and by his concern for his heart condition (he prefers to drive the few blocks to St. Victor's rather than walk). It all adds up: Bogardus fears mortality and wishes to leave something behind when he dies. He has no human relationships to sustain him—and hence his "edifice complex" (McCarey's attitude towards "buildings" is generally negative: see *Ruggles of Red Gap, Love Affair,* or even *Duck Soup*).

Indeed, were it not for the fact that Bogardus genuinely fears death and longs for some sort of memorial, it is altogether unlikely that the actions taken by Father O'Malley would convince Bogardus to donate the property. Those "actions" are three—and they hardly amount to a campaign of emotional "terrorism" (as Corliss and Richards imply). First, Father O'Malley simply allows Sister Benedict to believe that Bogardus *might* be willing to donate the building—at which point she finally musters up the courage to put the proposal to Bogardus. Of course, in doing so she does appeal to his sense of mortality ("This will live long after you're dust") but *she* does not harp on it: Bogardus does (he asks her to repeat the phrase). The second action that Father O'Malley takes is to suggest to Bogardus's physician that the cause behind Bogardus's hypochondria may be less physical than mental —and accordingly that the cure for Bogardus's complaints might well involve good advice rather than chemicals: maybe "doing good" will help to heal the old man's "bad heart." It is hardly a suspect suggestion, particularly when Bogardus's ills are so obviously psychosomatic; and furthermore O'Malley leaves it to the doctor to decide whether he should "change [his] prescription." The third and last action that O'Malley takes is to tell Mr. Bogardus what Sister Benedict had told him: that we pass through life but once and should do good works while we have the chance. It is said somewhat casually, as O'Malley and Bogardus chat on the street corner—and it is fairly clear at the time that Bogardus has already decided to donate the building to St. Mary's—in which case O'Malley can hardly be accused of arm-twisting or dishonesty. It is not even, as Richard Corliss and Jeffrey Richards suggest, a question of ends justifying means. The "means" in this case involves nothing more than empathy: Father O'Malley understands Bogardus's dilemma and suggests, both to Bogardus's doctor and to Bogardus himself, that Bogardus's own ends will be better served by donating the building. Father O'Malley is far "sneakier," if that's the word for it, in *Going My Way.*

The second context for the Sister Benedict/Father O'Malley conflict is the "Gallagher" sub-plot. Here again we have characters indulging in some sort of behavioral or emotional rigidity, although the members of the Gallagher family display their lack of flexibility in matters more sexual than financial. That is, the family is disrupted when Mr. Gallagher, fearing the responsibility of marriage, walks out on his wife; the disruption is perpetuated by Mrs. Gallagher who refuses to go look for her husband on the grounds that *he* was the one who walked out on *her;* and the disruption threatens to continue, even *after* Mr. and Mrs. Gallagher are reunited, because Patsy fears desertion. She has never met her father—does not know him *as* her father when by chance she sees her parents together—and in her ignorance she assumes that her mother no longer loves her: hence she intentionally flunks her final exams and begs Sister Benedict to help her become a nun. And once again the rigidity/flexibility issue is repeated in terms of reaction. Once again Sister Benedict adopts the more abstract and doctrinaire response: she flunks Patsy Gallagher for failing her finals and justifies the action by appealing to the necessity for "standards." And once again Father O'Malley exhibits

Mr. and Mrs. Joe Gallagher (William Gargan and Martha Sleeper) thank Father O'Malley (Bing Crosby) in *The Bells of St. Mary's.*

the more practical and immediate response. He hunts down Joe Gallagher in the first place, thus reuniting husband and wife; and then he urges Sister Benedict to graduate Patsy despite her failure, on the grounds that Patsy's self-confidence is of more pressing significance than the standards that Sister Benedict feels compelled to uphold. To be sure, at this juncture *both* Father O'Malley and Sister Benedict (like Patsy) are acting in ignorance. Neither one knows why Patsy failed. If anything, Father O'Malley could be faulted for refusing at the outset to give Sister Benedict any real understanding of Patsy's family situation (here is where Mrs. Breen's exaggeration has its negative effect: Father O'Malley hadn't trusted Sister Benedict to sympathise with Mrs. Gallagher's sexually shady past). But the rigidity/flexibility opposition is still clearly at issue.

Ironically, however, the antagonism between Sister Benedict and Father O'Malley is predicated less on the differences between them than on the similarities. It is not the case, for example, that Sister Benedict is incapable of loosening up. She does give boxing lessons on occasion—though she focuses as much on "bobbing and weaving" as on punching (the boxing *motif* recalls *Belle of the Nineties* and *The Milky Way*). She swings a pretty mean baseball bat. She gives writing assignments on the topic of "the five senses"—which indicates that she values the immediacy of life, however much she also values concepts and abstractions. She sings Swedish folk songs. She discourages Patsy's desire to become a nun on the grounds that Patsy should experience more of life before choosing to follow a religious vocation. Sister Benedict is even capable, when Father O'Malley informs her that she will be leaving St. Mary's, of admitting, at least intellectually, that it is possible for a person to become too attached to a place or institution (her attachment to St. Mary's echoes that of Bogardus to his office building in *Bells* and of Father Fitzgibbon to St. Dominic's in *Going My Way;* in all three cases the attachment is equated with disease). Likewise, Father O'Malley is capable of being rigid on occasion. He does withhold the facts of the Gallagher family from Sister Benedict, after all. And later on he withholds the fact of her illness from her—although he does so on the orders of Dr. McKay.

The similarity between Father O'Malley and Sister Benedict is most memorably evidenced, however, midway through the film when together they watch the grade-school kids rehearsing the annual Christmas pageant. The play itself is the familiar Nativity play, Joseph and Mary seeking shelter, followed by the visit of the wise men to the manger—but the kids improvise, within the general limits provided

Father O'Malley (Bing Crosby) and Sister Benedict (Ingrid Bergman) watch the children rehearse the Christmas play.

by the structure of the story, their own dialogue and gestures. As Sister Benedict points out, the children never perform the play the same way twice. Thus every enactment is unique; and yet, it seems clear, in every case the improvised quality of the performance is likely to underline, as it does so marvellously in the one performance we actually see, the most profound implication of the Christmas story: that in Christ we are reborn; that in Christ we can renew ourselves as the children renew the play with each performance of it. All of which is thematically to the point—but in the present context we should emphasise McCarey's *mise-en-scéne*, which is constructed in such a manner as to highlight, in immediate dramatic terms, the "identity" of Sister Benedict and Father O'Malley. McCarey cuts between reaction shots of Father O'Malley and Sister Benedict, together in a single frame (see still), and point-of-view medium shots and full shots of the play as Father O'Malley and Sister Benedict witness it. We thus *see* the unity of positive response that Sister Benedict and Father O'Malley demonstrate in their nearly identical reactions to the play: both are charmed and moved, both by the play *and* by the other's response. And by seeing it we assert an analogous unity of the viewer with the central characters: that is, we are *all* "viewers," of the play and of other "viewers," including Sister Benedict and Father O'Malley; and by "sharing" their vision of and response to the play we as spectators assert a significant measure of emotional identification. We demonstrate "empathy." And it is this sort of empathy that McCarey celebrates in *The Bells of St. Mary's*.

Furthermore, this empathetic understanding of the Sister Benedict/Father O'Malley relationship allows us, later on in the film, to understand Sister Benedict's agonised over-reaction to the fact of her transfer. Her sorrow at the thought of leaving St. Mary's is real enough, is made more real, indeed, when Father O'Malley tells her that she will not even be given another teaching assignment—but her reaction is all the more bitter for the fact that the transfer seems an act of intentional cruelty on Father O'Malley's part. She thought she knew him, thought they shared the same basic humane values and goals, and she assumes, in her sorrow and her ignorance, that Father O'Malley's apparently generous and easy-going manner was really only an act. It is a terrible way to feel about someone, as Sister Benedict admits in the chapel scene when she prays that she be forgiven her anger and cleansed of her bitterness, but she wouldn't feel that way, I submit, had it not been for the fact that she and Father O'Malley had previously been so in tune (quite literally at times) with one another. She just can't understand how or why he could do what he seems to be doing; and in her ignorance she invents motives for him—just as Patsy Gallagher, in *her* ignorance, invents motives to explain the fact that her mother seems set to desert her for a man; in both cases false inferences follow from a lack of immediacy. Characters are either unable (as Sister Benedict is unable) or unwilling (as Patsy is unwilling) to find out the truth: both of them prefer to suffer in silence, and both would prefer to stay at St. Mary's.

But *The Bells of St. Mary's* preclude that sort of stasis. The "spirit" of St. Mary's, the "resonance" that "rings" in the minds of the students and staff, is predicated on the fact that people must necessarily change and grow and move on. The educational mission of the school, as it is embodied in the school song and in Father O'Malley's graduation remarks, and as it is exemplified by the actions and ethics of the St. Mary's staff, is to encourage in the students just

Saying goodbye: Sister Benedict (Ingrid Bergman) bids farewell to the sisters of St. Mary's.

that sort of empathetic creativity which will make their lives rewarding and meaningful after they leave St. Mary's. Doing for others fulfils the self no matter where one does it. It is that sort of empathy which allows Father O'Malley to understand Mr. Bogardus. It is that sort of empathy which Sister Benedict exhibits when she finally decides to pass Patsy despite her failing marks (to be sure, by that point Sister Benedict knows that Patsy failed on purpose—but the marks still stand and Sister Benedict does ignore them). And finally, it is that sort of empathy which prompts Father O'Malley to disregard the doctor's instructions and tell Sister Benedict of her illness. Father O'Malley is attuned to the immediacy of her agony, knows how and why she is suffering, and he is flexible enough to do the right thing despite the doctor's prohibition. Sister Benedict must be told the reason for her departure from St. Mary's—and he tells her. It is another marvellous McCarey moment, rich with grace and feeling, and yet it celebrates a genuinely ethical position. Indeed, Father O'Malley's action allows Sister Benedict to recover her sense of identity—both with Father O'Malley and with St. Mary's. But now she understands that this sense of shared identity does not depend on physical presence. She will never "leave" St. Mary's because the spirit of St. Mary's will always be with her, will always find expression in the creativity of personal relationships—relationships which can transcend time and space. She can always "dial O—for O'Malley"; and therefore she need never fear to face the future. Thus, like Lucy and Barkley Cooper in *Make Way for Tomorrow*, Sister Benedict and Father O'Malley part company, perhaps forever, but in *The Bells of St. Mary's* the departure is cause for joy rather than agony. And in truth it is no departure at all but an affirmation of those qualities of action and insight which make life worth living in McCarey. What more can we reasonably ask of an artist than that?

My Son John:
The Case for McCarey

It must be conceded that *My Son John* and *Satan Never Sleeps*, McCarey's two "anti-Communist" films, are difficult to watch. In the case of *Satan Never Sleeps*, however, it is clear that the difficulty does not reside primarily, as most would have it, in McCarey's use of Communism as a metaphor for personal and social rigidity. It resides, rather, in the fact that McCarey's vision of life and its possibilities had become genuinely darker by the time he had made the film. The marriage which concludes the movie, for example—a marriage which binds a rapist and his victim together for the sake of the rape-

ance Nuyen and William Holden
Satan Never Sleeps.

conceived child—can hardly be described as symbolic of social or personal health. Indeed, the fact of the marriage is attributable to an over-rigid social structure which McCarey implicitly condemns. The rape victim is cast out by her father in order to save face: she has no real choice but to marry the child's father.

The problem with *My Son John* is of a similar sort. Again, it is not merely a function of metaphor. As George Morris points out in his often eloquent but ultimately inadequate defence of the film, McCarey's decision to set super-Americanism against anti-Americanism seems a perfectly legitimate and workable method for exploring the dangers of over-rigid behaviour and belief.[18] And in portraying the conflict between father and son, between the veteran and the college grad, between the super patriot and the Communist agent, McCarey continues to demonstrate the sort of detached but concerned evenhandedness which characterised his treatment of the family in *Make Way for Tomorrow*. In both instances, we are shown how readily certain self-destructive habits of mind can be passed down from one generation to the next: like parent, like child.

In *My Son John*, however, the conflict which nearly destroys the Jefferson family involves more than mere presence or absence. It is not just a matter of children who wish to ignore their parents, as it is in *Make Way for Tomorrow*. Rather, the quarrel between Dan Jefferson (Dean Jagger) and John Jefferson (Robert Walker) involves an aggressive and psychotic passion for conflict on the part of both men: Dan seeks to dominate while John seeks to aggravate. Thus Dan snidely refers to John's use of "two dollar words." Thus John purposefully avoids returning home to bid his two brothers *bon voyage* before they embark for Korea and the Korean War. Thus, a week later, John quite consciously chooses to spend his first afternoon home in a year conferring with an old professor rather than with his parents, and he adds insult to injury by having his folks drop him off at the local college on the way home from Mass. Furthermore, John justifies visiting the professor on the grounds that he needs advice on the commencement address that he has been invited to present at his alma mater, a speech of which his parents are ignorant until he asks to be dropped off, and to which they are rather pointedly *not* invited. Finally, and most importantly, there is the running battle between Dan and John over the speech that Dan is scheduled to give that week at the American Legion post.

Ironically but appropriately for such an "American" movie, the film's most revealing metaphor is not politics, however, but football.

The game is referred to throughout the film, both visually (various team pictures are found in the living room and kitchen of the Jefferson home, for example) and verbally. Thus Ben and Chuck, John's two younger brothers, see the Korean War as a kind of football game: they express the hope that guardian angels will run interference for them if the battlefield going gets tough. And Father O'Dowd uses the football metaphor when discussing the "nuance" with which John had served Mass as an altar boy: "He looked good doing it, like a Notre Dame quarterback." In neither instance is the football reference "necessary," given the context of conversation, although in both cases the metaphor is used rather self-consciously, with sufficient humour or self-mockery to indicate an awareness, at least on McCarey's part, that the metaphor is *just* a metaphor and is not to be taken or used literally. In which case we can understand these "unnecessary" football references as being "very necessary"—for providing a thematic context within which falsely "literalist" uses of the football metaphor (or of *any* metaphor) gain significance. Indeed, the tragedy in *My Son John* results from the fact that the characters in the film take their metaphors far too literally and are therefore incapable of transcending them. Put another way, the central characters in *My Son John* are run by and rely on various conventionalised patterns of action—and the football metaphor serves alternately as a general paradigm of overritualised human behaviour and as one of the several specific metaphors which dominate the history of the Jefferson family.

Much that we need to know about the relationship between Dan and his son John, for example, is set forth in the first scene of the film, which has Ben and Chuck tossing a football back and forth in front of the Jefferson house while they wait with their father for Lucille to finish dressing for church. Chuck motions Ben to go out for a long pass, but then he turns and flips the ball to Dan—who promptly fumbles it. The boys jokingly kid the old man about it ("You're getting kind of clumsy, eh boy?"); Dan replies that, when he played football, he played tackle and never handled the ball; at which point Ben agrees: "That's right, Pop. They always went through you." Dan's response to the jibe is significant—a testily perfunctory denial ("Is that so?"), after which he shifts the subject to the fact that Lucille (Helen Hayes) is once again behind schedule ("This happens every Sunday").

We need not go further to suggest that a clear-cut relationship exists between Dan's "clumsiness"—expressed here through the football metaphor and specifically in terms of Dan's inability either to carry the ball or to stop those who do—and his tendency to insist on a regularity of behaviour, here associated with religion and elsewhere with politics. In cause/effect terms, we can see that Dan's fear of being "run through" pushes him into an ideological/intellectual corner where convention either prohibits aggression (religion), ritualises it (football), or directs it outward in the name of some greater good (patriotism)—and Dan aligns himself in that corner in such a position that he avoids situations that could call his tactic into question. That is, he makes a living teaching elementary school, where even a muddled brain will not be challenged, and he spends his spare time drinking with his American Legion cronies, men who share, or so the film implies, the same crippled and crippling super-patriot vision.

Clearly the greatest threat to Dan Jefferson's fragile ego—perhaps the threat that pushed him over the line into paranoia in the first place—is not Communist aggression, however, but his first born son, John. One need not be a doctrinaire Freudian to suggest that John represents a negative, hyper-distorted image of his already warped father. As George Morris points out, there is a mirror between them in their first scene together—John first sees his father *in* the mirror—and McCarey's use of the shot/reverse-shot editing figure in *My Son John,* as opposed to his usual straight-forward two-shots, binds all the characters, but particularly Dan and John, in a demonic, face-to-face visual web: again, the mirror motif. Beyond that, the two men are, in the context of the film, rather alike in their appearance, their overcoats and hats contrasting with the military uniforms worn by Chuck and Ben, with Lucille's female clothing (she is first seen standing in a slip), and with Father O'Dowd's priestly regalia. They are also somewhat alike in their professions: Dan is an educator while John is known for his education (he has "more degrees than a thermometer," as his mother puts it to the FBI agent) even if he now works as a government bureaucrat. (Both father and son are thus civil—or uncivil—servants.) They are also alike in their politics—to the extent that neither one is really a political animal. That is, they both use politics for personal reasons, and each sounds equally hollow if impassioned when spouting the party line, even if the party lines in question are exact opposites of one another. More importantly, both men are known for their "clumsiness"—both physical and emotional. Thus at the film's beginning Dan drops the ball and yells so loudly at Lucille that a neighbour tells him to be quiet—there's a baby next door. Thus Dan is so angry at John's asking to be left off at the college that he rear-ends the car ahead of him (driven, it turns out, by Steadman [Van Heflin], the FBI agent). Thus John goes far out of his way to humiliate his father upon returning home that first evening back in town by singing Dan's "anti-Commie" song with all possible sarcasm. And later on, after he hits John over the head with the family bible and shoves him across the kitchen table (John rips his trousers in the fall), Dan tries to explain things to Lucille by suggesting that John is "clumsy." Lucille then sends Dan off to his Legion meeting—and when he returns home late that night he staggers drunkenly around the house, so drunkenly that he tries to parody John's mock-heroic performance of his own anti-Commie song—and he stumbles down the stairs for his trouble. At which point a slightly sarcastic Lucille wonders aloud: "Where does he [John] get his awkwardness?" And finally, both men are alike in their devotion to Lucille. Dan's love for his wife is never in question—and John's love for his mother is evidenced, intially, by the intimacy of their relationship when they are alone together (one could point out the frequent "bedroom scenes" between them) and, eventually, by the fact that John recants his Communism and confesses his sins. Indeed, the only time in the film when John and Dan effectively agree on something is when they both, at different times, urge Lucille to take the "goof insurance" pills prescribed by Dr. Carver. Neither of them wants to see Lucille crack up.

All of which serves to explain, I believe, the fervour of Dan's antipathy toward John. John is *too* much a mirror image of his father—and Dan clearly fears the prospect of being "replaced," generally, in the world, and specifically, in Lucille's affections. Dan's fear is so great in this regard that he seems almost eager to take John out in the backyard and give him "both barrels." To be sure, Dan's repeated threats to kill John are couched in the rhetoric of cold war politics, and Dan has invested more than enough emotion in patriotism to make him trigger happy at the thought of getting one of those "scummies" in his sights. But Dan's paranoia is so all-inclusive that politics serves as simply one among several false metaphors for stability.

In this respect, indeed, it is striking how apolitical, how thoroughly personal, Dan's "anti-Commie" song happens to be. There is nothing in it about the "evils" of Communism. It is rather concerned with a lack of gratitude, expressed through the metaphor of nourishment ("Don't bite the hand that's feeding you"); and the hostility of the song is aimed at eliminating the ungrateful interloper ("Go back to your

**The son and the father: Robert
Walker and Dean Jagger in *My Son
John*.**

home o'er the sea"). It attests to Dan's insecurity that he tries to hide
his personal anxiety behind the cloak of patriotism, but the syntax of
the verse, which forces Dan to substitute the personal pronoun "me"
for "Uncle Sammy," and the context of the song, Dan singing it
straight at John on the first evening of John's visit home, make it fairly
clear that Dan's motives are largely and specifically personal. The
song thus expresses Dan's fear of being maimed or castrated—and
the only solution is to eliminate the threat, either by ideologically
maiming the intruder (hence all of Dan's talk about "honouring thy
father and thy mother") or by physical violence, football style, if all
else fails. Which is precisely what happens when Dan confronts John
in the kitchen after John has sworn to his mother that he has never

been a Communist. Dan wants John to repeat the act of "self-castration" by swearing to a word-for-word belief in the bible and the commandments. John refuses. And in the scuffle that follows Dan hits John over the head with the good book and then shoves John into the kitchen table. It almost comes off as slapstick—both men are clumsy enough to make fools of themselves—but the emotional issues are so hot that laughter is out of the question. Indeed, it is the last time Dan sees his son John alive. In retrospect, the wound that John receives in the scuffle is fatal. It is the final break with his father; and John's ripped trousers eventually serve to blow his cover as a spy—at which point John becomes vulnerable, either to arrest, if he does not confess, or assassination, if he names names.

But Dan's self-righteous anger toward John only half explains what happens in *My Son John*. For all of the similarities between the two men, there are differences as well. And the primary difference is that John's dislike of his father is, by itself, nowhere near so strong as his father's dislike of him. John, in truth, does not care about his father one way or the other (not surprisingly) and John's sarcasm, while real and biting, is almost always a matter of response: Dan is the primary aggressor in each of their four conversations. Thus, despite the fact that John can't resist an opportunity to do battle when such opportunities arise (he eagerly agrees to edit Dan's speech), and despite the fact that John enjoys the hell out of getting his father's goat, particularly when he can do it on Dan's terms, John generally prefers to avoid his father altogether. Thus John's visit is not much of a visit (he spends very little time at home). But if John prefers to avoid Dan, why then does he come home at all? The answer, clearly, is Lucille— but *not* simply because John "loves" his mother. On the contrary, the issue is not John's love for Lucille but Lucille's love for John—and again the football metaphor helps put things in perspective.

Clearly the most harrowing scene in *My Son John* is the confrontation between John and Lucille which takes place after Lucille returns from Washington, D.C. She had taken the trip ostensibly to visit John and to return the trousers which John had ripped in the scuffle with his father. (She had donated them, at John's instruction, to Father O'Dowd's charity, but then John had asked her to retrieve them.) Her real purpose in visiting John, however, is to test his integrity. Her suspicions have been aroused, by the whole course of domestic events, the phone calls, the strange visitors, etc., but particularly by John's request that she retrieve the trousers and by his transparently false denial that he had left anything in them (he had: the key to the apartment of an already arrested cohort); and she hopes against hope that she is wrong. She isn't. John fails the test. He tells her, Why, yes, there was something, the key to *his* apartment, at which point she leaves his office with key in hand and goes (after talking to the FBI) to the apartment of John's accomplice. The key fits the lock. Lucille then returns home—followed closely by John, who wants to know *why* she left the capital so suddenly, and by Mr. Steadman of the FBI, who knows everything by virtue of wire taps and hidden cameras.

The scene in question takes place, then, after John and Lucille have it out. She tells him she knows the truth; he effectively admits to her charges, by pressing her for the incriminating key and by telling her that she cannot prevent him from delivering his propagandistic commencement address: "Mother, how do you plan to stop me?" She threatens to speak out publicly, at which point John threatens to have her committed. Steadman then enters and Lucille tries one more time to get John to confess. John is forced to berate her. She scolds him—Steadman mentions her other boys, the "two halfbacks"—at which point Lucille seizes a team photo of Ben and Chuck and begins reminiscing, asking John if he remembers the many games his brothers had "pulled out of the fire." John replies, "Yes, dear," in tones both respectful and remorseful. At this, Lucille looks away from the photo to John, recalls painfully that John had "never played," and asserts the belief, almost as if it were a question, that John had been "hurt" when Dan and Lucille "jumped up and down cheering" for Chuck and Ben. Then, as if to make things up to him, she asks John to remember that she used to whisper to him, telling him "to keep studying" and reminding him that "there are other goals." Lucille then shifts contexts once more, though she does not leave the football metaphor behind. Rather, she updates and "literalises" it. She tells John that the family is cheering for Ben and Chuck again: they are "fighting on God's side now" and she urges John to "get into the game." In her anxiety, indeed, she becomes a possessed if pathetic kind of cheerleader, chanting "my son John, my son John, my son John," as if there really were a football game in progress.

The most significant aspect of the scene in question is what it reveals about family relationships—among the Jeffersons generally, and between John and Lucille specifically. I have already remarked on the importance of football to the family as a whole: it served to displace private feelings into the realm of public ritual. Thus Dan could cheer on Ben and Chuck precisely because they were *not* mirror images—they were backs, he had played the line—and yet in cheering for them

Lucille begs her son John to "get to the game": Helen Hayes, Van Heflin, and Robert Walker.

Dan had had opportunity to express, if only vicariously, his general sense of anger and frustration. Football obviously served a similar function for Lucille. As she had told John earlier in the film, in the second "bedroom" scene, he was her favourite son, the one who represented her hopes of significant action in the world, action of the sort that housewives seldom have time for. She evidently felt guilty for favouring John, for pushing his education, for putting all her hopes for intellectual and social betterment in his hands, and in her guilt she denied John the sort of public approval that she gave to Ben and Chuck. Thus Ben and Chuck got cheers, as Lucille overcompensated for her favouritism; while John, her "favourite," only got surreptitious whisperings. At which point we can see the impossibility of John's position. To his father, John is a threat, a tomorrow Dan does not want to see; while, to his mother, John represents a promise, a tomorrow Lucille cannot stand *not* to see. It is no wonder, then, that

John is unstable, an instability perfectly captured by Robert Walker's edgily ambiguous performance.

Furthermore, the scene demonstrates the danger implicit in letting metaphors become reality—or of letting any reality rigidify into metaphor. We see the latter danger in the fact that Lucille's apparently once genuine "love" for John is submerged in and eventually replaced by her "hopes" for his education. The "present" of the relationship between John and Lucille is thus postponed for the sake of the "future"; accordingly Lucille is unable to face the "present" when confronted by the facts of John's activities. As a prisoner in a federal pen, John will never do the great deeds that Lucille had hoped for—and when her hopes are destroyed, her sanity collapses as well; hence her pathetic retreat into the ritual of cheerleading.

At which point we see how threatening the former danger can be: Lucille "goes mad" when she allows the metaphor of football to replace the reality of her circumstances. Rather than face facts, she tries to accommodate them to an imagined but inappropriate view of the world; and it simply doesn't work. Throughout the film, Lucille's tenuous hold on reality is evidenced by her obsessive vision of family perfection, of the sort symbolised by family rooting sections at high school football games. This desire for perfection accounts for the degree of her emotional investment in the farewell dinner for Chuck and Ben. Dan is almost pleased when John telegraphs his regrets. Lucille is crestfallen. Her lust for perfection accounts as well for her constant anxiety when John finally does arrive: she sees his visit as an opportunity to reconcile her favourite son and her husband and she does her best to stage manage John's visit so that a reconciliation can take place. She suggests that Dan and John talk, for example; she suggests that John look over Dan's speech; she tries to admonish John for being rude to Dan; etc., etc. And yet it is clear that Lucille's efforts are doomed. The perfection was never there to begin with—so it can't be reconstructed. Thus keeping John's old chair and his books in the front room will not help at all. If anything, the chair evidences past failure rather than positive accomplishment. As a youth, John would retreat to the chair and read till all hours—so that even John's appetite for learning can be seen as a tactic for avoiding family fact. The one fact that no one will face is the fact that the family *as a family* never worked. And it never worked because both Dan and Lucille, like Lucy and Barkley Cooper in *Make Way for Tomorrow*, were incapable of facing reality head on. Nursery rhymes or no nursery rhymes, the family was a failure from the beginning. Lucille's use of the nursery rhyme ("my son John") in her cheerleading routine, therefore, is only one more reminder of her inadequacy.

Far and away the most disturbing example of this tendency to confuse fact and metaphor, however, is evidenced in the behaviour of Lucille's son John himself. I have already remarked that John's behaviour towards his father is not sufficiently accounted for by reference to Oedipal conflict alone. And this is true because the focus of John's antagonism is not Dan at all but Lucille. John plays the game he plays not primarily for the purpose of outraging his father but for the purpose of testing his mother. In general, as we have already noted, Lucille's affection for John is characterised by her inability to express approval of his accomplishments. She can cheer for Chuck and Ben but not for her son John. If she talks about John at all, she talks about his past—about how she used to bounce him on her knee and sing nursery rhymes ("Teedle deedle dumpling, my son John"), how she fought for his education, how she used to bribe him with cookies so that he would learn his scripture, etc., etc. But clearly the most significant event in John's past occurred when he stole some pennies from a cookie jar. John had felt so guilty, as Lucille tells the tale, that he had retreated to his room, feigning sickness and cutting school. Rather than punish him, however, Lucille forgave him, telling him that she had been saving the pennies for him (for his education?) all along—at which point John's eyes had filled with tears and his illness was suddenly cured. It is, to the best of our knowledge, the only time in his life that John had felt truly loved—so it is hardly surprising that the equation of mother love and forgiveness should come to dominate John's behaviour. He is constantly being reminded of the incident, by Lucille in conversation and by the fact that the cookie jar has a place of honour right beside the kitchen sink. He cannot avoid seeing the jar and he cannot break with the pattern of action that the jar represents. The road to love is crime—and John commits the worst of all possible crimes by becoming a Communist spy. He doesn't care much for Communism one way or the other; but he does care very deeply for his mother and he seeks her love as best he can, by giving her opportunity to forgive him his trespasses.

It is, therefore, essential to John's altogether personal mission that he go out of his way—as he does—to arouse suspicion. If he is *not* suspected of sinful or even criminal activity, his mother will have nothing to forgive. We cannot account for John's activities in any other terms. If John really were a spy, were he dedicated to the overthrow of the government, he would hardly go to such lengths to antagonise not only his parents but Father O'Dowd and Dr. Carver as well. He would do far better to join Dan for a drink and a song at the American Legion post. But John is not much of a spy. No spy in his right mind would leave an incriminating key in his trousers and give the trousers away; and no spy in his right mind would then make such a foolish fuss over getting the trousers back. What happens is that John simply adopts the spy role to suit his personal purposes—and when the scheme backfires, when the FBI starts to close in, John panics: hence his anxiety about the stranger and the phone call, hence his transparent attempt to deceive his mother, etc., etc. If all spies were like John, there would be little need for an FBI.

All of which points to the basic futility of viewing *My Son John* in broadly allegorical terms. Such readings inevitably oversimplify characterisation by ignoring matters of motive. Thus Dan is seen as the embodiment of pure and perfect patriotism while John is seen as personifying the ungodly evils of Communism—and little critical effort is expended wondering how or why that might be true. Furthermore, and consequently, such readings inevitably over-simplify the significance of the film's conclusion. John loses his life and by extension the "argument." Therefore Dan's sort of patriotic fanaticism appears to be validated, in Robert Warshow's words, "as a higher form of wisdom."[19] Indeed, Warshow goes on to cite the words of Lucille herself to support the contention that the film upholds Dan's sort of stupidity. As Lucille puts it to Dan, just before her final confrontation with John, "You've got more wisdom than all of us, because you listen to your heart."

But such a reading simply does not work. To begin with, it ignores the fact of McCarey's sympathetic evenhandedness. It is very seldom the case that McCarey completely approves or disapproves of his characters. Even his best characters make mistakes (O'Toole in *Once Upon a Honeymoon* and Nicky Ferrante in *An Affair to Remember,* to cite two examples) and most of his less sympathetic characters (Effie in *Ruggles of Red Gap,* Nellie in *Make Way for Tomorrow,* the Ken character in *Love Affair* and *An Affair to Remember,* even von Luber in *Once Upon a Honeymoon*) are generally granted some measure of humanity. It is only in his more farcical moods that McCarey allows himself the leisure of an occasional scapegoat figure (Belknap-Jackson in *Ruggles,* Ferguson in *Six of a Kind,* Trentino in *Duck Soup,* Captain Hoxie in *Rally Round the Flag, Boys!*). For the most part, however, McCarey is careful to avoid schemes which depict specific characters as clear-cut examples of specific and completely debilitating vices. Thus the worst character ever seen in McCarey—Hitler in *Once Upon a Honeymoon*—is seen *on screen* only briefly. It would be altogether inconsistent, then, in so seriously "realistic" a film as *My Son John,* for McCarey to devote concerted attention to an out-and-out "evil" character. On the contrary, McCarey's very detailed explication of family dynamics among the Jeffersons has the effect of "humanising" the characters involved. We know why they do what they do—and our response, I would submit, is far more a matter of compassion than approval or disapproval. We regret that the characters in *My Son John* act as they do, mindlessly repeating their own mistakes, but we are hardly invited to assign blame. We are rather invited to observe—in the hope, perhaps, that we can better avoid such mistakes ourselves.

Furthermore, we must remark that Warshow drastically misrepresents the context of Lucille's statement. First of all, she makes the remark *after* visiting John in Washington, D.C. She is on the verge of hysteria, for discovering that John is involved in espionage, and her hysteria is made manifest only moments later when she confronts John downstairs and urges him to "get into the game." More important, however, is the fact that Dan himself, the film's embodiment, as Warshow reads it, of "stupidity," refutes Lucille's argument. Even Dan can see that Lucille has gone off the deep end, and he urges her not to "overdo" it. "When you talk like that," he tells her, "you're the one who's not thinking so straight." Warshow could not have put it better himself. The problem is that *none* of the characters in the film is all right or all wrong. Each has moments of lucidity and insight. But such moments are only exceptions which prove the tragic rule. By and large, the characters in *My Son John* are trapped beyond escape in habits of mind which obscure rather than promote understanding.

No doubt, the most difficult scene in the film—for McCarey, one suspects, as well as his critics—is the posthumous playing of John's tape-recorded commencement address/confession which closes the film. For Warshow the scene is totally unmotivated. He sees "no apparent reason" for John to repent his crimes—and he concludes that John's confession represents McCarey's final capitualation to Cold War didacticism.[20] Warshow is correct, I think, to imply that the scene is crucial to our understanding of the film. We cannot simply pass it over, as George Morris does, on the grounds that McCarey had to do a patch job on the film after the death of Robert Walker.[21] Walker did die before completing the film—but the shooting schedule quite clearly did not follow narrative chronology. Thus McCarey resorts to dubbing, to cover-up editing, to process photography, to the use of doubles, even to the use of footage taken from Hitchcock's *Strangers on a Train* which had also featured Robert Walker, but he does so throughout the film, not just in the final reel or two. Furthermore, it is clearly Walker's voice on the soundtrack while the tape recorder runs, and we can reasonably conclude that John would have died at the hands of Communist agents even had Walker survived to complete the shooting schedule. It is likely, then, that the posthumous confession corresponds to McCarey's original design, in which case we are required to deal with the closing scene in all of its implications, something which Warshow's allegorical reading of the scene by and large fails to do.

Clearly the "reason" for John's confession is completely personal and reflects the degree to which John's "present" is determined by his "past." Once again he has been caught with his hand in the cookie jar; once again his mother expresses some measure of forgiveness (by urging him to "get into the game"); once again John responds with heartfelt tears—he is hurt that she is hurt (McCarey emphasises the hurt by shooting Walker in close-up); and in both cases John repays forgiveness by returning to school, grade school in the former instance, his alma mater in the latter. The only really significant difference between the two "cookie jar" incidents is the fact of Lucille's emotional collapse the second time around. And her emotional collapse has a profound effect on John. His motive for spying in the first place was to re-affirm the fact of Lucille's affection. He never really wanted to hurt her. Thus her collapse affects John on two levels. It proves the degree of her concern for him (she would not be so torn-up if John did *not* matter to her) and it obliges John to show a similar sort of forgiveness or acceptance. And the only obvious means to that end is the tape-recorded confession (John clearly intended to give himself up to the FBI so he would not have been able to deliver the speech in person under any circumstances).

The personal aspect of John's confession is further emphasised by the language of the confession itself. By and large, John's posthumous monologue is a string of biblical and political clichés taken almost word for word from Lucille and Dan. John portrays himself as a rebellious son, seduced by the "narcotic" power of flattery into becoming a "native American Communist spy," and he begs God to have mercy on his soul. All of which pleases Dan and Lucille immensely—though none of it, we know, is really true. True or not, however, it is in John's eye the only scenario that his parents are likely to accept or understand, and by acting it out John once again

Trapped in the past: Lucille and Dan Jefferson at the end of *My Son John*.

demonstrates the tragic consequence of substituting metaphor (the Cold War) for reality. John talks about beginning a "new life"—but by so doing he only demonstrates how completely trapped he is in his old one.

It could be argued, on the basis of biographical evidence, that the apparently anti-Communist tone of *My Son John* accorded with McCarey's personal political views. I would venture the guess, indeed, that McCarey's beliefs were well enough known (he did testify before the House Un-American Activities Committee) that critics automatically read *My Son John* as if it were an allegorical rendering of McCarey's political opinions.[22] And even if we agree with George Morris that McCarey could have chosen any sort of "ism," political or otherwise, to stand as a metaphor for rigidity without much changing the film, we are obliged to account for the fact that McCarey *did not* choose to make John (or Dan, for that matter) a fanatic of some other stripe.

In so doing, however, we must distinguish between "professed intention"—what an artist might have said he intended to do in a particular work—and "realised intention"—the work he actually and eventually created. Hitchcock is a prime example of the fact that these two sorts of "intention" can often be widely and wildly divergent. And Hitchcock scholarship has repeatedly demonstrated the necessity and validity of ignoring professed intention whenever the texts themselves require it. The art of Alfred Hitchcock is far more profound and disturbing than Hitchcock has ever been willing to admit to an interviewer. And something similar needs to be said about "intention" in *My Son John*. It may well have been the case that McCarey intended *My Son John* as an anti-Communist statement of the sort condemned by Warshow and others—but the film he actually made is clearly and carefully something else again. The pattern of issues and motivation in *My Son John* is far too elaborate, too thorough, and far too typical of McCarey's general concerns to permit quirky political readings like Warshow's. And yet politics *are* an issue in *My Son John*, and we must therefore consider what thematic function they play in the film, particularly if we are going to refute naïve political readings of McCarey's apparent "intentions."

I have already suggested that politics in *My Son John* can *best* be understood by reference to character dynamics. Being a super-patriot allows Dan to express his sense of personal paranoia in relatively acceptable public terms. It is a desperate tactic and McCarey portrays it as precisely that. A secondary function of the ideological metaphors in *My Son John*, however, is to raise the general issue of personal and social flexibility—an issue of central importance to McCarey ever since *Putting Pants on Philip*. It is, of course, highly ironic that those characters in *My Son John* who most preach the cause of freedom—Dan Jefferson and Steadman, the FBI agent—are such poor examples of freedom in action. But the contrast between their words and their deeds only serves to underscore the importance of avoiding social and conceptual rigidity. Steadman, for example, may sermonise to Lucille about the God-given gift of liberty, but McCarey's *mise-en-scène* at that moment tends to emphasize the *distance*, both spatial and thematic, which exists between the foreground, dominated visually by barren trees and diagetically by Steadman's desire to confirm John's guilt, and the background, which is dominated by the almost fluid grace of the Jefferson memorial. Against that background, Steadman's motives seem barren indeed. And the same can be said of almost every instance of overt political sermonising in *My Son John:* context, either visual or thematic, almost always undercuts and qualifies the political rhetoric (compare the rigid, impersonal, long-shot *mise-en-scène* of the commencement scene in *My Son John,* for example, to the intimate, medium-shot *mise-en-scène* of the commencement scene in *The Bells of St. Mary's*). Thus it is necessary to understand the *whole* film if it is to be understood at all. To take its set speeches at face value is to drastically misread the text.

Ultimately, I believe the whole of *My Son John* can best be understood as a negative image of McCarey's normally positive social mythos. Thus McCarey usually sets positive foreground characters against a negative social background (as in *Love Affair* and *Once Upon a Honeymoon,* for example); but in *My Son John* he does just the reverse, projecting a foreground of unremitting emotional rigidity against a thematic background which reminds us that rigidity is not an absolute necessity. If the film has a problem, it is that the foreground is so immediate and intense that we forget that alternatives exist. Indeed, that is precisely what the film's characters do, and their doing it, their willingness to destroy freedom in the name of freedom, is the ultimate McCarey nightmare. The associative logic is clear: families like the Jeffersons, who use the language of freedom to satisfy their own emotional requirements, are the cause; and societies like the society of *My Son John,* autumnal, devoid of laughter, represented by Steadman-like political police, are the result. It is the worst of all possible worlds. But facing it squarely, as McCarey faced it squarely in *My Son John,* is an act of genuine artistic courage. If only McCarey's critics had understood that in 1952.

NOTES

1. See Robin Wood, "Democracy and Shpontanuity: Leo McCarey and the Hollywood Tradition," *Film Comment,* 12, No. 1 (1976), pp. 6-15; and Charles Silver, "Leo McCarey: From Marx to McCarthy," *Film Comment,* 9, No. 5 (1973), pp. 8-11. Renoir is cited in Wood and in Andrew Sarris, *The American Cinema: Directors and Directions 1929-1968* (New York: E.P. Dutton, 1968). Hawks praises McCarey in an interview which originally appeared in *Cahiers du Cinéma,* No. 56 (1956), rpt. in Andrew Sarris, ed., *Interviews with Film Directors* (New York: Avon, 1969), pp. 228-240. Ford's remarks on McCarey can be found in his Preface to Frank Capra's autobiography, *The Name Above the Title* (New York: Macmillan, 1971), where Capra's own praise of McCarey may be found. See also Peter Bogdanovich's discussion of McCarey in *Pieces of Time* (New York: Dell, 1974). McCarey has been interviewed in *Cahiers du Cinéma,* No. 163 (1965), pp. 11-21. Jean-Louis Noames' article "L'art et la manière de Leo McCarey" appears in the same issue of *Cahiers.* The McCarey interview has been reprinted in *Cahiers du Cinéma in English,* No. 7 (1967), pp. 43-54.

2. Robert Warshow, *The Immediate Experience* (Garden City: Doubleday, 1962).

3. Sarris, *The American Cinema,* p. 100.

4. Geqrge Morris, "McCarey and McCarthy: *My Son John," Film Comment,* 12, No. 1 (1976), pp. 16.

5. Jeffrey Richards, "Great Moments: Leo McCarey," *Focus on Film,* No. 14 (1973), pp. 34-46. A revised version of this essay appears in his book *Visions of Yesterday* (London: Routledge & Kegan Paul, 1973). There are significant differences between the two essays. Readers wishing to get Richards whole would do well to read both. Unless otherwise noted, I refer to the *Focus on Film* version of the piece.

6. Allen Eyles, *The Marx Brothers: Their World of Comedy,* 2nd ed. (New York: A.S. Barnes & Co., 1969), p. 77. The best discussion of McCarey's work on *Duck Soup* can be found in Joe Adamson, *Groucho, Harpo, Chico, and Sometimes Zeppo* (New York: Simon and Schuster, 1973).

7. Eyles, p. 85.

8. Raymond Durgnat, *The Crazy Mirror: Hollywood Comedy and the American Image* (New York: Horizon Press, 1970), p. 151.

9. Wood, p. 15.

10. Wood, p. 15.

11. Gerald Mast, *The Comic Mind: Comedy and the Movies* (New York: The Bobbs-Merrill Co., 1973), p. 254.

12. Stanley Cavell's discussion of screwball comedy in "Film in the University or Leopards in Connecticut," *Quarterly Review of Film Studies,* 2, No. 2 (1977), pp. 141-158, is essential reading. A key term in that discussion is "repetition." And while I use that term rather more specifically, in terms of technique rather than theme, I would like to acknowledge the general debt.

13. See James Agee, *Agee on Film* (New York: McDowell, Oblensky Inc., 1958), pp. 184-185; and Richard Corliss, *Talking Pictures: Screenwriters in the American Cinema* (Woodstock: The Overlook Press, 1974), p. 233.

14. Silver, p. 11.

15. Mast, p. 278.

16. Mast, p. 278.

17. Corliss discusses *Love Affair* and *An Affair to Remember* in his *Talking Pictures* discussion of Delmer Daves. See also Peter Lloyd, "Some Affairs to Remember: The Style of Leo McCarey," *Monogram,* No. 4 (1972), pp. 17-19.

18. Morris, p. 17.

19. Warshow, p. 167.

20. Warshow, p. 167.

21. Morris, p. 20.

22. Richards, *Visions of Yesterday,* p. 263.

LEO McCAREY
FILMOGRAPHY

by Gary Hooper and Leland Poague

Leo McCarey is the least appreciated of all those American film directors like John Ford, Howard Hawks and Frank Capra, who matured during the early sound era and through the Thirties. Most critics are content to pair McCarey with Capra (whose career parallels McCarey's to an astonishing degree) as purveyors of a "fantasy of goodwill," an unflattering and misleading catchphrase that serves to consign the two to a critical limbo of misinterpretation and, in McCarey's case, of outright neglect. Given the modern critical bias against sentiment—even legitimate sentiment—and McCarey's innate sense of human decency, this neglect is perhaps understandable if no less regrettable. Up to now there has been no serious attempt at a full-scale assessment of McCarey's life and work, with the result that only limited research into the facts of his career has been made available. Hence, this filmography is regrettably though necessarily incomplete, particularly regarding McCarey's early years at Universal and the Hal Roach studio.

The primary source of biographical data on Leo McCarey is McCarey himself, particularly in his 1965 "Cahiers du Cinéma" interview with Serge Daney and Jean-Louis Noames, translated and reprinted in "Cahiers du Cinéma in English," No. 7 (January 1967), p. 43 ff. (all references are to this edition); this information is supplemented by further anecdotes recorded by Peter Bogdanovich in his essay on McCarey included in "Pieces of Time" (New York: Dell, 1974), and the general outline of McCarey's overall career in Jeffrey Richards' "Great Moments: Leo McCarey," "Focus on Film," No. 14 (1973), pp. 34-36. It should be cautioned that these reminiscences are those of an old man who had long outlived his artistic reputation. Though remarkably free of bitterness, McCarey's memories are full of little inconsistencies attributable to nostalgia and the talents of a born storyteller.

The filmography proper has been collated from the following sources: Charles Barr, "Laurel and Hardy" (Berkeley: University of California Press, 1968); William K. Everson, "The Films of Laurel and Hardy" (New York: The Citadel Press, 1967) and "The Films of Hal Roach" (New York: The Museum of Modern Art, 1971); Kalton C. Lahue, "World of Laughter: The Motion Picture Comedy Short, 1910-1930" (Norman: University of Oklahoma Press, 1966); John McCabe, Al Kilgore, and Richard W. Bann, "Laurel & Hardy" (1975; rpt. New York: Ballantine, 1976); and the filmography by Jeffrey Richards and Allen Eyles appended to Richards' "Focus on Film" article. Whenever possible these primary sources have been cross-referenced with Andrew Sarris' "The American Cinema" (New York: E.P. Dutton, 1968), Paul Michael's "The American Movies Reference Book" (New York: Garland Books, 1969), and the files of "The New York Times." Grateful acknowledgment is tendered to these as well as to other sources cited in the text.

I. Apprenticeship

Leo McCarey was born 3 October 1898 in Los Angeles, California. After graduating from Los Angeles High School, he studied law at the University of Southern California. By his own account, McCarey was a poor lawyer because he was too young to inspire confidence in his clients and too inexperienced to ever win a case. Once, an angry client chased him out of a courtroom: "After about three blocks, I lost the client but I kept running out to Hollywood" (Bogdanovich, p. 194). According to Richards (p. 34), McCarey took a brief fling at songwriting before going into the movies, but this is unconfirmed. However, it might be noted that McCarey alludes briefly in the "Cahiers" interview (p. 50) to writing lyrics, but the reference is not followed up in the interview as published. Furthermore, in *Red Hot Rhythm*, McCarey's second sound feature film, for which he co-wrote the story, the central character is a songwriter/publisher, and McCarey received credit as co-author of the title songs of *An Affair to Remember* and *Satan Never Sleeps*. Whatever the exact course of McCarey's early years, however, he wound up at Universal Studios about 1918.

McCarey remembers that his first movie jobs were menial ones, but he was so eager and determined to learn the craft that any job was acceptable: "I started by being a script girl! At that time I didn't know that it was almost always girls who did this work. I was dying to work in cinema, I wanted absolutely to get past the studio gates, to be one of them (*sic*), I adored this métier" ("Cahiers" interview, p. 44). In this and other capacities, McCarey was able to study the techniques of film directing and scenario construction. Eventually he became an assistant to director Tod Browning on such films as *The Virgin of Stamboul* (with Priscilla Dean and Wallace Beery—1920) and *Outside the Law* (with Lon Chaney—1921). This union of the director of *Dracula* and *Freaks* with the director of *The Awful Truth* and *Going My Way* is provocative to speculate on. On the sur-

face, at least, two less compatible personalities are difficult to imagine. Perhaps McCarey's professional affinity for eccentric personalities was born and seasoned of this early relationship. McCarey calls it a "unique apprenticeship" to work with Browning, who "wrote, directed and edited his films himself" ("Cahiers" interview, p. 44).

McCarey's persistence and developing talents obviously impressed the studio for he was soon allowed to direct a feature film:

SOCIETY SECRETS (1921). *Dir:* Leo McCarey. *Sc:* Douglas Z. Doty (a story by Helen Christine Bennett). *Ph:* William Fildew. *With* Eva Novak *(Louise)*, Gertrude Claire *(Mrs. Kerran)*, Clarissa Selwynne *(Aunt)*, William Buckley *(Arthur)*, Ethel Ritchie *(Maybelle)*, L. C. Shumway *(George)*, Carl Stockdale *(Squire)*, Lucy Donohue *(Squire's Wife)*. *Prod:* Universal. 4,795 ft.

Unfortunately, nothing of *Society Secrets* beyond these bare production credits has survived. It may be the case that the film was so bad (as McCarey admits) that it was never put into general release; if it was, it wasn't considered worthy enough to generate any response in "The New York Times." At any rate, McCarey's career between 1921 and 1923 is as lost as *Society Secrets*. What he did in those two years before he joined Hal Roach is, and will probably remain, unknown.

II. PERFECTING THE CRAFT (THE HAL ROACH YEARS)

From 1923 to 1929 McCarey worked at the Hal Roach Studios as a writer, production supervisor, and occasional director of comedy shorts. In "The Silent Clowns" (New York: Knopf, 1975), Walter Kerr has characterised the Roach lot as "the most relaxed and friendliest in the business. [Roach] . . . encouraged his hirelings to doodle, to invent by amusing one another, to lend a hand in any capacity that offered itself" (p. 108). By all accounts it was common practice for various supervisors, writers, directors, and actors to help each other out when time or inspiration ran short: "Stan Laurel, generally held to be the swiftest improvisor after Chaplin, would answer a call to Charley Chase's set to help construct an elusive gag; Chase . . . would reply in kind by directing Laurel or any of their companions on the lot" (Kerr, pp. 108-109). (Chase directed under his real name, Charles Parrott; his brother James Parrott was the "official" director of many of the Laurel and Hardy shorts.) A classic example of this atmosphere of mutuality which prevailed on the Roach lot is a film called *The Call of the Cuckoo.* This 1927 two-reeler was directed by Clyde Bruckman and supervised by McCarey. Its nominal star was Max Davidson, its subject Davidson's problems with his "dream house." However, Laurel and Hardy, Charley Chase, and James Finlayson "guest star" and do improvised bits as lunatics from the asylum next door. Everson remarks on the "home-movie" atmosphere of these appearances ("The Films of Laurel and Hardy," p. 49).

McCarey's own catalogue of his various duties as a "supervisor" seems to fit the foregoing description to the nth degree: "This 'supervision' . . . was, in those days, the function of being responsible for practically everything in the film: writing the story, cutting it, stringing the gags together, co-ordinating everything, screening the rushes, working on the editing, sending out the prints, working on the second editing when the preview reactions weren't good enough and even, from time to time, shooting sequences over again" ("Cahiers" interview, p. 43). Such a multiplicity of tasks gathered under the umbrella of the simple term "supervisor" tends to render that term meaningless for the specific purpose of assigning adequate and accurate credits to individual films, especially when coupled with the dearth of scholarship on the silent film comedy short at this point in time. Even the most thoroughly researched production credits, those of the

Laurel and Hardy films, are subject to controversy. Lahue, Barr, and Everson agree that among *Habeas Corpus, We Faw Down, Liberty,* and *Wrong Again,* at least three were directed by McCarey. But which three? Barr lists *We Faw Down, Liberty,* and *Wrong Again,* while attributing *Habeas Corpus* to James Parrott (thus concurring with Bann); Lahue credits *Habeas Corpus, We Faw Down,* and *Liberty* to McCarey, and assigns no directorial credit in the case of *Wrong Again;* and Everson mysteriously, and we presume inadvertently, sidesteps the problem by referring in his book on Laurel and Hardy to the "three" films (p. 70) directed by McCarey, while credits for individual films list McCarey as director of all four. If such a minor problem concerning the credits for four short films cannot be resolved by respected and loving scholars, consider the problems inherent in the fact that McCarey was probably involved in the production of some three hundred shorts.

THE CHARLEY CHASE FILMS

ALL WET (1924). Jimmie Jump (Charley Chase) sets out on a domestic errand. Before his journey is over his car is stuck in the mud, sunk in a pool, pulled apart by a tow-truck, and he is cited for illegal parking. And, as it turns out, he ran the errand on the wrong day [as described by Gerald Mast in *The Comic Mind* (New York: Bobbs-Merrill, 1973), pp. 188-189]. *Dir:* Leo McCarey.
BAD BOY (1925). *Dir:* Leo McCarey.
HIS WOODEN WEDDING (1925). *Dir:* Leo McCarey.
INNOCENT HUSBANDS (1925). *Dir:* Leo McCarey.
THE RAT'S KNUCKLES (1925). "Jimmie Jump has invented a humane mousetrap that no one will buy. He eventually throws himself into the river as the result of his frustration" (Mast, p. 189). *Dir:* Leo McCarey.
WHAT PRICE GOOFY? (1925). *Dir:* Leo McCarey.
CRAZY LIKE A FOX (1926). *Dir:* Leo McCarey.

DOG SHY (1926). *Dir:* Leo McCarey.

MIGHTY LIKE A MOOSE (1926). A buck-toothed husband and his hooked nose wife, tired of the acrobatics required for even the simplest of kisses, both have plastic surgery performed on the same day, without either telling the other. After the operations they meet, do not recognise each other, and they indulge in some innocent flirtation. Before the situation is resolved Chase has to play both the "lover" and "husband" roles. *Dir:* Leo McCarey.

MOVIE NIGHT (1929). Charley tries to go to the movies but his pleasure is spoiled when his daughter, the ticket taker, and finally Charley himself all get the hiccups in turn. *Dir:* Lewis Foster. According to Mast, McCarey and George Stevens were "behind the camera" (p. 184) on *Movie Night,* but Mast does not specify their exact functions. It is likely that McCarey supervised and Stevens served as photographer.

THE LAUREL AND HARDY FILMS

Roach moved his distribution from Pathe to M-G-M in late 1927. We have no information on the distribution of the Charley Chase films, though we can safely assume that most of them, excepting perhaps *Movie Night,* were released through Pathe. All of the "official" Laurel and Hardy films listed below were released through M-G-M and produced by Hal Roach.

THE SECOND HUNDRED YEARS (1927). Laurel and Hardy are two convicts trying to escape. Their first attempt ends when they tunnel into the warden's office. Their second try succeeds when they literally paint their way out. Afterwards, they steal the clothes of two foreign dignitaries (who happen to be French prison officials), are mistaken for them, and the boys find themselves on a guided tour of their former residence. *Dir:* Fred Guiol. *Ed:* Richard Currier. *Story:* Leo McCarey. *Titles:* H.M. Walker. *With* James Finlayson, Eugene Pallette, Tiny Sandford. 2 reels.

The Second Hundred Years was the first "official" Laurel and Hardy two-reeler, released in October 1927. *Putting Pants on Philip* was the first one filmed, but it was held back from release until December 1927. This filmography lists the comedies in the order of their release. (See the Bann Filmography in *Laurel & Hardy* [1976] for further information on release dates.)

HATS OFF (1927). Laurel and Hardy attempt to deliver a bulky washing machine via an awesome flight of stairs. A precursor of their Academy Award winner, *The Music Box* (1932). *Dir:* Hal Yates. *Supervisor:* Leo McCarey. *Ed:* Richard Currier. *Titles:* H. M. Walker. 2 reels.

PUTTING PANTS ON PHILIP (1927). Hardy is dismayed to find that his Scottish nephew (Laurel) wears a skirt (i.e., a kilt) and is also an inveterate skirt-chaser. The film takes off from Hardy's desperate attempts to put pants on his charge, curb Philip's embarrassing libido, and maintain his own dignity before an ever-growing crowd of curious onlookers. *Dir:* Clyde Bruckman. *Supervisor:* Leo McCarey. *Ph:* George Stevens. *Ed:* Richard Currier. *Titles:* H. M. Walker. *With* Harvey Clark. 2 reels. McCarey says that *Putting Pants on Philip* was "my baby." As he put it in the "Cahiers" interview (p. 43): "I made it from beginning to end with no outside help at all . . . . I had to direct it, telling myself that at least I would be popular with the tailors!" As noted above, *Putting Pants on Philip* was the first film made by Laurel and Hardy as a "team." This may account for the fact that the two have character names (Hardy plays J. Piedmont Mumblethunder, Laurel the title character) and also for the fact that Stan's character is initially less fragile than it would generally be in the later films.

THE BATTLE OF THE CENTURY (1927). Laurel as a boxer, Hardy as his manager. Hardy takes out an insurance policy on his charge and then attempts to contrive an accident so he can collect.

However, the "perfect" plan goes awry when the conjunction of a banana peel and a pie vendor initiates an apocalyptic pie fight. *Dir:* Clyde Bruckman and Hal Roach. *Supervisor:* Leo McCarey. *Ph:* George Stevens. *Ed:* Richard Currier. *Story:* Hal Roach. *Titles:* H. M. Walker. *With* Eugene Pallette, Charlie Hall, Anita Garvin. 2 reels. We will see crooked fight managers in two McCarey features: *Belle of the Nineties* and *The Milky Way*.

LEAVE 'EM LAUGHING (1928). When Stan visits the dentist, Ollie goes along for moral support, and naturally gets *his* teeth pulled instead. During the mix-up, they overload on laughing gas. Once back on the street, they foul up traffic amidst gales of uncontrollable laughter. *Dir:* Clyde Bruckman. *Supervisor:* Leo McCarey. *Ph:* George Stevens. *Ed:* Richard Currier. *Story:* Hal Roach. *Titles:* Reed Heustis. *With* Edgar Kennedy, Charlie Hall. 2 reels.

THE FINISHING TOUCH (1928). Laurel and Hardy contract to build a house in one day. They do the job, but when the house begins to collapse under the weight of a single bird, a hassle develops between the irate owner and the builders which escalates and completes the demolition. *Dir:* Clyde Bruckman. *Supervisor:* Leo McCarey. *Ph:* George Stevens. *Ed:* Richard Currier. *Titles:* H. M. Walker. *With* Edgar Kennedy, Dorothy Coburn, Sam Lufkin. 2 reels.

FROM SOUP TO NUTS (1928). Stan and Ollie are itinerant waiters hired to serve at a society dinner. While the hostess struggles to eat her fruit salad, the boys proceed, with some help from a dog and a banana, to make the inevitable shambles of things. *Dir:* E. Livingston [Edgar] Kennedy. *Supervisor:* Leo McCarey. *Ph:* Len Powers. *Ed:* Richard Currier. *Story:* Leo McCarey. *Titles:* H. M. Walker. *With* Anita Garvin, Tiny Sandford. 2 reels.

YOU'RE DARN TOOTIN' (1928). As out-of-work musicians who face eviction from their apartment, Stan and Ollie seek solvency by playing on street corners. The pressures of failure finally vent

themselves when Ollie breaks Stan's clarinet in two and Stan, in turn, tosses Ollie's horn into the path of a truck. This leads to an episode of shin-kicking, and soon the entire populace partakes of an orgy of kicking and clothes-ripping. *Dir:* E. Livingston [Edgar] Kennedy. *Supervisor:* Leo McCarey. *Ph:* Floyd Jackman. *Ed:* Richard Currier. *Titles:* H. M. Walker. *With* Otto Lederer, Christian Frank. 2 reels.

THEIR PURPLE MOMENT (1928). Stan and Ollie attempt a night away from their wives. Stan's wife discovers his ingeniously concealed cache of mad money and substitutes worthless coupons for the cash. Out on the town, and fairly innocently living it up with two girls at a fancy restaurant, Stan and Ollie discover the switch. While they ponder a way out of their dilemma, waiters and wives converge on them. The film climaxes with a pie fight. *Dir:* James Parrott. *Supervisor:* Leo McCarey. *Ph:* George Stevens. *Ed:* Richard Currier. *Titles:* H. M. Walker. *With* Anita Garvin, Fay Holderness, Leo Willis, Tiny Sandford. 2 reels.

SHOULD MARRIED MEN GO HOME? (1928). Mr. and Mrs. Hardy's quiet Sunday together is disrupted by the arrival of Stanley, who promptly assaults the furniture and the Hardys' marital harmony. Banished to the golf-course, Stan and Ollie's run-ins with a short-tempered golfer lead to a mud fight. *Dir:* James Parrott. *Supervisor:* Leo McCarey. *Ph:* George Stevens. *Ed:* Richard Currier. *Story:* Leo McCarey and James Parrott. *Titles:* H. M. Walker. *With* Edgar Kennedy, Viola Richard, Edna Marian. 2 reels.

EARLY TO BED (1928). Upon receiving an inheritance, Ollie moves into a mansion and assigns Stan the job of butler. Ollie comes home late one night and drives Stan to distraction by ringing the doorbell and then hiding (the same gag crops up in *Duck Soup*). Eventually, Stan decides to quit and goes on an orgy of destruction: he wants to force Ollie to fire him. They make up after Ollie takes refuge in an ornate fountain ringed with Hardy-visaged gargoyles. *Dir:* Emmett

Flynn. *Supervisor:* Leo McCarey. *Ph:* George Stevens. *Ed:* Richard Currier. *Titles:* H. M. Walker. 2 reels.

TWO TARS (1928). Sailors on leave from their ship, Stan and Ollie rent a car and pick up two girls. After a run-in with a bubble-gum machine, the boys head for the open road where they encounter a traffic jam and are run down by Edgar Kennedy. Insults are added to injury and eventually every vehicle in sight is demolished. However, the boys somehow survive a final run-in with a locomotive. *Dir:* James Parrott. *Supervisor:* Leo McCarey. *Ph:* George Stevens. *Ed:* Richard Currier. *Story:* Leo McCarey. *Titles:* H. M. Walker. *With* Edgar Kennedy, Charlie Hall. 2 reels.

HABEAS CORPUS (1928). Laurel and Hardy are employed as grave-robbers by a mad scientist. The main action centres on their attempts to make a midnight snatch. The corpse turns out to be an undercover detective. *Dir:* James Parrott. *Supervisor:* Leo McCarey. *Ph:* Len Powers. *Ed:* Richard Currier. *Story:* Leo McCarey. *Titles:* H. M. Walker. *With* Richard Carle. 2 reels. (A take-off of Tod Browning?)

WE FAW DOWN (also known as WE SLIP UP—1928). Laurel and Hardy briefly escape their wives and head for a poker game. Before long they've been soaked by a street-sprinkler (we see the same gag in *Going My Way*) and are taken in to dry off by two flirtatious girls. The boys' escape from a jealous boyfriend is witnessed by their curious wives. Upon returning home, the boys do their best to establish an alibi, but the arrival of one of the flirts (bearing Ollie's vest) prompts Mrs. Hardy to grab a shotgun. In the chase which follows she lets go a volley and the entire male population of a building takes to its heels. *Dir:* Leo McCarey. *Ed:* Richard Currier. *Titles:* H. M. Walker. *With* Bess Flowers, Vivien Oakland, Kay Deslys. 2 reels.

LIBERTY (1929). Convicts once again, the boys escape and change to civilian clothes—only to switch pants in the process. Their attempts to get things right result in a series of embarrassing and

Laurel and Hardy in *Liberty*.

sometimes dangerous incidents. including Stan's run-in with a lively lobster and with record-store owner Jim Finlayson. The pants are finally exchanged atop a half-finished skyscraper. *Dir:* Leo McCarey. *Ph:* George Stevens. *Ed:* Richard Currier and William Terhune. *Story:* Leo McCarey. *Titles:* H. M. Walker. *With* James Finlayson, Tom Kennedy, Jean Harlow. 2 reels. Released in both silent and sound versions.

WRONG AGAIN (1929). Hearing of the theft of "Blue Boy," stable hands Laurel and Hardy naturally assume that the name refers to the race-horse they are tending and undertake to return it to its "owner" for the promised reward. The bulk of the film is a vivid series of demonstrations of how *not* to put a horse on a piano. *Dir:* Leo McCarey. *Asst Dir:* Lewis R. Foster. *Ph:* George Stevens and Jack Roach. *Ed:* Richard Currier. *Story:*

Ollie and Stan put "Blue Boy" on the piano in *Wrong Again*.

Leo McCarey and Lewis R. Foster. *Titles:* H. M. Walker. *With* Del Henderson, Josephine Crowell, Fred Holmes, Harry Bernard. 2 reels. Released in both silent and sound versions.

THAT'S MY WIFE (1929). Ollie's wife delivers an ultimatum: either the free-loading Stan moves out—or she does. Ollie protests that he will lose an inheritance if he is not married; but Mrs. Hardy leaves despite his plea. Ollie's rich uncle then appears unexpectedly, and Stan is forced to impersonate Mrs. Hardy. The scene then shifts to the Pink Pup cafe where Stan's bar-bell breasts, a drunk, and a thieving waiter help Stan and Ollie to make such fools of themselves that Uncle Bernal vows to leave his money to a dog-and-cat hospital. *Dir:* Lloyd French. *Supervisor:* Leo McCarey. *Ed:* Richard Currier. *Story:* Leo McCarey. *Titles:* H. M. Walker. *With* Vivien Oakland, Charlie Hall, Jimmy Aubrey, William Courtwright, Sam Lufkin, Harry Bernard. 2 reels. Silent, but with synchronized sound effects and music.

BIG BUSINESS (1929). Laurel and Hardy are Christmas-tree salesmen in July—with negligible success. They resolve to test the irresistibility of their sales technique on the immovable recalcitrance of Jimmy Finlayson. Business eventually escalates into all-out war, with both Finlayson's house and the salesmen's car reduced to rubble. *Dir:* James Wesley Horne. *Supervisor:* Leo McCarey. *Titles:* H.M. Walker. *With* James Finlayson, Tiny Sandford. 2 reels.

dog-eat-dog world of *Big Busi-*
s.

UNACCUSTOMED AS WE ARE (1929). An innocent accident leads to domestic chaos when Ollie invites Stan home for supper. Mrs. Hardy refuses to cook and walks out; the blonde next door tries to help but burns her dress; her policeman husband comes home just as she removes the dress, so she hides in a trunk; the husband has Laurel and Hardy carry the trunk to his apartment; and when the trunk is opened all hell breaks loose. *Dir:* Lewis R. Foster and Hal Roach. *Ed:* Richard Currier. *Story:* Leo McCarey. *Dialogue:* H.M. Walker. *With* Mae Busch, Thelma Todd, Edgar Kennedy. 2 reels. Laurel and Hardy's first "all talky"; no special silent version was filmed. Several silent films were shot before *Unaccustomed as We Are* was put into production (according to Bann, these include *Double Whoopee, Bacon Grabbers,* and *Angora Love*) but they were not released until after *Unaccustomed* was rushed into circulation.

DOUBLE WHOOPEE (1929). Like Marmaduke Ruggles in *Ruggles of Red Gap,* Laurel and Hardy are mistaken for visiting European celebrities—until it's discovered that they are really stand-in doormen. Once they assume their duties they wreak havoc among hotel guests and nearly prove the death of the real, Stroheim-like, Prince. *Dir:* Lewis R. Foster. *Ph:* George Stevens and Jack Roach. *Ed:* Richard Currier. *Story:* Leo McCarey. *Titles:* H.M. Walker. *With* Charlie Hall, Tiny Sandford, William Gillespie, Jean Harlow. 2 reels.

BERTH MARKS (1929). Laurel and Hardy are itinerant musicians (again) on their way to their next engagement. They almost miss their train; they wreak sartorial havoc among their fellow passengers (another clothes-ripping orgy); and the difficulty they experience trying to sleep in their upper berth almost causes them to miss their stop. They get off just in time—only to leave their instruments aboard the train. *Dir:* Lewis R. Foster. *Ph:* Len Powers. *Ed:* Richard Currier. *Story:* Leo McCarey. *Story Ed:* H.M. Walker. *With* Charlie Hall, Harry Bernard, Baldwin Cooke, Silas D.

Wilcox (and Paulette Goddard?). 2 reels. Released in sound and silent versions.

MEN O'WAR (1929). Two sailors out for a good time, Stan and Ollie do their best to uphold both the propriety and honor of navy manhood, despite various misunderstandings, sexual, financial, and nautical. The film concludes when Laurel and Hardy and their dates go down with the ship—their rowboat sinks when everybody else on the lake tries to climb aboard. *Dir:* Lewis R. Foster. *Ph:* George Stevens and Jack Roach. *Ed:* Richard Currier. *Story:* Leo McCarey. *Dialogue:* H.M. Walker. *With* James Finlayson, Charlie Hall, Harry Bernard, Anne Cornwall, Gloria Greer. 2 reels. Released in sound and silent versions.

PERFECT DAY (1929). The perfect day is far from perfect when plans for a country picnic fall prey to an escalating series of delays, pratfalls, mechanical catastrophes, and neighborhood hostilities. The film concludes, like so many other Laurel and Hardy shorts, with a submersion. When the car finally starts, the boys drive families and all into a six-foot-deep puddle. *Dir:* James Parrott. *Ed:* Richard Currier. *Story:* Leo McCarey and Hal Roach. *Story Ed:* H.M. Walker. *With* Edgar Kennedy, Kay Deslys, Isabelle Keith, Harry Bernard, Clara Guiol, Baldwin Cooke. 2 reels. Released in sound and silent versions.

THEY GO BOOM (1929). Laurel's efforts to minister to Ollie's head cold somehow result in the near total collapse of their small rented room. *Dir:* James Parrott. *Ed:* Richard Currier. *Story:* Leo McCarey. *Story Ed:* H.M. Walker. *With* Charlie Hall, Sam Lufkin. 2 reels.

BACON GRABBERS (1929). Laurel and Hardy do their level best to serve a summons on Edgar Kennedy, for the repossession of a console radio, and then they try for the radio itself—which Kennedy has no intention of returning. Before it's all over, both Kennedy's radio and Laurel and Hardy's car are smashed flat by a steamroller. *Dir:* Lewis R. Foster. *Ph:* George Stevens and Jack Roach. *Ed:* Richard Currier. *Story:* Leo McCarey. *Titles:* H.M. Walker. *With* Edgar Kennedy, Charlie Hall, Jean Harlow, Harry Bernard, Sam Lufkin. 2 reels.

THE HOOSE-GOW (1929). Another descent into chaos. Stan and Ollie are prisoners on a work farm. They try to escape but bungle the job; they are assigned to a ditch-digging crew and almost kill each other with pick-axes; they spoil and spill their food and must chop wood to get more; they proceed to chop down a guard platform which falls on the camp and demolishes the tents; officialdom arrives in the person of James Finlayson; back in the trench, Stan and Ollie go at it with the pick-axes again—only to puncture the radiator of Finlayson's car when Ollie throws Stan's ax away; they try to plug the leaking radiator with rice; the rice "cooks"; and the mush begins to fly as tempers finally give out all around. *Dir:* James Parrott. *Ph:* George Stevens, Len Powers, and Glenn Robert Kershner. *Ed:* Richard Currier. *Story:* Leo McCarey. *Story Ed:* H.M. Walker. *Titles Ed:* Nat Hoffberg. *With* James Finlayson, Tiny Sandford, Leo Willis, Dick Sutherland, Charlie Hall. 2 reels.

ANGORA LOVE (1929). Animals pop up frequently in McCarey (there are dogs, for example, in *Part Time Wife, Six of a Kind, The Awful Truth,* and *The Bells of St. Mary's*). In *Angora Love,* which anticipates these later McCarey films and also subsequent Laurel and Hardy shorts, particularly *The Chimp* (1932) and *Laughing Gravy* (1931), the animal is a stray goat which takes a fancy to Laurel and Hardy. Afraid to return the goat (for fear of arrest) the boys take the goat home and do their best to keep their unusual pet under wraps. The film concludes with a "battle of the century" water fight between Laurel and Hardy and their landlord. *Dir:* Lewis R. Foster. *Ph:* George Stevens. *Ed:* Richard Currier. *Story:* Leo McCarey. *Titles:* H.M. Walker. *With* Edgar Kennedy, Charlie Hall, Harry Bernard. 2 reels. *Angora Love* was the last Laurel and Hardy silent to be released.

NIGHT OWLS (1930). An ineffectual policeman threatens Stan and Ollie with arrest for vagrancy unless they stage a break-in at the home of his chief. The policeman (Edgar Kennedy) plans to recoup his reputation by chasing the "thieves" away. The boys do their bumbling best to slip quietly into the house, but they are foiled by such things as player pianos, etc. (all of which recalls a similar sequence in *Duck Soup*). The plan thus fails, and Kennedy is left, quite literally, holding the bag. *Dir:* James Parrott. *Ph:* George Stevens. *Ed:* Richard Currier. *Story:* Leo McCarey. *Story Ed:* H.M. Walker. *With* Edgar Kennedy, James Finlayson, Anders Randolph, Harry Bernard. 2 reels.

BLOTTO (1930). During prohibition, Stan and Ollie scheme to go out on the town and get "blotto." Mrs. Laurel overhears the plan and empties the bottle of contraband that the boys plan to take along, replacing the booze with a non-alcoholic brew of her own concoction. The boys get roaringly "drunk," get hysterically out of hand, and get their come-uppance when Mrs. Laurel, having followed them to the club, reveals the truth and blasts their Tin Lizzie taxi with a shotgun. *Dir:* James Parrott. *Ph:* George Stevens. *Ed:* Richard Currier. *Story:* Leo McCarey. *Dialogue:* H.M. Walker. *With* Tiny Sandford, Baldwin Cooke, Charlie Hall, Frank Holliday, Anita Garvin. 2 reels.

BRATS (1930). Laurel and Hardy play dual roles, two fathers, each with· a mirror-image son. When the two pairs find that they cannot get along in peace on the first floor, the kids are hustled upstairs to bed. While the fathers are systematically making a shambles of the den shooting pool, the sons are just as systematically making a shambles of their second-floor bedroom and bathroom. Ollie Jr. winds up submerged in the bathtub and inadvertently sets the tap flowing as he climbs out. Eventually the fathers try to exert control, and Ollie Sr. seems to have things well in hand when he lullabies the children. Before total calm prevails, Stanley Jr. asks for a glass of water. Ollie Sr. insists on fetching it from the bathroom, which has been

Boys will be boys in *Brats* (note the photo of Jean Harlow on the mantle).

filling with water for almost a reel, with predictable results. *Dir:* James Parrott. *Ph:* George Stevens. *Ed:* Richard Currier. *Story:* Leo McCarey and Hal Roach. *Dialogue:* H.M. Walker. *Titles Ed:* Nat Hoffberg. 2 reels.

BELOW ZERO (1930). Stan and Ollie are street musicians (accordian and bass viol) whose duet of "In the Good Old Summertime" in the dead of winter is not appreciated. Eventually their instruments are kicked into the street, just in time to be run over by the inevitable truck. Now destitute, they find a lost wallet and head for a nearby restaurant, inviting a policeman along to help celebrate their good luck. When the bill arrives, however, it turns out that the wallet belongs to the cop. Hardy escapes in a trash can, and Laurel takes cover in a rain-barrel. *Dir:* James Parrott. *Ph:* George Stevens. *Ed:* Richard Currier. *Story:* Leo McCarey. *Dialogue:* H.M. Walker. *Titles Ed:* Nat Hoffberg. *With* Charlie Hall, Leo Willis, Kay Deslys, Tiny Sandford, Blanche Payson, Frank Holliday. 2 reels.

HOG WILD (1930). To please his insistent wife, Hardy volunteers to erect a rooftop radio antenna, and reluctantly accepts Laurel's generous offer to lend a hand. Stan "helps" him to take several nosedives into a fishpool. The film climaxes with Ollie clinging to a ladder which is propped on the back seat of Stan's car while Stan speeds through city traffic. Once back on solid ground, Ollie learns that his wife's radio has been repossessed. As a topper, Stan's car is walloped by a streetcar. *Dir:* James Parrott. *Ph:* George Stevens. *Ed:* Richard Currier. *Story:* Leo McCarey. *Dialogue:* H.M. Walker. *With* Fay Holderness, Dorothy Granger, Charles McMurphy. 2 reels.

In all probability, the Laurel and Hardy shorts of 1930 bearing McCarey's name in the credits represent a backlog of McCarey-written plots and storylines, since by August 1929 (the release date of *The Sophomore*) McCarey had left Roach to direct feature films for Pathe.

Evidence suggests that McCarey was involved in at least one other film while at the Roach studio:

A PAIR OF TIGHTS (1928). *Dir:* Hal Yates. *With* Stu Erwin, Edgar Kennedy, Anita Garvin, Marion Byron. Gerald Mast attributes the film to McCarey and Stevens (p. 184) without specifying their precise functions. In "The Silent Clowns," however, Walter Kerr has classified *A Pair of Tights* as "a Laurel and Hardy comedy without Laurel and Hardy" (p. 333). If we take Kerr literally here, it is likely that McCarey supervised and Stevens worked the camera.

III. DIRECTED BY LEO McCAREY (FEATURE FILMS)

Unless otherwise noted, all subsequent films were directed by Leo McCarey.

THE SOPHOMORE (1929). When a college football star loses his tuition money in a crooked crap game, he works his way through school as a soda jerk and helps put on a big show. *Dialogue dir:* Anthony Brown. *Sc:* Earl Baldwin, Walter DeLeon (adaptation by Joseph Franklin Poland of story by Corey Ford and Thomas H. Wenning). *Ph:* John J. Mescall. *Ed:* Doane Harrison. *With* Eddie Quillan *(Joe Collins)*, Sally O'Neil *(Margie Callahan)*, Stanley Smith *(Tom Week)*, Jeanette Loff *(Barbara Lange)*, Russell Gleason *(Dutch)*, Sarah Padden *(Mrs. Collins)*, Brooks Benedict *(Armstrong)*, Spec O'Donnell *(Joe Collins' nephew)*, Walter O'Keefe *(Radio announcer)*, Lew Ayres. *Prod:* William Conselman for Pathe. Released in both silent (5,799 feet) and sound (72m) versions.

RED HOT RHYTHM (1929). All about the romantic entanglements of a shady music publisher. *Sc:* Earl Baldwin, Walter DeLeon (a story by William M. Conselman and Leo McCarey). *Ph:* John J. Mescall (part Technicolor). *Art dir:* Edward Jewell. *With* Alan Hale *(Walter)*, Kathryn Crawford *(Mary)*, Walter O'Keefe *(Sam)*, Josephine Dunn *(Claire)*, Anita Garvin *(Mable)*, Ilka Chase *(Mrs. Fioretta)*, Ernest Hilliard *(Eddie Graham)*, Harry Bowen *(Whiffle)*, James Clemmons *(Singer)*. *Prod:* William M. Conselman for Pathe. Released in both silent (6,981 feet) and sound (69m) versions.

WILD COMPANY (1930). A pampered young man finds himself on trial for murder. When he is released in the custody of his doting father, both men are forced to reassess themselves and their relationship. *Sc:* Bradley King (adapted by John Stone and Bradley King from the story "Soft Shoulders" by Philip Hurn). *Ph:* William O'Connell. *Art dir:* Stephen Gosson. *Ed:* Clyde Carruth. *Mus & lyrics:* Jimmy Monaco, Jack Meskill, Cliff Friend, Con Conrad. *With* Frank Albertson *(Larry Grayson)*, H.B. Warner *(Henry Grayson)*, Sharon Lynn *(Sally)*, Joyce Compton *(Anita)*, Claire McDowell *(Mrs. Grayson)*, Mildred Van Dorn *(Natalie)*, Richard Keene *(Dick)*, Frances McCoy *(Cora)*, Kenneth Thomson *(Joe Hardy)*, Bela Lugosi *(Felix Brown)*, George Fawcett *(Judge)*, Bobby Callahan *(Eddie)*. *Prod:* Al Rockett for Fox. 71m.

Adrift at sea: James Hall, Jeanette MacDonald, Kay Francis, Jack Oakie (front), and William Austin (back) in *Let's Go Native*.

LET'S GO NATIVE (1930). A musical farce with Jeanette MacDonald as a costume designer. When she goes broke, she leaves with her lover, the disinherited scion of a wealthy family, on a cruise ship. Romantic complications ensue because his childhood sweetheart is on board too. Further complications follow when they are shipwrecked on a tropical island. All complications are eventually resolved when the young man's grandfather shows up with his yacht to rescue the castaways. Once the rescue is effected, the island promptly sinks. *Sc:* George Marion Jr., Percy Heath. *Ph:* Victor Milner. *Songs:* Richard A. Whiting, George Marion Jr. *Dance dir:* David Bennett. *With* Jack Oakie *(Voltaire McGinnis)*, Jeanette MacDonald *(Joan Wood)*, James Hall *(Wally Wendell)*, Skeets Gallagher *(Jerry)*, William Austin *(Basil Pistol)*, David Newell *(Chief Officer Williams)*, Kay Francis *(Constance Cook)*, Charles Sellon *(Wallace Wendell)*, Eugene Pallette *(Sheriff)*. *Prod:* Paramount. 63 m.

PART TIME WIFE (1930). A golf-widower tries to learn the game in order to win back the attention of his wife. While doing so he becomes involved with a young caddy and his rare breed of dog. *Sc:* Raymond L. Schrock, Leo McCarey (the story "The Shepper-Newfounder" by Stewart Edward White). *Ph:* George Schneiderman. *Ed:* Jack Murray. *With* Edmund Lowe *(Jim Murdock)*, Leila Hyams *(Mrs. Murdock)*, Tommy Clifford *(Tommy Mulligan)*, Walter McGrail *(Johny*

Spence), Louis Payne *(Butler)*, Sam Lufkin *(Caddie Master)*, Bodil Rosing *(Maid)*, George (Red) Corcoran *(Chauffeur)*. *Prod:* Fox. 72 m. Released and reviewed by "The New York Times" (25 December 1930) as *The Shepper-Newfounder*.

INDISCREET (1931). The heroine's attempts to break up an affair between her sister and a shady character (with whom the heroine had previously been involved) nearly wrecks her current romance with a writer. *Sc:* DeSylva, Brown & Henderson (their story co-authored with Leo McCarey). *Ph:* Ray June, Gregg Toland. *Ed:* Hal C. Kern. *Mus:* Alfred Newman. *With* Gloria Swanson *(Jerry Trent)*, Ben Lyon *(Tony Blake)*, Barbara Kent *(Joan Trent)*, Monroe Owsley *(Jim Woodward)*, Arthur Lake *(Buster Collins)*, Maude Eburne *(Aunt Kate)*, Henry Kolker *(Mr. Woodward)*, Nella Walker *(Mrs. Woodward)*. *Prod:* Joseph M. Schenck for United Artists. 92 m.

THE KID FROM SPAIN (1932). Mistaken for the driver of a getaway car, the hero flees to Mexico where he masquerades as a bullfighter to elude the dogged detective who pursues him. *Sc:* William Anthony McGuire, Bert Kalmar & Harry Ruby (a story idea by Leo McCarey). *Ph:* Gregg Toland. *Ed:* Stuart Heisler. *Mus:* Alfred Newman. *Songs:* "Look What You've Done," "In the Moonlight," and "What a Perfect Combination" by Bert Kalmar, Harry Ruby,

Ben Lyon and Gloria Swanson in *Indiscreet.*

and Harry Akst; other songs by Kalmar and Ruby. *Dance dir:* Busby Berkeley. *Sound:* Vinton Vernon. *With* Eddie Cantor *(Eddie Williams)*, Lyda Roberti *(Rosalie)*, Robert Young *(Ricardo)*, Ruth Hall *(Anita Gomez)*, John Miljan *(Pancho)*, Noah Beery *(Alonzo Gomez)*, J. Carrol Naish *(Pedro)*, Robert Emmett O'Connor *(Crawford)*, Stanley Fields *(Jose)*, Paul Porcasi *(Gonzalez)*, Walter Walker *(The Dean)*, Ben Hendricks Jr. *(Red)*, Julien Rivero *(Dalmores)*, Theresa Maxwell Conover *(Martha Oliver)*, Sidney Franklin *(Himself)*, Leo Willis *(Robber)*, Harry Gribbon *(Traffic Cop)*, Betty Grable, Paulette Goddard, Toby Wing *(Goldwyn Girls)*, Edgar Connor, Harry C. Bradley, Eddie Foster. *Prod:* Samuel Goldwyn for United Artists. 90m.

DUCK SOUP (1933). Groucho Marx is the newly installed ruler of Freedonia while Harpo and Chico spy for Freedonia's arch-rival, Sylvania. Various romantic and diplomatic entanglements lead to Chico's trial for treason and all-out war with Sylvania. *Sc:* Bert Kalmar, Harry Ruby (additional dialogue by Arthur Sheekman and Nat Perrin). *Ph:* Henry Sharp. *Art dir:* Hans Dreier, Wiard B. Ihnen. *Ed:* Leroy Stone. *Mus & lyrics:* Bert Kalmar, Harry Ruby. *Mus dir:* Arthur Johnston. *With* Groucho Marx *(Rufus T. Firefly)*, Harpo Marx *(Pinky)*, Chico Marx *(Chicolini)*, Zeppo Marx *(Bob Roland)*, Margaret Dumont *(Mrs. Teasdale)*, Raquel Torres *(Vera Marcal)*, Louis Calhern *(Ambassador Trentino)*, Edgar Kennedy *(Lemonade Vendor)*, Edmund Breese *(Zander)*, William Worthington *(Minister of Finance)*, Edwin Maxwell *(Secretary of War)*, Leonid Kinsky *(Agitator)*, Verna Hillie *(Secretary)*, George MacQuarrie *(First Judge)*, Fred Sullivan *(Second Judge)*, Davidson Clark *(Second Minister of Finance)*, Charles B. Middleton *(Prosecutor)*, Eric Mayne *(Third Judge)*. *Prod:* Paramount. 68 or 70m.

SIX OF A KIND (1934). Trying to get away for a second honeymoon, a middle aged couple run afoul of an embezzler, a zany couple with a large dog, and a sheriff who maintains that everything he likes is either "illegal, immoral, or fatten-

Charlie Ruggles, Gracie Allen, Mary Boland, and George Burns in *Six of a Kind*.

ing." *Sc:* Walter DeLeon, Harry Ruskin (a story by Keene Thompson and Douglas MacLean). *Ph:* Henry Sharp. *Art dir:* Hans Dreier, Robert Odell. *Ed:* LeRoy Stone. *Mus:* Ralph Rainger. *With* Charlie Ruggles *(J. Pinkham Whinney)*, Mary Boland *(Flora Whinney)*, W.C. Fields *(Sheriff John Hoxley)*, George Burns *(George Edwards)*, Gracie Allen *(Gracie Devore)*, Alison Skipworth *(Mrs. Rumford / The Duchess)*, Bradley Page *(Ferguson)*, Grace Bradley *(Trixie or Goldie)*, William J. Kelly *(Gillette)*, Phil Tead *(Newspaper Office Clerk)*, James Burke *(Sparks)*, Dick Rush *(Steele)*, Walter Long *(Butch)*, Leo Willis *(Mike)*, Lew Kelly *(Joe)*, Alf P. James *(Tom)*, Tammany Young *(Dr. Busby)*, Verna D. Hillie, Florence Enright, William Augustin, Kathleen Burke, Irving Bacon. *Prod:* Paramount. 65m.

BELLE OF THE NINETIES (1934). Ruby Carter, the "Belle" of the title, must choose between love and love-of-money when she becomes involved with a villainous fight-promoter / saloon keeper, a gentleman millionaire, and a boxer known as "Tiger Kid." *Sc:* Mae West. *Ph:* Karl Struss. *Art dir:* Hans Dreier, Bernard Herzbrun. *Ed:* LeRoy Stone. *Mus:* Arthur Johnston. *Lyrics:* Sam Coslow. *Songs:* "When a St. Louis Woman Goes Down to New Orleans," "My Old Flame," "My American Beauty," "Troubled Waters." *With* Mae West *(Ruby Carter)*, Roger Pryor *(Tiger Kid)*, John Mack Brown *(Brooks Claybourne)*, Katherine DeMille *(Molly Brant)*, John Miljan *(Ace Lamont)*, James Donlan *(Kirby)*, Stuart Holmes *(Dirk)*, Harry Woods *(Slade)*, Edward Gargan *(Stogie)*, Libby Taylor *(Jasmine)*,

Warren Hymer *(St. Louis Fighter)*, Frederick Burton *(Colonel Claybourne)*, Augusta Anderson *(Mrs. Claybourne)*, Benny Baker *(Blackie)*, Morrie Cohan *(Butch)*, Rex Ingram *(Brother Eben)*, Tom Herbert *(Gilbert)*, Wade Boteler *(Editor)*, George Walsh *(Leading Man)*, Duke Ellington and his Orchestra *(Musicians)*, Tyler Brook, Eddie Borden, and Fuzzy Knight *(Comedians)*, Kay Deslys *(Beef Trust Chorus Girl)*, Frank Rice, Edward Hearn, Mike Mazurki. *Prod:* William LeBaron for Paramount. 70 or 75m.

RUGGLES OF RED GAP (1935). When his master loses him in a poker game, a proper English valet finds himself in Red Gap, Washington, where the Old West and modern civilisation exist uneasily side by side. Mistaken for gentry, Ruggles is treated royally until the snobbish "civilised" faction unmasks and attempts to ostracise him. The attempt fails when Ruggles declares his independence and opens his Anglo-American Grill. *Sc:* Walter DeLeon, Harlan Thompson. (adaptation by Humphrey Pearson of the novel by Harry Leon Wilson). *Ph:* Alfred Gilks. *Art dir:* Hans Dreier, Robert Odell. *Ed:* Edward Dmytryk. *Cos:* Travis Banton. *Mus:* Ralph Rainger. *Lyrics:* Sam Coslow. *Sound:* P. G. Wisdom. *Asst dir:* A. F. Erickson. *With* Charles Laughton *(Marmaduke Ruggles)*, Mary Boland *(Effie Floud)*, Charlie Ruggles *(Egbert Floud)*, ZaSu Pitts *(Mrs. Judson)*, Roland Young *(Earl of Burnstead)*, Leila Hyams *(Nell Kenna)*, Maude Eburne *(Ma Pettingill)*, Lucien Littlefield *(Charles Belknap-Jackson)*, James Burke *(Jeff Tuttle)*, Dell Henderson *(Sam)*, Leota Lorraine *(Mrs. Belknap-Jackson)*, Clarence Wilson *(Jake Henshaw)*, Brenda Fowler *(Judy Ballard)*, Augusta Anderson *(Mrs. Wallaby)*, Sarah Edwards *(Mrs. Myron Carey)*, Rafael Storm *(Clothing Salesman)*, George Burton *(Hank)*, Victor Potel *(Cowboy)*, Frank Rice *(Buck)*, William J. Welsh *(Eddie)*, Harry Bernard *(Cowboy)*, Alice Ardell *(Lisette)*, Rolfe Sedan *(Barber)*, Jack Norton *(Barfly)*, Jim Welch *(Saloon Customer)*, Willie Fung *(Chinese Servant)*, Libby Taylor *(Black Servant)*, Harry Bowen *(Photographer)*, Charles Fallon *(Waiter in*

Paris Cafe), Genaro Spagnoli *(Cabman)*, Carrie D'Aumery, Isabelle La Mal *(Effie's Guests in Paris)*, Frank O'Connor *(Station Agent)*, Ernie Adams *(Dishwasher)*. *Prod:* Arthur Hornblow Jr. for Paramount. 91m. *Fancy Pants* (1950), directed by Hal Roach alumnus George Marshall, is often mentioned as a remake of *Ruggles of Red Gap*. The films have little in common except that both were based on the same novel. Otherwise the films are remarkably dissimilar and the McCarey version seems not to have influenced George Marshall in the slightest.

THE MILKY WAY (1936). A mild-mannered milkman with a well-developed talent for ducking and an unearned reputation as a knockout artist is convinced by a crooked fight promoter that he is a tiger in the ring. The milkman is nursed though a series of fixed fights until he is scheduled to meet the champ—at which point the promoter plans to make a killing with the bookies. Much to the promoter's surprise, and with some dressing room help from the milkman's pet horse, the milkman triumphs. However, he promptly exchanges his middleweight crown for a partnership in his ex-boss's dairy business. *Sc:* Grover Jones, Frank Butler, and Richard Connell (a play by Lynn Root and Harry Clork). *Ph:* Alfred Gilks. *Ed:* LeRoy Stone. *With* Harold Lloyd *(Burleigh Sullivan)*, Adolphe Menjou *(Gabby Slaon)*, Verree Teasdale *(Ann Westley)*, Helen Mack *(Mae Sullivan)*, William Gargan *(Speed MacFarland)*, George Barbier *(Wilbur Austin)*, Dorothy Wilson *(Polly Pringle)*, Lionel Stander *(Spider Schultz)*, Charles Lane *(Willard)*, Marjorie Gateson *(Mrs. LeMoyne)*. *Prod:* E. Lloyd Sheldon for Paramount. 83m.

MAKE WAY FOR TOMORROW (1937). When an elderly couple are forced to give up their home, their children feel obligated to take them in, but not together as man and wife. Throughout their ordeal, Lucy and Barkley Cooper maintain the hope that they will eventually be together again. However, the best they can salvage is a brief reunion at their honeymoon hotel before

Barkley goes to live with a daughter in California and Lucy (without her husband's knowledge) goes to live in a rest home. *Sc:* Vina Delmar (the novel "The Years Are So Long" by Josephine Lawrence and the play by Helen and Nolan Leary). *Ph:* William C. Mellor. *Art dir:* Hans Dreier, Bernard Herzbrun. *Ed:* LeRoy Stone. *Spec eff:* Gordon Jennings. *Mus:* George Antheil. *Arrangements:* Victor Young. *Mus dir:* Boris Morros. *Song:* Leo Robin, Sam Coslow, and Jean Schwartz. *Sound:* Walter Oberst, Don Johnson. *Asst dir:* Harry Scott. *With* Beulah Bondi *(Lucy Cooper)*, Victor Moore *(Barkley Cooper)*, Fay Bainter *(Anita Cooper)*, Thomas Mitchell *(George Cooper)*, Porter Hall *(Harvey Chase)*, Barbara Read *(Rhoda Cooper)*, Maurice Moscovitch *(Max Ruben)*, Elisabeth Risdon *(Cora Payne)*, Minna Gombell *(Nellie Chase)*, Ray Mayer *(Robert Cooper)*, Ralph Remley *(Bill Payne)*, Louise Beavers *(Mamie)*, Louis Jean Heydt *(Doctor)*, Paul Stanton *(Hotel Manager)*, Dell Henderson *(Car Salesman)*, Ferike Boros *(Mrs. Ruben)*, Nick Lukats *(Boy Friend)*, Kitty McHugh *(Head Usherette)*, Terry Ray [Ellen Drew] *(Usherette)*, Ethel Clayton *(Woman Customer)*, Helen Dickson, Byron Foulger, Averil Cameron *(Bridge Players)*, Leo McCarey *(Passerby, Carpet Sweeper)*. *Prod:* Leo McCarey for Paramount. 92m. The screenplay for *Make Way for Tomorrow* has been published in John Gassner and Dudley Nichols (eds.), "Twenty Best Film Plays" (New York: Crown, 1943), pp. 433-476; in light of which it should be remarked that McCarey made some fairly drastic changes, cutting whole scenes and sequences from the pre-shooting script. Previously published credit lists for the film are based on pre-production credit rosters and are therefore inaccurate for including actors whose parts were cut from the finished film.

THE AWFUL TRUTH (1937). For complex reasons, a young couple goes through the motions of divorce. Various complications arise, including Ralph Bellamy and his mother, but the couple reconcile before the divorce becomes final. *Sc:* Vina Delmar (adaptation by Dwight Taylor of the play by Arthur Richman). *Ph:* Joseph Walker. *Art dir:* Stephen Gooson, Lionel Banks. *Interiors:* Babs Johnstone. *Ed:* Al Clark. *Cos:* Kalloch. *Mus dir:* Morris Stoloff. *Song:* "My Dreams Have Gone With the Wind" by Ben Oakland and Milton Drake. *Sound:* Edward Bernds. *Asst dir:* William Mull. *With* Cary Grant *(Jerry Warriner)*, Irene Dunne *(Lucy Warriner)*, Ralph Bellamy *(Daniel Leeson)*, Alex D'Arcy *(Armand Duvalle)*, Cecil Cunningham *(Aunt Patsy)*, Molly Lamont *(Barbara Vance)*, Esther Dale *(Mrs. Leeson)*, Joyce Compton *(Dixie Belle Lee)*, Robert Allen *(Frank Randell)*, Robert Warwick *(Mr. Vance)*, Mary Forbes *(Mrs. Vance)*, Paul Stanton *(Judge)*, Scott Colton *(Mr. Barnsley)*, Wyn Cahoon *(Mrs. Barnsley)*, Edgar Dearing *(Motor Cop)*, Mitchell Harris *(Jerry's Attorney)*, Alan Bridge *(Motor Cop)*, Leonard Carey *(Butler)*, Miki Morita *(Japanese Servant)*, Frank Wilson *(M.C.)*, Vernon Dent *(Police Sergeant)*, George C. Pearce *(Caretaker)*, Kathryn Curry *(Celeste)*, Edward Peil *(Bailiff)*, Bess Flowers *(Viola Heath)*, John Tyrrell *(Hank)*, Edward Mortimer *(Lucy's Attorney)*, Claude Allister, Zita Moulton, Byron Foulger, Bobby Watson. *Prod:* Leo McCarey for Columbia. *Assoc prod:* Everett Riskin. 90m.

THE COWBOY AND THE LADY (1938). An idealistic rodeo cowboy meets and marries a woman whom he believes to be a lady's maid. When he discovers that she is really the daughter of a rich politician with Presidential aspirations, he walks out on the marriage. All ends happily when the girl and her father follow him back to his ranch and they resolve their differences. *Dir:* H. C. Potter. *Sc:* S. N. Behrman, Sonya Levien (the story by Frank Adams and Leo McCarey). *Ph:* Gregg Toland. *Art dir:* Richard Day, James Basevi. *Ed:* Sherman Todd. *Mus:* Alfred Newman. *With* Gary Cooper *(Stretch Willoughby)*, Merle Oberon *(Mary Smith)*, Walter Brennan *(Sugar)*, Fuzzy Knight *(Buzz)*, Patsy Kelly *(Katie Callahan)*, Mabel Todd, Harry Davenport, Henry Kolker, Emma Dunn, Berton Churchill, Walter Walker,

Charles Richman, Arthur Hoyt. *Prod:* Samuel Goldwyn. *Rel:* United Artists. 91m. Following a serious illness, McCarey needed money to pay his doctor bills. At William Wyler's suggestion, he sold the story of *The Cowboy and the Lady* to Samuel Goldwyn. When asked by Goldwyn to direct the film, McCarey refused because he didn't like the story well enough.

LOVE AFFAIR (1939). A man and a woman, each involved with wealthy lovers, meet on shipboard. After a brief stop to visit his grandmother, they fall in love. Their love affair resurrects their romantic ideals and they agree to part for six months to test their feelings and their capacity for financial independence. Their scheduled reunion does not take place, however, because she is seriously injured in a traffic accident. But they are eventually reunited on Christmas Day. *Sc:* Delmer Daves, Donald Ogden Stewart (the story by Mildred Cram and Leo McCarey). *Ph:* Rudolph Maté. *Art dir:* Van Nest Polglase, Al Herman. *Ed:* Edward Dmytryk, George Hiveley. *Montage:* Douglas Travers. *Spec eff:* Vernon Walker. *Songs:* "Wishing" by B. B. DeSylva; "Sing My Heart" by Harold Arlen and Ted Koehler. *With* Irene Dunne *(Terry McKay)*, Charles Boyer *(Michel Marnay)*, Maria Ouspenskaya *(Janou, Michel's Grandmother)*, Lee Bowman *(Kenneth Bradley)*, Astrid Allwyn *(Louise Clarke)*, Maurice Moscovitch

(Maurice Cobert), Scotty Beckett *(Boy on Ship)*, Bess Flowers and Harold Miller *(Couple on Deck)*, Joan Brodel [Joan Leslie] *(Autograph Seeker)*, Dell Henderson *(Cafe Manager)*, Carol Hughes *(Nightclub Patron)*, Leyland Hodgson *(Doctor)*, Ferike Boros *(Boarding House Keeper)*, Frank McGlynn Sr. *(Picklepuss)*, Oscar O'Shea *(Priest)*, Tom Dugan *(Drunk)*, Lloyd Ingraham *(Doctor)*, Phyllis Kennedy *(Maid)*, Gerald Mohr. *Prod:* Leo McCarey for RKO Radio. 87m.

MY FAVORITE WIFE (1940). Just after his second marriage, the hero's first wife returns from seven years on a desert island. The inevitable reunion (and remarriage) is delayed by his jealousy, after he discovers that she did not spend those seven years alone but rather with a very debonair "Adam." *Dir:* Garson Kanin. *Sc:* Bella and Samuel Spewack (a story by Bella and Samuel Spewack and Leo McCarey). *Ph:* Rudolph Maté. *Art dir:* Van Nest Polglase, Mark-Lee Kirk. *Ed:* Robert Wise. *Mus:* Roy Webb. *With* Irene Dunne *(Ellen)*, Cary Grant *(Nick)*, Randolph Scott *(Adam Burkett)*, Gail Patrick *(Bianca)*, Ann Shoemaker *(Ma)*, Scotty Beckett *(Tim)*, Mary Lou Harrington *(Chinch)*, Donald MacBride *(Hotel Clerk)*, Hugh O'Connell *(Johnson)*, Granville Bates *(Judge)*, Pedro de Cordoba *(Dr. Kohlmar)*, Brandon Tynan *(Dr. Manning)*, Leon Belasco *(Henri)*, Harold Gerard *(Assistant Clerk)*, Murray Alper *(Bartender)*, Earl Hodgins *(Clerk of Court)*, Clive Morgan *(Lawyer)*, Florence Dudley *(Witness)*, Cy Ring *(Contestant)*, Jean Acker *(Witness)*, Bert Moorhouse *(Lawyer)*, Joe Cabrillas *(Phillip)*, Frank Marlowe *(Photographer)*, Thelma Joel *(Miss Rosenthal)*, Horace MacMahon *(Truck Driver)*, Chester Clute *(Little Man)*, Eli Schmudkler *(Janitor)*, Franco Corsaro *(Waiter)*, Pat West *(Caretaker)*, Cy Kendall *(Detective)*. *Prod:* Leo McCarey for RKO Radio. 88m. McCarey was scheduled to direct the film, but he was laid up by a serious automobile accident and Garson Kanin took over.

ONCE UPON A HONEYMOON (1942). While Hitler marches into Austria, an ex-burlesque queen assembles

harles Boyer and Irene Dunne in
ve Affair.

her honeymoon wardrobe. Her plans for a "happily-ever-after" marriage are called into question when a news correspondent informs her that her husband is a Nazi agent. The destruction of Poland allows her to see the light and upon her eventual arrival in Paris she agrees to spy on her husband at the request of the U. S. Embassy. She is caught, but escapes and sails for America with her newsman-lover. On the boat she meets her ex-husband and pushes him overboard in self-defence. *Sc:* Sheridan Gibney (a story by Leo McCarey and Sheridan Gibney). *Ph:* George Barnes. *Art dir:* Albert S. D'Agostino, Al Herman. *Ed:* Theron Warth. *Mus:* Robert Emmett Dolan. *With* Cary Grant *(Patrick O'Toole),* Ginger Rogers *(Katie O'Hara),* Walter Slezak *(Baron von Luber),* Albert Dekker *(Gaston Leblanc),* Albert Basserman *(Marshal Borelski),* Ferike Boros *(Elsa),* Harry Shannon *(Ed Cumberland),* Natasha Lytess *(Anna Beckstein),* Hans Conried *(Tailor),* Lionel Royce *(German Officer). Prod:* Leo McCarey for RKO Radio. 115m.

GOING MY WAY (1944). When a new priest arrives at St. Dominic's church, his non-conformist methods and progressive attitudes alienate the old priest who is nominally in charge. This antagonism is exacerbated when the old man discovers that his new assistant is there on orders from the Bishop to revive the parish. Outstanding problems include imminent foreclosure of the church's mortgage, a runaway teenage girl, and a gang of street toughs. Just as Father O'Malley seems to have everything under control, the church burns down. But with the help of the parishioners, the banker who holds the mortgage, and a Metropolitan Opera star, the church is rebuilt. *Sc:* Frank Butler, Frank Cavett (a story by Leo McCarey). *Ph:* Lionel Lindon. *Art dir:* Hans Dreier, William Flannery. *Ed:* LeRoy Stone. *Spec eff:* Gordon Jennings. *Mus dir:* Robert Emmett Dolan. *Songs:* "Swinging on a Star," "Day After Forever," and "Going My Way" by Johnny Burke and Jimmy Van Heusen; "Too-Ra-Loo-Ra-Loo-Ra" by J. R. Shan-

non; "Ave Maria." *With* Bing Crosby *(Father O'Malley),* Risë Stevens *(Genevieve Linden),* Barry Fitzgerald *(Father Fitzgibbon),* Frank McHugh *(Father Timothy O'Dowd),* James Brown *(Ted Haines),* Gene Lockhart *(Mr. Haines),* Jean Heather *(Carol James),* Porter Hall *(Mr. Belknap),* Fortunio Bonanova *(Tomaso Bozanni),* Eily Malyon *(Mrs. Carmody),* The Robert Mitchell Boy Choir *(Themselves),* George Nokes *(Pee-Wee Belknap),* Tom Dillon *(Officer Patrick McCarthy),* Stanley Clements *(Tony Scaponi),* Carl "Alfalfa" Switzer *(Herman Langerhanke),* Bill Henry *(Interne),* Hugh Maguire *(Pitch Pipe),* Robert Tafur *(Don Jose),* Martin Garralaga *(Zuniga),* Sybyl Lewis *(Maid at Metropolitan Opera House),* George McKay *(Mr. Van Heusen),* William Frawley *(Max),* Jack Norton *(Mr. Lilley),* Anita Bolster *(Mrs. Quimp),* Jimmie Dundee *(Fireman),* Julie Gibson *(Taxi Driver),* Adeline DeWalt Reynolds *(Mrs. Molly Fitzgibbon),* Gibson Gowland *(Churchgoer). Prod:* Leo McCarey for Paramount. 130m. The screenplay for *Going My Way* has been published in John Gassner and Dudley Nichols (eds.), "Best Film Plays of 1943-44" (New York: Crown, 1945), pp. 149-222.

THE BELLS OF ST. MARY'S (1945). A parochial school, threatened with demolition, gets a new parish priest. Various conflicts among parishioners and students, and between the priest and the nuns who run the school, complicate matters. Just when things are looking up (the old man who owns the building next door donates it to St. Mary's to replace the old class-room buildings) the Sister Superior is taken ill with tuberculosis. Father O'Malley is under doctor's orders not to tell her of her illness before she is transferred to a warmer climate, but he breaks the rules (once again) to tell her the truth. *Sc:* Dudley Nichols (a story by Leo McCarey). *Ph:* George Barnes *Art dir:* William Flannery. *Ed:* Harry Marker. *Spec eff:* Vernon L. Walker. *Mus:* Robert Emmett Dolan. *Songs:* "Aren't You Glad You're You?" by Johnny Burke and Jimmy Van Heusen; "In the Land of Beginning Again" by Grant Clarke and

George W. Meyer; "The Bells of St. Mary's" by Douglas Furber and A. Emmett Adams; "Ave Maria." *With* Bing Crosby *(Father O'Malley)*, Ingrid Bergman *(Sister Benedict)*, Henry Travers *(Mr. Bogardus)*, William Gargan *(Mr. Gallagher)*, Martha Sleeper *(Mrs. Gallagher)*, Joan Carroll *(Patsy Gallagher)*, Rhys Williams *(Dr. McKay)*, Richard Tyler *(Eddie)*, Una O'Connor *(Mrs. Breen)*, Ruth Donnelly *(Sister Michael)*, Bobby Frasco *(Tommy)*, Aina Constant, Gwen Crawford, Eva Novak *(Nuns)*, Matt McHugh *(Clerk in Store)*, Edna Wonacott *(Delphine)*, Jimmy Crane *(Luther)*, Dewey Robinson *(Truck Driver)*, Jimmy Dundee *(Taxi Driver)*, Joseph Palma *(Workman)*, Minerva Urecal *(Landlandy)*, Peter Sasso *(Blind Man)*, Cora Shannon *(Old Lady)*. *Prod:* Leo McCarey for Rainbow/RKO Radio. 126m.

THE KID FROM BROOKLYN (1946). A re-make of *The Milky Way*. *Dir:* Norman Z. McLeod. *Sc:* Grover Jones, Frank Butler, and Richard Connell (the play by Lynn Root and Harry Clork, subsequently adapted by Don Hartman and Melville Shavelson). *Ph:* Gregg Toland (Technicolor). *Ed:* Daniel Mandell. *Art dir:* Peggy Ferguson, Stewart Chaney. *Mus dir:* Carmen Dra2Mus supervisor: Louis Forbes. *Songs:* "I Love an Old-Fashioned Song," "You're the Cause of It All," "Hey, What's Your Name?," "Josie," and "Sunflower Song" by Sammy Cahn and Jule Styne; "Pavlova" by Sylvia Fine and Max Leibman. Dorothy Ellers sings for Vera-Ellen, Betty Russell for Virginia Mayo. *With* Danny Kaye *(Burleigh Sullivan)*, Virginia Mayo *(Polly Pringle)*. Vera-Ellen *(Susie Sullivan)*, Steve Cochran *(Speed McFarlane)*, Eve Arden *(Ann Westley)*, Walter Abel *(Gabby Sloan)*, Lionel Stander *(Spider Schultz)*, Fay Bainter *(Mrs. E. Winthrop LeMoyne)*, Clarence Kolb *(Mr. Austin)*, Victor Cutler *(Photographer)*, Charles Cane *(Willard)*, Jerome Cowan *(Flight Announcer)*, Don Wilson *(Radio Announcer)*, Knox Manning *(Radio Announcer)*, Kay Thompson *(Matron)*, Johnny Downs *(Master of Ceremonies)*,

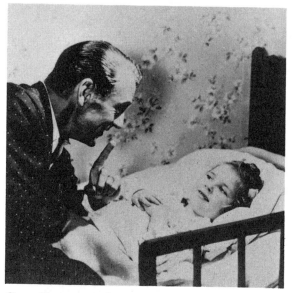

Gary Cooper and Lora Lee Michel in *Good Sam.*

Torben Meyer, Jack Norton, William Forrest *(Guests)*, Ralph Dunn, Billy Nelson *(Seconds)*, Karen X. Gaylord, Ruth Valmy, Shirley Ballard, Virginia Belmont, Betty Cargyle, Jean Cronin, Vonne Lester, Diana Mumby, Mary Simpson, Virginia Thorpe, Tyra Vaughn, Kismi Stefan, Betty Alexander, Martha Montgomery, Joyce MacKenzie, Helen Kimball, Donna Hamilton, Jan Bryant *(The Goldwyn Girls)*, Jimmy Kelly *(Specialty Dancer in "What's Your Name")*, Eddie Cutler, Harvey Karels, Al Ruiz *(Specialty Dancers in "Old Fashioned")*, John Indrisano *(Boxing Instructor)*. *Prod:* Samuel Goldwyn for RKO. 114m.

GOOD SAM (1948). Gary Cooper portrays a good Samaritan whose Samaritanism is called into question when he can't afford a house big enough for his own (somewhat extended) family. Sam's patience is rewarded, however, and even after he loses the hard-earned house money to muggers the bank comes through with a loan. *Sc:* Ken Englund (a story by Leo McCarey and John Klorer). *Ph:* George Barnes. *Art dir:* John B. Goodman. *Ed:* James McKay. *Mus:* Robert Emmett Dolan. *With* Gary Cooper *(Sam Clayton)*, Ann Sheridan *(Lu Clayton)*, Edmund Lowe *(H.C. Borden)*, Ray Collins *(Rev. Daniels)*, Joan Lorring *(Shirley Mae)*, Clinton Sondberg *(Mr. Nel-*

son), Minerva Urecal *(Mrs. Nelson)*, Louise Beavers *(Chloe)*, Dick Ross *(Claude)*, Matt Moore *(Mr. Butler)*, Netta Packer *(Mrs. Butler)*, Todd Karns *(Joe Adams)*, Carol Stevens *(Mrs. Adams)*, Lora Lee Michel *(Lulu Clayton)*, Bobby Dolan Jr. *(Butch Clayton)*, Ruth Roman *(Ruthie)*, William Frawley *(Tom Moore)*, Irving Bacon *(Tramp)*, Harry Hayden *(Banker)*, Tom Dugan *(Santa Claus)*, Dick Wessel *(Bus Driver)*, Almira Sessions *(Landlady)*, Sarah Edwards *(Mrs. Gilmore)*, Ingrid Dawson, Jane Allan, Marta Mitrovich, Ruth Sanderson, Franklin Parker, Sedal Bennett, Mimi Doyle, Jack Gargan, Bess Flowers, Florence Auer, Gary Owens, Stanley McKay, Bert Roach, Joseph Crehan, William Haade, Ann Lawrence, Bob Tidwell, Joe Hinds, Francis Stevens, Ida Moore. *Prod:* Leo McCarey for Rainbow/RKO Radio. 114m.

MY SON JOHN (1952). A family is torn apart by the conflict between a super-patriot father and his Communist agent son. The son's commitment to Marxism is personally motivated, however, and his mother's agony, coupled with pressure from the FBI, prompts his recantation. He is eventually murdered by his former accomplices but not before recording a graduation address to his alma mater. *Sc:* Leo McCarey and Myles Connolly (adaptation by John Lee Mahin of the story by Leo McCarey). *Ph:* Harry Stradling. *Art dir:* Hal Pereira, William Flannery. *Ed:* Marvin Coil. *Mus:* Robert Emmett Dolan. *With* Helen Hayes *(Lucille Jefferson)*, Van Heflin *(Steadman)*, Robert Walker *(John Jefferson)*, Dean Jagger *(Dan Jefferson)*, Minor Watson *(Dr. Carver)*, Frank McHugh *(Father O'Dowd)*, Richard Jaeckel *(Chuck Jefferson)*, James Young *(Ben Jefferson)*, Nancy Hale *(Nurse)*, Todd Karns *(Bedford)*, Francis Morris *(Secretary)*, William McLean *(Parcel Post Man)*, Fred Sweeny *(Cleaner)*, Russell Conway *(FBI Agent)*, Lee William Aaker *(Boy)*, Vera Stokes *(Secretary)*, Douglas Evans *(Government Employee)*, Gail Bonney *(Jail Matron)*, Irene Winston *(Ruth Carlin)*, David Newell *(FBI Agent)*, Erskine Sanford *(Professor)*, Margaret Wells *(Nurse)*,

Cary Grant and Deborah Kerr in An Affair to Remember.

David Bond, Eghiche Harout *(College Professors)*, Jimmie Dundee *(Taxi Driver)*. *Prod:* Leo McCarey for Rainbow/Paramount, 90m. Out-takes from Hitchcock's *Strangers on a Train* were used to complete the film after the death of Robert Walker. Some of the credits listed above obviously do not correspond to the finished film. They are included for the light, however dim, which they cast on McCarey's original design which had to be abandoned when Walker died.

LET'S DO IT AGAIN (1953). A remake of *The Awful Truth*. *Dir:* Alexander Hall. *Sc:* Mary Loos and Richard Sale (the play by Arthur Richman). *Mus & Lyrics:* Ned Washington and Lester Lee. *With* Jane Wyman *(Constance Stuart)*, Ray Milland *(Gary Stuart)*, Aldo Ray *(Frank McGraw)*, Leon Ames *(Chet Stuart)*, Valerie Bettis *(Lily Adair)*, Tom Helmore *(Courtney Craig)*, Mary Treen *(Nelly)*. *Prod:* Oscar Saul for Columbia. Irene Dunne's "Gone with the Wind" number seems to have become a dance called "Zambesi Puberty Ritual." That one change aside, and despite the fact that we have not seen the film, it is our best guess, based on the general trend of Columbia re-makes to mimic their orig-

inals, that McCarey's influence probably lingers on in *Let's Do It Again*.

AN AFFAIR TO REMEMBER (1957). A remake of *Love Affair* incorporating. scenes deleted from the original script. *Sc:* Delmer Daves, Leo McCarey, Donald Ogden Stewart (uncredited) (the story by Leo McCarey and Mildred Cram). *Ph:* Milton Krasner (CinemaScope, De Luxe colour). *Art dir:* Lyle R. Wheeler, Jack Martin Smith. *Ed:* James B. Clark. *Spec eff:* L. B. Abbot. *Cos:* Charles LeMaire. *Mus:* Hugo Friedhofer, conducted by Lionel Newman, from orchestrations by Edward B. Powell and Peter King. *Songs:* "An Affair to Remember" by Harry Warren, lyrics by Leo McCarey and Harold Adamson, sung by Vic Damone. *Asst dir:* Gilbert Mandelik. With Cary Grant *(Nickie Ferrante)*, Deborah Kerr *(Terry McKay)*, Richard Denning *(Ken)*, Neva Patterson *(Lois)*, Cathleen Nesbitt *(Janou)*, Robert Q. Lewis *(Announcer)*, Charles Watts *(Hathaway)*, Fortunio Bonanova *(Courbet)*, Walter Woolf King *(Doctor)*, Jack Raine *(English TV Commentator)*, Dino Bolognese *(Italian Commentator)*, Jack Lomas *(Painter)*, Dorothy Adams *(Mother)*, Robert Lynn *(Doctor)*, Patricia Powell *(Blonde)*, Alena Murray *(Airline Stewardess)*, Minta Durfee *(Ship Passenger)*, Matt Moore *(Father McGrath)*, Louis Mercier *(Marius)*, Geraldine Wall *(Miss Webb)*, Sarah Selby *(Miss Lane)*, Nora Marlowe *(Gladys)*, Alberto Morin *(Bartender)*, Genevieve Aumont *(Gabrielle)*, Jesslyn Fax *(Landlady)*, Tommy Nolan *(Red Head)*, Theresa Emerson, Richard Allen, Tina Thompson, Scott Morrow, Kathleen Charney, Terry Ross Kelman, Norman Champion III *(Students)*, Mary Carroll, Suzanne Ellers, Juney Ellis *(Teachers)*, Don Pietro *(Page Boy)*, Paul Bradley *(Bit Man)*, Tony De Mario *(Waiter)*, Michka Egan *(Waiter on Ship)*, Bert Stevens *(Maitre D')*, Brian Corcoran *(Young Boy)*, Priscilla Garcia *(French Child)*, Marc Snow *(Ship's Photographer)*, Anthony Mazzola *(Page Boy)*, Helen Mayon *(Nurse)*. *Prod:* Jerry Wald for 20th Century-Fox. 115m.

Paul Newman and Joanne Woodward in *Rally Round the Flag, Boys!*

RALLY ROUND THE FLAG, BOYS! (1958). The political issue raised when a small town becomes the site of an army missile base is complicated by the domestic squabbles of Grace and Harry Bannerman. As a notorious do-gooder she is chosen to be spokesperson for the town in its attempt to stop the base while he becomes a military public relations officer when he is called back into active duty. *Sc:* Claude Binyon and Leo McCarey (the novel by Max Shulman). *Ph:* Leon Shamroy (CinemaScope, De Luxe Colour). *Art dir:* Lyle R. Wheeler, Leland Fuller. *Ed:* Louis R. Loeffler. *Spec eff:* L. B. Abbot. *Cos:* Charles LeMaire. *Mus:* Cyril J. Mockridge, orchestrations by Edward B. Powell. *Mus dir:* Lionel Newman. *Songs:* "Seein' as How You're Mah Boojum" by Leo McCarey. *Asst dir:* Jack Gertsman. With Paul Newman *(Harry Bannerman)*, Joanne Woodward *(Grace Bannerman)*, Joan Collins *(Angela Hoffa)*, Jack Carson *(Capt. Hoxie)*, Dwayne Hickman *(Grady Metcalf)*, Tuesday Weld *(Comfort Goodpasture)*, Gale Gordon *(Col. Thorwald)*, Tom Gilson *(Opie)*, O. Z. Whitehead *(Isaac Goodpasture)*, Murvyn Vye *(Oscar Hoffa)*, Ralph Osborn III *(Danny Bannerman)*, Stanley Livingston *(Peter)*, Jon Lormer *(George Melvin)*, Joseph Holland *(Manning Thaw)*, Burt Mustin *(Milton Evans)*, Percy Helton *(Waldo Pike)*, Nora O'Mahoney *(Betty O'Shiel)*, Richard Collier *(Zack Crummitt)*, LeRoy Prinz Jr., Nick Venet *(Delinquents)*, Jesse Kirkpatrick *(Conductor)*, John Roy *(Air Force General)*, Richard

Cutting *(Hotel Clerk)*, Billy Benedict *(Bellboy)*, Sammy Ogg *(Delinquent)*, Jack Ging *(Hoxie's Driver)*, Charles Tannen *(TV Director)*, Edward Canutt *(Soldier)*. *Prod:* Leo McCarey for 20th Century-Fox. 106m.

SATAN NEVER SLEEPS (G.B. THE DEVIL NEVER SLEEPS) (1962). A retiring priest and his replacement are stranded in their Chinese mission when Red Army troops over-run the area. Things are complicated by a young Chinese girl who's in love with the new priest, and by the leader of the Chinese troops, a former altar boy at the mission, who lusts after the girl. The Commander eventually imprisons the priests, rapes the girl, and recants his communism in favour of escape to Hong Kong and matrimony after his parents are shot on the orders of his superiors. *Sc:* Claude Binyon, Leo McCarey (a novel by Pearl S. Buck). *Ph:* Oswald Morris (CinemaScope, De Luxe colour). *Prod design:* Tom Morahan. *Art dir:* Jim Morahan, John Hoesli. *Ed:* Gordon Pilkington. *Mus:* Richard Rodney Bennett. *Title song:* Harry Warren, Harold Adamson, Leo McCarey. *With* William Holden *(Father O'Banion)*, Clifton Webb *(Father Bovard)*, France Nuyen *(Siu-Lan)*, Weaver Lee *(Ho-San)*, Athene Seyler *(Sister Agnes)*, Edith Sharpe *(Sister Theresa)*, Martin Benson *(Kuznietsky)*, Robert Lee *(Chung Ren)*, Burt Kwouk *(Ah Wang)*, Lin Chen *(Sister Mary)*, Marie Yang *(Ho-San's Mother)*, Andy Ho *(Ho-San's Father)*, Anthony Chin *(Ho-San's Driver)*. *Prod:* Leo McCarey for 20th Century-Fox. 120m. Filmed in Great Britain. According to McCarey ("Cahiers" interview, p. 54), he left the film in disgust at constant studio interference with his work and "modifications" to his script, and the final week's shooting was left to an assistant. The released version of *Satan Never Sleeps* was edited without McCarey's supervision or approval, which may explain (if not excuse) the bizarre aspects of the film's ending.

MOVE OVER, DARLING (1963). A remake of *My Favorite Wife*. *Dir:* Michael Gordon. *Sc:* Hal Kanter and Jack Sher (the screenplay by Bella and Samuel Spewack and the story by Bella and Samuel Spewack and Leo McCarey). *Ph:* Daniel L. Fapp (CinemaScope and De Luxe colour). *Art dir:* Jack Martin Smith and Hilyard Brown. *Ed:* Robert Simpson. *Spec eff:* L. B. Abbott and Emil Kosa Jr. *Cos:* Moss Mabry. *Mus:* Lionel Newman, orchestrations by Arthur Morton and Warren Barker. *Songs:* "Move Over, Darling" by Joe Lubin, Hal Kanter, and Terry Melcher; "Twinkle Lullaby" by Joe Lubin. *Asst dir:* Ad Schaumer. *With* Doris Day *(Ellen Wagstaff Arden)*, James Garner *(Nick Arden)*, Polly Bergen *(Bianca Steel Arden)*, Chuck Connors *(Stephen Burkett/Adam)*, Thelma Ritter *(Grace Arden)*, Fred Clark *(Mr. Codd)*, Don Knotts *(Shoe Salesman)*, Elliott Reid *(Dr. Herman Schlick)*, Edgar Buchanan *(Judge Bryson)*, John Astin *(Clyde Prokey)*, Pat Harrington, Jr. *(District Attorney)*, Eddie Quillan *(Bellboy)*, Max Showalter [Casey Adams] *(Desk Clerk)*, Alvy Moore *(Waiter)*, Pami Lee *(Jenny Arden)*, Leslie Farrel *(Didi Arden)*, Rosa Turich *(Maria)*, Herold Goodwin *(Bailiff)*, Alan Sues *(Court Clerk)*, Pat Moran *(Drunk)*, Bess Flowers *(Woman)*, Rachel Roman *(Injured Man's Wife)*, Jack Orrison *(Bartender)*, Kelton Garwood, Joel Collins *(Ambulance Attendants)*, Sid Gould *(Waiter at Pool)*, Ed McNally *(Commander)*, James Patridge *(Skipper)*, Christopher Connelly *(Executive Seaman)*, Billy Halop, Mel Flory *(Seamen)*, Emile Meyer, Brad Trumble *(Process Servers)*, Michael Romanoff *(Floorwalker)*, John Harmon *(Cab Driver)*. *Prod:* Aaron Rosenberg and Martin Melcher for 20th Century-Fox. 103m. The picture began as *Something's Got to Give* with Dean Martin and Marilyn Monroe.

INDEX